MOSES
THE LAW-GIVER

BY

WILLIAM M. TAYLOR

WIPF & STOCK · Eugene, Oregon

Wipf and Stock Publishers
199 W 8th Ave, Suite 3
Eugene, OR 97401

Moses the Law Giver
By Taylor, William M.
Softcover ISBN-13: 978-1-7252-9085-3
Hardcover ISBN-13: 978-1-7252-9087-7
eBook ISBN-13: 978-1-7252-9086-0
Publication date 11/2/2020
Previously published by Baker Book House, 1886

This edition is a scanned facsimile of the original edition published in 1886.

FOREWORD

THE Bible Biography books by William M. Taylor remain unexcelled in their field. The author speaks of these outstanding Bible personalities with warmth, zest, and penetrating insight. He writes of them as they were, without magnifying their excellencies, or apologizing for their faults. At the same time he repeatedly points out the lessons from their lives for life in our day and age.

The contents of these books consist mainly of the exposition, defense, and application of the Scriptural narrative. It was said that Taylor's sermons were so constructed that every sentence was a definite step toward his goal. This is true of the chapters in these books. The style is such as to inspire any preacher or speaker. The result is an outstanding homiletical and expository series of biographical sermons with warm and spiritual applications. These books furnish excellent material for series preaching.

William M. Taylor was born, educated and ordained in Scotland. He was one of the greatest preachers of his day. He is especially known for his expository writings on the parables and miracles.

At the age of 42 years Taylor came to America, and for twenty years was the famed preacher of the Broadway Tabernacle in New York City. He was Lyman Beecher lecturer in Yale Seminary and L. P. Stone lecturer in Princeton Seminary. He was a preacher in the front rank, and enjoyed an international reputation. He died in 1902.

THE PUBLISHERS

CONTENTS.

		PAGE
I.	The Birth of Moses	7
II.	Training and Choice	24
III.	The Burning Bush	41
IV.	First Appearance Before Pharaoh	61
V.	The Ten Plagues	77
VI.	The Passover	95
VII.	The Crossing of the Red Sea	111
VIII.	Marah, Elim, and Sin	128
IX.	Rephidim	149
X.	Jethro's Visit	164
XI.	Sinai and the Decalogue	182
XII.	The Golden Calf—Aaron's Weakness	198
XIII.	Intercession	214
XIV.	The Tabernacle, and its Symbolism	232
XV.	The Mosaic Legislation	253
XVI.	Final Incidents at Sinai	274
XVII.	Murmurings	292
XVIII.	Miriam and Aaron's Sedition	307
XIX.	The Report of the Spies	323
XX.	The Korahitic Conspiracy	339
XXI.	The Sin of Moses, and the Death of Aaron	358
XXII.	The Brazen Serpent	374
XXIII.	Balaam	388
XXIV.	Deuteronomy	408
XXV.	Death and Burial of Moses	434
XXVI.	Characteristics of Moses	451
INDEX		469

MOSES THE LAW-GIVER.

I.

THE BIRTH OF MOSES.

Exodus ii., 1–10.

BEFORE the descendants of Abraham could take formal and permanent possession of the land which had been promised by God to their father, three things were, apparently, indispensable. It was necessary that they should become numerically strong; that they should become acquainted with the arts and sciences in the highest stage to which human development had then attained; and that they should be trained into courage and endurance, so as to be able to thrust out the Canaanites from before them. The two former of these were secured by their residence in Egypt; the latter was attained by the discipline of bondage, and by the experiences through which they were led during their sojourn in the wilderness. Their extraordinary increase made them a multitude; but their common hardships under slavery, their common deliverance under the leadership of Moses, and their common endurance of the discomfort of the desert, unified them into a nation fitted to become the depository of God's truth.

Egypt is generally regarded as one of the mothers of civilization; and in at least two directions her influence has told with unparalleled effect upon the history of later times. From her, through the medium of Phœnicia, Cadmus received the letters which he introduced to Greece, whose literature is even yet an inspiration in poetry, patriotism, and political government. By her, too, kindly at first, but more harshly as the years went on, that nation was nurtured, whose sacred books, blossoming into the beauty of the New Testament Scriptures, have put the benevolence into our modern life, and incarnated themselves in the Christian Church.

At the time when Joseph rose into prominence as the prime minister of this singular country, its lower province was ruled by a dynasty of foreign birth. This may partly account for the great favor which was shown to the gifted young Hebrew; while the generation which had profited by his forethought and energy would, we may be sure, make no objection to the granting of the land of Goshen to his brothers and their families. But years flew on. Joseph died, and a new dynasty from Upper Egypt, flushed with the glory of conquest, took possession of the throne. Naturally, therefore, its representative would be inclined to treat with coldness those who had been specially honored by the expelled monarch. And this course, so easily explicable on mere general principles, was rendered, in the view of the king, the more imperative by the fact that they had grown into a formidable people. The seventy that went down at first with Jacob* had, in the course of two hundred years, multiplied so amazingly, that, two years after the Exodus,† the full-grown males numbered six hundred and three thousand five hundred and fifty; so that if we add women and children, the entire number at the time of their departure from Egypt would be little short of a million

---

* Exod. i., 5. † Ibid., xxxviii., 26.

The Birth of Moses.

and a half. We may, therefore, safely say that at the date of Moses's birth they must have amounted to somewhere about three-quarters of a million. Under any circumstances, such a number of foreigners maintaining their tribal distinctions and their traditional religion must have constituted to a king an element of danger. But though they were mainly shepherds, some of them had learned the arts in which the Egyptians were so eminent. A few had become expert in working with the precious metals,* and at least the leaders among them had become proficient in the art of writing. All this must have made them objects of great anxiety to the king. Indeed, he felt them to be so formidable that he dared not make upon them an open and fair attack, but had recourse to cunning craftiness.† Knowing well the decimating influence of enforced labor, as it is seen even at this day in the same land among the Fellahin, he made them slaves, not to individual masters but to the State, and exacted from them the most exhaustive service. He compelled them to make bricks, and to build cities; and he set over them tyrannical and violent overseers, who "made their lives bitter with hard bondage, in mortar, and in brick, and in all manner of service in the field." What that means may be inferred from a modern fact; for it is said that when the canal which joins the Nile to the sea at Alexandria was made, one hundred and fifty thousand men were forced to labor on it, and of these twenty thousand perished before it was completed. There has been discovered, also, a painting on a Theban tomb, which though it is now regarded as having no reference to the Hebrews, may yet help to illustrate the nature of their toil. "In this picture some of the laborers are seen transporting the clay in vessels; some intermingling it with straw; oth-

---

* Exod. xxxi., 3.   † Exod. i., 10.

ers are taking the bricks out of the form and placing them in rows; and still others, with a piece of wood on their backs and ropes on each side, carry away the bricks already dried, while the taskmasters are beside them, some standing, others sitting, with their uplifted sticks in their hands." Besides this, a learned Egyptologist (Chabas) has translated some papyri, which, under the hieroglyphic "Aperiu" (by him identified, whether correctly or not I am incompetent to determine, with Hebrews), speaks of a foreign race as employed on public works. In one of these the writer, making a return to his superior officer, says, "I have obeyed the command which my master gave me, to provide sustenance for the soldiers, and also for the Aperiu who carry stone for the great Bekhen of King Rameses. I have given them rations every month according to the excellent instructions of my master."*

The labor was most oppressive, but the purpose of the king was not accomplished; for the more the Israelites were afflicted, the more they multiplied and grew. Pharaoh knew not that the people whom he sought to reduce both in numbers and in resources were the wards of God; and in his overweening estimate of his own sovereignty, he forgot that there was another King, "who doeth according to his will in the armies of heaven and among the inhabitants of the earth." So, foiled in one direction, he set to work in another, and enacted yet more brutal measures. He attempted to prevail upon those who assisted at the birth of the Hebrews' children, to murder all the males as they were born; but in that he was out-witted by the shrewdness of women, who would rather brave his wrath, than lend themselves to his diabolical designs. Then he

---

* See Kitto's "Daily Bible Readings," vol. ii., pp. 6-12; "Commentary, Critical, Experimental and Practical, on the Old and New Testaments," by Jamieson, Fausset, and Brown, vol. i., p. 273.

gave commandment to his people that every boy born in a Hebrew household should be cast into the river Nile, which, as the great source of the prosperity of the country, had come to be regarded among them with religious reverence. It is not likely, however, that this cruel edict could be long enforced. It does not seem to have existed at the birth of Aaron, who was only three years older than Moses. And it could not have been in operation long after the preservation of Moses, otherwise it would be impossible to account for the large number of the Israelites at the time of the Exodus. But we cannot forbear remarking on the fact that it happened to be in force just at the time when Moses was born; and that in consequence of its existence, through the efforts made by his parents to preserve his life, the future deliverer of the Hebrews was introduced into the palace of the king's daughter, there to receive a training which helped to fit him for his after-work. Thus does cruelty out-wit itself; and by the very crushing nature of his oppression, the king opened a way into his court for him who was at length to be the emancipator of the race that he was seeking to extirpate.

The parents of Moses both belonged to the tribe of Levi. If the genealogical table given in Exodus vi., 16-20, be taken as complete, then Amram was the grandson of Levi, and Jochebed his daughter; so that Amram married his own aunt. But we know that these tables were constructed on artificial principles, and that frequently three or four generations are overleaped in order to bring the number within certain limits, as is the case, for example, in those three fourteens in the first chapter of Matthew. We know, also, that the terms daughter, sister, son, brother, were often used in the sense of our generic word descendant. Therefore, it is not likely that Amram and Jochebed were so nearly related as nephew and aunt; but we may simply conclude that they were, the one a son, and the other a daughter, of collateral branches of the tribe of Levi.

We have no particulars regarding them that can throw any light on their characters, save those which this narrative has furnished; but from them we may infer that they were earnest in their piety, simple in their habits, strong in their affection, and sagacious in their conduct. Moses was not their first-born; for, as we learn from a subsequent chapter,* Aaron was three years old at his brother's birth; and judging from the activity and astuteness which Miriam manifested in securing that his mother should be the nurse of her infant brother, she must have been at least eight or nine years of age at this time.

The birth of a baby in a home is commonly a joyous event; but in this case the advent of the little one would create deep anxiety; for the question would immediately arise, whether they were to allow him to be thrown into the Nile, or whether they should endeavor to preserve him alive. Here, however, in addition to the strength of the parental instinct, Amram and Jochebed were impelled to attempt to conceal their infant, by his surpassing beauty. Every mother, indeed, is apt to think her child supremely fair; but something more than this maternal idealization is implied in the words, "he was a goodly child;" for Stephen† has translated the phrase into "divinely fair;" and as beauty was regarded as a mark of God's favor, it may be that the parents of Moses were led to hope that some special protection would cover him from harm. The author of the Epistle to the Hebrews has thus explained their conduct: "By faith, Moses, when he was born, was hid three months of his parents, because they said he was a proper child, and they were not afraid of the king's commandment."‡ But, as we read

---

* Exod. vii., 7. † Acts vii., 20. ‡ Heb. xi., 23.

THE BIRTH OF MOSES.

his words, the question rises, "Faith in what?" and some, thinking that faith always presupposes the reception of some particular word from God, have conjectured that, before the birth of the little one, a divine intimation was given to Amram or to Jochebed, to the effect that he would become the deliverer of his people. There is nothing improbable in that, in itself considered, for a similar announcement was made to Manoah and his wife, in the case of Samson. But we have no record of it here, and it is safer to hold that their faith was manifested by their refusal to obey the royal edict, out of regard to that prior law which God has written in every parent's heart. Nor let any one suppose that such a view of the case depreciates their faith; on the contrary, it sets it on a higher pedestal than if it had rested on some special and supernatural announcement. These Hebrew parents were a pious pair, who sought simply and only to do right, and looked to God for his blessing and protection. They did not know what was going to happen, any more than other parents do in similar circumstances; but, happen what might, they would not destroy their child; and therein lay their faith. Would to God the same faith were as strong in multitudes among ourselves!

It was no easy task, as we may well believe, to conceal their infant for three months. It involved unbroken silence, great watchfulness, and agonizing suspense. We can understand how the father and mother held their peace. But how could Miriam keep the secret about the little stranger? and by what means was Aaron preserved from letting fall even one unfortunate word about his new brother? The prudence of these little people is remarkable, and ought to be a pattern to the children in our modern homes, who not unfrequently make the secrets of the household the common property of all their companions.

But this concealment could not be maintained indefinitely. Not always could the mother hush those cries which, if heard by any one outside, would have drawn punishment upon the parents and death upon the babe. Not forever could she bear the agony that shot through her heart when a visitor came to her door, or a neighbor looked in upon her dwelling. Something else must be attempted; and after thought, which would often, if not always, end in prayer, she determined on the plan which she would adopt.

"She took for him an ark of bulrushes." The bulrush is the papyrus or paper-reed of the ancients. It grows in marshy places, and was once most abundant on the banks of the Nile; but now that the river has been opened to commerce, it has disappeared, save in a few unfrequented spots. It is described as having "an angular stem from three to six feet high, though occasionally it grows to the height of fourteen feet; it has no leaves; the flowers are in very small spikelets, which grow in thread-like, flowering branchlets, which form a bushy crown to each stem."[*] It was used for many purposes by the Egyptians, as for example, for shoes, baskets, vessels of different sorts, and boats; but it was especially valuable as furnishing the material corresponding to our paper, on which written communications could be made. To obtain this last fibre, the coarse exterior rind was taken off, and then with a needle the thin concentric layers of the inner cuticle, sometimes to the number of twenty in a single plant, were removed. These were afterward joined together with a mixture of flour, paste, and glue; and a similar layer of strips being laid crosswise in order to strengthen the fabric, the whole sheet was subjected to pressure, dried in the sun, beaten with a mallet, and polished with ivory. When completed and written over, the sheets were united into one, and rolled on a slen-

---

[*] Smith's "Dictionary," article REED.

The Birth of Moses.

der wooden cylinder. Thus was formed a book, and the description of the process gives the etymology and primal significance of our own word "volume."

From some portion of this useful plant Jochebed made a little chest, using slime to make the different parts adhere to each other, and pitch to make it water-tight. Then, with many tears and kisses and prayers, she put the baby into it, and laid it among the reeds by the brink, or, as the word literally is, the "lip" of the river. She did not put it in the water, but on the bank among the long reeds which grew so luxuriantly there, and among which it might seem to have been drifted up and then left stranded by the current. If, as has been commonly supposed, the residence of the Pharaohs at this time was at Zoan, or Tanis, on the Tanitic branch of the Nile, near the sea, there would be no danger from crocodiles, since these animals are never found there. It is possible, too, that there may have been some place in the neighborhood which was known to be frequented by the members of the court, and so Jochebed selected that, with the feeling, half of hope and half of mysterious premonition, that something might occur similar to that which actually happened. But though she prayed and trusted, she also used appropriate means; for she stationed the demure little Miriam "afar off to see what would be done to him," putting her so near that she might observe everything, and do what was required, and yet so far away that she would not be in any way associated with the child.

How long Miriam thus watched the record does not state; but as she stood looking on, she saw the king's daughter, with her maids of honor, coming down to wash at the river. At first sight it seems to be improbable, as altogether contrary to modern custom in the East, that a princess should thus go to bathe in the open river; but Wilkinson gives, from one of the ancient monuments—which are the most recent and valuable additions to Biblical evidences, and one of which may possibly ere long adorn our own city— a picture of a bathing scene, in which an Egyptian lady of rank is seen attended by four female servants.*

As she passed along by the edge of the river, the daughter of Pharaoh, observing the little bulrush box, sent her maid to fetch it; and when she opened it, she saw a beautiful but weeping babe! What woman's heart could resist such an appeal? And if, indeed, she were the great Thermuthis, who had been married, but was childless, we have another reason why, though she recognized the little one as the son of one of the Hebrews, she made it evident that she designed to keep him for her own.

But now was the time for Miriam's diplomacy; and nobly did she act her part. Her heart, indeed, must have been full of palpitating interest in the result of her efforts, yet there was no manifestation of over-eagerness to excite suspicion; and in the most unaffected and nonchalant way, as if the baby-boy had been of no consequence to her, and she was only seeking to do the princess a kindness, she came forward and said, "Shall I go and call to thee a nurse of the Hebrew women, that she may nurse the child for thee?" The offer was accepted, and with willing feet the little messenger went and called her mother, to whom Pharaoh's daughter gave back her own child, with these words, "Take this child away and nurse it for me, and I will give thee thy wages." Wages! Had she but known the heart of her to whom she spoke, she needed not to have referred to any reward; for what could be more delightful to the mother than to have her little one restored to her arms, with the assurance that now she might have no fear of his being put to

---

* Wilkinson, vol. iii., p. 389. Quoted by Jamieson in commentary on the passage.

death! Who may attempt to describe the joy of Amram's household on that memorable night; when to the happiness of having the child, there was added the delight of feeling that their treasure was secure under the protection of the king's daughter! Who may tell of the thanksgivings that went up to God because he had crowned their confidence in him with such abundant blessing! And how would Miriam rejoice that now her tongue was let loose, and she could talk to all around her of her little brother without endangering his life! How she would recount again and again the adventures of the day, and finish up, in her ecstasy, with a song which was the prelude and prophecy of that glowing anthem chanted by her and her attendant maidens, with timbrels and with dances, on the Red Sea shore!

But one Egyptian mark, which clung to the little one through his eventful life, and by which his fame has become the heritage alike of Jew and Gentile and Mohammedan, was the name he bore. The princess called him Moses, "because," she said, "I drew him out of the water." The etymology of this word was long matter of perplexity; but it is now ascertained that it comes, not from a Hebrew term at all, but is—like Zaphnath-paaneah, the name which had been given to Joseph—of purely Egyptian origin. It is *Mosu*, which, as Dr. Crosby of this city has said, means two things—first, "drawn out," and secondly, "brought forth." So Pharaoh's daughter, wanting to call this her child, although it was not her own, and unable to speak of him as "brought forth," could yet, in the other sense of the word, give him this name, and she said, "I drew him out of the water, and so I have a right to call him Mosu;" although that is the common name to give to one's own child.*

---

* See "Lecture on History and the Old Testament in God's Word, Man's Light and Guide," p. 134.

But now, leaving this interesting narrative for the time, let us pause to gather up and carry with us two practical thoughts.

We are reminded then, in the first place, by the slavery of the Hebrews in Egypt, of the bondage of sin. Throughout the Scriptures the circumstances of Israel in Egypt are referred to as typical of the servitude under which the sinner is held. There is more than guilt in wickedness. It would indeed be bad enough, even if that were all, but there is slavery besides. Our Lord himself says, "Whosoever committeth sin is the slave of sin;"* and there are no taskmasters so exacting as a man's own lusts. Look at the drunkard! See how his vile appetite rules him! It makes him barter every comfort he possesses for strong drink. It lays him helpless on the snowy street in the biting winter's cold. It sends him headlong down the staircase, to the injury of his body and the danger of his life. If a slave-holder were to abuse a slave as the drunkard maltreats himself, humanity would hiss him from his place, and denounce him as a barbarian. And yet the inebriate does it to himself, and tries to sing the while the refrain of the song which ends, "We never, never shall be slaves." The same thing is true of sensuality. Go search the hospitals of this city; look at the wretched victims of their own lusts who fill the wards, and then say if man's inhumanity to himself be not, in some aspects of it, infinitely more terrible than his oppression of his neighbors. Visit our prisons, and see how avarice, fashion, frivolity, and the love of standing well with their companions, have held multitudes in their grip, forcing them—nay, I will not say forcing them, for they sin wilfully—but leading them to dishonesty day by day, until at last the inner servitude gives place to an

---

* John viii., 34.

external imprisonment. I tell you, friends, the setting of slaves to make bricks without straw is nothing to the drudgery and the danger—as of one standing on the crater's edge —that dishonesty brings upon a man when once it has him in its power. And it is the same with every kind of sin. But this slavery need not be perpetual; for the Great Emancipator has come. Jesus Christ has said, "Ye shall know the truth, and the truth shall make you free;" and Paul has affirmed that "the law of the spirit of life in Christ Jesus hath made us free from the law of sin and death that is in our members." To him, then, let enslaved ones repair. He only can set them at liberty. If they will follow him fully their lives will be perpetual jubilee, and their joy will be to labor for the manumission of those who have been in bondage like their own. Jesus is the great liberator. His work on earth and in heaven is one long and loving exposition of the text which he read that day in the synagogue of Nazareth: "The spirit of the Lord God is upon me; because the Lord hath anointed me to preach good tidings unto the meek; he hath sent me to bind up the brokenhearted, to proclaim liberty to the captives, and the opening of the prison to them that are bound; to proclaim the acceptable year of the Lord."* In that acceptable year we are privileged to live; but let us see that we improve it, for when he comes again, it will be to proclaim "the day of vengeance of our God;" and woe to them who are his enemies then!

But we have here, in the second place, a beautiful instance of the minute providence of God. You must have been struck, as you have read these opening verses of the biography of the greatest of Old Testament worthies, with their simplicity and truthlikeness. Here is no mention of prodi-

---

* Isa. lxi., 1, 2; Luke iv., 18.

gies such as those which were said to attend the birth of Cyrus, and such as mythology delighted to tell concerning Romulus and Remus. It is a plain unvarnished story. There is no word of any miracle. The incidents are such as, allowing for the differences between ancient and modern life, might have happened among ourselves. And yet see how they fit into each other, altogether irrespective of, and indeed independent of, human calculation. There is the edict of the king which took this particular shape, and was enacted at this particular time. There is the placing of the ark of bulrushes in that special spot, and the coming of the princess and her observation of it at the moment; all converging toward the preservation of the child. Now these were not lucky accidents or happy coincidences. Had it been the case of a single fortunate occurrence, we might have talked of chance; but the coalition of so many acts of so many agents indicates design. When you come to a great railway junction, at which trains arrive from north and south and west, in time to be united to another that is just starting for the east, and you see the connection made, nobody talks of a happy coincidence. There was a presiding mind guiding the time of the arrival of the train in each case, so that the junction was reached by all at the required moment. Now, at the birth and preservation of Moses, one feels himself standing at the meeting-place of many separate trains of events, all of which coalesce to save the life of the child, and to put him in the way of securing the very best education which the world could then furnish. Why should we speak of accident in this case any more than in the other? No! there was a presiding providence here; and all these things were arranged under the supervision of Him who maketh even man's wrath to praise him, and who at the very blackest hour of his people's darkness was preparing a Deliverer.

The Birth of Moses.

And yet we must not imagine that God was more in these things than he is in our common lives. The phrase "special providence" is liable to be misunderstood. The teaching of this book is, not that God overrules some things more than others, but that he is in all alike, and is as really in the falling of a sparrow as the revolution of an empire. I prefer, therefore, to speak of the universality of providence; and I would have you not to forget that God was as truly in the removal of the little ones that were taken away, as he was in the saving of Amram's son; and that there were lessons of love and warning from the one, no less than of love and encouragement from the other. Nay, more, I would have you to remember that God is in the daily events of our households precisely as he was in those of the family of the tribe of Levi long ago. The births and the bereavements; the prosperity and the adversity; the joys and the sorrows of our homes, are all under his supervision. He is girding us when we know it not; and his plan of our lives, if we will only yield ourselves to his guidance, will one day round itself into completeness and beauty. Every one of us here has as really been preserved from childhood to this hour by the providence of God, as Moses was delivered on the occasion before us. It is not only when one is snatched out of visible danger, that we should speak of God's care. The protection is as real, though we may not be so conscious of it when no danger is seen. Many remarkable stories have been told of the preservation of children from peril, and every one remembers the incident in the life of John Wesley, when, while yet a little boy of four or five years old, he was saved from his father's burning rectory. But the continued life of every little child is as much due to the watchful care of God's providence as was that of Moses or of Wesley. Yes, and I will add, the taking from us of little children is as much a matter of providence and love as the preservation to us of those who survive. I have lived long enough, and have known both experiences sufficiently to be able to bear this testimony. So that they who are bereaved are not to feel themselves God-forsaken because their Moses has been taken away.

But, while all that is true, we may surely say that the life which God has prolonged ought to be spent in his service. Now that comes home to us. We are here, through all perils of existence, safe thus far; and, as we look back, we can say with Addison,

> " Unnumbered comforts to my soul
> Thy tender care bestowed,
> Before my infant heart conceived
> From whence these comforts flowed.
>
> " When in the slippery paths of youth
> With heedless steps I ran,
> Thine arm unseen conveyed me safe,
> And led me up to man.
>
> " Through hidden dangers, toils, and death,
> It gently cleared my way,
> And through the pleasing snares of vice—
> More to be feared than they.
>
> " When worn with sickness, oft hast Thou
> With health renewed my face;
> And when in sins and sorrows sunk,
> Revived my soul with grace."

And what return are we making for all this? It will not do to content ourselves with singing about it; but the life which God has prolonged should be spent entirely for God. You know the story of the Frenchman who, having been twice foiled in his attempt to commit suicide, threw away the pistol which had thus repeatedly missed fire, saying, "Surely, I am intended for something great;" and gave himself then and there to a course which ended in his becoming one of the leaders of his nation. So let your preservation to this hour lead you, my hearers, to consecrate your remaining days to God. Goodness with him is greatness. Holiness with him is excellence. Therefore seek these. If you have never sought them before, begin to seek them now. God has kept you alive for a great purpose; see that you do not miss it. Beware that you receive not this grace of God in vain.

II.

TRAINING AND CHOICE.

EXODUS ii., 11-15; ACTS vii., 22-29; HEBREWS xl., 24-27.

A NEW sorrow came ere long to Jochebed and her husband. The time arrived when the king's daughter claimed Moses as her own, and his departure for the palace would be almost as painful to his parents as it had been for them to leave him in his frail bulrush-ark by the river's brink. But now, again, their faith would triumph over their fear; and trusting that He who had preserved their son from death at first would keep him uncontaminated by the corruptions of court life, they would send him away with a benediction, while nightly the prayer would ascend from their hearts, that the God of their fathers might shield him from all harm.

The son of a king's daughter must be educated in a royal manner. Accordingly, we are not surprised at the statement made by Stephen,* to the effect that Moses was "learned in all the wisdom and knowledge of the Egyptians." That was the first-fruits of the spoil which the despised Hebrews were yet to take from their oppressors, and we are able now to form some definite idea of its value. The extreme dryness of the Egyptian atmosphere has preserved almost in perfection monuments of that early civilization, and the diligence of modern scholars has discovered the key for the deciphering of the inscriptions on them, which had been for ages regarded as absolutely incomprehensible. It may be

---

* Acts vii., 21.

worth while, therefore, to indicate some of the departments of knowledge in which it is probable that Moses was instructed.

According to tradition, he studied at the Temple of the Sun in Heliopolis, a structure which had been then only recently restored by Thothmes III.,* who also, it is said, set up in front of it those two granite obelisks which were afterward removed to Alexandria; and one of which, during the last week† has been so singularly preserved from shipwreck, after having been abandoned by those who were attempting to convey it to England. At this seat of learning Moses would be initiated into the arts of reading and writing; for the priestly and military castes among the Egyptians seem to have been addicted to literature. Many papyri have been preserved containing works in history and religion; and some romances of a purely imaginary character have been discovered. There are also collections of letters by celebrated persons, kept as models of style, and specimens of literary exercises analogous to the orations of the Greek and Roman rhetoricians. They had two sorts of characters: the one, known as hieroglyphics, which were long thought to be symbols of the objects for which they stood—but it is now admitted that they were in the majority of cases purely phonetic, representing either syllables or letters; the other, usually known as the hieratic, were cursive, and differed from the hieroglyphics much as our ordinary letters differ from capitals. They were hieroglyphics, abbreviated and altered for the convenience of the scribe; and in them all the books on papyrus that remain are written.‡

---

* "The History of Egypt," by Samuel Sharpe, vol. i., p. 51.
† This discourse was preached October 21, 1877.
‡ "Encyclopædia Britannica" (9th edition, American reprint), vol. vii., p. 629.

To these, now elementary but then advanced, accomplishments, Moses would add a knowledge of arithmetic, in which were used both the duodecimal and decimal scales of notation. In geometry he would be taught so much at least as to make him familiar with the theory, if not also the practice, of land-measuring—an acquirement which was specially valuable in Egypt, because the annual inundations of the Nile obliterated every boundary mark on the surface of the soil. In mathematics he would be instructed in trigonometry as well as geometry, for a papyrus exists containing exercises which extend beyond the essential and elementary problems of that science. This would be crowned with some acquaintance with astronomy; for that the Egyptians knew something of that subject is evident from the fact that the pyramids are so exact in their orientation, that the variations of the compass may be ascertained from their observation; and indeed, if the ingenious calculations of Mr. Piazzi Smyth may be accepted regarding the great pyramid, it would appear that they were already acquainted with some of those facts and relations which have been boasted of by us as among the most wonderful discoveries of our men of science. This much at least is indisputable, that from the remotest antiquity they used a year of three hundred and sixty-five days, and in later times they invented a very ingenious astronomical period, to bring their calendar from time to time into accordance with the real year of three hundred and sixty-five and a quarter days.*

It is probable, also, that Moses would be trained to acuteness of observation and accuracy of representation in the art of painting, for there remain on the monuments many specimens of rare excellence in this department. They con-

---

* "Encyclopædia Britannica" (9th edition, American reprint), vol. vii., pp. 625, 632.

sist, for the most part, of delineations of common scenes and daily occupations, executed with what we should now call pre-raphaelite minuteness, and characterized by definiteness of outline and correctness of detail, but without any attempt at perspective. They are remarkable, also, for the freshness and durability of the colors; but that may be owing in some degree to the fineness of the Egyptian atmosphere, which does not effect such productions so injuriously as that of our damper climate.

In architecture, there was a constant education for a youth of observing habits, in the buildings by which he was surrounded. They were distinguished by massiveness, sublimity, and strength, rather than by beauty. Everything the Egyptians built was colossal and enduring; and the Pyramid of Cheops, which was perhaps a thousand years old when Moses first beheld it, is as stable as ever to-day, though since then thirty centuries have run their course. Such structures could not be reared without some skill in mechanics; and of the six elementary powers known to us, they seem to have used the wedge, the lever, and the inclined plane, but not the screw, the pulley, or the wheel and axle—a fact which makes their achievements in building all the more wonderful in our eyes. In medical science they were not so advanced as in other departments, though there has been found in a mummy a tooth filled with gold, and perhaps also with cement, which shows some proficiency in dentistry; and it is not improbable that Moses received some instruction in anatomy. He was also, it is likely, trained in chemistry and a knowledge of metals, for the Egyptians had copper mines among the mountains of Sinai, and gold mines in the Nubian Desert. They were familiar with the use of iron, while their skill in the manufacture of bronze became celebrated. They used the blowpipe, the bellows, the syringe, and the siphon; and their knowledge of metallurgy, as well as the influence of that on Moses's education, is attested by the fact that he was able in the wilderness to reduce a golden image to powder.

But, studying at a religious temple, he would be sure to acquire a liking for that music which had such a prominent place in their sacred services. The harp, the lyre, the flute, the tambourine, and the cymbals were largely used in their public solemnities. Dancing also was common in their worship; and we have in these facts an explanation of the freedom and ease with which Moses sang his grateful psalm on the Red Sea shore, and Miriam answered him with timbrels and with dances. We never hear of music in the tents of Abraham and the early patriarchs, and therefore it is not improbable that this also was one of the finest of the spoils which Moses brought with him from his house of bondage.

For amusements, the students had games of chance; and a favorite pastime was draughts, which was played apparently with equal relish by people of all ranks, for Rameses III. is represented more than once as playing it in the palace at Thebes.

From these facts we may form to ourselves some idea of the nature of the intellectual training which Moses received, and are prepared to accept the statement of Philo when he says, regarding him, "He speedily learned arithmetic and geometry, and the whole science of rhythm and harmony and metre, and the whole of music by means of the use of musical instruments, and by lectures on the different arts."[*]
But in religious matters he would be taught many things which either he could not receive at the time, or must have rejected afterward; for their system was one of sublime truths mingled with the strangest errors, and consisted of

---

[*] Quoted by Thornley Smith, in "Moses and his Times."

what one has called "a refined morality, an abject form of worship, and popular superstitions coarse to the last degree."* Their representation of the attributes of deity by certain animals degenerated into the grossest sort of idolatry, and the worship of four-footed beasts and creeping things was common among them; yet they seem to have recognized the doctrines of human immortality and personal responsibility, and therein they were superior to some among ourselves who call themselves the advanced thinkers of the age. But much of that Egyptian wisdom, as James Hamilton has said, "was the merest foolishness; and if Moses ever mastered it, it would seem to have dropped from the memory of his more enlightened years, as the baby gewgaws drop from the open hand of manhood; for of their historical mythology there is no more trace in the Book of Genesis, than there is in the worship of Jehovah trace of their ridiculous idolatry."†

But Stephen, in his address to the council, spoke also of Moses as "mighty in words and deeds;" and therefore many are prepared to accept the tradition preserved in the pages of Josephus, to the effect that he was appointed general of the Egyptian army in a war with the Ethiopians, and gained repeated victories over the enemies of his foster-mother's nation. The historian goes on to tell that he besieged a city afterward known as Meroe, but could not take it; when Tharbis, the daughter of the king, seeing him fighting with great courage, fell in love with him and sent him a proposal of marriage, which he accepted on condition that she would find means to transfer the city to his hands. Having thus gained the fortress, he consummated the mar-

---

* "A Manual of the Ancient History of the East," by François Lenormant and E. Chevalier, p. 327.
† "Moses, the Man of God," by James Hamilton, D.D., p. 24.

riage and returned to Egypt. This story can hardly be received as it stands, for it is very improbable in some of its details, and not creditable to any of the parties concerned; yet it may be held as indicating that Moses at first took his place alike among the scholars and the warriors of the land, as one of the leading princes.

But though this was the case, there seems to have been within his soul a secret and silent reserve which kept him from committing himself to the side of the oppressors of his people, and which, while gathering up everything that might be of service to him in his future career, was only waiting for an opportunity to strike a decisive blow for the emancipation of his kinsmen. Lange has suggested, and James Hamilton has beautifully elaborated, the historic parallel in this respect between Moses, the hero of the Exodus, and William the Silent, the savior of the United Provinces: and we cannot help remarking on the irony of Providence, by which it is so frequently brought about, that the oppressor makes a rod for his own back, and trains the champion who is to become his chastiser.

But reticent and self-restrained as he was, Moses allowed himself to be surprised into an act which at once revealed his purpose, and, as it seemed, rendered it impossible for him to attain it. Visiting his kinsmen at their toil, he happened to see one of the taskmasters inflicting the bastinado on a Hebrew, and he was so provoked that he lost his self-control and slew the assailant. Much has been said and written in defence of this act: as for example, that Moses was the Goel, or nearest of kin, and so had a right to take revenge; and even the gentle Hamilton has held him up to admiration as being the father of chivalry in this act. But neither of these views can be accepted. Moses knew he was doing an illegal thing, else why did he "look this way and that way," and only attempt to slay the Egyptian when he thought that there was no witness? why, again, did he hide the body in the sand? Nothing is gained by seeking to vindicate every action even of a godly man; and we shall miss the force of this incident as a warning to ourselves, if we do not frankly admit that Moses here acted not only rashly and hastily, but unlawfully. He thought, however, that he had covered every trace of his misdeed when he had buried the body in the sand; but he soon discovered that he had miscalculated. For on the following day, when he saw two Hebrews fighting, he interposed in the interests of peace, saying, "Wherefore smitest thou thy fellow?" but was met with the retort, "Who made thee a prince and a judge over us? intendest thou to kill me, as thou killedst the Egyptian yesterday?" So it was out. That which the slaves knew, the taskmasters would soon hear; and what the taskmasters heard, would be speedily transmitted to the king. Therefore, he would stay no longer; and, without a farewell word to brother, or sister, or father, or mother, he fled from the face of Pharaoh, and dwelt in the land of Midian.

Thus, by his hasty act, Moses banished himself from the vicinity of his people for forty years; and though his sojourn in the wilderness, equally with his education in Egypt, was lifted up and utilized when he came to the crowning work of his life, we may not shut our eyes to the fact that but for his lack of self-restraint he might have become an earlier benefactor to the people whom he desired to liberate. Stephen tells us that "he supposed that his brethren would have understood how that God by his hand would deliver them."[*] But in such matters a vague supposition is not enough. He was running, in this instance, before he had been sent; and he discovered by the result that neither was he as yet com-

---

[*] Acts vii., 25.

petent to be the leader of the people, nor were the people ready to rise at his call. He had not yet acquired sufficient command of himself, and they had not as yet been stung into mutiny by their oppression; so he was sent to the wilderness to learn to rule his own spirit, and they were sent back to the brick-yards to smart for forty years longer beneath the taskmasters' rods. When they met again they would both be wiser; for Moses would do nothing without taking with him the elders of Israel, and the people would hail his presence as that of their emancipator. There is thus a long distance often between the formation of a purpose and the right opportunity for its execution; and we should not always regard promptitude as wise. The providential indicators of duty are the call within us, and the willinghood of those whom we would benefit, to receive our blessing; and if either of these is absent, we should pause. Above all, we should not allow the passion of a moment to throw us off our guard and lead us into sin, for we may be sure that in the end it will only retard our enterprise and remove us from the sphere of our activities. The ripening of a purpose is not always the mark of the presence of an opportunity. "Raw haste" is always "half-sister to delay;" and wrong-doing can never help forward, directly at least (however God may afterward overrule it), a good cause. A man's first battle is with himself; and only when he has conquered on that field is he competent to lead others in their warfare.

But while we cannot approve of the rashness of the manner in which it was indicated by Moses, we must admire his decision itself; for now at length he fully and conclusively gave up all the advantages of an Egyptian prince, and cast in his lot with the people of God. Josephus has a mythical story, which tells that when Moses was a child his foster-mother took him to the king and introduced him as the heir to the kingdom; whereupon the monarch took him in his arms and caressed him, and at length put his own diadem on his head. But Moses took it, and in a seeming passion threw it on the ground and trod it beneath his feet. Thus he despised the treasures of Egypt. But that is all imaginary; and the true sublimity of this divine record is seen in the absence from it of all such tales. It was by the incidents which we have now reviewed that Moses, as we believe, first publicly indicated his determination to abjure Egypt for Israel; and so to this we must apply the apostle's words, "By faith Moses, when he was come to years, refused to be called the son of Pharaoh's daughter; choosing rather to suffer affliction with the people of God, than to enjoy the pleasures of sin for a season; esteeming the reproach of Christ greater riches than the treasures in Egypt; for he had respect unto the recompense of the reward. By faith he forsook Egypt, not fearing the wrath of the king; for he endured, as seeing him who is invisible."*

Now let us analyze this choice, and see all that it involved. It was made by him after he was "come to years," and in the full maturity of his powers. The impulsive ardor of inexperienced boyhood had nothing to do with the formation of this resolution. It is delightful, no doubt, to see the young, ere yet they are caught in the currents of human activity or tainted with the contamination of worldly men, taking their stand upon the side of Christ; and the very hoisting of his banner thus early will be a means of preserving a lad amid the snares to which he shall be afterward exposed. But, from the nature of such cases, they are the results of careful and judicious home-training; and the faith which they manifest, real though it be, is more emotional than intellectual. There comes a time, however, for every

---

* Heb. xi., 24-27.

one, when this traditional belief has to be exchanged for a personal conviction; and in such an hour, often one of agony and conflict, it is well to recur to the example of Moses here. He was now probably forty years of age. He had received the best education which the world then could furnish. He was possessed of mental powers of the highest order; and yet after examination searching and thorough, he chose to cast in his lot with the people of God. Religion —the religion of Christ—is not, therefore, the thing of blind fanaticism which many would represent, else had not intellects like those of Moses and Paul been found in the service of the Lord. The Bible has nothing to fear on that score. Even if it were to come to a counting of heads among the great ones of the earth, and men should say, We cannot accept a system which has so few master-minds among its followers, we should not need to be afraid. For how many do you reckon Moses for? and who among our modern philosophers is worthy to be named in the same breath with Paul? Then, as you step down through the centuries, you find that the epoch-making men have been those who have stood most firmly on the side of God. That cannot be a childish choice which was made by such a one as Moses in the ripe vigor of his powers.

Again, this choice was not made by one who had nothing to give up. It is often said, sneeringly, by those who read that the disciples forsook all and followed Jesus, that they did not lose much—only a few battered boats and a few frail nets. Be it so, we answer; but what is to be said of that which Moses forfeited? He stood on the very steps of the Egyptian throne. There was before him, if he pleased to abjure Jehovah, the very grandest position which earth then had to give—all that riches and rank and power and splendor could offer. It was as if there had come to him the same arch-tempter who, nearly two thousand years later, confronted Christ; and as if he had shown him also "all the kingdoms of the world and the glory of them," and had said, "All these things will I give thee, if thou wilt fall down and worship me." But he, too, spurned the offer and stood firm. Nor did he refuse in ignorance of what he was giving up. It is easy, comparatively, for a poor man to say, I do not want a palace or a throne, for he has never known either; but it is a harder thing for one who has been accustomed to luxury and comfort to give them up at the call of duty. Yet this harder thing it was that Moses did; and by the doing of it, he places himself side by side with him who said so nobly, "What things were gain to me, those I counted loss for Christ; yea, doubtless, and I count all things but loss for the excellence of the knowledge of Christ Jesus my Lord." This was no cheap sacrifice. It involved comfort, competence, earthly prospects of the most alluring character, and all that men usually hold dear.

Moreover, this choice was not made at a time when it was fashionable to be among the followers of Jehovah. The worshippers of the true God, then, were for the most part slaves, and to join them was to share their oppression. In this case, indeed, Moses did not come beneath the taskmaster's lash, or swelter in the brick-yard under the vertical sun. But he escaped these only by betaking himself to the kindlier shelter of the desert. For this choice, he had to give up fellowship with kinsmen and friends, and to take his place among those who were "persecuted, afflicted, and tormented."

Now all these things go to show that it was made only under an intensely strong conviction that he was doing right; and we can find no adequate explanation of it save in the words of the inspired writer. It was by faith; "for he had respect unto the recompense of the reward." It was by faith; "for he endured, as seeing him who is invisible." That accounts for it all. Beyond the boundary of earth and time he saw a glory and a greatness which dazzled into dimness the glittering pomp even of an Egyptian royalty; and he gave up the latter that he might secure the former. Through the veil which conceals the spirit-realm from mortal sight, his soul-eye saw the living throne of the eternal God; and that, for him, rectified all the variations of earth, so that the compass of his conscience trembled sensitively, yet steadily, to Him. In His light he saw clearly the relative position of earthly and heavenly things—the infinite ratio between the temporal and eternal—and he reckoned that the light afflictions, which are but for a moment, are not worthy to be put in the balance over against that "far more exceeding and eternal weight of glory."

The perfect eye is that which best combines the telescopic and the microscopic in itself; that which sees farthest, and at the same time sees most distinctly the minute objects which are close at hand. And that is the truest intellectual perception which unites in it the vision of the far and the near. One of the most thoughtful of modern poets has thus expressed himself:

> "God has conceded two sights to a man—
> One, of men's whole work, time's completed form;
> The other, of the minute's work, man's first
> Step to the plan's completion."

And we know that, for all success in any department of earthly labor, we need the combination of these two—the far sight and the near. But now, if man be indeed immortal; if there be an eternity before him; if on the threshold of that eternity there be a throne of judgment whereon One sits to whom he is accountable for every deed done in the body; and if by the decision of that Judge regarding his earthly character and conduct his eternal destiny is fixed, what momentous importance is added thus to these two sights, the far and the near, in their combination and in their relation! The far sight, that takes in eternity and Him who is invisible, what is that but the faith which we have seen as the inspiring principle of the grandest human life of which ancient history can boast? The near sight, that observes the things of to-day, and can distinguish the precious from the vile, the good from the evil, what is that but the same faith which led the son of Amram to give up the Egyptian throne for a banishment in Midian, because there was godlessness in the one and communion with the Invisible in the other? Thus the faith of the man of God, so far from being irrational and absurd, is only an application to the relation between this life and that which is to come, of the principles on which men act, in seeking the honors and rewards of earth. Even if it be only the medal of a boat-race, or the trophy of an international shooting-match that is to be gained, they who strive for it will give up present enjoyments, and go into active training for a while, in order, if possible, to secure the victory. "They do it for a corruptible crown." But the far sight of faith beholds an incorruptible crown as the recompense of its reward; its near sight marks what, in the present, is inconsistent with the ultimate attainment of that glory; and by the final choice of the man, the latter is sacrificed for the former. Thus, what the student is doing for his scholarship, and the merchant for his wealth, and the statesman for his office, and the author for his fame, that the believer is doing for his recompense of the reward. It is not a question, then, of rationality, as between the conduct of the Christian and other men. It is a question, rather, as to the relative value of the things which he gives up and those which he is seeking to attain. Moses thought the reproach of Christ was greater riches than the treasures in Egypt. If he was right in so thinking, his choice was every way rational. But was he right? Was he right? Let the nobleness of his character, the influence of his writings, and, more especially, his appearance in glory by the side of Jesus on the Mount of Transfiguration, answer. He *was* right in his estimate; he *was* justified in acting on it; and this decision was the first step in that ascending ladder of which the other rounds were Horeb, Sinai, Pisgah, Heaven.

Now, at some time or other, every man has to make a decision similar to that of Moses. The story of Hercules, told by Xenophon in his "Memorabilia," repeats itself in every human life; and each soul, as it wakes to the consciousness of responsibility, must choose between "the pleasures of sin" and "the reproach of Christ." It may be that some one in the audience to-night is, even at this moment, hesitating between the two; and I would seek, in all faithfulness and affection, to help him to a right decision. I will not deny that there are pleasures in sin. There must be so, else it would never be committed. There is a joy in the wild throb of sensual indulgence, and in the exhilarating excitement of the intoxicating cup. The miser must have some delight in his gold, and the gambler in his game. But admitting all that, what is such pleasure worth? On the testimony of those who know it best, it is short-lived; and brief as it is, it leaves a sting behind—for it is true of every form of sin, as of the wine-cup, that "at the last it biteth like a serpent, and stingeth like an adder." Morever, it palls upon the palate, and the oftener it is enjoyed there is the less enjoyment in it; while it is procured at an expense which no human arithmetic can reckon, and no sum of money can represent. The body is enfeebled by it into disease; the intellect is shattered by it into imbecility; the moral nature is hardened by it into insensibility; the man has given himself for it, and what remains as the result? On earth, nothing more than that which remains in the hand after the bubble has burst—nothing better than that which remains on the hearth after the thorns have burned; and in eternity, the portion of those where there is weeping and wailing and gnashing of teeth.

Over against this set now the reproach of Christ. It is true that, following him, we must bear a cross; it is true that we must endure hardness as good soldiers; but then, along with these, there is within us the testimony of a good conscience, and a joy which one who knew the very worst of the tribulations has described as "unspeakable and full of glory." Nor is that a fleeting thing. It abides and it increases the longer it stays, so that we may say that Jesus keeps the best wine for the last. Moreover, it is a wholesome thing; for it uses the body without abusing it; it stimulates the intellect; it quickens the affections, and ministers to health in every department of our nature. Then when death comes, it brings to the Christian an abundant entrance into the presence of his Lord, and the enjoyment of his eternal recompense. The pleasure of sin is external and evanescent; Christian happiness is internal and permanent. The one is galvanic, lasting only while the sin-battery works, and requiring evermore a stronger charge; the other is calm, natural, and ever increasing—like the light, which waxes on to its meridian glory. In the one, the joy is for a moment, and the pain is perennial; in the other, the pain is temporary, while the happiness is everlasting. The one is destructive; the other is salutary. The one terminates in hell, the other leads to heaven.

Now, with these things before you, why should you hesitate a moment in making your choice? If you wish your life to resemble the course of the sun, rising in beauty, going forth in power, and shining more and more unto the perfect day; if you would have your death resemble his setting; if, like him, you would go down in a sea of gilded glory, and set only to shine on in the firmament beyond, then follow the example of Moses and choose Christ even with his reproach; but if you wish to waste your strength, to blast your intellect, to make your influence on others blighting and destructive, and to destroy your soul eternally, then you will give yourself up to the pursuit of the pleasures of sin.

There was once a king in Jerusalem who sounded every "depth and shoal" of pleasure, and drank of every cup of human joy. If there be any element of permanent satisfaction in life apart from God, he surely might have found it; for, with every possible advantage, he made deliberate search for it; but still, from each new voyage of discovery, he returned with this melancholy result: "Vanity of vanities; all is vanity and vexation of spirit." Listen to him, my friend, if you will not hearken to me; listen to him as, worn and weary, and wounded too, from his life-long pursuit, he cries back to you, half in mocking irony, and half in solemn earnestness: "Rejoice, O young man, in thy youth; and let thy heart cheer thee in the days of thy youth, and walk in the ways of thine heart, and in the sight of thine eyes: *but know thou, that for all these things God will bring thee into judgment.*"

III.

THE BURNING BUSH.

Exodus ii., 16; iv., 17.

THE region to which Moses fled from the face of Pharaoh seems to have been the eastern portion of that peninsula from the centre of which the range of Sinai rears its bare and jagged granite peaks to the sky. It is true, indeed, that the land of Midian, properly so called, lay on the other side of the Elanitic Gulf. But the people whose territory it was were shepherds, migrating from place to place, according to the changes of the seasons and the exigencies of their flocks; so that, although their head-quarters were on the eastern border of Edom, their wanderings extended north as far as Gilead and Bashan, while they embraced on the south wide tracts of country along both the shores of that which is now known as the Gulf of Akabah.*

Here Moses found a home, in a manner which illustrates at once the habits of the people, his own inherent hatred of oppression, and the minute particularity of the providence of God. Resting beside a well, which was the most likely place for meeting any of the inhabitants of the country, he saw seven young women approach and draw water for their flock. But just as they were about to lead the cattle to the troughs which they had filled, a company of selfish and ill-mannered shepherds came, and attempted to steal from them with violence the results of their labor, by driving them away and taking possession of the water for their own

---

* See Alexander's "Kitto's Cyclopædia," article Midian.

herds. On this Moses, stung into indignation by the injustice of the rude fellows, and moved also, perhaps, by that regard for woman which he had learned in Egypt, where alone at that time among the nations she had anything like her true position,* stood up in defence of the maidens, and enabled them so to hold their own that their work was speedily performed.

It has been supposed, from his success in this chivalrous interference on behalf of the oppressed, that Moses must have been accompanied by some of his kinsmen from Egypt; but there is no necessity for accepting any such hypothesis. The bully is invariably a coward; and the conscience of the wrong-doer is so thoroughly in alliance with the champion of the right, that it is commonly an easy thing to overcome him. None the less, however, is Moses to be commended for his prompt and decisive resistance to such a wanton and unjustifiable iniquity. It was not a great thing, indeed. Only a few troughs of water. Just as John Hampden's ship-money amounted only to a few shillings. But there was a great principle underneath: and, as we shall always see, Moses was never wanting in the defence of the right. Faithful here in that which was least, he had at length an opportunity of showing his fidelity in that which was greatest. And small, apparently, as this service was, it brought with it a great reward.

For the damsels whom he had thus assisted were the daughters of Reuel, or Raguel, the patriarch and priest of his tribe, who, on learning of the stranger's kindness to them, insisted on receiving him into his home as a guest. The result was that Moses abode with him, and ultimately obtained Zipporah, one of the seven sisters, for his wife.

---

* "Encyclopædia Britannica" (9th edition, American reprint), vol. vii., p. 624.

The members of this household seem to have been very highly regarded by Moses; for on at least one occasion of importance Jethro's advice was implicitly followed by him, and Hobab accompanied the tribes in their march through the wilderness. But as some difficulty exists as to their number and identity, this may be the best place to investigate and, if possible, to settle these questions. In the third chapter of Exodus, the father-in-law of Moses is called Jethro. In the Book of Numbers* we have mention made of Hobab, the son of Raguel, Moses's father-in-law, and, in the Book of Judges,† Heber the Kenite is said to have been of the children of Hobab, Moses's father-in-law. Perhaps the meaning of the name *Jethro* may help us to a solution of the difficulty. *Jether* signifies excellence, and *Jethro*, his excellency; so that we may suppose that it was the official title of the Priest of Midian, just as Pharaoh was that of the King of Egypt. If this view be accepted, then Reuel, or Raguel, will be regarded as the proper name of the patriarch, and Hobab will be taken as that of the son of the priest, and the brother-in-law of Moses. But in that case it will be asked, How comes it that, in the Book of Judges, Hobab is called Moses's father-in-law? and the answer to that inquiry must be found in the latitude of meaning in which all terms signifying relationship were used in the East; so that, as Dr. Douglas has affirmed, the same word may be rendered father-in-law or son-in-law, as the connection may require.‡ Reuel, Raguel, and Jether, Jethro, are thus names of the same person, whose daughter, Zipporah, became the wife of Moses; and whose son, Hobab, was in later days the companion and counsellor of Moses in his journeyings with his people through the wilderness.

---

* Numb. x., 29. † Judges iv., 11.
‡ See Fairbairn's "Imperial Bible Dictionary," article RAGUEL.

So far as we can gather from the narrative, Raguel seems to have been a worshipper of the true God, something after the stamp of that Melchizedek whom Abraham honored, and, it may be also, having spiritual kinship to the patriarch of Uz, whose trials and triumph are so dramatically told in the Book of Job. If this were indeed the case, then Moses must have had much profitable fellowship with those among whom his lot was cast; and in their common worship of the one living and true God, there would be a bond of union between them of the tenderest kind. Yet the son of Amram could not forget his kindred. Often would his thoughts recur to Egypt, where his brethren were toiling under the most cruel bondage; and as he felt within him the consciousness that he had lost, by his own rashness, the opportunity of working out their deliverance according to his most cherished ambition, he would be apt to sink into despondency, if not even into despair. But ever as he remembered God, his hopes would revive within him, and there would rise before him the vague yet comforting anticipation of the time when, in some way, the Lord would break in pieces the oppressor, and let the oppressed go free. Some evidence of this alternation in him between depression and trustfulness is furnished by the names which he gave to the two sons who were born to him in Midian. The first he called Gershom, saying, with a feeling of isolation, which is at no time so keenly felt as when one cannot have any of his own kindred to rejoice with him in his joy, "I have been an alien in a strange land."* The second he named Eliezer, with a heart that seemed fuller, at the moment, of the thought of his mercies than of his miseries; for he said, "The God of my father was my help, and delivered me from the sword of Pharaoh." Thus at length, in spite of temporary deviations,

---

* Exod. xviii., 3.

his soul came back to habitual dependence on Him for whom he had suffered the loss of all things, and in whom he found more than compensation for the comforts he had forfeited.

There was much, also, in the solitude of his shepherd-life that would stimulate him to devout meditation. Here amidst "the sleep that is among the lonely hills," he communed with himself, with nature, and with God; facing for himself those "obstinate questionings" which continually arise when one seeks to fathom the mysteries of being. A very different university was this from that at which he studied among the worshippers of the Sun at Heliopolis; yet more helpful to him even than the education which he had received in Egypt, would be his musings upon the mountain sides, as he rose from the thunder-riven peaks to Him who before the mountains were brought forth is, from everlasting to everlasting, God. Like the Scottish boy, who in the intervals of his shepherd-life mapped out for himself with beads the distances of the stars, and designated himself "God Almighty's scholar," Moses was now under the special tuition of the Lord. His books were the silent stars and giant hills; the shrubs that grew at his feet, and the flocks that went on beside him, browsing on the grass; and often and often would he pore lovingly over the pages of man's first Bible—Nature. But most frequently, perhaps, he would look within and try to read himself; for of the prophet, fully more than of the poet, one must be able to say,

> "He saw through life and death, through good and ill;
> He saw through his own soul;"

and after awhile there was to come to him the vision which would open to him as a scroll, "the marvel of the everlasting will."

Forty years had this discipline continued, when, leading

his flock away to that wild region, afterward known as the
Mount of God, which lay to the north of the Sinaitic range,
and was called Horeb, he saw a flame flashing from an
acacia-bush. At first he was filled with alarm—much as
one would be now on the parched prairie at the least appearance of fire; for there, too, it would spread rapidly, and
carry desolation before it. But pausing a moment to look,
he was amazed to discover that, though the flame was bright,
the bush was unconsumed. The lambent glory played
harmlessly on the branches, and seemed only to make their
verdure more conspicuous. So he turned aside to see the
great sight, and found it greater than he had first supposed;
for as he advanced, a voice came to him from the bush, saying, "Moses, Moses. And he said, Here am I. And he
said, Draw not nigh hither: put off thy shoes from off thy
feet; for the place whereon thou standest is holy ground.
Moreover he said, I am the God of thy father, the God of
Abraham, the God of Isaac, and the God of Jacob."* We
have, therefore, no need to ask who this mysterious one was.
The angel of the bush is the God of Abraham; and we have
thus another of those symbolic manifestations which prepared the way for the appearance of the great "mystery of
godliness," God manifest in human flesh. But it differs
from those which were given to Abraham and Jacob in this,
that whereas to the patriarchs God appeared under a human form, he makes himself known here to Moses in a
flame of fire. We have in this the prelude of the Shechinah
glory over the mercy-seat, by the veiling of which from all
save the high-priest, and even from him save when he bore
the blood of atonement, the Lord would instruct his people
in the majesty of holiness; and in the command, "Draw
not nigh hither," there is the first indication of that restric-

---

* Exod. iii., 4–6.

tion in men's approach to God which is so characteristic of the Mosaic ritual. Thus, the system which Moses was to introduce was designed to educate men, through reverence, into liberty. It was not so noble as the patriarchal dispensation that went before it, "for Abraham talked with God as a man talketh with his friend;" and it is far outshone by that under which now we live, for in Christ we may draw near to God with full assurance of faith. "Draw not nigh," is the first utterance of the one; "Come near," is the first and last exhortation of the other.

But though thus inferior to the Gospel, the Mosaic economy was not the less necessary in the education of men. Its restrictions were like the framework of the horn lantern, through which the light of God's truth shone dimly, it is true, but by which, also, it was kept from being extinguished by the rude blasts of idolatry and unbelief; and it is interesting to note, in this first divine utterance to Moses, the germ of the dispensation which goes by his name.

But in remarking on that arresting word of God, let us not lose sight of the symbolism of the vision. The bush burning, yet not consumed, has always been regarded as an emblem of Israel in Egypt. The fire could not waste those with whom God dwelt; and so we have here set before us, in material figure, the same truth which was taught by the presence of the mystic fourth with the three Hebrews in the Babylonian furnace, and which has been illustrated by the whole martyrology of the Christian Church. And perhaps I am not wrong in supposing that this aspect of the vision was that which made it to Moses, as he looked back upon it in after-life, fullest of consolation and support; for, in his farewell blessing of the tribes, he could find no richer benediction of the sons of Joseph than to wish for them "the good-will of Him that dwelt in the bush." The Church of Scotland, therefore, has not made an inappropriate or unwarranted use of this emblem, when, looking at her own history, how she was cradled in persecution, and nurtured amidst the assaults of Claverhouse and his dragoons, she has put upon her banner a representation of the burning bush, with the legend, "Nec tamen consumebatur;" yet it was not consumed. But it is true of every branch of the Church of Christ as well as that—yea, of every individual believer; for where God resides, there evil is impotent to harm.

Let us not fail to observe, also, the foundation which there is in the words, "I am the God of Abraham," for the argument which the Saviour draws from them for the resurrection of the body.* God does not say, I was the God of Abraham, but speaks of himself as being still in that relation to the father of the faithful; therefore, Abraham was then existing; his spirit was still in covenant union with God; and at length, in his full identity, he would appear among the ransomed. We scarcely think that all that was seen by Moses; but the reference to his great ancestors would remind him of all the revelations which God had made of himself through them, and specially of the promises which he had made to their descendants; and so it was a fitting preparation for the commission which was to follow.

But "Moses hid his face; for he was afraid to look upon God." It was not the fire he feared, but Him whose presence was half concealed and half revealed in its flame. The God whom he had been prone, like too many of us, to regard for the most part as an abstraction, and speak of as the Eternal, the Almighty, the Absolute, had come to him as a living person, who could speak to him, and look him through; and he did as we should have done, and as instinctively we try to do yet, whenever we have a vivid sense of his presence: he covered his face. He shrunk into him-

---

* Matt. xxii., 23–32; Mark xii., 24–27.

self; for he could not bear to stand naked and open to his sight. It was a crisis in his history. The meeting of the personality within me with the personal God; the discovery that, behind and above nature, there is a living God, who says "thou" to me, and to whom I can say "thou;" the confronting of my spirit with the Spirit of God; that is for me the supreme experience of existence, out of which I come with a new life-commission, and from which I draw inspiration through all my after-wanderings in this wilderness world; and the first thing it will make me do is to hide my face. The earliest effect of true knowledge is humility; and the eldest daughter of faith is reverence. Ah! would that God might thus reveal himself to the self-confident philosophy of these days!

The Lord, referring with deepest tenderness to the sufferings of his people in their house of bondage, indicates his will that Moses should become their emancipator in these words: "Come now, therefore, and I will send thee unto Pharaoh, that thou mayest bring forth my people, the children of Israel, out of Egypt." But he who, forty years ago, was so eager to become their deliverer that he ran without being sent, is now strangely reluctant to undertake the work. He had learned more of his own insufficiency; and there was perhaps also in him something of the *vis inertiæ* which accompanies advancing years, and makes one increasingly unwilling to enter upon a struggle with oppression. At all events, he offers four distinct excuses for declining the work to which the Lord here called him, and only under a species of constraint does he consent to undertake it.

The first excuse was his own personal unworthiness; and that was removed by God's assurance, "Certainly I will be with thee;" accompanied by such pledge of his success as is contained in the promise that after he had brought the people out of Egypt he should serve God with them in that very spot.

The second excuse was his inability to answer the Israelites if they should ask him, "Who sent you? What is his name?" And that was met by these far-reaching words, "I AM THAT I AM: Thus shalt thou say unto the children of Israel, I AM hath sent me unto you." This is that mysterious name which the Hebrews could not bring themselves to write, and which now—as many scholars say incorrectly—we pronounce Jehovah; the one, eternal, personal, unchangeable God. It is not here used for the first time, but it is here for the first time employed in its distinctive and peculiar sense, as indicating not the Almighty merely, but the Deliverer. It is the name of the Lord as the Saviour, and so it ought to be specially dear to the saved. Perhaps it was not entirely unknown to Moses, for it entered into the name of his mother Jochebed (which signifies *Jehovah, my glory*); and Ewald* has "conjectured that, in the small circle of her family, a dim conception had arisen of that divine truth which was through the son of that family proclaimed forever to the world." Slowly after this it made its way into the faith of the people, and we see an evidence of that in the fact that Hoshea's name was changed to Joshua; while for us Christians it is forever enshrined in the precious word "Jesus," which means *Jehovah that saves*. The whole after-life of Moses was inspired by this name; and it was the foundation on which the nation of Israel was reared. The movement which the son of Amram was to inaugurate was no mere struggle for emancipation from civil slavery. It was religious, and not political, in its character; and this word, uttered from the flaming bush, was Israel's charter of independence. Admirably has Maurice said,

---

* Quoted by Stanley, "Jewish Church," vol. i., p. 97.

"The more we read of that nation, the more we shall feel that it could not have had for its basis any abstraction or logical formula. It stood upon no conception of the unity of God; it stood upon no denial of the Egyptian faith, or any other; it stood upon no scheme of making the speculations of priests or hierophants the property of the people. Either it stood upon this Name, or both it and all that have grown out of it are mockeries and lies from first to last; roots, branches, flowers, fruit, all are rotten, and all must be swept away. 'The Lord God of the Hebrews, the God of our nation, the God of Abraham, Isaac, and Jacob, the God of our family, has established and upholds the order of human existence, and of all nature.' This is the truth which Moses learned at the bush, the only one which could encounter the tyranny of Pharaoh or the tricks of the magician; the only one which could bring the Jews, or any other people, out of slavery into manly freedom and due obedience."*

The third excuse offered by Moses was that the people would not believe him, but would say that the Lord had not appeared unto him; and God took that stumbling-block out of his way by showing him two miracles which he was to perform in Egypt, and which were at the same time signs to himself of the success which would follow from his obedience, and the evil which would result from his refusal to do what God was now commanding him. Calling attention to the rod that was in his hand, the Lord commanded him to cast it on the ground, and forthwith it became a serpent, from which he fled in terror. But at the word of God he put forth his hand and caught it, and it became again a rod in his hand. The asp, a kind of serpent, played a conspicu-

---

* "The Patriarchs and Law-givers of the Old Testament," by Frederick Denison Maurice, p. 166.

ous part in Egyptian mythology. It was the emblem of one of their goddesses, and, in particular, the sign of royalty. So the flight of Moses from it was an apt illustration of his unwillingness to encounter the pride and power of Pharaoh in the effort to emancipate the Hebrews; while its becoming a rod in his hand was an indication of the ease with which the might of Egypt could be turned by God into weakness.

The other miracle was more solemnly suggestive in its teachings even than that. Putting his hand into his bosom, he took it out leprous; and returning it again into his bosom, he brought it forth as healthy as ever. This miraculous infliction and removal of the most loathsome of all diseases was a sign to Moses, and through him to the Israelites, before whom it was to be repeated, of the danger which they incurred by refusing to obey the word of God, and of the deliverance that would come if they followed his injunctions. God also intimates that when Moses reached Egypt, he would compel the people to listen to his words, by turning the water of the Nile into blood.

Driven thus from all the outworks which he had so skilfully thrown up, Moses falls back on his first difficulty—his own incompetency—and selects a special feature of that for a new excuse. "O my Lord, I am not eloquent, neither heretofore nor since thou hast spoken unto thy servant; but I am slow of speech, and of a slow tongue." Possibly that was the real truth. Standing and talking with the great I AM, Moses was not likely to say anything that was not correct. He was a thinker, rather than a speaker. Fluency was not his forte. He saw too much in a moment to be able to give utterance to it all at once; and so his lack of readiness in the use of language was the result of the richness of his thought, rather than of its poverty. When the bottle is full, its contents flows out less freely by far than when it is two parts empty. So, very often, the fluency of one speaker is due to the fact that he sees only one side of a subject; while the hesitancy of another is the consequence of his taking in at a glance all the bearings of his theme, and of his desire to say nothing on it that will imperil other great principles with which it is really, but not to all minds visibly, connected. No better illustration of the truth of these remarks can be given, than the difference between Moses and his brother Aaron, whom the Lord here designates as his colleague and interpreter. So long as Aaron was the spokesman of Moses's thought, we cannot but admire him; but when he was left to himself, the eloquent orator became, as many another merely eloquent orator has become, the willing dupe in the hands of a maddened people, and the very moulder of the golden calf which they set up to worship. Speech is noble only when, like an honest currency, it represents the gold of thought; but when it is merely inflated fluency, it is then like the rags of a dishonest currency, which is the symbol of poverty, and not of wealth.

The Lord met Moses's plea by reminding him that he was not sending him in his own strength. "Who hath made man's mouth? or who maketh the dumb or deaf, or the seeing or the blind? have not I the Lord? Now therefore go, and I will be with thy mouth, and teach thee what thou shalt say." That ought to have been enough; but now, driven from every refuge, Moses plainly acknowledges that he does not want to go, saying, "O my Lord, send, I pray thee, by the hand of him whom thou wilt send." And then, to let him know that he had crossed the line that marks disobedience from humility, the Lord showed his displeasure, and put an end to the conference by saying that he would give him Aaron to be his assistant, and by renewing the command to him to go to Egypt and begin the enterprise. "Thou shalt take this rod in thy hand, wherewith thou shalt do signs;" and, thus accoutred, he sets out to enter on a conflict with the mightiest empire then upon the globe! It was, to human view, like going to shiver the pyramids into fragments with a baby's hammer! But, as we advance, we shall discover that, when God is in the case, it is all one whether we work with a rod or with a mighty army, and that human weakness is irresistible in its might when the strength of God is made perfect in it.

It is time, however, that we should draw to a close by giving prominence to the practical lessons which this history suggests. Let us learn, then, in the first place, not to be impatient for the discovery of our true life-work. Moses was eighty years old before he entered upon that noble career by which he became the emancipator and educator of his nation. Two-thirds of his days were gone before he really touched that which was his great, distinctive, and peculiar labor, and his enterprise was all the more gloriously accomplished by reason of the delay. Nor is this a solitary instance. The Lord Jesus himself lived thirty years, during most of which he was in training for a public ministry which lasted only two-and-forty months. John Knox never entered a pulpit until he was over forty years of age; and much of the fire and energy of his preaching was owing to the fact that the flame had been so long pent up within his breast. Havelock was for a dreary while a mere lieutenant, held back by the iniquitous system of purchase which was so long in vogue in the English army; but, as it happened, that was only a life-long apprenticeship, by which he was enabled all the more efficiently to become, at length, the savior of the Indian Empire. So let no one chafe and fret over the delay which seems evermore to keep him from doing anything to purpose for the world and his Lord. The opportunity will come in its own season. It does come, sooner or later, to every man; and it is well if, when at length he hears the voice calling "Moses! Moses!" he is ready with the answer, "Here am I."

For while I would comfort you with the assurance that the hour will come, I do not mean that you should be idle until it strikes. No; for if you adopt such a plan, the certainty is that you will not hear its stroke, or that you will not be ready to begin at its call. The true principle is to do with your might that which is lying at your hand day by day, in the firm conviction that you are thereby training yourself into fitness for your future vocation. Moses was as observant as a shepherd as he had been diligent as a student; and when at length his higher work opened up before him, he saw how it lifted up into itself and utilized all the knowledge which he had acquired in his lower pursuits. He might not be able to discover, during his forty years' musings in the wilderness, how his sojourn in these wild regions was to be of any after-service; yet, as we proceed with his history, we shall have cause to remark that, as his Egyptian learning stood him often in good stead, his knowledge of the Sinaitic peninsula was of equal value. When he consecrated himself to the great work of his life, he discovered, as many since his day have done, that the energizing flame which marked the acceptance of his sacrifice infolded and glorified both that which was behind him in the past, and that which was before him in the future. It was because he had been so diligent in the two preparatory stages of his career, that he was so efficient in the latest and ripest achievements of his life. He was all the more able—though in his humility he knew it not—to be the leader of his people from their house of bondage, because he had been so faithful and so earnest alike in Egypt and in Midian.

You see, then, to what my remarks are tending. Be not impatient of delay. Seek not to vault by one sudden leap into the throne of your peculiar power. But prepare yourself for wielding your sceptre when it comes, by doing with all fidelity the duties of your present sphere. Men fail in the world to do anything to purpose, not because the opportunity never comes to them, but because when it does, they are not able to take advantage of it; inasmuch as they have been trifling when they ought to have been working. Multitudes, when they hear of one being as suddenly called to some post of usefulness, as Moses was to his great work of deliverance, exclaim, "What luck! Oh, if I could only have such a chance!" But there has been neither chance nor luck in the case; for the envied one has been all the while steadily making himself in the lower sphere for efficiency in the higher, and God has only done with him what you do with a diligent clerk in your store, when, seeing his faithfulness and ability, you promote him to a more important office. Here, therefore, is the harmonizing principle between contentment and ambition. The true man is eagerly anxious to do his best in some high calling for God, yet he does what he can where he is, and is content until it is God's time for him to rise; and when that time comes, he is ready. The men who vault at once into greatness, like those who become suddenly rich, very commonly squander their influence, and make themselves ridiculous. But he who waits, and works while he waits, will surely emerge at length, and his work will be worthy of his place. The leap is all the greater because of the race that goes before it; the current becomes all the stronger at the last because it has been so long held back by obstacles; and the noblest work is done by him who has had to wait for long before he could get at it. As our own poet has sung in stirring strains:

> "The heights by great men reached and kept
> Were not attained by sudden flight;
> But they, while their companions slept,
> Were toiling upward in the night.

> "Standing on what long we bore
>   With shoulders bent and downcast eyes,
> We may discern—unseen before—
>   A path to higher destinies.
>
> "Nor deem the irrevocable past
>   As wholly wasted, wholly vain,
> If, rising on its wrecks, at last,
>   To something nobler we attain."*

But, in the second place, this case of Moses reminds us that our best life-work is that on which we enter under a feeling that it is absolutely essential that we should do it. Moses tried in every way to put away from him the office to which God called him. But still it came back upon him. He felt that he must go; and when that irrepressible *must* shaped itself in his soul, he went, and carried all before him. We see the same thing in Jeremiah. The man of Anathoth did not covet the honor of the prophetic office. Like Moses here, he said to Jehovah, "I cannot speak, for I am a child;" but still the Lord strove with him, until at length that which was at first an outward constraint became an inner impulse, and he could say, "His word was in mine heart, as a burning fire shut up in my bones; and I was weary with forbearing, and I could not stay." And we hear the same thing in Paul's words: "For though I preach the Gospel, I have nothing to glory of; for necessity is laid upon me: yea, woe is unto me, if I preach not the Gospel." It is the irrepressible in a man that makes him great. So long as the work he undertakes is performed because he must do something, there is nothing remarkable either about him or about it; but when he enters on it because it is something that *he must do*, then prepare yourself for something noble. Is it not just in this that the quality which we call genius peculiarly

---

* Longfellow.

resides? If a man thinks that he would like to write in verse, or to paint something, or to make a speech, or what not, his work will never be heard of. But if there is in him a song which insists on singing itself out, or a painting which will not let him rest until he has put it on the canvas, or a truth, the utterance of which he cannot hold back, then he is sure to be at length a poet, an artist, or an orator. That was a wise old minister who, on being consulted by a youth who desired to become a preacher of the Gospel, said to him, "Young man, don't become a minister if you can help it." It is the man who cannot help being a preacher who will be most effective always in the pulpit. The work which we can help doing is not for us. If Moses could have successfully excused himself, he would have been no fit man for the great crusade on which he entered. But it was because, in spite of all his reluctance, there was within him the overmastering sense that God had called him to be Israel's deliverer, that he was at length so successful. Ah! have we not here the cause of so many failures in moral and religious enterprises? The men who have inaugurated them have done so for personal eclat, or pecuniary profit, and not because of this inner impulsion. There has been no vision of the burning bush to set their hearts on fire with a flame which they could not extinguish. That is the explanation of the fact that so many educated for the ministry, and for a time occupying pulpits, are now retired. That is the "open secret" that reveals why so many Sabbath-school teachers are listless and indifferent, and so many more have given up the work entirely. That is the reason why so many reforms in Church and in State that promised so much in the beginning, have been at length like "clouds without rain, and wells without water." Write it on your hearts, then, my hearers; grave it on the palms of your hands; keep it continually before your eyes: that is your life-work which you feel you must do, which you cannot run away from, and which you are constrained to do by an irrepressible and irresistible impulse; if you have no such impulse, then go to Midian and seek solitary communion with God until you have. Moses ran away at the first difficulty, when he attempted the work of deliverance forty years before; for then he took it up because he must do something: but from this time on he is indomitable, because now the something is that which he *must* do.

Finally, when we enter upon such a work, we may rely that God will give us everything that is necessary for its performance. There was much in the revelation of God to Moses, resulting as it did in the revelation of Moses to himself, that was fitted to qualify him for his work; and we cannot fail to note the parallel which in this respect exists between him and the prophet Isaiah and the Apostle Peter. To each of these their true vocation came, as here to Moses, through a vision of the glory of God, and in them, also, it led to the deepest personal humility. But in the promise, "Certainly I will be with thee," there was all that the great leader needed. His miracles were the consequence of Jehovah's presence, and everything else was contained in this assurance. So when we enter on work to which God has called us, and from the undertaking of which we cannot escape, we too may fall back on the persuasion that God is at our side; for that which was the personal benison of Moses here is the common inheritance of every Christian. "Lo, I am with you alway, even unto the end of the world:" such was the declaration of Jesus to his followers when he sent them to disciple the nations; and when we engage in anything which has for its end the glory of Christ and the welfare of humanity, we may rely on his co-operation. Do we need anything more? Ah, if we but relied less on human expedients, and more on that unseen yet real Presence, our success would be far greater. At the late meeting of the American Board, the question was asked by one of the secretaries, in a very noble paper, "Shall we have a missionary revival?" And I answer "Yes, when we have more faith in the presence with us of our regal and all-powerful Lord." The deliverance of Israel from Egpyt did not seem more Utopian when Moses set out to accomplish it, with nothing in his hand but his rod, than the conversion of the heathen nations seem to-day; yet it was God that effected the one, and he is to accomplish the other. All things are possible to him; what we need is but the faith of Moses to go forth and act as if we believed that God is with us. That is all. But we need all *that:* we all need that; and when we have it in our churches, we shall see mightier wonders on the fields of paganism than Moses wrought by the banks of the Nile. Nor let any one lose his sense of individual responsibility when we speak of the work of the churches. Whatever you are called to do, he will help you to accomplish. Go, then, in this thy might, and each of you may be a Moses in his own little sphere, confronting infidelity and immorality, and rescuing some captives from the taskmaster's oppression. Would that some one here, and now, might hear the call, and answer with reverent promptitude, "Here am I; send me—send me!"

IV.

FIRST APPEARANCE BEFORE PHARAOH.

Exodus iv., 18; vii., 7.

IN our desire to present a clear and connected view of the conference between Jehovah and Moses at the burning bush, we were compelled to omit all reference to two matters of detail which have often proved perplexing to the devout reader of the narrative. It may be well, therefore, before we go farther, to pause a little over them, if haply we may be able to clear away all difficulty from them. The first is connected with the demand which the Lord instructs Moses to make of Pharaoh in these words: "Thou shalt come, thou and the elders of Israel, unto the King of Egypt, and ye shall say unto him, The Lord God of the Hebrews hath met with us: and now let us go, we beseech thee, three days' journey into the wilderness, that we may sacrifice to the Lord our God."* Now, looking at these words in the light of the after history, it must be confessed that they have an appearance of diplomacy, as if they were intended to deceive Pharaoh as to the real end which Jehovah had in view. But when we go deeper into the matter, we discern in them a true purpose of mercy to the Egyptian king. The demand is made in the most moderate fashion; so that, if there had been any disposition in his heart to comply with it, he might have found it all the more easy to do so. Everything harsh and defiant is avoided, so that no occasion is furnished for Pharaoh's anger; while at the same time

---

* Exod. iii., 18.

it is a clear and unmistakable assertion that the Hebrews ought to have the liberty to serve their God wheresoever he might ask them to sacrifice to him. This is God's common mode of procedure. He speaks to men of the near and the comparatively small; and according as they respond to him in regard to these matters, he leads them on to the higher and the greater, or drives them away from his presence altogether. In the case before us, the request which he instructed Moses to make was so small that no right-minded man would have rejected it. Had it been complied with, negotiations of a peaceful sort might have been opened; difficulties might have been removed by mutual consultation; and the Exodus might have been accomplished in an amicable manner, without any of those desolating judgments with which it was ultimately accompanied. Thus the presentation of the demand in this mild form, so far from being a piece of cunning policy, was in reality a merciful probation given by God to Pharaoh; and if he had possessed the wisdom to improve it by granting the favor which was asked, no plagues had been sent to waste his land, but, instead, the richest blessings which the Lord could bestow would have descended on him and on his people.

The second difficulty springs out of the statement, which accompanies the declaration, that the Israelites should go out of Egypt laden with spoils. These are the words: "And I will give this people favor in the sight of the Egyptians: and it shall come to pass, that, when ye go, ye shall not go empty: but every woman shall borrow of her neighbor, and of her that sojourneth in her house, jewels of silver, and jewels of gold, and raiment: and ye shall put them upon your sons, and upon your daughters; and ye shall spoil the Egyptians."* But if they were to borrow, when there was no in-

---

* Exod. iii., 21, 22.

tention whatever of returning that which they received, what becomes of the honesty of the transaction? Now, in reply, it will not do to say that they had already been defrauded by their oppressors of far more than the value of these spoils, for they were not commissioned to ask wages of any sort. Neither, again, must we say that the Hebrews did not know, when they borrowed these things, that they were not coming back to Egypt, and so must be held as having acted in good faith; for God at the bush gave Moses the instructions which we have just quoted, and the reader's difficulty is that *He* should have so spoken. But all perplexity is removed when we know that the term rendered here "borrowed" means simply to "ask," so that this difficulty is one which has been created by our generally admirable translation. How the word "borrow" came to be used here is more than I can explain; but the fact is indubitable that the original verb, which is a very common one, always* means "ask" or "demand." The request would be natural enough, coming from those who had been so long enslaved; but the Egyptians would have declined to comply with it had it not been for the influence on them of calamities which they could not but trace to supernatural agency, and for the infliction of which on them they blamed the obstinacy of their own king. Thus understood, all difficulty vanishes from the history, and we are prepared to go on with the narrative with unabated confidence in the divinity of its authorship.

After his return from Horeb to Midian, Moses requested permission of his father-in-law to revisit Egypt, and ask after his brethren whom he had left behind him there. He said no word even to him of the marvellous vision of the burning bush, and the equally marvellous conference with Jehovah

---

* Except in these two instances: 1 Sam. i., 28; 2 Kings vi., 5. See "Speaker's Commentary," *in loco.*

to which that vision led. These were, as yet, personal matters, and the impression produced on his soul was too deep to be talked about even with those who were nearest him in his home. When one is caught up into the third heaven, the words he hears there are commonly unspeakable; and he who is always telling of the glory of his secret communion with God is thereby only revealing that he knows not wherein the true glory of such fellowship consists. When one comes down from the mount, the face may shine, but the lips are usually silent. Never, so far as appears—save to his brother Aaron, in the frank confidence of his first interview with him after their long separation—did Moses give any account of that wonderful colloquy which he was permitted to hold with the great I AM: and it would be well if the same reverent reticence were observed by many among ourselves.

Jethro offered no objection to Moses's proposal, but simply said to him, "Go in peace." So he took his wife and his two sons, and set them on an ass, while, with his rod in his hand, he strode on by their side. Three things intervened between his leaving Midian and his arrival in Egypt, and each of them had its own importance as preparing him for his arduous enterprise. First, he was encouraged and instructed by the Lord. Lest he should fear that some remnant of the old difficulty from which he fled at the first should meet him, he was assured that all the men were dead who had sought his life. And that he might not be cast down by the antagonism which he would have to encounter, he was forewarned that Pharaoh would not let the people go. He must not tremble before imaginary dangers, but neither must he expect immediately favorable results. Ah, how many of our despondencies and disappointments spring from these two causes! We fancy enmities where none exist; and we look for such effects from our labors as God has not unqualifiedly promised, forgetful that the opposition of the ungodly to us is as really a testimony to our fidelity as would be their submission. If we expect too much, we only court disappointment. If we fear what has no existence, we put an arrest upon activity.

But the manner in which the Lord here speaks of Pharaoh's resistance is peculiar; and as the same phraseology is of frequent recurrence in the narrative, we may as well consider it here once for all. He says to Moses, "See that thou do all those wonders before Pharaoh, which I have put in thy hand: but I will harden his heart, that he shall not let the people go." It is somewhat remarkable that the hardening of Pharaoh's heart is ascribed in this history ten times to God, and that in an equal number of passages it is affirmed that Pharaoh hardened his own heart. It is to be noted, also, that up till the sixth plague it is always said that Pharaoh hardened his own heart, and that it is only after that we read, as a matter of history, that the Lord hardened it. This will help us, I think, to a right understanding of the subject, in so far as it can be comprehended by finite minds. These, then, are the facts: In the outset of this contest, and on till the fifth plague, Pharaoh, in the exercise of his free agency, resisted God's demand. This repeated resistance had in itself a hardening influence, so that each time he rejected the demand of Jehovah his heart was left more indurated than it had been before. But at length he passed the boundary of God's forbearance, and, as a judicial punishment upon him, that which had been, up till this point, the natural consequence of his conduct, was confirmed by the decree of God, who gave him over "to a reprobate mind to do those things which are not convenient." At first, the hardening was Pharaoh's own act; later, its increase was the fruit of his repeated resistance; and then, last of all, it was the punitive infliction of Jehovah. This seems to me to be the full truth on the subject; and the fact that the Lord here speaks thus early of his hardening Pharaoh's heart, is to be accounted for by the purpose which he had here in view, which was to keep the faith of Moses from fainting when he should see the first manifestations of Pharaoh's rage; for he was to understand that what in the beginning was pride would in the end become perdition.*

The second experience of Moses on his way to Egypt was somewhat mysterious. When he came to a halting-place on his journey, the Lord met him, and either threatened him with death by violence, or visited him with a sudden and dangerous bodily disease. This led him, as it would seem, to earnest self-examination, which resulted in the recollection that, to please Zipporah, he had neglected or postponed the circumcision of his younger son. In the circumstances in which he was now placed, such a repudiation of the covenant which God had made with Abraham appeared to be, as it really was, a heinous sin, and was at once recognized by him as the cause of his affliction. Accordingly, to save his life, he prevailed upon Zipporah to perform the rite herself; and when she laid at his feet the evidence that she had done so, she exclaimed, in the excitement of her feelings and with a tone of displeasure in her voice, "Surely a bloody husband art thou to me." But when she saw his speedy recovery, she changed her tone, and repeated in gratitude what she had formerly said in anger.

The third incident of his journey was his meeting with his brother Aaron, whom God had directed where to find him. No doubt, after their affectionate salutation, they asked each other of their welfare, and each would have much to say to the other of the incidents of those forty years in Egypt and

---

* On this whole subject, see "Keil and Delitzsch on the Pentateuch," vol. i., p. 453-457.

in Midian. But the hearts of both were heavy for their enslaved kinsmen, and the younger brother did not care to record anything of their interview but this: "Moses told Aaron all the words of the Lord who had sent him, and all the signs which he had commanded him." That was enough for Aaron. Possibly he too had received some special communication from Jehovah, which prepared him for ready acquiescence in the proposal of his brother, thus confirmed by miracle, that they should go in company into Egypt and begin their emancipation work. At all events, he makes no objection and interposes no delay. So, together, they go to Goshen, and there assemble the elders of Israel. Moses is wiser now than he was forty years ago. He will not begin to fight merely "for his own hand." He will not resist individual instances of oppression, in the hope of thereby rousing the slumbering spirit of the people. But he assembles the elders, and through them seeks to understand what the views and feelings of the people are. From them he learned that their oppression continued as burdensome as ever; and it seemed now that the set time of their deliverance had indeed come, for when the people saw the signs which Moses wrought before their eyes, "they believed; and when they heard that the Lord had visited the children of Israel, and that he had looked upon their affliction, they bowed their heads and worshipped."

But the end was not so near as it appeared to be; for when the two brothers went in before Pharaoh and made the demand which God had instructed them to present, they were met with disdainful defiance. Professing utter ignorance of Jehovah and indifference to him, the king flatly refused to let the Hebrews go; and pretending that the presence of Moses and Aaron was hindering the people at their work, he sent for the taskmasters, who were Egyptians, and their officers or scribes, who were Hebrews, and commanded them to withhold the straw which they had been in the habit of supplying to the brickmakers, and at the same time to insist on receiving an undiminished quantity of bricks. This branch of work was apparently a government monopoly in ancient Egypt, as nearly all the bricks that are now found are stamped with a king's name. They were made of clay mixed with chopped straw, and then hardened by the sun. At first the straw was given to the Hebrews; but now they had to go and find it for themselves in the fields, where it was left by the reapers, who cut the stalks close to the ears. Very soon, however, all the meadows in their neighborhood would be bared, and then they would be compelled to scatter over all the land in search of the very materials for their work. Of course, they could not keep up their tale of bricks, and equally, of course, the officers were beaten; for then, as now, Egypt was ruled largely by the stick. An appeal to Pharaoh brought no relief. He was bent on giving them something else to think of than sacrificing to their God, and he cruelly taunted them with idleness, alleging that as the reason why they wished to serve Jehovah. Thus the people were discouraged, and upbraided the two brothers with being the authors of their misery.

Dispirited and disappointed, Moses returned unto God, and cried to him in passionate ejaculation: "Lord, wherefore hast thou so evil entreated this people? Why is it that thou hast sent me? for since I came to Pharaoh to speak in thy name, he hath done evil to this people; neither hast thou delivered thy people at all." In answer to this natural but sad complaint, God renewed in, if possible, stronger language than ever the assurances which he had already given to his servant. He indicated, moreover, that the time had come for the execution of his judgments upon Pharaoh, and based the certainty of their infliction on the declaration, "I am Jehovah." Indeed, no one can read the opening verses of the sixth chapter of Exodus without remarking the prominence which is given in them to this significant name. Four times the Lord repeats the words, "I am Jehovah;" and in connection with the first occurrence of them, he adds, "I appeared unto Abraham, unto Isaac, and unto Jacob, by the name of God Almighty, but by my name JEHOVAH was I not known unto them." This declaration has caused great perplexity to the commentators, yet a very little penetration will enable us to discover its meaning. Many names for deity occur in the Hebrew writings, the principal of which are *Elohim* (sometimes abbreviated into *El*); *El Shaddai*, or God Almighty, which refers especially to the attribute of power; *Adonai*, or Lord; and *Jehovah*, which designates God as he stands in relation to men as their deliverer and redeemer. When the word *God* or *Lord* is printed in the English Bible, in small capitals, we may know that it is the equivalent of Jehovah in the original; but when it is printed in ordinary type, it is then the translation of some other name. Now, when the Lord says that he was known to the patriarchs as El Shaddai, and not as Jehovah, we are to understand that he uses the term name, not of the letters which form the word, but of the true significance of the word. The patriarchs did know the word Jehovah;* but the people were now to find out all the faithfulness, and tenderness, and covenant-keeping deliverance which the word implied. Thus the statement, which seems at first so startling, must be taken not as an absolute, but as a comparative negation. Formerly, the chief aspect in which God revealed himself was that of power; now he is about to manifest himself as the faithful performer of his promises— "the same yesterday, to-day, and forever"— unchangeable in his purposes as in his essence. Pharaoh had asked,

---

* Gen. xii., 7, 8; xxii., 14.

"Who is Jehovah, that I should obey his voice?" The Lord replies, "I AM," and he proceeds to unfold his meaning to him in that desolating series of miracles, all of which were wrought by him, that he might fulfil the word which he had spoken to his servant Abraham. Fitly, therefore, does he here connect his new promise to Moses with his old covenant with the Father of the faithful. He was now about to deliver the Hebrews from slavery, to adopt them as his own peculiar people, and to give them the secure possession of the land of Canaan; and he would have Moses understand, for his own consolation and support, that this was no sudden determination on his part, but only the fulfilment of a covenant which had been ratified four hundred years before.

This assurance was enough for Moses himself, and served, for the time at least, to remove all his misgivings; but when he went with it to his kinsmen, "they hearkened not unto him for anguish of spirit, and for cruel bondage." They could not see farther than the present; and because the first attempt of Moses to work out their deliverance had resulted in an aggravation of their misery, they had lost heart, and would listen to him no more. Worse than all, this rejection of him by his kinsmen reacted sorely on Moses himself; and when a new commission came to him, "Go in, speak unto Pharaoh, king of Egypt, that he let the children of Israel go out of his land," he made this desponding reply, "Behold, the children of Israel have not hearkened unto me; how then shall Pharaoh hear me, who am of uncircumcised lips?" This brought new consolation to him from his Lord, who once more encouraged him by associating formally his brother Aaron with him in his mission, and by repeating the assurance that Pharaoh would be humbled, and compelled to let the people go. And so, fortified by these promises, the brothers went together a second time into the presence of the king. And there we must leave them for the present, while we seek to extract for ourselves the practical lessons of the history over which we have now come.

We may learn, then, in the first place, that he who would lead others into obedience must himself be exemplary. This seems to me to be the practical significance of that scene in the inn, around which so much obscurity still hovers. The purpose of God in calling Moses was to make him, humanly speaking, the emancipator and educator of Israel; and one of the first and most important qualifications which he needed for that work was reverence for law. Hence means were taken to recall to his attention the fact that he had neglected to claim the covenant blessing for his son, by obeying the command which God had given to Abraham for himself and for his seed after him. He had, perhaps, yielded to the importunities of his Midianitish wife in the matter; and he might have been tempted to think that it was a very slight thing after all. But he must learn to know no one but God, when duty is in the case; and in the very outset of his ministry, he must have it impressed upon his heart that nothing is little which God has thought it important enough to command. There is a temptation to be encountered at the beginning of every enterprise; and according as we meet that, we demonstrate our fitness or unfitness for entering upon the undertaking. The burning bush and the scene in the inn correspond, in the life of Moses, to the baptism, and the conflict with Satan in the wilderness, in the history of the Lord Jesus; and the greatest danger to which we are exposed at such testing-times is that of thinking that the matter in question is one of no great importance. The making of bread out of stones was a little thing to him who had the power of Omnipotence at his call, even as the circumcision of his son was a small affair to Moses; but if Jesus had yielded to do the one, at Satan's bidding, he could have been no Saviour of sinners; and if Moses, at the urgency of Zipporah, had consented to continue to neglect the other, he would never have become the emancipator of the Hebrews. This is the great law: "He that is faithful in that which is least, is faithful also in much; and he that is unjust in the least, is unjust also in much." How could Moses have taken such a stand as he afterward did with Aaron, with the people, and with the rebellious company of Korah, Dathan, and Abiram, if he had not first learned to take it with himself? We cannot have it too frequently repeated that our first battle is with ourselves, and that it is commonly over something which may seem to be a trifle. But that intensifies the danger; for it helps to make us unconscious of the test to which at the moment God is subjecting us; and so our only safeguard is to seek in everything, however apparently unimportant it may be, to be loyal to the will of God. Friends, will you lay this to heart? When you are starting out on some new and noble work, with aspirations kindled at some flaming bush of divine revelation to your soul, "be not high-minded, but fear." Look for some test to be administered to you just then, and look for it in no great affair, but rather in some such common thing as the getting of your daily bread, or in some such domestic matter as the government of your children; for by these God may be determining your fitness for the work you covet: and if you fail in the trial, there will come no second probation. When Gideon led his forces down to the river and made them drink, each man did as he liked best; and yet, unknown to them all, God was thereby dividing the self-indulgent from the self-forgetting, and choosing the latter for the enterprise of honor which was to rout the Midianites. That was not the last time that drinking was made a test of fitness, and there may be those before me now who have been rejected because they preferred appetite to duty.

But we may learn, in the second place, that when God begins to work for a soul's emancipation, the first effect is frequently an increase of its misery. When Moses demanded from Pharaoh the liberation of the Hebrews, the tyrant increased their burdens; and in like manner, when the soul rises to expel evil from its domain, it then for the first time discovers the full bitterness of its bondage. Its earliest impulse thereon is to blame the truth which awakened it to a sense of its degradation, for causing the misery which it only revealed. The preacher is accounted cruel when he has been only faithful; and his hearer accuses him of personal malice when he has been only holding up a mirror wherein the angry one caught a glimpse of himself.

But all these are hopeful signs. They are indeed, when rightly regarded and fostered, the prophecies of a coming conversion. The docile slave, who is contented with his condition, is petted and made much of by his master; but if he tries to run away, he is immediately put into fetters. So, when we are roused to battle with sin, it is then that, most of all, we feel its power. It is easy to float with the current, but it is hard to row against the stream; and thus it comes, that the agony and efforts of the awakened sinner are considered by him to be more oppressive than any experience of his former iniquities. But the truth should not be blamed for that, and neither the sinner nor the Moses preacher should fall into despair because of that. It is the invariable accompaniment of emancipation. The outgoing tenant does not care how dreadfully he abuses the house which he is so soon to quit. And Satan does his worst on the soul just as he is about to be expelled from its possession. You remember the history of the child demoniac, who had been brought for cure to the nine disciples during the absence of the Lord, and the other three on the Mount of Transfiguration, and whose father came to Jesus just as

He descended into the valley. He told a pitiful story, and, moved with compassion, the Lord said, "Bring thy son hither." Then we read, "And as he was yet a coming, the devil threw him down, and tare him."* It was poor spite in the demon. It was atrociously cruel; yet it was, after all, a confession of defeat in the presence of the Conqueror, and so a forerunner of cure. Now, it is the same with those aggravations of misery which the sinner feels in the moment of his awakening, and just when he thinks he has accepted God's salvation. The first stage of the convert's experience is one of joy, corresponding to the gladness of the Israelites in hearing the first message of Moses and Aaron to them; but the next is one of conflict, corresponding to that of the Hebrews when their straw was taken from them, and their tale of brick undiminished. Let the anxious soul fully understand this, and its perplexity will cease; for the added burdens and the cynical sneers that imputed idleness as a motive for worship, will all be accepted as the forerunners of its complete deliverance. When the city of Man-soul has to be given up by Satan, he will seek first to set it on fire; but before the flames can make head, he is in full retreat, and the great Emancipator has taken possession.

Finally, we may learn that there are only two ways of knowing Jehovah. The Israelites up to this time had never had God revealed to them as Jehovah; and now they were to learn to know him as such, by his bringing them out of the house of bondage. Pharaoh exclaimed, in haughty disdain, to Moses, "Who is Jehovah?" and he had his answer in the plagues and death which devastated his land. The obedient know Jehovah as the deliverer; the disobedient know him as the destroyer. There is no middle term. Jehovah is the very best friend, or the very worst enemy,

---

* Luke ix., 42.

a man can have: the very best friend, because his faithfulness, wedded to his omnipotence, makes his promises all yea and amen; the very worst enemy, because his faithfulness, wedded to his omnipotence, makes his threatenings certain to be fulfilled. Which is he to you? And oh! remember that there is a point beyond which it may be impossible for you to have him as your friend. Pharaoh hardened his own heart at first; and then, in judgment, God confirmed that hardening and made it constant. So it may be with you, my hearer, if you persist in your disobedience to his commands. The capacity may be extirpated in you by disuse, and God may deliver you "to your own heart's lusts." I dare not say that he has done so in the case of any of you, but I must warn the disobedient among you that there is a possibility that he may do so; and I must urge upon them immediate submission as the only safeguard. Very solemn, in this connection, are the lines written by the late Dr. Joseph Addison Alexander. Let me leave their awful warning with you, as the application of this discourse:

> "There is a time, we know not when,
>   A point we know not where,
> That marks the destiny of men
>   To glory or despair.

> "There is a line, by us unseen,
>   That crosses every path;
> The hidden boundary between
>   God's patience and his wrath.

> "To pass that limit, is to die—
>   To die as if by stealth;
> It does not quench the beaming eye,
>   Or pale the glow of health.

> "The conscience may be still at ease,
>   The spirits light and gay;

That which is pleasing, still may please,
  And care be thrust away.

"But on that forehead God has set,
  Indelibly, a mark,
Unseen by men : for men as yet
  Are blind, and in the dark.

"Oh, where is this mysterious bourne
  By which our path is crossed?
Beyond which God himself hath sworn
  That he who goes is lost.

"How far may we go on in sin?
  How long will God forbear?
Where does hope end, and where begin
  The confines of despair?

"An answer from the skies is sent—
  'Ye that from God depart,
While it is said to-day, repent,
  And harden not your heart.'"

V.

THE TEN PLAGUES.

EXODUS vii., 8-x., 29; xii., 29, 30.

BEFORE proceeding to describe and comment upon the contest—so brief, and so decisive, yet in every respect so peculiar—which was carried on between Moses, as the representative of Jehovah, and Pharaoh, as the head of the world-power of his time, we have two preliminary remarks to make. In the first place, it is to be noted that only such a series of supernatural disasters as the ten plagues can account for the escape of the Israelites from their Egyptian oppressors. On the one hand, it is incontrovertible, that the posterity of Abraham were held in galling servitude for generations in the land of Ham. On the other, it is equally indisputable that they are found at length emancipated and settled in the land of Canaan. How is this to be explained? Evidently their liberation was not the voluntary act of the Egyptian king. It was not the manner of the Pharaohs thus to loosen their grasp on those who were in their power. Even in this nineteenth century of the Christian era, men speak of the emancipation of her slaves by England, and the setting free of his serfs by the Russian emperor, as exceptionally noble things: but in those early days such a generosity of justice was absolutely unknown; and if it were to be asserted that Pharaoh of his own free will, and out of regard to the natural rights of the Hebrews, had given them their liberty, everybody would feel that such an act was far more improbable than the occurrence of a physical miracle. Again, their deliverance could not have been the result of their own uprising, for they had not spirit enough to rebel against their masters; and if they had attempted such a thing, and had succeeded in it, they were not the people to have kept silence regarding it, but would have emblazoned it with unmistakable distinctness on their national annals. Furthermore, the escape of the Hebrews could not have been the consequence of any overthrow of Egypt by foreign enemies who sought to make their emancipation a means of weakening the Pharaohs; for not only is there no hint of anything of that sort in the sacred history, but in neither of the reigns to one or other of which the Exodus has been assigned by Egyptologists, is there on the monuments any indication of such an occurrence.* Unless, therefore, we admit that Egypt was severely crippled, and sorely terrified by such a series of desolating calamities, coming one after another, as is here recorded, it is absolutely impossible to account for the Exodus of the Israelites. Whether these judgments were or were not miraculous, is a question which will fall to be discussed at a future stage of our investigations; but in the mean time I call your attention to the fact that, apart from the exhaustion and terror and humiliation of Egypt, which only such a rapid succession of plagues could have produced, the exodus of the Hebrews becomes an insoluble enigma. The cause which is here assigned is the only one adequate to account for the result; and if we refuse to accept that, we leave one of the most marked and most impressive events of ancient history not only unexplained, but inexplicable.

But we must bear in mind, in the second place, that the contest on which Moses was now about to enter was not one merely for national independence. It is true, indeed, that it issued in the emancipation of the Hebrews, and in

---

* See "Speaker's Commentary," vol. i., p. 275.

the establishment of that sentiment of nationality which in the Jews has survived many centuries of expatriation and oppression. It is true, also, that it was the first step in the direction of that theocratic system which was codified in the Sinaitic law, and localized at length in Palestine. And every one will be forward to admit that the psalm which Moses chanted on the Red Sea shore became the national anthem of the Israelites, to which they recurred in all times of special trial or triumph. All that Tell was to the Swiss, or Bruce and Wallace to the Scotch, or Washington to the Americans, Moses was to the Hebrews. But he was also infinitely more, and their temporal deliverance was but the outward accessory and accompaniment of his prophetic mission. His commission came to him at the flaming bush, where he accepted the personal and eternal I AM, as the only sovereign of his heart, and the only king and ruler of the universe; and it was because he was the legate and representative of the one living and true God, that he was the emancipator of the oppressed. His mission was religious rather than political; or, if political at all, it was so only because it was religious. In a day when the nations of the earth had degenerated into the most debasing idolatry, he was sent to the very seat and head-quarters of the evil, to meet it with the positive declaration of the unity and supremacy of Jehovah; and we shall lose sight of the full magnitude and significance of the conflict in which he engaged, if we think of it mainly as a struggle for social and civil emancipation. It was, in his age, a battle quite similar to that which Elijah fought, in a later generation, with Ahab; and to that which, with more spiritual weapons, the Lord Jesus himself inaugurated during his public ministry on earth. That I am not wrong in this, will appear if we put into juxtaposition the following passages from the history of each. Hear what the Lord says at different times to

Moses: "The Egyptians shall know that I am Jehovah, when I stretch forth my hand upon Egypt, and bring out the children of Israel from among them." "That thou mayest tell in the ears of thy son, and of thy son's son, what things I have wrought in Egypt, and my signs which I have done among them; that ye may know how that I am the Lord." "Against all the gods of Egypt I will execute judgment: I am Jehovah."* Listen now to what Elijah says to God on Mount Carmel: "Jehovah, God of Abraham, Isaac, and of Israel, let it be known this day that thou art God in Israel, and that I am thy servant, and that I have done all these things at thy word. Hear me, O Lord, hear me, that this people may know that thou art Jehovah God, and that thou hast turned their heart back again."† Then open your ears to these words of Jesus, in his unparalleled prayer, "that they all may be one; as thou Father art in me, and I in thee; that they also may be one in us, that the world may believe that thou hast sent me."‡ Thus the personal existence and unity of God came uppermost in the mission of all the three. They were all alike witnesses for the supremacy of the only God, amid abounding idolatry; and the glories attendant on each of their histories were largely the accessories of this great design.

When we remember all this, we shall easily understand how at each of these three eras, and in connection with each of these three names, we have a dispensation of miracles; for only by deviating in individual instances from the established course of things which he is always maintaining, can Jehovah indicate that the natural and the supernatural are alike from him. Moreover, the perception of this identity in the mission of these three gives a new significance to their

---

* Exod. vii., 5; x., 2; xii., 12.   † 1 Kings xviii., 36, 37.
‡ John xvii., 21.

conference in glory on the Mount of Transfiguration; for it was as if the two great generals had come for a brief space to their old battle-field, to share with the commander-in-chief in the honor of that final victory which he was to win over the enemies whose strength they knew so well, and so they spake of "his decease which he should accomplish at Jerusalem." Let it be understood, then, that Moses enters in before Pharaoh as a legate of the Truth. That is his main object, and he becomes an apostle of freedom only because liberty and truth go ever hand in hand.

Now, let us mark the course which here the conflict took. At the first formal interview Moses made his demand and showed his credentials, for the rod which Aaron cast upon the ground became a serpent. But as the magicians whom Pharaoh called at the sight of this miracle did something like it, the king refused to accept it as the signature of God, even although the serpent into which Aaron's rod had been changed did, contrary to all nature, swallow up the others.

This sign was followed by the first of the plagues; for as Pharaoh was going to the Nile, perhaps for some idolatrous purpose, Moses met him and renewed his demand that Israel should be let go, threatening at the same time that he would turn the river into blood. But the king would not hear, and so Aaron's rod was stretched out and "all the waters that were in the river were turned into blood." That which was the pride and idol of Egypt became now an object of loathing, and "all the Egyptians digged round about the river for water to drink, for they could not drink of the water of the river." But because the magicians did on a small scale what seemed to be as really a miracle as that which followed on the word of Moses, Pharaoh would not relent. So the second plague was sent, and the land was covered with frogs. In the bedchambers and on the beds, in the ovens and in the kneading-troughs, these croaking abominations were found. But because the magicians were able, by their sleight-of-hand, to produce an imitation of this miracle, the king would not admit, at first, that it had come from Jehovah. At length, however, he besought Moses to have the frogs removed, and promised to yield to his demand; but when "he saw that there was respite," he hardened his heart as before. This brought upon him the plague of gnats, a species of mosquito, which was exceedingly distressing both to man and beast; but though his magicians failed even to imitate the production of these insects, Pharaoh was now more stubborn than before. Therefore the gnats were followed by the flies, which corrupted all the land, save the district of Goshen, which was now for the first time exempted from the influence of the plagues. Under the influence of this distressing visitation Pharaoh came so far as to say that the people might go and sacrifice to Jehovah, provided they did not leave Egypt. But Moses replied that they could not safely offer there in sacrifice animals which the Egyptians accounted holy; and then the king appeared to consent that they should go into the wilderness, "Only," he adds, as if reluctant to let them go at all, "ye shall not go very far away."

That, however, was only a momentary relenting; for when the flies had gone his penitence went with them, and then there came in succession a pestilence among the cattle, and a loathsome cutaneous disease upon the people themselves. These were followed by a fearful and long-continued thunder-storm, in the course of which hail fell so heavily that the trees were broken, and the barley and flax, which were then upon the ground, were completely ruined. Pharaoh was reduced by these to the same humiliation in the presence and under the pressure of the calamity, as before; but when "he saw that the rain and the hail and the thunders were ceased, he sinned yet more." And thus an eighth plague —that of the locusts; too familiar, alas! to our own Western farmers from recent experience—came upon the land. "And they did eat every herb of the land, and all the fruit of the trees which the hail had left; and there remained not any green thing in the trees or in the herbs of the field." It seemed almost as if the force of this chastisement, combined with the entreaties of some of his own servants, had at last prevailed over the royal pride. But no; for when the locusts were removed the king was as defiant as ever; and although after a visitation of darkness, such that "the people saw not one another, neither rose any from his place for three days," he sent for Moses and Aaron, with the intention of yielding so far as to let the people go if they would leave their families and flocks in Egypt, he became so infuriated at the demand that not a hoof should be left behind, as to say to Moses, "Get thee from me, take heed to thyself, see my face no more; for in that day thou seest my face thou shalt die." And it was as he requested—Moses saw his face no more. But ere long he had to meet a greater enemy; for now came the last and severest of these terrible calamities, entering into every home save those of the Hebrews, who were instructed how to ward it from their dwellings, and ordered, also, to hold themselves in readiness to march out of Egypt amid the consternation and preoccupation which it caused among their oppressors. It was a fearful judgment, and no language can portray it so vividly as the sublime words of the record itself: "At midnight the Lord smote all the first-born in the land of Egypt, from the first-born of Pharaoh that sat on his throne, unto the first-born of the captive that was in the dungeon; and all the first-born of cattle. And Pharaoh rose up in the night, he, and all his servants, and all the Egyptians; and there was a great cry in Egypt, for there was not a house where there was not one dead."*

---

* Exod. xii., 29, 30.

The issues of this great infliction will come up for consideration in a future discourse; meanwhile we must look for a little at the general characteristics of these plagues, and at the effects which they produced on all concerned.

The candid reader of the narrative must admit that the historian intends to produce the impression that these plagues were miraculously inflicted. Indeed, having regard to the issues raised in the contest, it is impossible to see how they could have had any place in it at all unless they are to be so regarded. The very matter to be established was the personal existence and supremacy of Jehovah. The ground on which the demand of Moses was based was not that the Hebrews had a right to their civil freedom, though that was true, but rather that Jehovah had the prior claim to their service, and that Pharaoh too was bound to yield him obedience. The great reason constantly assigned by God for Pharaoh's submission to him was, "*I am Jehovah.*" This involved an assertion of his sovereignty over the universe; and he could prove that he was the upholder of the common order of nature only by deviating from that order in certain previously indicated instances. When we put the matter in this light, you will see in a moment that the whole objection, which in these days is urged so much, as to the antecedent impossibility of miracles, is at once disposed of. For if there be an intelligent and personal Cause sustaining the common order of nature, it is just as possible for him to deviate in exceptional cases, and for a worthy end, from that order, as it is for him to carry it continuously on. So, if the being of God be admitted at all, the possibility of miracles is involved in that admission. But Pharaoh admitted in the abstract the being of Deity, only he contended that the god whom he worshipped was the true God; and now by this series of miracles Jehovah demonstrated that he alone is the ruler of the universe.

It has been attempted by some, indeed, to show that these judgments were all of such a sort as occur naturally in Egypt. The blood-water they would resolve into the red color of the Nile at certain stages of its rise; and the frogs, the gnats, the flies, the thunder and the hail, are all visitations that might have come in the ordinary course; while the darkness "that might be felt" is not unlike that produced by a sand-storm in the present day. But suppose we admit all that—as, save in the instance of the water, I am disposed to do—what the better are we? Does that dispose of the miracles? That only shows what multitudes of other cases go to establish that God in his miracles makes the natural the basis of the supernatural. But it is very far, indeed, from reducing the occurrences to merely natural events; for, observe, they were all completely under the control of Moses as the agent of Jehovah. They came at his word, and they went at his intercession. In this particular they were precisely similar to the drought which Elijah foretold before Ahab; and they who would reduce them to the level of mere natural occurrences are not only shutting their eyes to the meaning of the whole contest, but are leaving the fact of the Exodus, and the whole after-religious history of Israel, without adequate explanation. Without this supernatural foundation the history of Israel becomes, in itself, a moral miracle so astounding as to be harder of belief than that the Nile was changed into blood. With this accepted, all that comes after is at once easily accounted for.

But if we contend that the plagues were miraculous, must we not also admit that the works of the magicians were supernatural? This is, in fact, conceded by many eminent authors, among whom even such an orthodox expositor as Kurtz is to be included. But holding a miracle to be an effect out of the usual sequence of secondary causes and effects, and produced by the direct agency of God, I cannot admit that the magicians performed works worthy of that name; and the record over which to-night we have traversed seems to me, when rightly read, to confirm the opinion which I have just announced. Let a careful analysis of these chapters be made, and the following things may be inductively gathered from them, namely, that the magicians could only go a certain length in their reproductions (allowing, for the moment, that they were reproductions) of the works of Moses; that on all the occasions on which their feats were successful, intimation was given either of what Moses had done, or of what he was about to do, in time to allow opportunity on their part for preparation; and that in the case in which they failed this intimation was not given, and so they were taken unawares, having had no information furnished them, and consequently having no preparation made. Now, does not all this look as if they had, in the successful instances, prepared themselves by some natural means to produce something like what Moses was to do; but that, on this new occasion, being taken by surprise, they only made a feint of attempting to counterfeit it, and immediately covered their retreat by saying, "This is the finger of God?" Indeed, if this explanation be not accepted, it will be hard to see what there was more difficult in the bringing of the gnats than in the production of the frogs. Nay, if it be allowed that they really and truly changed a rod into a serpent, which was a virtual act of creation—since it was the bringing of serpent-life out of that which had in it no germ of serpent-life—it will be impossible to tell why those who could do that divine work could not perform the other. Hence, putting all these things together, we are compelled to conclude that the wonders done by the magicians were not miracles at all, but mere feats of legerdemain similar to those which are common to this day among the jugglers of the East.

But some will say, "Is it not affirmed that the magicians did so? and does not that imply that they did the same things as Moses?" To such a question the obvious reply is, "No; for in the very instance in which they failed the same words are employed, 'The magicians did so with their enchantments, and they could not.'" What is, to my mind, conclusive on the point, however, is the fact already adverted to, that some of the works done at the word of Moses were virtual creations. Now, if there be one power which may be regarded as more peculiarly and incommunicably divine than another, it is that of creation; yet here, if these magicians did real miracles, we are required to believe that created spirits — it makes no matter whether human or demoniacal — working in antagonism to God, did exercise this divine omnipotence. The thing is absurd. Even if we admit, what indeed it concerns us not to deny, that evil spirits can produce physical effects just as the will of man can, yet it is inconceivable either that they should have a power that is distinctively divine, or that God should delegate that power to them for the mere purpose of contending with it—as if one, in a game of chess, should match his right hand against his left. Clearly, therefore, whatever those works of the magicians were, they were not miracles in the only sense in which we can employ that term. They were no more than feats of conjuring; for, as Dr. W. L. Alexander has said, "The jugglers of India will for a few pence do tricks with serpents far more wonderful than making them rigid, so as to resemble staves; and any juggler could make water in a tank resemble blood; or, when the country was already swarming with frogs, could cover some place that had been cleared for the purpose with these reptiles, as if he had suddenly produced them."[*] And, I may add, if

---

[*] Alexander's "Kitto," vol. i., p. 750.

the magicians had removed the plagues, that would have been something to the purpose, and would have clearly demonstrated their superiority to Moses; but the fact that they never attempted anything of that kind shows that their power was only that of conjurers, inferior in many respects to Hartz and Heller among ourselves.

Another feature of this series of supernatural judgments is its climactic character. Each calamity rises above that which went before it, adding new elements of terror, until at length the culmination is reached in that universal bereavement when "there was no house in which there was not one dead." The first blow fell upon the Nile; the next three affected the physical comfort of the people; the next decimated the cattle; the next affected the health of the nation; the next two swept away the food of the community; the darkness carried terror into the hearts of the individuals, and the destroying angel sent death into their homes. Now, if with this very striking feature of these plagues we combine the fact that, from the first up till the ninth, the demand of Jehovah for the unconditional submission of Pharaoh was repeated and refused after each, we have brought before us a most important principle of the divine administration. The Lord does not visit the first act of disobedience with his severest punishment, but marks his displeasure by a comparatively light affliction; yet if that be disregarded, a heavier is sure to follow; and so on and on, until at length "he who, being often reproved, hardeneth his neck, is suddenly cut off, and that without remedy." It is a serious thing, therefore, for a man, or for a community, to disregard even the slightest affliction from Jehovah's hand; for each arrow that is taken from his quiver is more destructive than that which went before it, and hardened resistance to his will brings down upon itself accumulated and accelerated wrath. It was bad enough to have the blessing of pure water changed into a curse, but that was as nothing to the death of the first-born; and if the first had been heeded, the last had not been inflicted. So, from the consideration of this chapter of ancient history, new emphasis is given to the solemn words of Jeremiah: "If thou hast run with the footmen, and they have wearied thee, then how canst thou contend with horses? And if in the land of peace wherein thou trustedst, they wearied thee, then how wilt thou do in the swellings of Jordan?"

But now, turning for a moment or two to the results produced by these plagues, we can see that they were calculated to prepare the mind of Moses himself for the arduous work which lay before him in the leading of the tribes through the wilderness. That enterprise would task to the utmost his courage, his patience, and his faith; and reluctant as he was to undertake it at the first, he might have been often tempted to give it up in despair, had he not been fortified at the very outset with the assurance which the sight of these plagues produced within him, that the Lord whom he served was indeed Jehovah, and had the resources of the universe at his command. We may rely upon it that this early experience had much to do with the fostering within him of those qualities of meekness, calmness, fortitude, and forbearance which, as we shall see in the sequel, came out so conspicuously in his march through the desert. Already the Lord was fulfilling to him the promise, "Certainly I will be with thee;" and this foretaste of his faithfulness strengthened him forever afterward. Thus the Lord not only "brake the head of leviathan in pieces" for him, but gave the monster "to be meat to the people inhabiting the wilderness." A similar effect would be produced on the Hebrews themselves; and they needed this quickening of their faith even more than Moses did, for their protracted slavery had resulted in a great debasement both of their intellectual and religious life. They might, and did sometimes, forget what they had seen done for them by God in Egypt; but always when it was recalled to their recollection they would rise to faith in the majesty of God; while the fact that they themselves experienced the effects of the first four plagues would tend to produce in them a holy fear of offending him who was, in one aspect of his character, "the great and dreadful God." It is probable, also, that a salutary impression was wrought on the minds of many of the Egyptians themselves; for not only did the servants of Pharaoh expostulate with him on his stubbornness, but multitudes of the common people joined themselves with the Hebrews, and went forth with them when they left the land of Goshen.

But the pre-eminent design of these wonders was to demonstrate the glory of Jehovah as contrasted with the vanity of the Egyptian idols; for almost every one of the miracles tended to bring into contempt some object which the Pharaohs and their people worshipped. This is clear from the following summary, which I take from Dr. William L. Alexander:* "The devouring of the serpents by the serpent into which the rod of Moses had been turned, was directed against the serpent-worship of Egypt; the turning of the water into blood was an assault on their sacred river, the Nile; the plague of the frogs, the gnats, the flies (or scarabæi), all tended to bring objects of idolatrous worship among the Egyptians into contempt; the murrain among the cattle was directed against their Apis-worship; the plague of boils, brought on by the casting of ashes from the altar into the air—a rite which they followed to arrest evil—showed how God could reverse their omen, and make what they used for good to turn to evil; the hail and storm plague was directed against their worship of the elements, or of deities supposed

---

* Alexander's "Kitto," vol. i., p. 751.

to preside over them; the plague of locusts showed that this great scourge, which they were accustomed to trace to the wrath of their deities, was entirely in the power of Jehovah; the plague of darkness poured contempt on their worship of the sun-god; and the death of the first-born wound up this terrible series, by showing that in the hand of Jehovah alone was the life of all his creatures. A mighty and a memorable lesson was thus read out before both Egyptians and Israelites, which could not but have its effect in weakening among the former the attachment of many to their idols, and confirming the latter in their reverence for Jehovah as the only true God."

I have left myself but little time for practical application, but I may not let you go without seeking to give brief emphasis to three lessons, which seem to me to be enforced by this history.

We may learn, then, in the first place, that repentance which springs only from fear is always transient. After each of the plagues, from that of the frogs to that of the darkness, Pharaoh promised to let Israel go; and on one occasion he came so far as to say to Moses, "I have sinned against the Lord your God, and against you." But it is noticeable that this state of mind was evoked only by the presence and pressure of calamity, and that so soon as the plague was removed he became more hardened in his obstinacy than before. His professions of repentance and promises of amendment were thus like those of the child under the rod of chastisement: they were designed to mitigate the infliction, and when the punishment was over, they went for nothing. Now, this is always the case when fear alone predominates over the soul; and in proof of that assertion, I need only remind you of the parallel cases of Saul and Ahab, neither of whom had in his heart even one spark of love to God. I would not, indeed, disparage fear as a motive of action. Terror may awaken a man to thought, and may rouse him to self-examination; but unless it yield at length to love, no permanent improvement will be produced on the life of the individual; for fear, of itself, will drive away God, and it is only when we are assured that God loves us, and have thereby produced in us the beginning of love to God, that we will repair to him. True and permanent penitence, therefore, has its root in faith in God's love. It is born now at the cross of Christ, where, though the evil of sin is made tremendously apparent, the very blackness of the cloud of judgment only brings into stronger relief the rainbow of mercy which shines out of it. Love grapples the soul to God, fear drives it away from him; and so the penitence which springs only from the feeling of present punishment, or the fear of future punishment, is never lasting. True repentance has, as its constituent elements, not only grief and hatred of sin, but also an apprehension of the mercy of God in Christ. It hates the sin, and not simply the penalty; and it hates the sin most of all because it has discovered God's love. Ah, how much of our penitence is like this of Pharaoh! and how many are saints on a sick-bed, but as wicked as ever when they recover! During an epidemic of cholera in the village where I first labored as a minister, the churches were filled to overflowing by suppliants who had never before entered them; but when it had passed, they relapsed into worse carelessness than ever: and there may be some here to-night who, when they were dangerously ill, or when they were laying a dear little one's body in the grave, vowed to God that they would yield themselves to him; while now they are as far from his service as ever. Let me beseech such hardened ones to beware. Their case is perilously like that of Pharaoh; and they have need, ere it be too late, to awake to their great danger. Remember God loves you; and if you would know how much

The Ten Plagues. 93

he loves you, go to Calvary, and see there the sacrifice he made that he might be able righteously to forgive you. Let that reveal to you the magnitude of your guilt, and the majesty of his mercy. Lay hold now of his love; for, unless you do that, your repentance will be as "a morning cloud, or as the early dew," that goeth away.

But we may learn, in the second place, from this subject, that the root of unbelief is in the heart rather than the head. Scepticism is not so much an intellectual thing as an immoral thing. There are exceptions; but for the most part a man does not believe, because he does not want to believe. We sometimes hear men say that if they had seen the miracles of Jesus, they would certainly have accepted him. But Pharaoh saw real miracles. He never thought of questioning their genuineness; and if he had, the words of his own magicians, "This is the finger of God," would have reproved him. Yet he did not submit himself to Jehovah. Rather, he was determined to oppose him at all hazards. He preferred his own royal pride to the humility of obedience; and so, the miracles notwithstanding, he resisted Jehovah. In the same way the Scribes and Pharisees saw Christ's miracles, but were not thereby induced to become his followers. They would not join his ranks, not because they disputed the reality of his miracles, but because they rebelled against the searching inwardness of his doctrines. And, in these days of ours, many men profess that they cannot believe in Jesus because of intellectual difficulties; when the truth is, that they will not believe in him, because their lives are condemned by his words. Even if they were to see miracles wrought in his name before their eyes, it would make no difference to them; they do not wish to have him as their Lord, and that is all. Ah, there are none so blind as those who will not see! And for all its intellectual pretensiveness, infidelity springs from a heart that is wrong with God, far more frequently than from a head which is unusually acute.

Finally, we may learn from this subject that the issue of a conflict with God must always be disastrous to his adversary. Pharaoh made nothing out of his resistance. He was defeated all along the line, and only courted his own destruction. True, it did not come all at once. Long years of arrogant oppression of God's people preceded this dreadful Nemesis. But it came at last, and it was crushing when it did come. Let not the warning be lost upon us. Our antagonism cannot harm God, but it will destroy ourselves. Do not forget these words: "The nation and kingdom that will not serve thee shall perish: yea, those nations shall be utterly wasted." And that is as true of individuals as of nations. Oh, why will you break yourselves against the thick bosses of the Almighty's buckler, when by timely obedience you may have that buckler spread over you as a shield?

VI.

THE PASSOVER.

EXODUS xii., 1–51; 1 COR. v., 7, 8.

FULLY to understand the position of the Hebrews on the night of the Passover and the Exodus, it is necessary for us to go back a little way in the narrative. The first three plagues fell on them equally with the Egyptians; but when Moses, as the legate of Jehovah, threatened Pharaoh with the visitation of swarms of flies, he was commissioned to say in the name of God, "I will sever in that day the land of Goshen, in which my people dwell, that no swarms of flies shall be there;"* and from that point on, the children of Israel were exempted from the terrible inflictions by which the Egyptians were desolated. No pestilence fell on man or beast among them; the lightning and thunder and hail which spread terror and destruction elsewhere were unknown in Goshen; the locusts which devastated the fields in other districts did no damage among them; and the thick darkness which for three days wrapped its impenetrable mantle round the rest of the land did not interfere with their convenience, for "all the children of Israel had light in their dwellings."† Thus, while the minds of their oppressors were engrossed with their own sufferings, the Hebrews were at peace; and when the Egyptians were prevented from moving from place to place, by storm or darkness, the slave population of Goshen had ample opportunity to make prep-

---

* Exod. viii., 22. † Ib. x., 23.

arations for that departure from their house of bondage which Moses assured them was so near. During the days when Pharaoh and his people were crippled and confined by the plagues which came upon them, Moses and Aaron were doubtless busy among the tribes; and it was on the occasion of one such interview that the ordinance concerning the Passover, contained in the first part of the twelfth chapter of Exodus, was given. I cannot but think that if this consideration had been duly weighed, Bishop Colenso, who has pressed his arithmetic so strongly into the service of unbelief, would not have insisted on some of his objections to the credibility of this narrative so confidently as he has done. That ingenious sceptic has alleged, that as Moses received his command about the Passover on the very day on which it was to be observed, he could not possibly have communicated it in time to every head of every household among the people; and further, that the notice to start at once in the middle of the night could not have been circulated among the tribes in so brief an interval. But who told this mitred rationalist that Moses received his instructions from Jehovah, and gave them to the people, on the very day on which the Passover was to be eaten? Let us look at the record itself, and see what materials it furnishes for settling the date of the ordinance. It runs in this wise: "Speak ye unto all the congregation of Israel, saying, in the tenth day of this month they shall take to them every man a lamb."* Here, then, is an order given for the tenth day of the month; but the Passover was to be eaten on the fourteenth; so that, at the very least, it must have been received and proclaimed *four days* before the Exodus. But as it is likely that some little interval must have come in, even between its publication and the tenth day to which it refers, we may not err in

---

* Exod. xii., 3.

dating its reception by Moses, and its promulgation among the people, at the beginning of the month. No doubt we are reminded that, a little farther down, the author of the ordinance says, "I will pass through the land of Egypt this night."* But every candid interpreter must see that the phrase "in this night" refers not to the night of the day on which the words were spoken, but rather to that of the day to which, throughout, reference is made by the speaker. And if we bear in mind that the Exodus was immediately preceded by those three days of darkness during which the Egyptians could not move from their place, while to the Hebrews it was light, we shall see in that fact an admirably guarded opportunity for the organizing of the slave population for their departure. Of course Colenso will sneeringly answer that he does not believe in any such nonsense as that preternatural darkness. But happily we are responsible only for the consistency of the narrative as it is, and not as it would be if every element of the miraculous were eliminated from it; and when we defend our position by a reference to this divine work and the facilities which it afforded to the Israelites, we are not to be put out of court by an objection, on *a priori* grounds, to the very possibility of miracles. If that objection holds, then the whole Bible goes, and all the bishop's arithmetical calculations to prove its falsity are just so many works of supererogation; but if that objection be repelled, and this series of judgments which fell on Egypt, but from which the Hebrews were exempt, be admitted as historical, then we have in them opportunities ample enough, if improved, for the preparation even of so many lambs for the hasty yet sacramental meal of an escaping and delivered nation.

Let it be understood, then, that on some day between the

---

* Exod. xii., 12.

first and the tenth of the month Abib, which corresponds to the latter part of our March and the former part of our April, Moses communicated to the people through their representatives, called here "the elders of Israel," the injunctions which are here recounted. They were to be carefully obeyed by every household in connection with their exemption from the plague which inflicted death on the firstborn, and with their departure from their house of bondage. These injunctions were substantially as follows: On the tenth day every head of a house was to choose a lamb or a kid, a male of the first year, without any disease or physical defect. If his family were not sufficient to consume the whole lamb, he might unite with his neighbor in its participation; and if any part of it should after all be left, that was to be burned with fire. The lamb was to be kept from the tenth to the fourteenth day of the month, and then it was to be killed in the latter part of the afternoon.* The blood was to be preserved in a basin, and was, with a bunch of hyssop, to be sprinkled on "the two side-posts and the upper door-post" of the tents or houses in which they were. Then the carcass was to be cooked entire by being roasted, and not boiled, and was to be served with bitter herbs. They were to eat it with unleavened bread, having, at the same time, their loins girt and their staves in their hands, so as to be ready at a moment's notice to set out on their journey. Special significance was attached to the sprinkling of the blood, as being not simply the sign of their deliverance from the last plague, but also, in some sense, the means of ensuring their safety; for thus it was ordained, "None of you shall go out at the door of his house until the morning, for the Lord will pass through to smite the Egyptians; and

---

* Literally, between the two evenings; that is, some time between the beginning of afternoon and sunset.

when he seeth the blood upon the lintel and on the two side-posts, the Lord will pass over the door and will not suffer the destroyer to come unto your houses to smite you." Moreover, it was intimated, thus early, that a similar feast should be observed on the same day of the same month annually among them, whereby the remembrance of the deliverance from Egypt, which God had wrought out on their behalf, should be perpetuated among their descendants from generation to generation.

These commands were reverently received and implicitly obeyed by the Hebrews. No one among them said, "We have escaped five of the plagues without the observance of any such rites, and why should we be required to do anything now?" Neither was the objection started in any household, that there was no apparent efficacy in the blood of a lamb sprinkled on their door-posts, to keep away death from the family. They had seen in these latter months testimonies enough to the faithfulness of God in the fulfilment of his word as spoken by Moses, and now the simple promulgation of his ordinance was sufficient. "They bowed the head and worshipped," and they went and did as they were commanded. That which was in all the years of their national history a commemoration of their deliverance, was at first a prophecy of their emancipation and an ordinance issued in anticipation of their Exodus. Therefore their obedience was an expression of their confidence in God; and so of them, also, as of Moses, it was true that "through faith they kept the Passover and the sprinkling of blood, lest he that destroyed the first-born should touch them."*

Let us endeavor to reproduce somewhat the scenes of that much-to-be-remembered night. The full moon shone clearly out over the Egyptian landscape—for in arranging

---

* Heb. xi., 28.

for a midnight journey to be hastily made by his chosen people, even such a minute matter was thought of, and the date on which the moon was at the full was deliberately selected. All was quiet in the streets of the city wherein for the time the Pharaoh had his residence; but out in the quarter occupied by the Hebrew brickmakers there was unwonted life. No one, indeed, could be seen running about among the huts; but lights gleamed out through every aperture, and in every dwelling there was a feast. As you neared their habitations you might have seen by the moonlight the big blood-stains on the door-posts; and if you could have passed within each entrance, you would have found that everything available had been packed into the kneading-trough, from which the unleavened bread had been taken to be hastily baked upon the fire; while the members of the family were standing all ready for a journey, and eating their meal with as much of eager hurry as is manifested by modern travellers in the restaurant of a railway station. But if you had asked them whither they were going, not one of them could have given you a reply; and if you had requested them to go forth with you and look upon the beauteous night, they would have pointed you to the mystic blood upon the lintel, and would have said, "We pass not out from beneath that until Jehovah summons us." Nor had they long to wait for his command; for hark! a shriek of agony is heard, distinct and loud as from some broken-hearted mourner, and another and another rises, long and clear, until the night is filled with lamentation. And while they gather at their doors, within them—yet near enough to see what is passing without—the royal messengers appear, with rage in their hearts and fury in their eyes, crying for Moses, and saying to him in the king's name, "Rise up, and get you forth from among my people." Nay, multitudes of the Egyptians themselves, roused by the grief of that awful night, beseech the Hebrews to depart immediately, saying, "We be all dead men." But they will not move until they have heard the word sent down from Moses through their elders; and then, laden with jewels of silver and jewels of gold, and raiment, which the terrified Egyptians gave them for the asking, they march out from Rameses—a nation born in a day. What a transformation that night has made upon them! Yesterday a horde of slaves, to-day a host of exultant freemen; yesterday a multitude of units, to-day a united people. By this one journey they have put Egypt and bondage behind them; they have begun that national life which neither Midianite nor Philistine, neither Assyrian nor Persian, neither Grecian nor Roman could destroy, and which, after eighteen centuries of dispersion through Gentile lands, beats yet with inextinguishable ardor in the breast of every Jew; for still, as on that paschal night, these scattered ones do eat their food with sandalled feet and tightened girdle, ready at any favorable opportunity to return to Palestine and claim their own again. Verily, it was a night much to be remembered.

But now, leaving the history for the time, let us look for a little at the Passover feast, with which this deliverance was connected. We are impressed, in the first place, with its sacrificial character. The lamb chosen by each household head was to be slain as "the sacrifice of the Lord's Passover;"* and in a remarkable passage occurring later in the history, the Lord speaks of it as "my sacrifice."† Moreover, in the permanent form which it assumed in the afterlegislation of Moses, it was, like other sacrifices, to be slain at the holy place, and its blood was to be sprinkled on the altar. Therefore, although at its first observance the head of the family was the priest, and the home was the sanctuary, it was as really a sacrifice as when, in later days, it was slain

---

* Exod. xii., 27. † Ib. xxxiv., 25; see also Exod. xxiii., 18.

at the Temple and the blood was sprinkled upon the altar. The Israelites were sinners as well as the Egyptians, but for their first-born God was pleased to accept the substitution of a lamb; and the putting of its blood upon the door-posts was designed to have an influence both toward him and toward them. So far as they were concerned, it was a sign to them of his sparing mercy, and an assurance that they would be delivered; so far as he himself was concerned, it was the emblem of a greater satisfaction which was to be rendered in the offering of a greater Lamb. And so he said, "When I see the blood, I will pass over you, and the plague shall not be upon you to destroy you, when I smite the land of Egypt."*

Further, this feast was designed as a memorial, for it was to be kept throughout their generations; and so, even in connection with the directions for its first observance, there are repeated injunctions concerning its annual celebration; others were added at a later date, yet its perpetual annual observance was no after-thought, but was evidently intended from the first. This was the birth-night of their national independence, and at the same time the date of their formal entrance as a people into the service of Jehovah. Now, if you will bear in mind that they were ere long to enter into covenant with their God, not for themselves only, but for their descendants also, you will see how this memorial came to be of importance. For the true value of every memorial lies in the educational service which it renders to the people among whom it is set up. The monuments of a nation are an epitome of its history; and their real worth is not in the artistic taste which they foster, or in the architectural adornments wherewith they beautify our cities, but in the scenes which they commemorate, and in the qualities of character for which those in whose honor they were reared were most

---

* Exod. xii., 13.

distinguished. They are worth preserving, therefore, not simply as memorials of the past, but as stimulating each successive generation to emulate the virtues of those whose names and fame they are designed to perpetuate. Now, just such an educational purpose the Passover was designed to serve through all the years of Israel's history. There were changes, indeed, in some matters of detail, but in its great outstanding features the perpetual Passover was identical with that of Egypt; and ever as the children, on their way to Jerusalem, inquired of their elders, "What mean ye by this service?" the answer would bring out this old story of a wonderful deliverance wrought out for their fathers in Egypt by the mighty hand and outstretched arm of Jehovah. Thus it is we account for the fact that in all the succeeding crises of their history we find the Jews turning with one accord to the scenes of this memorable night. The remembrance of these things lay so imbedded in the nation's heart, that whenever any great deliverance was spoken of they invariably reverted to them; and the song which Moses led and Miriam answered struck the key-note of all their hymns of thanksgiving. When their faith was faint, they called to mind these "days of old," and remembered these "years of the right hand of the Most High;"* and when they wished to call in the most earnest and believing fashion on their God, they cried, "Awake, awake, put on strength, O arm of the Lord; awake, as in the ancient days, in the generations of old. Art thou not it that hath cut Rahab, and wounded the dragon? Art thou not it which hath dried the sea, the waters of the great deep; that hath made the depths of the sea a way for the ransomed to pass over?"† Thus, through the constant observance of this ordinance, their literature, their religion, their character as a people were large-

---

* Psa. lxxvii., 10.   † Isa. li., 9, 10.

ly moulded; and in an age when books were almost unknown, the constant representation of this first great scene in their history served all the purposes which to-day are answered by our children's histories and our public schools. Nay, the impression made was all the deeper, because some of the most significant things were re-enacted before the eyes of the young people themselves.

But we must not neglect to add that this feast had a typical significance. In one sense, indeed, every fact in history has a bearing on the future; so that the words of Bacon, quoted in this very connection by Fairbairn, are undoubtedly true: "All history is prophecy." But the record with which we are now concerned was designed by God to be a prophetic parable, as well as a faithful conservator of actual fact. It is all true, for everything actually occurred as it is here described; but it is also symbolical, and points to a higher truth in the spiritual sphere. So the typical significance of the history as a whole gives a typical character also to the Passover. I doubt not John had this ordinance in mind when, pointing to Jesus, he said, "Behold the Lamb of God that taketh away the sin of the world;" and there is no question whatever as to the meaning of Paul when he affirms that "Christ our Passover is sacrificed for us." Now, in this view of the case, it is interesting to trace the points of resemblance between the type and the antitype; and though in all such things one is in danger of running the parallel into the ground by insisting on minute matters which have neither significance nor importance, yet we cannot be far wrong when we enumerate such coincidences as the following: The lamb was to be "without blemish;" so Christ was "holy, harmless, undefiled, and separate from sinners:" the lamb was to be slain, and its blood sprinkled on the door-posts; so Christ died for us, and, if we would be saved through him, we must make personal appropriation of his atonement: the Hebrews were to keep under the blood all that night; so we must not only come to Christ, but abide in him—that is, we must keep ourselves in the faith of his doctrine, in the imitation of his example, in the obedience of his precepts, and in the manifestation of his spirit: the lamb of sacrifice was also one of food, and their sacrifice became their sacrament; so Christ, the lamb of sacrifice, is also the bread of life; we eat his flesh and drink his blood, and he is to our believing souls what food is to the body: and, finally, this lamb was to be eaten by the people with their loins girt and their staves in their hands, ready at a moment's notice to arise and go; so the life of the believer here is one of transit, he is not to be in this world forever, and he must be always ready to leave it for a better. It would be easy to expand each of these analogies indefinitely, but I prefer to leave them all thus sharply defined before your minds, while I seek to extract from this ordinance, as it was afterward enlarged into a seven-day festival, some great principles which shall be profitable to us not only for doctrine but for life.

For this purpose I shall avail myself of the words of Paul, to which I have already incidentally alluded. They are to be found in 1 Corinthians v., 7, 8, and are as follows: "For even Christ our Passover is sacrificed for us: therefore let us keep the feast, not with old leaven, neither with the leaven of malice and wickedness, but with the unleavened bread of sincerity and truth." The apostle is giving advice in a case of discipline, and counsels that the wicked person should be cast out of the church, because "a little leaven" would soon "leaven the whole lump." But the reference to that familiar proverb naturally suggests to him, as a Jew, the fact that during the feast of the Passover all leaven was excluded from every dwelling among the people; and he proceeds to draw a parallel between the great national festival and the Christian life. He affirms that Christ has been sacrificed for us as our paschal lamb; and that as among the Jews a feast of seven days was connected with the slaying of that victim, and was characterized by the putting away of all leaven, so our whole Christian life should be a feast to the Lord, during which we should serve him with sincerity and truth. Now, accepting this as the true exposition of the spiritual significance of the Passover, I find in it three things of prime importance to ourselves.

In the first place, we see that the Christian life begins in the acceptance by the soul of deliverance through the sacrifice of Christ. "History," says Bunsen, "was born on the night when the children of Israel went forth out of Egypt;" and whether we agree with the universality of his statement or not, we must at least admit that the national life of the Israelites, as a theocracy, began at the Exodus. Now, the command to observe the Passover and the sprinkling of blood was the test by which each family was tried, and which determined for each whether its members were content to go forth under the leadership of Moses, or to remain in bondage. The willingness or unwillingness to accept deliverance from the doom of the first-born in God's way settled whether the man and his family should become free men under God, or should continue slaves under Pharaoh. From the moment of their observing the Passover, they were no longer the bondsmen of Egypt, but the children of God, soon to be baptized by him "in the cloud and in the sea." So the keeping of this Passover marked a new departure for them. It was the commencement of a new era to them, and therefore the month in which it happened was to them the beginning of months. But Christ was slain for us in the same sense that the Passover was slain for the Hebrews. His death was vicarious, his blood was atoning; and from the moment of a sinner's acceptance of salvation

The Passover.

through faith in him as the Lamb of God, he is a new creature. Old things are passed away, and all things are become new. He is no more the slave of sin, but has become the child of God. His relation to God is changed. He has been set right with the divine justice, for there is no condemnation to him. His iniquities are forgiven; he is accepted as righteous. Nay, more: he is renewed in the spirit of his mind, so that whereas he formerly loved sin, he now hates it; and whereas he formerly hated God, he now loves him; and he desires evermore to show forth the praises of him who hath called him from darkness into his marvellous light. The song of Moses was the anthem of the emancipated Hebrews; the song of the Lamb is the grander chorus of the throng of ransomed sinners. In the death of Christ the believer dies with him to sin; and the key-note of his after-life has been struck for him by Paul, when he says, "God forbid that I should glory, save in the cross of the Lord Jesus Christ, by which the world is crucified unto me, and I unto the world." Thus the Christian dates his new birth from the moment of his acceptance of deliverance through the sacrifice of his Lord.

But, in the second place, the exposition given by Paul of the Passover in its relation to Christ implies that the Christian life should be a feast. On the night of the departure from Egypt there was no convenience for keeping the feast of unleavened bread, but ever afterward, when the Passover was observed, it was associated with a seven days' festival. Now, what these seven days were to the Israelites, that his whole life is to be to the Christian; that is to say, his entire life is to be consecrated to the service of God, and characterized by gladness. The feasts of the Jews were all times of joy, and each had its own peculiar charm. Passover had the joy of deliverance; Pentecost had the gladsomeness of harvest-home; and Tabernacles had the delight of settled rest after the wanderings in the wilderness. So when Paul says, "Let us keep feast," he means to give to the Corinthians, under a figure, the same exhortation as he gave to the Philippians when he wrote to them plainly, "Rejoice in the Lord always, and again I say, Rejoice." There is nothing of gloom about the Gospel, and there ought to be nothing of the morose or the ascetic about the Christian life. Who has a better right to be joyful than the man who knows that his sins are forgiven, that his heart is renewed, and that he himself is adopted into the family of God? The joy of the world is a baseless thing. It has nothing lasting about it. But that of the Christian is both elevating and enduring. It rests upon a foundation stable as the throne of God himself; and just as the unbeliever, if he knew the real character of his life and destiny, would be forever sad, so the Christian, if he were rightly to apprehend the blessings that belong to him, would be forever glad. Be joyful, then, my brethren. Count up the riches that are yours in Christ, and then no earthly affliction will distress you. There is no grinning mummy seated at the table to which he invites you; and your joy in him may be perennial.

But, finally, observe that the Christian life, according to Paul's view of it, as typified by the paschal feast, should be characterized by sincerity and truth. Perhaps at first the unleavened bread was used because of the haste which the people had to make; but afterward its absence from the dwelling during the paschal feast became specially significant, and the Jews were accustomed to make the most careful examination of their houses, that every particle of leaven in them might be discovered and cast out; and so the Christian should expel everything of insincerity and falsehood from his heart. We cannot serve Christ and Belial. We cannot go in two opposite directions at one and the same time. We cannot live as Christians, and yet live in sin. Hypocrisy is the mark, not of a Christian, but of a deceiver; and every one who has named the name of Christ should depart from all iniquity. For a time, indeed, falsehood may impose upon men. The Church may be deceived, the neighborhood may be misled, but the Lord cannot be for one moment deluded. He knew the hollowness of the heart of Judas from the beginning, and through the most cunning mask which one may wear he sees the real face. It is useless, therefore, to try to hide anything from him. But, worse than that, the effort is dreadfully injurious to the individual himself; for truth is the girdle of character, and when that is unloosed the whole falls to pieces. It matters not how many talents and other excellences a man may have, if he have not truth; if he be acting a part, there is no soundness in him, and all the other qualities crumble at length into ruin. He who is trying to live two lives is hardening his conscience, and thereby fitting himself for the commission, without a quiver, of the most flagrant offences. There are no such sinners as those who have been flaming professors of attachment to Jesus Christ, for the insincerity of every day has petrified their hearts into utter insensibility. For the same reason, there are none whom the minister of Christ finds it so hard to reach as the hypocrite. He is familiar with all truth. You cannot say anything to him that he has not often heard before. His ears have become accustomed to the warnings of the Gospel, and his heart has become accustomed to resist them; and, from sorrowful experience, I deliberately say that there is more hope of the conversion of an open and abandoned prodigal than there is of that of one who has made and persisted in an insincere profession of attachment to Christ.

But this personal danger is not the only evil of hypocrisy; it paralyzes the church with which the insincere one is connected. Just as a non-conductor will stop at itself the electric current, so a hypocrite breaks up the fellowship of those Christians among whom he is at the time. He mars their happiness, and he hinders their usefulness. Because Achan has hidden away in his tent the wedge of gold and the Babylonish garment, Israel must be defeated by the men of Ai; and who can tell how many of the discords and divisions in the Church, or how many of its defeats in its conflict with evil, ought to be traced to the hypocrites within its pale?

Nor is this all; hypocrisy is a terrible dishonor to the Lord. There was no make-believe about his sacrifice. The agony of the garden and the anguish of the cross were real. He did not feign to love us. He loved us to the very death. And is it to such a love as that that we dare to offer the hollow mockery of hypocrisy as a return? Nay, more—the men of the world themselves expect something better from the follower of Jesus than such insincerity. One such said to Peter, as he listened to his denial, "Did not I see thee in the garden with him?" Ah! how deep that arrow went into Simon's heart. He had been in the garden; he had seen the Saviour's agony there; he had there made an ardent profession of attachment to him, and even drawn a sword in his defence; he had there beheld the treachery of Judas, and the indignities done to Jesus by the Roman soldiery—and yet now he was repudiating all connection with him! It was not what the men of the world would have done. The very question carried in it a sneer of contempt. And still the insincere one is the object of the world's scorn. He brings the Church into derision; he puts a stumbling-stone in the pathway of the inquirer; he gives occasion of perplexity to the young Christian; he hangs like a clog on the chariot-wheels of the Gospel; and, above all, he wounds the heart of the Lord Jesus, by repeating in an aggravated form the weakness of Peter and the treachery of Judas.

VII.

THE CROSSING OF THE RED SEA.

EXODUS xii., 37-39; xiii., 17-22; xiv.; xv.

WHEN Pharaoh commanded the Hebrews to go forth from among his people, Moses, knowing that, as on the former occasions, there would come a reaction, made immediate arrangements for the departure of the tribes. They set out from Rameses, a host numbering six hundred thousand men, besides women and children. This, according to the usual average of population, would give a total of about two millions four hundred thousand, to which must be added the mixed multitude that accompanied them from Egypt, and their flocks and herds. Their first halting-place was Succoth, which could not well have been more than fifteen miles from Rameses. Here they took time to bake unleavened cakes of the dough which they had brought away with them, and probably, also, halted long enough to make their final plans for their march. The name of the place signifies booths, and may have in it some reference to the temporary huts which they erected for their shelter. It is, besides, the term which in after-days was used to designate the feast of Tabernacles, so that, as Stanley* remarks, this, their first resting-place, must have sunk deeply into their remembrance, and must have been recognized by them as the first step which involved the whole. Here was settled for them the route which they were to follow. They might have taken

---

* "Jewish Church," vol. i., p. 108.

the direct road into Canaan, by which they could have reached the promised land through Gaza in a few days. But that would have brought them into immediate conflict with the Philistines, and their faith was not yet strong enough to sustain them in the presence of such fierce enemies. Besides, it was in the purpose of God that the Egyptians were to be humbled by the destruction of their army, and that the people were to be trained into courage by the revelation to be given from Mount Sinai; so they were not permitted to take the straight road to Palestine. But that they were not entirely destitute of faith is manifested by the fact that they took with them the bones of Joseph; for that was no relic-worship, but, indeed, the declaration of their belief that their destination was to be the land which God had promised to give to Abraham their father. Joseph had been dead now a hundred and forty years; but he died prophesying that God would surely visit his people, and bring them out of Egypt into the land which he sware to Abraham, to Isaac, and to Jacob; and in that expectation he "gave commandment concerning his bones." During successive generations his words must often have been the theme of converse in the Hebrew households; and now, by taking with them his embalmed remains, they served themselves heirs to his faith, and went forth in the sure confidence that they would find a grave for them in the land of promise. Thus they left Egypt, not only to escape from slavery, but also to set out for Canaan. Nor let us fail to observe that they moved forward with deliberation. "They went up," as our version has it, "harnessed, out of Egypt." But the word rendered "harnessed" may mean either fully armed, or in five companies; and, adopting the latter interpretation as the correct one, we see already the marshalling genius of Moses at work; for thus they could move both with precision and haste. Nothing so retards progress as confusion; but where large numbers are concerned, the more order there is, the better speed they make.

From Succoth they went forward another stage to Etham, which is described as "in the edge of the wilderness;" and to this place, as in every after-movement in their journeyings, they were miraculously led by a pillar which had in the daytime the appearance of a cloud, and during the night that of fire. We are told that in the campaigns of Alexander the Great he caused to be set up beside his tent a lofty pole, which had at the top a cresset filled with combustible materials, which were always burning. Thus every one could distinguish his head-quarters in the day by a cloud of smoke, and in the night by the flaming fire. But we must not confound this pillar with any such contrivance. This cloud was miraculous. The fire here, as in the burning bush, was the symbol of the presence of Jehovah. So that in very deed

"Their fathers' God before them moved,
An awful guide, in cloud and flame."

At this place the people were commanded not to go round the head of the gulf, so as to reach at once its eastern shore, but to turn and keep along its western border. Thus runs the record: "The Lord spake unto Moses, saying, Speak unto the children of Israel, that they turn and encamp before Pihahiroth, between Migdol and the sea, over against Baal-Zephon; before it shall ye encamp by the sea." Much controversy has been carried on as to the situation of these places; and, indeed, the determination of the route by which the Israelites left Egypt, and the settlement of the locality at which they crossed the western arm of the Red Sea, are among the most difficult questions in Scriptural geography. It is impossible, without the aid of a map, to make the subject either intelligible or interesting; and, even if we were to go elaborately into it, we should have to admit at the end that absolute certainty is unattainable. The opinions of those who may be supposed to be well qualified judges in the case may be reduced to two. The first is that of those who, placing Rameses on the opposite side of the Nile from Memphis, make the first journey to Succoth, take a northerly direction, and identify Succoth with the modern Birket-el-Hadji, or Pool of the Pilgrims, which is about ten miles to the north-east of Cairo, and is at this day the rendezvous of the pilgrims from all parts of Egypt on their way to Mecca. From Succoth they make the route go eastward to Etham, which they locate near the end of the gulf, not far from Suez, but slightly to the north-west. At Etham they suppose that the turn was made at a right-angle southward, and that they went forward until they came to Ras Atakah, a lofty ridge, which they identify with Pihahiroth, while they regard Baal-Zephon as Suez. "There," says an eloquent exponent of this opinion, "within the bend of Jebel Attakah, between that ridge and the sea, they would be completely shut in when overtaken by Pharaoh, having the curving range of the mountain on their right and before them, the sea on their left, and Pharaoh and his host behind them."* This would make them cross the ocean at a point twelve miles below Suez, and some probability is given to this view of the case by the fact that the name Ras Atakah signifies the Cape of Deliverance. The other opinion is that of those who regard Rameses as the capital of Goshen, and place it at the western extremity of the Wady-et-Tumeylat; Succoth they place at a point a little to the north-west of the Crocodile Lake, and Etham they locate still farther to the north-east, at the very edge of the wilderness. Then they make the turning an actual retracing of their steps for

---

* Rowlands, in Fairbairn's "Imperial Bible Dictionary," article PIHAHIROTH.

some distance to a point north of the Bitter Lakes, whence the route leads southward through Serapeum, and along the edge of the Bitter Lakes down to Suez, where they suppose the crossing was made. Those who adopt this view affirm that there is evidence that the sea once extended much farther north than it does now, and included in it the whole basin of the Bitter Lakes; while they allege that in the immediate neighborhood of Suez there is at present a camel ford which at low-water can be safely crossed, and which is broad enough to furnish ample room for the passing, within the required limit of time, of a multitude that numbered two millions and a half, while it is also wide enough to hold at once the whole army of Pharaoh. Of these two theories I prefer the latter. Great names are to be found on both sides; but since the taking of the surveys in connection with the making of the Suez Canal, the preponderance of authorities seems to be in favor of that which I have adopted.

The pursuit by Pharaoh was no mere after-thought, suggested by the knowledge that the Hebrews had taken a southern direction in their march. As I read the narrative, he determined to follow them almost from the first. But when he learned that they had not gone directly into the wilderness, he thought he saw an opportunity of speedily cutting off their retreat, and so he quickened his march, resolved to fall upon them from behind, while they had mountains on their right and in front of them, and the sea on their left. His force was composed of chariots which could advance with great rapidity, and each of which contained a charioteer and a warrior. We may not wonder, therefore, that when the Israelites became aware that the army of Pharaoh was in hot pursuit of them, "they were sore afraid." They recalled the cities of the dead which they had often seen in the land of their bondage, and looked with horror at the prospect of their carcasses being left to whiten on the sand. So they said to Moses, "Because there were no graves in Egypt, hast thou taken us away to die in the wilderness? Wherefore hast thou dealt thus with us, to carry us forth out of Egypt? Is not this the word that we did tell thee in Egypt, saying, Let us alone, that we may serve the Egyptians? For it had been better for us to serve the Egyptians, than that we should die in the wilderness." But Moses had not lost his faith, for he calmly bade the people stand still and see how God would save them, and assured them that their enemies would be utterly destroyed. Yet that he knew not precisely how their salvation was to be effected, is evident from the fact that he must have gone to God earnestly in prayer; for the answer came in this fashion: "Wherefore criest thou unto me? speak unto the children of Israel, that they go forward: But lift thou up thy rod, and stretch out thine hand over the sea, and divide it: and the children of Israel shall go on dry ground through the midst of the sea. And I, behold, I will harden the hearts of the Egyptians, and they shall follow them: and I will get me honor upon Pharaoh, and upon all his host, upon his chariots, and upon his horsemen." Now the night came down to spread its shield over the fugitives. The two hosts were encamped near each other, and between them the pillar of the cloud miraculously came. To the Hebrews it was bright, thus enabling them to see how to arrange their movements, for its brilliancy would be as dazzling as that of the electric light. But to the Egyptians it was dark, like a dense mist or fog, thus preventing them from seeing anything, and making it difficult for them to advance. Besides, toward the morning the fiery, flashing eye of the Eternal looked out upon the host of Pharaoh and troubled it; so that in the confusion caused by restive horses and colliding chariots, many wheels were broken, and they drave heavily. It would seem, also, from the psalm which celebrates this memorable deliverance, that a terrible thunder-storm was raging; in the midst of which, through the parted ocean, the people passed over into safety. No description could more graphically reproduce the scene to the eye of the imagination than that which the Hebrew poet has given, and I quote it here in the rugged sublimity of that Scottish version which early association makes so dear to me:

> "The waters, Lord, perceived thee,
> The waters saw thee well;
> And they for fear aside did flee,
> The depths on trembling fell.
>
> "The clouds in waters forth were poured,
> Sound loudly did the sky;
> And swiftly through the world abroad
> Thine arrows fierce did fly.
>
> "Thy thunder's voice alongst the heaven
> A mighty noise did make;
> By lightnings lightened was the world,
> Th' earth tremble did and shake.
>
> "Thy way is in the sea, and in
> The waters great thy path:
> Yet are thy footsteps hid, O Lord,
> None knowledge thereof hath.
>
> "Thy people thou didst safely lead,
> Like to a flock of sheep;
> By Moses' hand and Aaron's thou
> Didst them conduct and keep."

Thus their way was miraculously made for them. Some, indeed, would resolve the whole phenomena into an ebb-tide made lower than usual, and held longer than usual by a strong east wind; but as the effect came at once on the outstretching of Moses's rod, it was clearly supernatural. It is quite immaterial, so far as the miracle is concerned, whether the divine power was put forth directly upon the sea, or indirectly through the force of the wind upon it; for the coming of the wind at once, in connection with the symbolical act of Moses, is as much a miracle as the immediate division of the waters, without the intervention of any secondary cause, would have been. Still, as the record declares that the Lord caused the sea to go back by a strong east wind all that night, we unquestioningly receive that statement as a full history of the case. Only, let it be understood that we cannot take the supernatural out of the narrative without destroying it altogether; and they who consider the calm dignity of the record will be the first to admit that it bears the stamp of credibility upon its face. For the rest, let it be noted that the people passed through deliberately. "They *walked* upon the dry land." They were in haste, but there was no confusion. They passed through safely, for the waters on either side were as a wall, or a defence unto them, so that their enemies could not come near them. But that mode of speech does not necessarily imply that the waves stood up on each side of them like perpendicular fortifications; and all the requirements of the narrative are met if we suppose that the simple continuance of the water at its ordinary depth kept the charioteers of the Egyptians from outflanking them, and compelled them to take the rear. Furthermore, they all passed through. No one was left behind. "There was not one feeble person among their tribes"*—and not one fell into the hands of their foes. So Moses also could say, "Those that thou gavest me I have kept, and none of them is lost;" and when they stood upon the farther strand, they recognized that they were fully and

---

* Psa. cv., 37.

finally severed from Egypt, and were committed to follow Moses as their leader forever after. Hence, Paul says, "They were all baptized unto Moses in the cloud and in the sea;" for this was their initiation into discipleship to Moses, even as baptism is our initiation into discipleship to Christ. Nor can I help remarking, as this first recorded baptism comes up before us, on the fact that, so far as appears, it was not immersion. Sprinkled the tribes might be, as the clouds poured down water, or the spray was dashed upon them by the fury of the wind—but their baptism in the sea was contemporaneous with their "walking upon dry land in the midst of it." It is a very small matter; but when esteemed brethren assure us that the word baptize always and everywhere means immerse, it becomes important to remark that in the very earliest case in reference to which the term is applied, it very evidently can have no such significance. There was an immersion here, indeed, but it was that of the Egyptians; and no one will be very eager to follow their example.

Toward the morning, when the tribes were well-nigh over the gulf, Pharaoh, not realizing that the path which they took had been made for them by miracle—or presuming that it would be as good for him as for them—led his host after them. But when he had advanced sufficiently to have his whole army in the sea, Moses, at the command of God, stretched his hand over it, and the waves, let loose from the leash in which so long they had been held, flowed back into their former channel, and submerged them all. "There remained not so much as one of them." Long had the oppressor boasted of his might. For generations the Egyptian rulers had lorded it with a high hand over the helpless captives. They had bruised them with rods, and beaten them with the scourge; they had strangled their children at the birth, and given their little ones to the maw of the crocodile;

they had ground them with hard bondage, and exacted from them "day labor, light denied;" and for more than a century it seemed as if Jehovah heeded not. But he had put the tears of the slaves into his bottle; and when the hour of doom rung out, for each of these diamond drops there was a victim. The retribution had been long in coming, but it was thorough when it did come; and the arrears which had been accumulating for generations were all exacted from that which had accepted the gains of its predecessors, and thereby become also the heirs of their responsibility. Nor has this been a solitary case in history. The victims of the Indian mutiny were not the beginners of Indian oppression: the citizens over which the thunder-storm of civil war burst in this land were not those who had begun negro slavery. But they had accepted the position; they were content to continue to draw its gains, and let the thing drift on; and lo! there came at length a tragedy as deep and dark as this in the Red Sea. Let us learn wisdom from all such events, and seek to understand that retributive providence which, in punishing an evil, lets the full judgment fall on those who have it last in hand, and are determined to keep it at all hazards. The Saviour affirmed that on the Jews of his generation would come "all the righteous blood shed upon the earth, from the blood of Abel unto the blood of Zacharias, the son of Barachias, whom they slew between the temple and the altar." They might have averted it by accepting Him, but they chose the other alternative; and you see the result even yet in the destruction of their city, and their own dispersion among the nations. But similar instances are continually occurring, and we may be sure that if in any way we act unjustly or oppressively, the penalty will fall either on our heads or on the heads of those who shall come after us. Robbery and repudiation may be profitable to-day to some; but when the Red Sea is to be crossed—and it must be crossed some time—the robbers will find themselves submerged.

The effect of this deliverance on the Hebrews was like that which is produced upon a man by his escape from death, say in a railway accident, or some other catastrophe. They felt that they had been at the point of destruction. They had, as it were, looked in at the open door of death; and they came back again with shuddering awe. They were subdued and solemn; while, at the same time, their consciousness that God was near them in the mystic cloud filled their souls with reverence; so we read that "they feared Jehovah, and believed Jehovah, and his servant Moses." But when this first feeling of awe-struck solemnity had passed, there came a happy gratitude, which Moses voiced for them in that outburst of song that has come down through the centuries, jubilant with the gladness of the Exodus, and which will hold its place as the foremost hymn of praise, until the day when it shall be surpassed by the fuller and more fervid chorus of "the song of the Lamb."

I cannot attempt its exposition here. I only call you to note the remarkable circumstance that it is presumably the oldest poem in the world; and that, in sublimity of conception and grandeur of expression, it is unsurpassed by anything that has been written since. It might almost be said that poetry here sprang full-grown from the heart of Moses, even as heathen mythology fables that Minerva came full-armed from the brain of Jupiter. Long before the grand old ballads of Homer were sung through the streets of the Grecian cities, or the foundation of the seven-hilled metropolis of the ancient world was laid by the banks of the Tiber, this matchless ode, in comparison with which Pindar is tame, was chanted by the leader of the emancipated Hebrews on the Red Sea shore; and yet we have in it no polytheism, no foolish mythological story concerning gods and goddesses, no gilding of immorality, no glorification of mere force; but, instead, the firmest recognition of the personality, the providence, the supremacy, the holiness, and the retributive rectitude of God. How shall we account for all this? If we admit the divine legation and inspiration of Moses, all is plain; if we deny that, we have in the very existence of this song a hopeless and insoluble enigma. Here is a literary miracle, as great as the physical sign of the parting of the sea. Even if you deny the latter, you cannot get rid of the former. When you see a boulder of immense size, and of a different sort of stone from those surrounding it, lying in a valley, you immediately conclude that it has been brought thither by glacier action many, many ages ago. But here is a boulder-stone of poetry, standing all alone in the Egyptian age, and differing entirely in its character from the sacred hymns either of Egypt or of India. Where did it come from? Let your rationalist furnish his reply; for me it is a boulder from the Horeb height whereon Moses communed with the great I AM — when he saw the bush that burned but yet was not consumed — and left here as at once a witness to his inspiration, and the nation's gratitude.

But Moses and the people had not all the music to themselves; for his sister Miriam, catching something of the fervor of her brother's soul, led the women even as Moses led the men; and at every pause in the psalm they came in with the chorus, to the accompaniment of the timbrel and the dance, "Sing ye to the Lord, for he hath triumphed gloriously; the horse and his rider hath he thrown into the sea."

It was a gladsome time. Will Israel ever forget the goodness of her God to her in this great deliverance? Ah, me! The very next verses tell of murmuring. But that we must reserve for a future time, while we return to glean a handful of lessons from this stirring story.

We may learn, then, in the first place, that God is the daily guide of his people. So soon as the Hebrews left Egypt, the pillar of cloud and fire came to show them the way. That was a miracle. But the perpetual miracle of his providence remains; and, though we cannot see him, he is hedging our way on either side: though we know it not, he is guiding us. Which of us, on taking a broad and comprehensive survey of his life, will not admit that these statements are true? We thought, as we came along, that we were merely following the bent of our own inclinations; but now we see that the whole has been planned for us from the beginning, and that through our years, as through the ages, "one increasing purpose," of which, at the moment, we were ignorant, has been running. We will all admit that. But the difficulty most commonly felt is that we have no visible conductor to decide for us, in our present perplexity, the way we ought to take; and there are many who would be glad to hear some voice from heaven, or to see some pillar of cloud, by which they might be delivered from all uncertainty. But that would be no gain to us in the end; for it is through leaving us, as it were, to ourselves, always, of course, under his own supervision, that God trains us into strength. He who is always told what he must do never knows what he should do. Moral thoughtfulness is created by the necessity under which we lie to take charge of ourselves.

Still, conceding all that, there are certain great principles which, rightly understood and acted upon, will be of great service to us in times of anxiety. First of all, we must take the case to God in prayer. No matter though it may be a trifle in the eyes of others, if it be important enough to trouble us, he will not ridicule our uneasiness, but give us grace according to our day. Then, we must remember that the first open door is not always the best or the safest for us. Multitudes, when they are in difficulties, welcome the earliest outlet. But God would not take the Hebrews through the wilderness to Gaza, though that would have been the shortest way, because they had not courage enough to face the Philistines. So, when an apparent way is opened, let us ask whether there is anything that will be likely to endanger our principles, or to render it probable that we shall fall into evil habits, if we take it; and if there be, let us avoid it. Suppose, for example, one is out of employment, and he is offered work where he would be among the Philistines; he ought to pause, and remember that the first offer is not always that which God means us to accept.

Again, hesitancy as to duty always means, in God's vocabulary, "*Stand still!*" "He that doubteth is condemned if he eat." That is a rule which one may make universal. Once more: when a door opens in front, and that which is behind us shuts, then God says "Go forward!" If I may speak from my own experience, I would testify that these principles have been of great value to me throughout my life; and I have, therefore, all the more confidence in commending them to you. In general, it may be said that when the principles of God's Word harmonize with our taking the position which his providence appears to open to us, we are safe in accepting it; but when either of these elements is wanting, we had better be cautious. The navigator finds his position by taking the point where latitude and longitude cut each other; and we shall find our guidance in the intersection of the precept of the word, with the indication of providence; and for both, like the mariner, we must look to the Sun. Believe me, he who looks up to God in prayer, and looks out over providence for the answer, will not be long in perplexity.

In the second place, we may learn that when God leads us into danger, he will take us safely through it. Had the Israelites gone of their own accord to encamp at Pihahiroth, they would have had no claim on the divine protection ; but because God had taken them thither, he stood near to help them. Thus it makes all the difference in the world, when I am in danger, whether I am there for my own pleasure and of my own motive, or on the business and at the bidding of the Lord. In the former case, I have no warrant for his protection ; in the latter, I may be sure that he will put himself between me and the peril, and make himself indeed my shield. This principle is far-reaching, and may be applied by us to business, to amusements, and, indeed, to every department of life. To go into danger thoughtlessly, is rashness ; to go into it wantonly, is foolhardiness ; but to go into it because only thereby can I follow my Master, and do what he commands, is true courage ; and at such times I shall always find him at my side. Thus, it would be reckless in the extreme for me to go wilfully and spend a whole evening in some haunt of wickedness ; and, though I might be able to keep myself pure, I may be sure that some evil would be the outcome. But suppose there came to me a telegram from over the sea, telling me that the son of a dear friend was lying at a certain house, which I knew to be one of the worst dens in the city, I could go then with all safety, because the pillar and the cloud would be between me, and harm while I was seeking to save the lost. Pharaoh tried to cross the sea without warrant, and he was drowned ; but the Hebrews, following their God, went over on dry land. Faith is one thing ; presumption is another. To expect that God will keep me, no matter though I go recklessly into danger, is *presumption;* to go through that danger on his service, is *courage.* Young men, will you mark well that distinction, and act upon it through life ? for it may save you from making shipwreck of your souls.

Finally, after deliverance there should come a song. Gratitude is an imperative duty ; and one of its first and finest forms is a hymn of thanksgiving and praise. It is true that it will not be worth much if it expends itself only in song; but wherever the psalm is sincere, it will communicate its melody also to the life. Too often, however, it does not give even a song. You remember how only one of the ten lepers returned to thank the Lord for his cleansing; and perhaps we should not be far wrong if we were to affirm that a similar proportion prevails to-day between the thankful and the ungrateful. Yet it would be wrong if we were to leave the impression that such gratitude as this of Moses is almost unknown. On the contrary, the pages of our hymn-books are covered with songs which have been born, like this one, out of deliverance. Many of the finest of David's Psalms are the utterances of his heart in thanksgiving for mercies similar to those which Moses celebrated; and some of the noblest lyrics of Watts and Wesley, of Montgomery and Lyte, have had a similar origin. Nor is this all; we can see that in all times of great national revival there has been an outburst of song. At the Reformation, no result of Luther's work was more remarkable than the stimulus it gave to the hymnology of the Fatherland. In fact, that may be said to have been as good as created by the Reformation; and in our own country each successive revival of religion has had its own special hymn. But we have not all the genius of Wesley, or the inspiration of Moses or of David; and what shall we do then? We can at least appropriate the lyrics of those who have gone before us, and use them in as far as they meet our case; and I can conceive no more pleasant or profitable occupation for the household than the singing of those hymns which have become dear to us because of the personal experiences which we can read between the lines. But we can do better still than that; for we can set our daily deeds to the music of a grateful heart, and seek to round our lives into a hymn—the melody of which will be recognized by all who come into contact with us, and the power of which shall not be evanescent, like the voice of the singer, but perennial, like the music of the spheres. To this hymnology of life, my hearers, let me incite you now; for only they who carry this music in their hearts shall sing at last, on the shore of the heavenly land, that song of "pure concent" for which John could find no better description than that it was "the song of Moses, the servant of God, and the song of the Lamb." But to sing of deliverance you must accept deliverance. Open your hearts, therefore, for the reception of salvation, and then David's experience will be yours. "He hath put a new song into my mouth, even praise unto our God. Many shall see it and fear, and shall trust in the Lord."

VIII.

MARAH, ELIM, AND SIN.

EXODUS xv., 23–xvi., 36.

AFTER crossing the Red Sea, the Israelites were led into "the wilderness of Shur." This name signifies a wall, and is believed to be the ancient designation of that wall-like mountain range which runs north and south to the eastward of Suez, and which is now called Jebel-er-Rahah. It is the continuation, in a northerly direction, of the great chain of Jebel-et-Tih; and by the Arabs who live in the interior of the wilderness, on its eastern side, it is still called Jebel-es-Sûr. It is mentioned in the history of Hagár, of Abraham,* and of the descendants of Ishmael; and is generally described as "before Egypt," because to one standing in that land and looking eastward it would appear to be directly in front. In the book of Numbers† it is called the wilderness of Etham, and so we are led to conclude that the whole of the district of which Jebel-er-Rahah forms the great backbone or range was called Shur; while that part of it which skirts the edge of the Red Sea, at the upper end of the Gulf of Suez, and extends up on the eastern side of the Bitter Lakes, was known by the name of Etham. Into this region, then, the tribes went for three days; marching through a district which is now a tract of sand or rough gravel, with here and there some sickly shrubs, and not a fountain near. Probably they had taken with them a supply of

---

* Gen. xvi., 7; xx., 1; xxv., 18. † Num. xxxiii., 8.

water from Ayoun Mousa, which seems to have been their first halting-place on the eastern shore of the gulf; but that would be speedily exhausted, and then they would be reduced to the greatest straits. At the end of the third day's journey, however, they saw what seemed from a distance to be an oasis, with abundance of water; but when they came up to it, and sought to quench their thirst at its fountains, they found that the water was so bitter that they could not drink it. This was a sore trial to them, and they vented their disappointment in murmurs against Moses. Just as before, when they saw the Egyptians coming down upon them at Pihahiroth, so now again they upbraided their leader for bringing them into trouble, and said unto him, "What shall we drink?" This conduct of theirs was at once unreasonable, ungrateful, and unbelieving. It was unreasonable, because Moses was only God's lieutenant, and was himself a sharer in their affliction. It was ungrateful, for Moses had from the first done everything in his power for them—and that not for any profit or glory which he might gain for himself, but simply and only for their good. It was unbelieving, because they might have reasoned that he who, three days before, had divided the sea to make a pathway for them, would not forsake them now, but would somehow make provision for their wants. Yet even as we thus analyze their guilt, we feel that we are condemning ourselves; for all our fretting at the providence of God is, in the light of the cross of Calvary, as bad as this dissatisfaction of the Israelites at the waters of Marah, since we may always say, with the Christian apostle, "He that spared not his own son, but delivered him up for us all, how shall he not with him also freely give us all things?"

But Moses met their discontentment with patience, because he met it with prayer. He did what the people themselves ought to have done. He went to God with their trouble. This became his habit; for long before Paul lived and wrote he acted upon the principle of that disciple's words, and "in everything, by prayer and supplication, made his requests known unto God." The result here was that "Jehovah showed him a tree, which, when he had cast into the waters, the waters were made sweet." The place where this miracle was wrought is almost universally identified with the modern Howarah, which is situated in the Wady Amarah, and is between thirty and forty miles south of Ayoun Mousa. It is thus described by a recent traveller: "It is a solitary spring of bitter water, with a stunted palm-tree growing near it, and affording a delicious shade. The quality of the water varies considerably at different times; and on the present occasion it was not only drinkable, but palatable. It is, however, only fair to state that Mr. Holland, who had visited the well on several former occasions, pronounced such purity of the water to be quite exceptional."*

Some have suggested that the berry of the Ghurkud was used for the purpose of sweetening the fountain, and that the whole thing is to be resolved into the operation of natural law. But, unfortunately, neither the fruit nor the wood of the shrub just named has any such property as that which is thus ascribed to it; and so we must look for the virtue which healed the spring not in the tree, but in God. The tree, like the salt used in a similar instance by Elisha, or the clay employed by the Saviour to anoint the eyes of the blind man, was only an outward sign to assist the faith of the people; but the effect which was consequent upon its being cast into the water was due not to any natural qualities which it possessed, but solely to the agency of God. That this was indeed the case, is evident from the fact that, in connection with the cure of the waters, "the Lord made for

---

* The "Desert of the Exodus," by E. H. Palmer, M.A., p. 45.

them a statute and an ordinance," which would have been meaningless if the healing of the spring had not been produced by his own direct and immediate energy. It ran in this wise: "If thou wilt diligently hearken to the voice of the Lord thy God, and wilt do that which is right in his sight, and wilt give ear to his commandments, and keep all his statutes, I will put none of these diseases upon thee which I have brought upon the Egyptians; for I am the Lord that healeth thee." This was a general covenant, which embraced in it all that was ultimately proclaimed from Sinai. The special precepts were to be afterward given; but now a pledge was exacted from the people that they would receive and obey everything that God should enjoin. There was given them, also, a promise of special preservation from calamity, which was conditioned on their perfect obedience to his commandments; while both the pledge on their part and the promise on his were enforced with the assurance, "For I am Jehovah-Rophek."

Deliverance increases obligation, and the observance of God's statutes secures new blessings. Because God hath healed us, he has a claim upon our allegiance; and the more loyal we are to him, the more immunity from calamity will he secure for us. He did not lay this ordinance upon the people until after he had cured the waters; but having so blessed them, he looked for their gratitude in their obedience; and the more of that he received, the more would he continue to bless them. Thus, through our varied necessities and deliverances, God increasingly reveals himself to our souls; and so even our troubles become useful, in giving us deeper insight into his heart. At the burning bush, he called himself to Moses simply Jehovah; on the Red Sea shore, through the miracle of salvation to Israel and destruction to Egypt, Moses saw him to be Jehovah—my strength; at Marah, he made himself known as Jehovah-Rophek; and at Rephidim, Moses, seeing yet farther into his grace, built an altar which he called Jehovah-Nissi—the Lord my banner. So out of every trial we come with some new and significant affix to the name Jehovah; while, at the same time, we are laid under deeper obligation to walk in all his statutes and ordinances blameless. They know God best who have been most frequently delivered by him in time of trial, and they ought to serve him best.

From Marah they moved forward, under the guidance of the mystic pillar, and came to Elim, identified by some with the Wady Ghurundel, six miles to the south of Howarah, and described as the most extensive watercourse in the western desert. The nearness of this wady to Marah, however, is made by others an objection to its being the veritable Elim; and they have preferred to locate the oasis of the Palm-trees in the Wady Useit, which is a few miles farther south, and in which there are two palm-trees at this day. From Elim, where their peace and plenty under a pleasing shade must have been all the sweeter to them after their experiences at Marah, they went to that encampment by the Red Sea which is specified in the record of their journeyings preserved in the book of Numbers,* and which is thought to have been at the farther end of the Wady et Taiyebeh, near the headland of Ras-Selima. The valley is described as beautiful; full of tamarisks and other shrubs, and having water in it; which, however, is inferior to that of Ghurundel. The place at which the tribes halted must have been of "considerable importance as the starting-point of the roads to the copper-mines of the Wady Mughara, Sarabit el Khadim, and the Wady Nasb.†"

At this point they turned away from the sea, into the in-

---

* Num. xxxiii., 10.
† See "Speaker's Commentary," vol. i., p. 316.

terior of the wilderness. They passed, probably, out of the plain of Murkhah by the Wady en Nusb, and encamped at the head of the latter, where it broadens out, and where there is a fine spring of water. This was the wilderness of Sin, at which they arrived a month after their departure from Egypt; and where, for the first time, the full privation of the desert life stared the people in the face. Moses, indeed, who had lived for forty years in the wilderness, must have known what was before them. Even in the most favorable circumstances, the victualling of an army is always a difficult matter to arrange for; and very frequently it is in the commissariat department that the strength or the weakness of a general is first manifested. We know, too, from the partial experience of last summer, that if a large city like this should be isolated by the stopping of its railway communications and the blockading of its harbor, we should have a famine upon us in little more than a month. But the isolation of the wilderness was complete; and, therefore, the courage and faith of Moses in leading two millions and a half of people into it, stand forth as amazing. He was not ignorant of the character of the desert; he knew that without miracle it would be impossible to provide in it for such a multitude; and that he was willing, in these circumstances, to go forward with his people, is an evidence that his faith was even superior to that of Abraham when he left his native land and went out, not knowing whither he went. It might be supposed, indeed, that the people could have lived upon their flocks and herds; but pastoral tribes do not slay their cattle save on very special occasions. They depend rather on their produce; and, as Kitto has remarked, "We are to recollect that their flocks and herds were not the common property of all, but were undoubtedly the private property of a comparatively small number of persons;"* while it is not to be forgotten that, even supposing these had been given up to the wants of the multitude, that supply would have been speedily exhausted. So we cannot wonder that when the provisions which they had brought with them had been consumed the people were at their wits' end. As on the former occasions, they blamed Moses and Aaron for their misery; and, in their thoughtless passion, they cried, "Would to God we had died by the hand of the Lord in the land of Egypt, when we sat by the flesh-pots, and when we did eat bread to the full; for ye have brought us forth into this wilderness, to kill this whole assembly with hunger."

We are not told in so many words that Moses went to the Lord with this complaint; but, judging from his conduct in similar cases, it is every way probable that he did. At all events, the Lord was near with his assistance, and sent the people two sorts of supplies, the one temporary, and the other permanent. He furnished flesh for them by bringing into that region an immense flock of quails; which, being exhausted with their flight, were easily killed or captured. These birds, which resemble partridges, are still found in the desert of Arabia; and the miracle of their appearance now consisted in the fact that they were brought into the district of the wilderness of Sin just at the moment when they were most needed. The Egyptians had a way of preserving wild fowl by drying them in the sun; and even at this day, in Lower Egypt, quails, after having been skinned, are buried for a short time in the hot sand, by which means they are kept from putrefaction.† It is likely, therefore, that, by one or other of these methods, the tribes were enabled to store some of this abundant supply for future use.

---

* "Daily Bible Readings," vol. ii., p. 114.
† Ib., vol. ii., p. 115.

At a later date, we know that when a similar provision of quails was made for them, "They spread them all abroad for themselves around the camp;"* and it is not unlikely that something of the same kind was done by them in the present instance. Thus God gave them flesh to eat.

Their bread came to them in another form; for, on the following morning, "The dew lay round about the host, and when the dew that lay was gone up, behold, upon the face of the wilderness there lay a small round thing, as small as the hoar-frost on the ground." The people knew not what to make of this, and asked "Man hu" (what is it?), when, to their astonishment, their leader told them that it was the bread which God had provided for them. He then commanded them to gather it, at the rate of an omer for every man; and gave instructions that every day's supply was to be consumed on its own day. Its appearance was like that of coriander-seed, and its taste, when they had prepared it either by baking or by boiling, was like that of wafers made with honey. Some very remarkable things came out in connection with this rich supply of nutritious food. In the first place, we read that the people "gathered, some more, some less, and when they did mete it with an omer, he that gathered much had nothing over, and he that gathered little had no lack." The Rabbins explain this statement as meaning that whatever quantity a man might gather, when he measured it in his tent he had just as much as was needed to give an omer for every member of his house; and Calvin supposes that the gatherings of all were placed in a heap, and then measured out in the ratio commanded; but the former interpretation seems to me to represent more accurately the sense of the passage, while it gives us a beautiful illustration of the divine economy. He who, when he fed the mul-

---

* Num. xi., 34.

titudes on the mountain-side, would have the fragments gathered that nothing should be lost, would not let his bounty here run to waste, but furnished only what was necessary. Again, some of the people, in defiance of Moses' command, attempted to hoard it from day to day, but found that it became corrupt; for the Lord's purpose was to train them into constant dependence upon himself. Still further, the people, apparently of their own accord, collected, on the sixth day, a double supply; while a small minority of them went out on the seventh day, as usual, and found none. The rulers of the congregation—that is, as we understand, the heads of the tribal families—were surprised at the procedure of the former; and Moses himself was indignant at the conduct of the latter, saying unto them, "How long refuse ye to keep my commandments and my laws? See, for that the Lord hath given you the Sabbath, therefore he giveth you on the sixth day the bread of two days: abide ye every man in his place; let no man go out of his place on the seventh day." From all this, then, the following things seem evident: First, that Moses had issued no command on the subject of the Sabbath; for if he had, it is inconceivable, on the one hand, that the rulers should not have known it, and, on the other, that he should not have mentioned it himself in his rebuke of those who went out on the seventh day: second, that the people, in gathering a double portion on the sixth day, were acting in observance of a precept already known by them: and, third, that God, in preserving their double portion over the Sabbath without corruption, stamped the action of the people in this matter with his own approval. It follows, therefore, that the observance of the seventh day as a day of rest does not date from Sinai, and is not merely a part of the Jewish ritual, but is an ancient and primeval institution. Perhaps in Egypt it had been too largely neglected by the tribes, and that may account for the fact that some of the people took no note of it; but the better portion of the Hebrews seem to have remembered it, and the giving of the manna was used as an occasion of emphasizing the holy character of that day, which was made for no separate nationality, but for man as man. Again, we have a supplementary note inserted, as it were, at the close of this singular history, either by Moses himself on his final revision, or, as seems more probable, by Joshua, to the effect that this supernatural food was continued to the people for forty years, until they came into the borders of the Land of Canaan. During those years, as we shall find, many changes came and went, and the whole generation which had reached maturity at the date of the Exodus passed away; but all through them, in spite of the weakness, the wavering, the murmuring, and even the rebellion of the people, God gave them day by day this daily bread—"for his mercy endureth forever." Finally, the Lord commanded that a pot of this manna was to be preserved, that after-generations might see how he had fed them in the desert; and when the tabernacle was set up, we shall find that this golden vessel was put in the very holy of holies itself.

In another portion of the Pentateuch we are told that God's design in giving the Hebrews this wondrous bread was that he "might make them know that man doth not live by bread alone, but by every word that proceedeth out of the mouth of the Lord doth man live;" and again, "That he might humble them, and that he might prove them, to do them good at the latter end."* He wanted to teach them that it was always safe to depend on him when they were obeying his commands; and, at the same time, to warn them against presuming wantonly on the continuance of his favor. He humbled them even while his gifts were so remarkable.

---

* Deut. viii., 3, 16.

"I could not understand this for a time," says the good John Newton; "I thought they were rather in danger of being proud when they saw themselves provided for in such an extraordinary way. But the manna would not keep; they could not hoard it up, and were, therefore, in a state of absolute dependence from day to day. This was well suited to humble them, and so it is with us in spirituals."

But now, some will ask what relation this manna had to the substance which is still called by the same name. There is a plant or shrub in the peninsula of Sinai—a species of tamarisk—from the trunk and branches of which a kind of gum exudes, and forms small white grains. In cool weather it preserves its solidity, but in hot weather it melts rapidly. Its taste is generally compared by travellers to that of honey, and it is found in the district between Elim and Sinai. Its resemblance to the substance described in the text, therefore, in color, taste, and shape, is exact. But its difference from it in other respects is quite as remarkable; for it is the exudation of a shrub, whereas the Bible manna lay like dew or hoar-frost upon the ground; its production is confined to the months of May and June, whereas the food of the tribes was found by them all the year round; the whole quantity of the turfa manna gathered in a season does not exceed seven hundred pounds, whereas more than that would be required by the Israelites in a single day; its production is restricted to the district between Elim and Sinai, whereas this was furnished to the Hebrews, wherever they went, for forty years; it keeps sweet and good for more than a day, whereas this became corrupt on the morrow; it comes from the shrub during the season on all days alike, whereas this was not given on the Sabbath. It is impossible, therefore, to pare down this narrative so as to make it mean that the children of Israel were fed by a merely natural product. But in the resemblance of the manna to that which was apparently indigenous to the place, we have a feature which is common to this with other miracles. When Christ fed the multitudes on the mountain-side, he did not set before them dainty rarities, but gave them loaves and fishes such as they were commonly accustomed to eat; and when he replenished the empty jars at Cana, he did so not with an unheard-of variety of wine, but with the kind of beverage ordinarily drunk on such occasions, only so much better in quality than what was ordinary as to call forth remark. So, when he provided for his people in the wilderness, he gave them wilderness food, sending them the quails of the district, and a substance similar to, only better than, that which, at the particular season at which they had arrived, might have been gleaned in small quantities by some of them from the tamarisks of the wady. Thus we may sum up the matter in the words of Keil: "We can neither deny that there was some connection between the two, nor explain the heavenly manna as arising from an unrestricted multiplication and increase of this gift of nature. We rather regard the bread of heaven as the production and gift of the grace of God, which fills all nature with its powers and productions, and so applies them to its purposes of salvation as to create out of that which is natural something altogether new, which surpasses the ordinary productions of nature both in quality and quantity, as far as the kingdom of nature is surpassed by the kingdom of grace and glory."*

It is impossible, now, to read this narrative without connecting it with the Saviour's discourse to the Jews which John has preserved for us in the sixth chapter of his Gospel, and from which it appears that, over and above the supply of a present and pressing necessity, this manna was design-

---

* "Commentary on the Pentateuch," by Keil and Delitzsch, vol. ii., pp. 73, 74.

ed, like the brazen serpent and the water from the rock in Rephidim, to prefigure and prophesy the coming of him in whom the wants of the soul would be as fully met as those of the body were by the well-known miracles to which I have referred. These signs are thus connected with and dependent upon the one great miracle of the Incarnation. They were the forecast shadows of that "coming one" to whom all Scripture testifies; and they help us not only to identify him as the "sent of God," but also to understand the work he did and the words he spake. They are to the gospel history what allegorical pictures are to a book, and by the study of them we may learn more of him of whom that history tells. When, therefore, we hear him say, "I am that bread of life. Your fathers did eat manna in the wilderness, and are dead. This is the bread which cometh down from heaven, that a man may eat thereof and not die. I am the living bread which came down from heaven," we understand him to mean that he is himself to the souls of men what the manna was to the bodies of the Israelites. And in this view of the case we may easily run through the parallel. For as the manna was heavenly in its origin, so Jesus Christ is he "which cometh down from heaven, and giveth life unto the world;" as the manna was abundant in its supply, so Jesus Christ is bread for every man; as the manna was easily obtained, so Jesus may be received by any believer; as the manna had to be gathered and eaten by each for himself, so Jesus has to be appropriated by each soul to himself; and as the manna was given day by day, so we must continually resort to Jesus for those supplies of grace which we require for the constantly emerging exigencies of life.

But now, leaving the facts of this wonderful history, let us see what great principles we can derive from them for our guidance and support through life. And, first of all, I think we may learn that we are not done with hardship when we have left Egypt. This may be regarded as a universal law so long as we are in the present life, and may be illustrated as really in common and secular matters as in spiritual things. The school-boy is apt to imagine that he is a slave. He is under tutors and governors; and as he grinds away at his studies, not seeing any relation between them and what he is to do in the future, he is tempted to think that the drudgery of the Hebrews in the brick-yard was nothing to that which he has to undergo, and he longs for the day when he shall be a free man, and enter upon the active duties of life. His emancipation from the dry and uninteresting labors at which he has so long been held marks an epoch in his history, and he sings over it a song as sincere, if not as exalted, as that of Moses at the sea. The burial of the books by our graduating classes may be in the main a foolish freak; but yet it is the expression, in its own way, of relief from that which has hitherto been felt to be a restraint, and each of those who take part in it is intensely jubilant. But after he has entered on the active duties of the work to which he devotes himself, the youth has not gone far before he comes to Marah, and his first experience is one of disappointment. Ah! well for him then if he cries to God, and finds the healing tree which alone can sweeten its waters of bitterness! So it is, also, with every new enterprise in which a man engages. After his first victory comes something which empties it of half its glory. Pure and unmingled success is unknown in the world, and would be, let me add, a great calamity if it were to be enjoyed; for then the man would become proud and forget God, and lose all remembrance of that precious influence by which the disappointments in our experience are transmuted into means of grace. If we knew it, we have as much to be thankful for in our Marahs as in our passings through Red Seas of difficulty. Surely there is here a lesson at once for instruction and for comfort to us in our own national history. We have come through the fiery flood of war, and we have sung our song of gratitude to him who, by that bloody baptism, committed us to follow on in the course of justice, of integrity, of true national union, and of hearty brotherhood throughout the land; and if now we are made to drink of the bitter waters of disappointment, it is not that we should murmur against him whose cloud-pillar has led us to our Marah, but rather that we should, in trustful prayer, cry to him for the healing wood which alone can make the fountain sweet. The lesson of the hour, therefore, which God sends us from this timely history, is that there should be less murmuring against Moses and Aaron, and more earnest supplication to the Lord himself.

But, in our desire to give expression to the national bearings of this old history, let us not forget its spiritual application. The young convert imagines that when he has found Christ, his whole after-experience is to be that of comfort. But he knows not what he thinks. He will never be done with disagreeables until he has entered heaven; and his first three days' journey will bring him to some bitter fountain. The Slough of Despond is not far from the city of Destruction, and every one who runs away from the former is in danger of falling into the latter. When, therefore, those who have just begun the Christian life have to encounter disappointment, let them not think that some strange thing has happened unto them. Others have been there before them, and though all have not found the waters equally bitter, yet they have been to all distasteful; and the purpose of bringing them through this experience is to teach them to depend not on external things alone, but on that indwelling Spirit who can and who will make all things work together for their good, and bring for them meat out of the eater, and sweet out of the bitter. An early difficulty, surmounted by the help of God, is a blessing rather than a calamity. It is a revelation at once of our own weakness and of God's favor; and it will lead us, in all similar times, to look for relief not to the fountains of earth, but to him who has said, "If any man thirst, let him come unto me and drink." Let the young Christian who is startled at the bitterness of Marah, therefore, take heart again. Let him not look back to Egypt, with its full-lipped river of delight; but rather let him look up to him who sits upon that throne from out of which proceeds "a pure river of water of life, clear as crystal." Nor will he look in vain, for these are his words of gracious promise: "When the poor and needy seek water, and there is none, and their tongue faileth them for thirst, I the Lord will hear them, I the God of Israel will not forsake them. I will open rivers in high places, and fountains in the midst of the valleys: I will make the wilderness a pool of water, and the dry land springs of water."*

In the second place, and to prevent misapprehension, we may learn that life is not all hardship. There are Elims, with their springs of water and their palm-trees' shade, as well as Marahs. In the history of our Lord himself we have the baptismal glory and the Mount of Transfiguration, as well as the darkness of Gethsemane and the anguish of the cross; and if Paul was long in prison, and was "in labors abundant, and in stripes above measure," we must not forget his revelations in the Arabian desert, and his being caught up into the third heaven to hear unspeakable words. No man's experience is either all sunshine or all shadow. Life is of a checkered pattern. In some the dark preponderates, in some the light; but in all the two are interblended. The dark is there to remind us that we are still on earth; the light is there as a foretaste and earnest—if,

---

* Isa. xli., 17, 18.

through faith in Christ, we choose to make it such—of the inheritance on high. How true that is in ordinary life you need not that I should prove to you. It is matter of universal experience. You are proving it now. Some are at Marah, some are at Elim. We all know the general features of both; but we must all remember that they are only stations on our way. We cannot be forever either at the one or at the other. Soon the pillar of the cloud shall move again, and bring to us either a new difficulty or a new deliverance. But the comfort is that God is in both. He will make the bitter sweet, and the pleasant safe. So long as he is with us, adversity has no power to destroy us, and prosperity has no charm to tempt us. At Marah he is the Lord the healer, and at Elim he is the Lord the shade. So in either he is our benefactor, and in both alike we may sing the good old psalm of providence, "The Lord shall preserve me from all evil, he shall preserve my soul. The Lord shall preserve thy going out, and thy coming in, from this time forth, and even for evermore."

In the third place, we may learn that every great leader may lay his account with opposition even from those who profess to follow him. What a hard place was this of Moses here! He had consecrated himself to the deliverance of his people, and had been instrumental in humbling and destroying their oppressor, and in securing their emancipation; yet, as each new difficulty emerges, they turn in threatened mutiny upon him, and taunt him with bringing them away from the Egyptian flesh-pots. But this has not been a singular experience among the world's benefactors. Every great reformer has had to go through a wilderness to the promised land of his success; and always some of those who left Egypt with him have turned against him before he had gone far. For reform means, not only that others should amend, but that we ourselves should put away the evil of our doings from before God's eyes. It means, therefore, for leader and followers alike, self-sacrifice, disinterested service of our generation, consecration not to any party, but to the common weal; and they whose hearts are in the flesh-pots cannot understand or appreciate such lofty principles. When the multitude, full of enthusiasm for Jesus Christ, wanted to take him by force and make him a king, you may depend upon it they were seeking, not his glory, but their own interests; and it was because he would not open up to them the paths to personal aggrandizement which they sought, that, just at that moment, so many went back, and walked no more with him. Ah, how often all this has been repeated in the world's history! I think of the almost mutiny of his men against Columbus, as day after day he steered westward and saw no land; I think of the trouble which Luther and Calvin had so often with their own followers, and of the banishment, at one time, of the latter from that Geneva which, even to this day, is the creation of his greatness; I think of the curs that yelped at the heels of the Father of his Country, when he was following that course which now the universal voice of posterity has applauded; I think of the difficulties which have embarrassed many meaner men, in lower works of reformation, which have at length benefited and blessed the world, and I blush for the selfishness of those who prefer their own interest to the welfare of the community, while, at the same time, I honor the conscientious courage which determines to go on, in spite of opposition in the front and dissatisfaction in the rear. Oh! ye who are bravely battling for the right, the pure, the benevolent, whether it be in the sweeping out of corruption from political offices, or in the closing of those pestilential houses which are feeding the intemperance of our streets, or in the maintenance in the churches of the faith once delivered to the saints—take heart of grace from Moses here. Go with your causes to the Lord, and *be sure* that they who are on his side are always in the end victorious. You may be long in the wilderness, but even while you are he will sustain you there, and at last the Jericho, which is the stronghold of the enemy—though you may not be there to see it, and though some younger Joshuas may have taken your place—will fall down flat before the forces whom you have disciplined and trained.

Finally, we may learn that the true theory of life is to follow the word of God. I recall your attention to the design of the manna, as described in the passage which I have quoted to you from Deuteronomy, "He fed thee with manna, which thou knewest not, neither did thy fathers know; that he might make thee know that man doth not live by bread alone, but by every word that proceedeth out of the mouth of the Lord doth man live." Now, you may remember that when Satan tempted Jesus to use his divine power in turning the stones of the desert into bread, the Lord made answer, "It is written, man shall not live by bread alone, but by every word of God;" that is to say, life does not consist in eating and drinking—life is not the gratification of the body in any way, but the obedience of the soul to God. There is, doubtless, in the words as used by Christ more than that: there is strong faith in the providence of God that when we are following him food will not be withheld from us. But, while we look at the faith, there is some danger of our forgetting the very suggestive definition of life which is here given us. Life is to follow the word of God, no matter though it may bring privation to the body; or, as Paul has said, "If ye through the spirit do mortify the deeds of the body, ye shall live." The great design of life is not to eat bread or to gratify appetite. These are only means to a higher end, that end being the honor and the glory of God, whose we are, and whom we ought to serve. Not, indeed, that we should be anchorites, and seclude ourselves from the world in monastic solitude. No; but that we should seek to make the body our servant, and not ourselves to be the body's slaves. That is the great turning question of life: Am I to be the body's? or is the body to be mine, and mine for God? and according as I answer that question, I will be a glutton, a drunkard, an adulterer, or a servant of the Lord. Ah, how often is the young man tempted into sensuality by the words of his companions, "Come, let us see life!" But that is not life—that is death. Life is something higher, nobler, more glorious by far: life is to obey every word of God. To follow the mere body is to lead an existence lower than that of the animals, for their instincts regulate them; but if man will not obey either reason or religion, there are no such instincts left to guide him. To follow the body is to be carnally-minded, and that is death. Ask yourselves, then, this question, What is the aim of my life? do I live to eat and drink? or do I eat and drink in order to live and glorify God? The appetite is not sinful, if you keep it in its place; but if you look on its gratification as the great end of your lives, you are making yourselves the slaves of your bodies, and there is no slavery more galling. If even such a man as Paul declared that he kept his body under, and brought it into subjection, lest that by any means when he had preached to others he himself should be a castaway, how much more ought we? The body is a good servant, but it is a bad master; and if men will so far yield to Satan as to seek, at his bidding, out of stones to make bread for it, they may by-and-by find that instead of bread they have received a scorpion. He only can be truly said to live who, by faith in God's word and obedience unto him, seeks constantly to serve the Lord. My hearers, and especially you, young men, will you lay that to heart? Life is not, as the gourmand fancies, to enjoy the pleasures of the table; it is not, as the drunkard madly sings, to drink the flowing bowl; it is not, as the sensualist declares, to give loose rein to the lowest passions of our nature—all that is mere animalism. Life is to know God, to love God, to serve God; and when bodily famine comes to us, as we pursue that course, we may rely upon it that he will provide for us even angels' food. Better, ten thousand times over, the liberty wherewith Christ makes us free, though we fare only on manna, than the slavery of Egypt, with its flesh-pots—for there is life in the one, and death in the other.

IX.

REPHIDIM.

EXODUS xvii., 1-16.

FROM the Wilderness of Sin the children of Israel journeyed, according to the commandment of the Lord, and pitched in Rephidim. In the enumeration of the stations at which they sojourned in the wilderness, which is contained in the book of Numbers,* two places, named respectively Dophkah and Alush, are mentioned between the Wilderness of Sin and Rephidim; and, amid the many controversies which have been raised in connection with the geography of the Sinaitic peninsula, it is difficult, if not, indeed, impossible, for one who has not himself visited the locality to come to any very satisfactory conclusion as to the route which is thus indicated. But, after reading all that is of importance on the matter, I may give the result at which I have arrived. Identifying, as we have already done, the station in the Wilderness of Sin with the broad part of the Wady en Nusb, we suppose that, on leaving that, the Hebrews took the road which passes Sarabit el Khadem, and encamped in Dophkah, which may be the Wady Sih, since both names mean the same thing; or which may be somewhere in the great plain now called Debbet er Ramleh. Thence they went up the valleys el Burk and Berah to Alush, which it is easy to identify with the modern Elush; and from this point they made their way by the Wady Sheykh to Rephidim, which we suppose to have been the

---

* Num. xxiii., 12-14.

large open space immediately outside or north of the pass which leads into the district of Horeb, properly so called. This site is about twelve miles from Mount Sinai, and corresponds in every respect with the requirements of the narrative. It is true, indeed, that in the rainy season a large torrent runs from the Sinaitic region down through the valley Es Sheykh, and thence through the Feiran to the sea; but we must remember that the tribes arrived here long after the rainy season had passed, and that any ordinary supply of water would be speedily exhausted by such a multitude. Moreover, though we do not set much store by traditional identifications, nor even by the similarity of modern to ancient names, we may mention that near the entrance of the pass to which I have alluded there is an insulated rock, called the Seat of Moses, which may be the stone on which the leader sat when Aaron and Hur supported his hands. Again, there is a spring here, called Bir Musa, the well of Moses, which may have been originally Bir Massa, the well of provocation; and nearly opposite that, on the west side, there is a valley called the Wady Charibeh, which may be a corruption for Meribah. Hence, although the English explorers do, for the most part, identify Rephidim with Wady Feiran, we are disposed to agree with those who fix it at the site which we have described, because the Feiran is almost universally conceded to have been occupied by the Amalekites, and therefore it would have been impossible for the Israelites to have ascended it without coming much sooner than they did into collision with their enemies; who, in that case, also, must have attacked them in front, and not, as we know they did, in the rear.*

When the people came to this place, they found no water,

---

* Deuteronomy xxv., 17, 18. See Fairbairn's "Imperial Dictionary," art. REPHIDIM.

or the supply which existed on their arrival was speedily exhausted; and, as usual, they "did chide with Moses," alleging that he had caused all their hardships by bringing them out of Egypt, the bitterness of whose bondage, in other respects, was forgotten, for the moment, in the fact that they had always had there abundance of bread and plenty of water. In vain did he remind them that Jehovah was their leader, and that they were really tempting him. Indeed, that only exasperated them the more, until "they were almost ready to stone him." In this emergency he cried unto the Lord, and was commanded to take with him the elders of Israel, and the rod with which he had smitten the River Nile, and to go forward to a rock in Horeb, which would be pointed out to him, and which, when smitten by him, would give forth water. Everything was done by him according to these instructions, and very soon a rivulet—if I should not rather say a river—ran down through the valley to the encampment. As the people heard the welcome sound of its approach, they would hasten forth to refresh themselves at its margin, and would rejoice in its presence, even before they learned the story of its marvellous origin; for they had not seen the smiting of the rock. The miracle was witnessed only by the elders, and it was wrought some miles away from Rephidim. In the valley of the Ledja, which runs between Mount Sinai and Mount Catherine, a large block of red granite, having on its face a number of horizontal fissures, at unequal distances from each other, is pointed out as the rock which was smitten by Moses. But, while some travellers aver that it bears every mark of the action of water, others ridicule the very idea of its having had any connection with this miracle; and so it is impossible to say anything definite regarding it. More important, however, than the identification of the precise spot, is the fact that the undoubted source of this miraculous river was somewhere in

Horeb, and therefore at an altitude sufficiently great to admit of its flowing down through the valleys, just as the ordinary winter-torrents do now. If, therefore, we may suppose that the stream continued to run during the residence of the tribes in the vicinity, we can understand how, on at least their first journeyings from Horeb, by way of Mount Seir to Kadesh Barnea, the water followed them; and so a little light, perhaps, is cast upon the assertion of the apostle that "they drank of the rock that followed them."* That there was a certain permanence in this stream seems to be implied in the language of Moses, many years later, when, speaking of the destruction of the golden calf, he says, "I burnt it with fire, and stamped it, and ground it very small, even until it was as small as dust: and I cast the dust thereof into the brook that descended out of the mount."† It is impossible, also, on any other theory to explain the psalmist's words, "He clave the rocks in the wilderness, and gave them drink as out of the great depths. He brought streams also out of the rock, and caused waters to run down like rivers."‡ So we may conclude that the rock was situated at such a height, and in such a relation to the Sinaitic valleys, as to furnish water to the tribes in other encampments than that at Rephidim. Thus, again, the extremity of the tribes was God's opportunity, and their murmuring, perpetuated in the names Massah and Meribah, was rebuked by his mercy. Thus, also, the rock becomes a finger-post, pointing to him whose cross was the altar from beneath which came those fertilizing waters which Ezekiel§ saw, and which gave life to everything they touched. If the Epistle to the Hebrews be the key to the hidden meaning of the ritual which Moses introduced, the Gospel by John is as truly the interpreter of much that is

---

* 1 Cor. x., 4.   † Deut. ix., 21.
‡ Psa. lxxviii., 15, 16.   § Ezek. xlvii., 1–12.

spiritually significant in the history of the pilgrimage of the people through the wilderness; for in the discourses of our Lord which it preserves there are such references as enable us to understand more fully the higher import of these ancient miracles. We have already seen how the manna was made by him to illustrate the true bread of life; and now, as we hear the rush of this new-born river through Rephidim, we cannot fail to be reminded of the words, "Whosoever drinketh of this water shall thirst again: but whosoever drinketh of the water that I shall give him shall never thirst; but the water that I shall give him shall be in him a well of water springing up into everlasting life."* That rock was Christ; for the stream which refreshed Rephidim came from him, from whom also, stricken for us, the blessings of salvation flow, full, free, and perennial, for all who choose to avail themselves of his mercy.

The supply of water had not been long furnished to them, when the people were attacked by a wild Arab tribe, who, as we learn from the account given in Deuteronomy, fell upon them in the rear, and "smote the hindmost of them, even all that were feeble behind them, when they were faint and weary."† These enemies are called Amalekites, and were probably the descendants of Amalek, one of the grandsons of Esau.‡ They belonged to the common stock of Edomites, but they formed, to some extent, a tribe by themselves, and occupied the western parts of Mount Seir. Their attack on Israel was probably dictated by religious animosity, for in the passage which I have already quoted it is said that "they feared not God." The Hebrews had not invaded their territory, or in any way menaced their possessions; but, acquainted, from their relationship to Esau, with the promises made to the seed of Jacob, and aggravated by hearing

---

* John iv., 13, 14.   † Deut. xxv., 18.   ‡ Gen. xxxvi., 12.

of the great things which Jehovah had done for his people in Egypt, they determined, in a spirit of envy, to destroy them, simply and only because God had adopted them as his own. They came at what appeared to them to be a favorable opportunity to lay their hand, as it were, on the very banner of Jehovah; and sought, if possible, to exterminate the people whom he had promised to protect. Their attitude was thus one of stern defiance to the Almighty, and that accounts at once for the manner in which they were met by Moses, and for the terrible denunciation which was pronounced upon them by the Lord. It was the first collision between heathenism and the people of God, and so Moses bestirred himself for the encounter. Calling Joshua, who is here mentioned for the first time, and who must have been now about forty-five years old, he commanded him to collect an army of picked men, and go forth to fight with Amalek, while he himself, with his rod in his hand, ascended one of the neighboring hills, accompanied by his brother Aaron, and by Hur, the father of Bezaleel, and, according to tradition, the husband of Miriam. While Joshua and the people were fighting, Moses stood holding the rod with his hands, and it was observed that the battle seemed to turn with the uplifting or falling of the wonder-working staff. When he held up his hands, Israel prevailed; and when he let them down, Amalek prevailed. But the constant elevation of his arms in one position made them weary, so Aaron and Hur "took a stone and put it under him, and he sat thereon; and Aaron and Hur stayed up his hands, the one on the one side, and the other on the other: and his hands were steady until the going down of the sun." This was not, as some have imagined, a sign to the army for the direction of the fight, but rather a direct appeal to God on their behalf; and many have seen in this procedure an illustration of the intercession of Jesus Christ in heaven for his Church militant on the earth. But that analogy will not hold in all respects, for Christ's hands are never weary; he needs no Aaron and Hur to support him, and his pleading never ceases. We prefer, therefore, to regard the whole as enforcing the necessity of uniting prayer with conflict in our contests with our spiritual enemies. Admirably has Keil said here, "As the heathen world was now commencing its conflict with the people of God, so the battle which Israel fought with this foe possessed a typical significance."* It furnishes the law for success in all spiritual warfare, namely, that we must unite the courage of Joshua with the prayer of Moses. A praying soldier is always the most formidable. This is true even in the warfare of earth. The piety of Gustavus Adolphus gave a keener edge to his sword; and when some specially difficult work was to be done during the Indian mutiny, the call was for Havelock and his "saints." But this is particularly true of the good fight in which the Christian is engaged; for the apostle, after enumerating all the pieces of our armor, adds, as specially important, "praying always with all prayer."†

Perhaps, also, we have set before us here the importance of a division of labor in the army of the Lord, and we are taught that while some are fighting others should be praying. In this regard, those Aaron and Hur societies which stay up the hands of the minister, and make earnest supplication for all who are engaged in any department of Christian activity, are among the most useful, as they are, also, among the least ostentatious helpers of the host of the Lord.

The result of this conflict was that Amalek was utterly discomfited; and, to strengthen the confidence of the peo-

---

* "Commentary on the Pentateuch," by Keil and Delitzsch, vol. ii., p. 81. † Eph. vi., 18.

ple that God would similarly help them in all their struggles with their enemies, Moses was commanded to write the history of this victory in a book—or rather, for the original word has the definite article prefixed to it, *the* book—which he had already begun, and which was to be a full and faithful chronicle of all their history. Moreover, for this bitter and unprovoked attack, which emanated from their hatred of himself, the Lord declared that he would utterly destroy Amalek; and at a later day* he bound Israel "to blot out the remembrance of Amalek from under heaven." So we read of their defeat by Gideon, and of their partial destruction by Saul; but it was not until the days of Hezekiah that they were finally annihilated.†

To deepen yet further the impression produced by the words of the Lord, Moses built an altar, not for sacrifice, but simply as a monument, for he called it "Jehovah, my banner," saying as he did so, "Because the Lord hath sworn that the Lord will have war with Amalek from generation to generation;" or rather, as some of the best scholars translate the words, "Because the hand of Amalek was upon the banner of the Lord, the Lord will have war with Amalek from generation to generation."

Many valuable lessons might be drawn from this history, such as the following: that the people of God may expect conflict in the world; that in their conflicts they must combine prayer with courage; and that those who wilfully and wantonly assail them on the Lord's account may expect not only signal defeat, but prolonged chastisement. These, however, will come up on other occasions, and may be conveniently reserved for future treatment, while we devote the remainder of the present discourse to a few considerations sug-

---

* Deut. xxv., 17-19.
† Judg. vi., 3; vii., 12. 1 Sam. xiv., 48. 1 Chron. iv., 42, 43.

gested by the name given to this altar, "Jehovah-Nissi—the Lord my banner."

A flag is in itself a simple thing enough. A piece of bunting, or of silk, having on it an emblematic device, such as a certain number of stars and stripes, or the cross of St. Andrew, combined with those of St. George and St. Patrick —that is all! and, when so regarded, it is "nothing in the world." But when we view it as a symbol, it forthwith acquires transcendant importance. It becomes then the mark of nationality, and all the sentiments of patriotism are stirred in us by the sight of it. We think of the struggles of our fathers, when for the first time it fluttered over them in the breeze, as they resisted injustice and oppression. We recall the many bloody fields over which, amidst the smoke of battle, its streaming colors waved their proud defiance. The memories of a hundred years have woven themselves into its texture; and, as it floats serenely over us, we see in it at once the aggregated result of our history in the past and the bright prophesy of our greatness in the future. Now, it is quite similar with the banner which God has given us, that it may be displayed because of the truth, and which, as this inscription declares, he is himself. Its value consists in that which it symbolizes or suggests. Let us see, then, what this affix to the name Jehovah here implies.

In the first place, it means that Jehovah is our token of decision. The raising of a banner indicates that the person who sets it up has made his choice of, and has determined to adhere to, the cause of which it is the symbol. Now, there are two parties in the world. The one is that of truth and love and holiness, the other is that of error and selfishness and sin; and they are in constant antagonism with each other. Nay, the more earnest the age is, the more intense is their opposition to each other, and the more difficult does it become for any one to avoid connecting himself openly with the one or the other. In seasons of prevailing indifference, when no great issues are raised, and lukewarmness is the characteristic of all alike, one may be tempted to tamper with the matter and stave off decision, with an effort to stand well with both. In the opening days of the first French Revolution, it is said that a timid trimmer fixed a cockade beneath the lappel of his coat on one breast, and a tricolor in the corresponding portion on the other; and that when he met a royalist he exposed the cockade, and shouted "Long live the king!" but when he met a republican he showed the tricolor, and cried "Long live the republic!" That, however, sufficed only for a short time; for as the strife increased, every man was forced to make a decision between the two. So sometimes, in times of indifference, it has been possible for men to seem to combine the services of God and mammon; but happily, as I think, for us, we have fallen on an earnest age. Never was Christianity more positive and aggressive than it is to-day. It is pushing its claims directly and distinctly before all thoughtful minds. Caring less, perhaps, than in former times for minor matters, it is calling more attention than ever to the person and work of Christ, and no inquirer can leave the subject alone. How otherwise shall we explain the appearance, within the last few years, of so many works devoted to the consideration of the life of our Lord? Men feel more and more that they must give some answer to the question, "What think ye of Christ?" and the force of the Christian view of the subject, illustrated, as that has been, by some great spiritual revivals, both in the Old World and in the New, has provoked a corresponding intensity in the antagonists of the truth. It is, therefore, becoming impossible even to seem to be neutral here. From the midst of earnest controversy in thoughtful and inquiring circles, from the midst of eager collision between principle and interest in business, from the midst of the constant conflict between good and evil in our city streets, from the midst of the increasing antagonism between Christian integrity and dishonest selfishness—nay, even from the debates in our halls of legislation, the cry is raised, "Who is on the Lord's side?" and it becomes us all to hoist our flag, and display to the world in its expanding folds this old inscription, "Jehovah-Nissi—the Lord is my banner." When Hedley Vicars, the Christian soldier, was converted, he knew that he should be made the butt of much ridicule, and the victim of much petty persecution by his comrades; so he resolved to be beforehand with them, and in the morning on which he made his decision he took his Bible and laid it down open on his table. Very soon a fellow-officer came in, and, looking at the book, exclaimed, "Halloo, Vicars! turned Methodist?" To which he made reply, "That is my flag; and, by the grace of God, I hope to be true to it as long as I live!" That was his Rephidim, and there he too conquered Amalek by raising the banner of the Lord. So let it be, dear friends, with you. "If Jehovah be God, follow him." Do not go about as if you felt that you required to apologize for being his disciples. You have no need to hang your heads for him. Hoist your flag, then, full in the sight of all your adversaries; and when they know that you are resolute, they will be deterred from attacking you. They who are timid are always most furiously assailed, for there is the greater likelihood of getting them to capitulate at length; but bold decision wards off assault. The worldling will not waste his ammunition on those whom he cannot bring down; and when the scoffer sees that a man is determined, he lets him alone. Take your stand, then, boldly with the people of God. Raise your banner; see that you never lower it before any earthly influence, and be ready to defend it with your lives.

Again, this name means that Jehovah is our mark of distinction. He who has crossed the ocean, and seen vessels daily coming into sight, knows how the nationality of each is recognized by the flag she shows. Each country has its own symbol, and to those who are acquainted with its history that symbol connects itself at once with the peculiar characteristics of the people to whom it belongs. So the Christian is different from other men; not, indeed, in the sense of having any external badge constantly about him, but in that of having a distinct and easily recognized character. When, in travelling through the midland counties of England, one comes on the stately residence of some duke or earl, and sees the flag floating in quiet dignity from its turret, he knows from that indication that the proprietor is himself within the walls. Now, the distinguishing peculiarity of the Christian is that God, to whom he belongs, is, by his spirit, dwelling within him, and that shows itself in many ways. It is apparent in the love by which he is animated for all who are in suffering, in sorrow, or in want. It is seen in the purity of speech and conduct which he maintains; in the earnestness of his devotion to the will of Christ, and in the eager efforts which he makes to attain to that perfection of character which he sees in his Lord. Thus the very graces of holiness are the indications of God's presence in the heart, and that is the special distinction of the child of God. Look at the Israelites here, and when you ask what was the difference between them and other nations, you will find it in the fact that God was in the midst of them. So the Christian is the temple of the Holy Ghost; and in the measure in which he is bringing forth the fruit of the Spirit, he is waving the banner which Moses described when he called this altar "Jehovah-Nissi."

Still again, this name implies that Jehovah is our joy. When we make demonstration of our enthusiasm, we raise a whole forest of flag-staffs, and fix on each an appropriate banner. Let it be the commemoration of some victory, or the celebration of national independence, or the welcome to some foreign prince who has visited our shores, and the whole city is gay with flags, while the emblems of many nationalities are seen fluttering in friendly fellowship from the mastheads of the ships in the harbor. So we are reminded, by the inscription on this altar, that "the joy of the Lord" is "the strength" of the Christian. His life is one of constant gladness; his characteristic is what I may call a calm enthusiasm, or, to use the phrase of Jonathan Edwards, a "quiet rapture." It is a mistake to think of the religion of Jesus as a gloomy thing. Because he is reconciled to God, because God, by his spirit, is dwelling in his heart, and because he has the well-grounded hope of spending eternity with God, the Christian cannot but be joyful, even though he should be suffering affliction in the world. It was because the apostles had hoisted this banner that "they departed from the presence of the council, rejoicing that they were counted worthy to suffer shame for his name." It was because the Hebrews had hoisted this banner that they "took joyfully the spoiling of their goods, knowing in themselves that they had in heaven a better and an enduring substance." It was because they had raised this banner that martyrs and confessors in every age were enabled to give such radiant testimony to the truth that God never forsakes those that put their trust in him.

Great has been the enthusiasm which that banner, first unfurled here by Moses, has everywhere evoked; and great has been the joy which its adherents everywhere have manifested, even when, to human view, they have been "destitute, afflicted, and tormented." Therefore, my hearers, if you wish to obtain pure, perennial, and incorruptible happiness, which the prosperity of the world cannot overlay nor its adversity destroy, come raise with me to-night this old flag, which has braved the battle and the breeze for over thirty centuries, and march forward from this good hour under the leadership of him whose name it bears.

Finally, this inscription reminds us that God is the protector of his people. There is nothing of which a nation is so jealous as the honor of its flag, and he who is in reality a citizen has a right to the protection of the government. The man who wraps himself in the flag of this republic has the whole power of the republic pledged for his security. Great Britain has few prouder chapters in her recent history than that which tells of the expedition to Abyssinia some years ago. A great force was landed on the Red Sea shore; a long, troublesome, and dangerous march of many days was made into an enemy's country; a fierce assault was successfully attempted on a hitherto impregnable fortress; many lives were lost, and fifty millions of dollars were spent—and all for what? Because a brutal tyrant was keeping in horrid imprisonment two or three men who had a right to the protection of the British flag; and you can hardly conceive what an outburst of joy broke forth from the nation when the news came that they had been set free, and that the insulting monarch had been made to bite the dust. But what is the power of the British empire, or the might of this great republic, in comparison with omnipotence? Yet he who sincerely raises this banner has God's pledge that he will protect him. Listen to these words: "I give unto them eternal life; and they shall never perish, neither shall any pluck them out of my hand. My Father, which gave them me, is greater than all; and none is able to pluck them out of my Father's hand." "No weapon that is formed against thee shall prosper, and every tongue that shall rise against thee in judgment thou shalt condemn." "In the world ye shall have tribulation; but be of good cheer, I have overcome the world." "Fear not; for I am with thee: be not dismayed; for

I am thy God: I will strengthen thee; yea, I will help thee; yea, I will uphold thee with the right hand of my righteousness."* These are the words of him who cannot lie, and who has the resources of infinite wisdom and power at his command. Why, then, should you hesitate to enlist into his army? If you have not done so before, do it now. You can never have a better opportunity. The close of the old year calls you to reflection, and the near approach of the new year makes for you a natural boundary between the past and the future. Come, then, and let the time past of your life suffice to have wrought the will of the Gentiles. Up with the banner of your new Lord, Jehovah Jesus! Raise it in firm decision, with quiet earnestness and with humble prayer; keep it with unflinching fortitude, and be ready to die rather than dishonor it.

> "Take thy banner, and beneath
> The battle-cloud's encircling wreath
> Guard it, while life lasts with thee!
> Guard it—God will prosper thee;
> In the dark and trying hour,
> In the breaking forth of power,
> In the rush of steeds and men,
> His right hand will shield thee then."†

---

* John x., 28, 29; xvi., 33. Isa. xli., 10; liv., 17.

† I trust Mr. Longfellow will forgive me for the slight alteration which I have made on the third line in the above stanza of his spirit-stirring hymn, that I might appropriate it to the battle of life. But that I may not be guilty of giving currency to an impure text of such a classical poem, let me say here that in the original it reads thus:

> "Guard it, till our homes are free."

X.

JETHRO'S VISIT.

EXODUS xviii., 1–27.

THE eighteenth chapter of the Book of Exodus contains an account of a visit paid by Jethro, the father-in-law of Moses, to the camp of the Israelites, and the character of the parties combines with the important results which issued from their interview to make the occasion one of the most interesting connected with the wilderness history of the tribes. At first sight it would seem that Rephidim was the scene of this patriarchal greeting, for the narrative comes in between the account of the victory over Amalek and that of the journey to the desert of Sinai; and many of the best expositors believe that the incidents here recorded did occur while yet the people were on the outside of that narrow and rocky defile which forms the entrance into the region of Horeb, properly so called. To me, however, it rather seems as if the story of this visit belongs to a later period, and is inserted here out of its chronological position because of certain important reasons which, under the guidance of divine inspiration, weighed with the mind of the writer. It is not a matter of much consequence, and no vital principle is affected by its settlement either way; for we know that in some of the gospel narratives the order of time has been made by the evangelists in many instances to give way before other and higher considerations. We do not suppose, therefore, that this chapter has fallen by some literary accident out of its proper place; but rather that it has been by its author deliberately inserted here, although it really belongs to a period subsequent to that at which it is introduced.

My belief is that the Israelites had moved into the district of Horeb, and had encamped in the plain, in which they remained for a whole year, and from which they witnessed the giving of the law; and that it was some time during their residence there that Jethro came with Zipporah and her sons to Moses. I am led to this conclusion by the fact that in the fifth verse of the narrative the locality is described as "the wilderness where Moses encamped at the Mount of God." Now this can mean only one place. The Mount of God is pre-eminently and emphatically Sinai; and therefore, all other considerations to the contrary notwithstanding, we are shut up to the inference that the encampment here referred to was not Rephidim, but Sinai. This view of the matter is confirmed by the words of Moses in the first chapter of the Book of Deuteronomy, where, describing what must be held to be the same change in the mode of his administration which he here initiated, he places it clearly in Horeb, and not long before the removal of the people from the base of Sinai.* Moreover, in this chapter itself there are certain expressions which seem to refer to the promulgation of the law and the establishment of the divine oracle as things already past; for Moses speaks to Jethro of "the people coming to inquire of God," and of his making them "to know the statutes of God and his laws;" while Jethro uses language which appears to imply that Moses had already begun "to bring their causes unto God."† Besides, the time which elapsed between the arrival of the people at Rephidim and their journeying to Sinai would hardly admit of the occurrence of all the events here enumerated, especially when we take into consideration the conflict with Am-

---

* Deut. i., 6, 9–17. † See Exod. xviii., 15, 16, 19.

alek, of which that valley was the scene, and which occupied at least one whole day. It is true, indeed, as some one has suggested,* that many questions of dispute might arise among them as to the disposal of the spoil which was taken from their enemies; but no one can read the words of Jethro without perceiving that his advice to Moses was founded not upon the sight of the proceedings of a single day, and that one of exceptional hardship, but rather on his observation, for some considerable time, of the wearing character of the constant routine of duties which Moses had undertaken, and which he was endeavoring daily to perform. For these reasons, therefore, I am disposed to conclude that the narrative contained in the eighteenth chapter of Exodus belongs chronologically to a later date than that of the encampment at Rephidim, and has its scene rather in the valley at the base of Sinai.† But if that be so, how has it been inserted here? To that question three answers may be given, no one of which excludes the others, and in the union of which we may probably find the true solution. It may have been brought in at this point in order to contrast the joy of a truly pious man like Jethro, at the deliverance of the Israelites, with the envy, malice, and ferocity of the Amalekites. All the neighboring tribes were not so bitterly hostile as the descendants of Ishmael, but those among them who retained their knowledge and worship of the true God were moved with gratitude at the manifestation of the goodness of the

---

* See Murphy, *in loco*.

† To these considerations might be added the fact that the chapter contains such a repetition of particulars regarding Jethro and the family of Moses, as suggests that it stands apart from the general narrative, and was probably written at first on a separate roll. It is only fair, however, to add that Canon Cook, who notes this characteristic of the chapter, considers that it stands in its true chronological position. See "Speaker's Commentary," *in loco*, vol. i., p. 325.

Lord to the Hebrews; and so the Gentiles were not rejected simply and only as Gentiles, but rather as idolaters. There is something, to my mind, exceedingly significant and suggestive in the introduction just here, between the defeat of Amalek and the giving of the law, of the account of Jethro, Moses, Aaron, and the elders of Israel keeping sacramental feast together before the Lord; and it seems to hint that, while the Jews were to be entirely isolated from the degrading idolatry of the heathen generally, they were yet to be generous and brotherly in their recognition of those who sincerely sought to serve the one living and true God. If this had been better remembered by the people in later days, there would have been fewer apostasies into idolatry on the one hand, and a less rigid exclusivism observed by them on the other.

But another reason for the placing of this narrative here may have been because the writer was about to enter on that section of his history which records the giving of the law, and desired that nothing should interrupt its continuity. The incidents of Sinai were to stand alone, and nothing was to be allowed to divert the attention of the reader from them even for a moment; therefore, before he entered upon the description of them, he dismisses the personal reminiscences connected with the visit of his father-in-law. These were too pleasant, and in their results too important, to be left out altogether, yet they must not be permitted to break in upon a more momentous history, or to withdraw the mind from the tremendous majesty of the revelation from Sinai.

Again, jealous for the honor of Jehovah, the inspired author may have desired to keep clearly distinct before his readers the measures which he adopted at mere human suggestion, and those which he inaugurated at the bidding of Jehovah. The suggestions of Jethro were those of a wise man, the law from Sinai was that of God, and the two are in nowise to be confounded; so, before we move forward to that valley over which the voice of the Eternal rolled his words of thunder, we are permitted to hear and to enjoy the counsels of the Midianitish priest. Too valuable to be entirely overlooked, they must not be overlaid beneath the grandeur of Sinai; while, on the other hand, they must not be put on a level with the utterances of God.

Having thus obtained a distinct idea of the true chronological position of this chapter, and of the probable reasons which led to its insertion here, let us go on to the consideration of its contents.

It would appear that, after the incidents which occurred at the inn,* and which led to the circumcision of her youngest son, Zipporah was sent back by Moses to her father's care. He was going to Egypt, on a mission which he felt sure would task his faith and courage to the utmost; and though, at first, it had been apparently his intention to take his family with him, yet the spirit manifested by Zipporah on the occasion referred to convinced him that her presence would be a hinderance rather than a help to him in his work; and, therefore, having a regard at once to his own efficiency and to her safety, he let her return, for the time, to her father's house. It is probable, also, that he appointed the Mount in Horeb, where God had met with him at first, and where he had assured him that he would bring his people to worship, as a place of tryst, to which Jethro was to bring his family, whenever he should hear of the arrival of the Israelites in that locality. So the good old man, having learned of the escape of the Hebrews, and their encampment in Horeb, set out from his Midianitish head-quarters, and, travelling after the manner of his people, reached the wilderness

---

* Exod. iv., 24–26. See above, p. 66.

of Sinai in safety. When he came near the outskirts of the camp, he sent on a messenger to announce his arrival to Moses; and the leader at once "went out to meet him, and did obeisance and kissed him; and they asked each other of their welfare, and they came into the tent." It is a touching Oriental picture, and illustrates the confidential character of the friendship which existed between these two members of God's own aristocracy. Moses does not take airs upon him, or assume any superiority over Jethro on the ground of the great things in which, during the interval of their separation, he had been so distinguished an actor. Nor does Jethro come to him with cringing sycophancy, as if now he dared hardly speak to his old acquaintance and friend. They are the same to each other as when they parted, only their separation has given them a higher opinion of each other, and a stronger affection for each other; and so there is not, on either side, the slightest suspicion of insincerity, as they run to lock themselves in each other's arms. They began again with each other just where they had left off, and sat down to tell each other of God's doings with them since they saw each other last. On the one hand, Jethro would have much to say concerning Zipporah and her sons; and Gershon and Eliezer would chime in with the story of their adventures, each trying to outdo the other in the marvellous things he had to tell. On the other, Moses would recount at length the story of his controvesy with Pharaoh; his turning of Jannes and Jambres to confusion; the desolation of Egypt by the plagues; the Passover; the Exodus, and the crossing of the sea; and, standing at the door of the tent, he would point to the pillar of cloud and fire, as he told the miracle of their guidance, and rehearsed the incidents of Marah and Rephidim. Doubtless, too, he would dwell with all the ecstasy of enthusiasm on the goodness and the glory of Jehovah, whose simple instrument he had been throughout; for, as he concluded, Jethro broke forth into praise, saying, "Blessed be the Lord, who hath delivered you out of the hand of the Egyptians, and out of the hand of Pharaoh; who hath delivered the people from under the hand of the Egyptians. Now I know that the Lord is greater than all gods; for in the thing wherein they dealt proudly he was above them." Then, as the priest of God, he offered a burnt-offering and sacrifices, and sat down with Moses, Aaron, and the elders to the holy feast.

It is rather singular that, throughout the narrative, there is no mention made of Zipporah and her sons, except the statement that Jethro brought them to Moses. This may be owing to the Oriental custom of virtually ignoring woman, or it may be explained by some peculiarity in the character of Zipporah herself; for, so far as appears, she had little sympathy with the grand work in which her husband was engaged, and perhaps would have been better pleased if he had never left his shepherd-life in Midian. But it could not be caused by any lack of affection for her, or appreciation of her, on the part of Moses; for, at a later date, he stood up on her behalf even against Aaron and Miriam. Still, we cannot conceal our disappointment that, while so much is made—and very properly made—of Jethro, there is no remotest reference to the reception by Moses of his wife and their sons. With that exception, however, we cannot but admire everything in this patriarchal greeting.

Nothing tests a man more than his bearing toward his former friends after he has passed through some experiences which have brought him great honor and prosperity; and when, as in the present instance, he comes back with his old frankness and cordiality, and is not ashamed of his old piety, he is a great man indeed. Too often, however, prosperity deteriorates character, and honor freezes the heart. The head swims on the giddy height, and the son returns a comparative stranger even to his father's house; while the family worship, which used to be so enjoyed, is smiled at as a weakness of the old people's, and avoided as a weariness by himself. Old companions, too, are passed without recognition; or, if recognized at all, it is with an air of condescension, and with an effort like that which one makes to stoop for something that is far beneath him. The development of character also estranges us from those whom we once knew intimately, and who were once, it may be, the better for our fellowship. But the consolation in all such cases is that there can be no value in the further friendship of those who can thus forget the past. He is the really good friend—as well as the truly great man—who, in spite of his deserved eminence, resumes with us at the point at which we separated, and carries us at length with him to the throne of grace, to acknowledge there our obligations to the Lord. There are men whom one meets from time to time with whom he has always to begin anew. They are like a book in which you never get fully interested, and which, whenever you take it up, you must commence to read again at the very preface; until, in absolute disgust, you cast it away from you, and never lift it more. There are others who are like a well-beloved volume, with a book-mark in it, which you can open at any moment, and resume where you broke off; and which, though you may be often interrupted, you contrive to read through to the end. Such a friend was Moses to Jethro, and Jethro to Moses; and though there came a final separation of the one from the other on earth, they would renew their conference in heaven, where still they would tell one another of the goodness which the Lord had shown to them. Compared with such frank, confidential, and mutually helpful friendships, that of the successful worldling and his fawning parasite is but as tinsel is to gold.

That Jethro was deeply solicitous for the welfare and honor

of Moses, appears from the wise advice he gave him. He found that Moses had taken upon him the sole responsibility for the administration of justice among the people; and, as the crowd of suitors continued with little apparent diminution from morning till evening, he saw at once that such a course would speedily break down the strength of his friend, while it must also fail to satisfy the disputants. Therefore, with admirable common-sense, he recommended him to divide the labor with others, rising in regular gradation from rulers of tens to rulers of thousands, who should judge the people at all seasons, and bring only hard matters to him. He advised that he should be for the people to Godward, bringing their causes unto God, and teaching them God's statutes and ordinances, alike in reference to their daily walk and their individual work; but he urged him to relegate the settlement of all minor matters to judges taken from among the people themselves. From the reference made to this arrangement in the Book of Deuteronomy, it appears that these subordinate judges were chosen by the suffrage of the tribes; but Jethro manifested his own sterlingness of character, as well as his thorough acquaintance with human nature, by urging that the persons so chosen should be "able men, such as fear God, men of truth, hating covetousness." The election was by the people, but the appointment was made by Moses; and it is probable, therefore, that he exercised a veto on their choice whensoever he considered it to be necessary for the best interests of the tribes that he should do so. Cavillers have objected to the arrangement suggested by Jethro, that it would create at once between seven and eight thousand judges; but they arrive at that result by taking the individual as the unit; whereas, in the East generally, and specially among such tribes as that to which Jethro belonged, and in which his experience was obtained, the unit is the family; and the lowest of these justices, therefore, would have jurisdiction over ten families. Next came the rulers over fifties, to whom the dissatisfied among the tens might appeal, and who were likely to have the largest share of the work; then came the rulers over hundreds, and then the rulers over thousands; and only such causes as ran through the whole ascending series without satisfactory settlement were brought before Moses himself. It was an excellent plan, which, with the approval of God, Moses adopted; and which the accumulated wisdom of thirty intervening centuries has done very little to improve upon. Thus Jethro lent his sagacity to Moses, and Moses helped to stimulate the piety of Jethro, for true friendship is always reciprocal in its advantages. But the pathways of the two men—so far as earth was concerned—diverged again; and so, after this brief and profitable season of fellowship with each other, Moses let his father-in-law depart, and he went away into his own land.

It is time now, however, that we should look for some lessons from this narrative that shall be appropriate to our modern life. And, first of all, we may learn here that public duties do not absolve a man from domestic responsibility. It may be unavoidable that one who has great work laid upon him should for a season be separated from his household; but in all ordinary cases a man's family should be under his personal supervision, and husband and wife should dwell together. It was not good either for Moses or Zipporah to be so long absent from each other, and certainly the effect on Gershom and Eliezer would be positively injurious; so, though it might be hard for Jethro to part with them all, he recognized that it was right for them to be with Moses, and interposed no objection to the reunion of his son-in-law's household, but did everything in his power to bring it about. No doubt Moses had many and pressing calls on his time and his strength. The leader of such a host, however much he might bring the exertions of others into requisition, had no sinecure. But there was one responsibility which he could not delegate to any man, and that was the responsibility for the ruling of his own house, and the godly upbringing of his sons. Nobody could attend to these matters but himself—neither Jethro, nor Aaron, nor Joshua, nor Hur could relieve him of these duties. God would hold him personally accountable for their performance; and we may well believe that the visit of Jethro, with his wife and sons, would be the means of quickening his conscience in regard to these home responsibilities. But how many among ourselves require some patriarch to come to us, and, as it were, reintroduce us to our wives and children! We have not left our homes, indeed; it is not quite with us, in this respect, as it was with Moses and Zipporah, who had been separated from each other for many months. We live beneath the same roofs as our families; we do some of our eating and all of our sleeping in the home beside them; we pay the bills; we say now and then an honest word of commendation to one or other of the household band; we preside at the breakfast-table and the dinner-table—and what else? We cannot honestly add much more. Yet we lay "the flattering unction" to our souls that we are model husbands and fathers; and we imagine, too, that we are training our children into habits of industry and frugality. What a miserable delusion! Business is important enough in its own place, and public work for the city and for the country is not to be neglected. But it seems to me that in these days men—ay, even Christian men—are too largely forgetting that their first obligation is to their homes. When the apostle wrote, "It remaineth that those that have wives be as though they had none," he did not mean that when you sit down to the morning meal you should bury yourself in the newspaper, and become entirely oblivious of those who are seated at the table with you, and of her who is even at the moment ministering to your comfort; neither did he mean that you should come home, after your weary business day, cross, testy, and cantankerous, such a son of Belial that you cannot be spoken to; and that when dinner is over you should go to sleep on the sofa, or adjourn with a masculine friend to the smoking-room, utterly forgetful of her whom you have solemnly vowed to make the companion of your life and the sharer of your lot; and indifferent, also, to the welfare of the children, who are left to be dragged up by some foul-tongued nurse or some cynical tutor. How many of the domestic tragedies which are constantly shocking the community and rending households in twain have had their origin in just such thoughtless indifference as that? Oh, my friends! we could do with a little less courting before marriage, if we only had a good deal more after it; and if parents were to be slightly less solicitous about getting the very most out of every bargain they make in the store, and a great deal more anxious to become acquainted with their own children, and to lead them into ways of holy happiness, the profiting would appear unto all men. What is the good of your money to you if you neglect your son, and let him grow up unregulated and revengeful, so that at the least provocation he shoots down the imagined author of the offence? Would you not, when that occurs, willingly offer the half of your fortune to wipe out its consequences? And yet it would have been far more sensible to have sought to prevent its causes, even if you should not have made the half of those thousands which you now call your own. Let me ask every father and every husband here to ponder well the appeal which I am now making. Your wife and children are of infinitely more importance than success in business, or the gaining by you of some public office; yet is it not true that you are largely a stranger to those under your own roof? You give them no confidences;

you never say a word of endearment to them; you only want to be let alone and left to yourself when you come home; and so you know just as little of the inner life and disposition, just as little of the dangers and temptations, just as little of the aptitudes and tastes of the members of your own family, as if they were in Kamtchatka and you in New York. Let me, therefore, Jethro-like, bring back to you to-night your wife and children; and let me urge you to register the resolution, at the commencement of this new year, that you will begin your home-life anew, on a different principle from that which you have heretofore followed, and that you will give to wife and children the foremost place in your affection and your care. Think how the sons of Eli brought his gray hairs with sorrow to the grave; remember that the sons even of Samuel lived to shame the name of their father; and learn, I beseech you, this great lesson, that even public usefulness, as well as business success, is too dearly purchased by the sacrifice of the highest welfare of your children.

But, in the second place, we may learn that division of labor is necessary to permanent efficiency. It may seem to you that if you are thus to recognize the paramount importance of home-life, there will be no time left for business; and that, in these days of active competition, the upshot must be either that you must retire, or you will fail. But just here comes in the valuable advice of Jethro as to the appointment of subordinates; and I have no hesitation whatever in saying that it is because business men in these days insist on doing everything themselves, that they are so exhausted by the work of the day as to be unfitted for any home discipline or enjoyment. We recognize the value of the principle of division of labor in manufactures, because there it cheapens the manufactured article; but we fail to see its importance in our own work, because there, in the first instance, it involves additional outlay. We cannot get a man competent to be the head of a department without paying him a handsome salary; for responsibility means character, and character always commands its price. So, to divide our work into so many departments, and to put over each a thoroughly capable man, whom we will hold to a rigid account, requires the immediate expenditure of a large amount of money, and we say we cannot afford it. But all that is a short-sighted policy, for, in the long run, the greater amount of business done will more than reimburse the original outlay; and, in addition, you can go home, not to fret and worry over trifles, but to be the companion of your wife and the guide and director of your children. Moreover, instead of breaking down hopelessly under the strain of carrying everything on your own shoulders, and requiring to go abroad for years, or, it may be, to leave business altogether, your strength remains unimpaired—nay, perhaps it even increases; and you have the satisfaction of seeing your home happy, and your children growing up to follow in your footsteps, and to declare that their God is dearer to them because he is the God of their father. You may tell me that I know nothing about business, and, indeed, I will plead guilty to such ignorance; but I know enough to understand that health is better than success, and that many a man would give nine-tenths of the fortune he has earned, if he could only thereby get back the health which he wrecked in earning it; while not unfrequently a great concern which was created and carried by a single man has gone to ruin when he died, or has left his widow or his children with a responsibility which they could not face, and which they were willing to sell to some adventurer for a tithe of its value.

One said to me, when I began my ministry, "Never do yourself what you can get another to do for you as well as you can do it yourself;" and, though I confess that I have not acted on the maxim as much as I ought to have done, I see the wisdom of it more clearly, the longer I live. "Divide et impera" was the maxim of the old Roman general—divide and conquer; and by dividing our labor into many sections, and holding some one responsible for each, we shall do more, we shall do it better, and we shall work longer, than would be otherwise possible. This is one of the best safeguards against that overwork which is slaying so many commercial men to-day; and if you read the memoirs of such employers as Brassey, Stephenson, Sir Titus Salt, Sir William Fairbairn, and the great contractors who seem almost to have girdled the world by their enterprise, you will discover that they never could have done so much if they had not taken Jethro's advice to Moses, and applied it to their several pursuits.

Finally, we may learn here what those qualities are for which we ought to look in the men whom we place in positions of responsibility. Nothing could be finer than Jethro's enumeration, alike in the characteristics which he names, and in the order in which he mentions them. He urges that the judges to be appointed shall be distinguished for ability, piety, truthfulness, and disinterested integrity. It may seem strange, at first sight, that he puts ability before piety; but we have only to think a moment or two to be convinced that the old sheik was right. The man who has piety and nothing else may fill a humble niche in private life with great honor; but in a place of responsibility, his piety will not make up for the lack of ability. Therefore ability stands first; but inasmuch as a man's bearing toward God determines also the direction of his ability among his fellow-men, after the ability comes the piety. The one is the engine of the steamship, the other is the compass; and both alike are necessary, though the engine is first in the order of erection. Richard Cobden used to say that "you have no security for a man who has no religious principle;" and even they who have no great regard for the Lord Jesus themselves are glad to get a good Christian into their service; for, like Laban, they can say, "We have learned by experience that the Lord hath blessed us for your sake." It is true, indeed, that in recent times among ourselves some who seemed to be God-fearing men have proved dreadfully unfaithful to the trust that was committed to them; but that must not bring the value of real piety to a discount among us, for the very outcry that has been raised is a proof of the comparative rarity of such occurrences, while the worth of the genuine thing furnished the temptation to counterfeit it. Perhaps old Samuel Johnson was as rash as he was rude when, hearing a man at table make a blatant profession of his atheism, he turned to his hostess and said, "Pray, madam, have you counted your spoons?" Yet there is a connection of the closest kind between a man's creed and his life; and, other things being equal, the God-fearing man ought, for every place that involves responsibility, to be preferred.

Properly speaking, piety carries in it truth and honesty; yet these are so important that Jethro gives them a separate place. Truth is the very girdle of character; and where that is loosed, everything else falls to pieces. The man who can tell a deliberate lie is fit for any other violation of the Decalogue; while he who changes his color with every change of circumstances, as the trout does in every several pool, is utterly unreliable. You may be sure that there is something worse behind, and that, if you could withdraw the veil, you would discover that he is scheming for his own aggrandizement; for falsehood and covetousness go commonly hand in hand.

Friends, does it not strike you, as you read these verses, that the human nature of to-day is extraordinarily like that of Jethro's time, and that the counsels which he tendered to Moses are the most appropriate which can be given yet to those who, whether in business, in Church, or in State, have to do with the selection and appointment of office-bearers to places of trust? On the day of President Hayes's inauguration, somebody sent him a postal card which referred him to these verses, and doubtless they were excellently fitted to give him direction; but we have to do with ourselves, and it is, to my mind, infinitely more important at present that the great mass of our citizens, who being at the bottom of the pyramid have by far the most in their power, should understand and act on this old advice. The glib-tongued orator, the party manipulator, the hungry office-seeker, too often carries the day with the people over ability and piety and truth; and as for disinterestedness, I am ashamed to say that it seems to be one of the lost virtues in American politics. Men want everywhere to serve themselves; and the honor of the State or the welfare of the community is of no moment to them, provided only they can secure their personal aggrandizement. Now this is all wrong. The office should seek the man, not the man the office. The commanding ability of a citizen in the place he holds in business life, the character he has made in his mercantile transactions, and the fact that he has no objects of his own to seek, ought to point him out to his fellow-citizens as the person best fitted to serve them in Legislature or Congress. I hope the day is coming when the very seeking of an office will disqualify a man for holding it; when the citizens shall call for those to represent them and serve them who are prominent in everything that is noble and magnanimous; and when the whole race of lean and hungry ones that take to politics for selfishness and not for patriotism will disappear from the midst of us. But, if that day is ever to come, we must begin at the bottom and work up toward it, and every citizen must lay to heart the advice of this old Midianitish chief. In a tree, rottenness begins at the top, but life springs from the root. So we must look here not to Cabinet or President, but to ourselves; for with what face dare we complain of any appointment that may be made in Washington, when we have ourselves sent the owner of a gambling-house to represent us in the Legislature?

You say, perhaps, that this is preaching politics. But I reply by asking, How can I do anything else from such a text? and by asserting that the preaching of the Gospel from our pulpits will be of very little service unless they who listen to it begin themselves to preach it in their conduct, both in business and in political life. I should despise myself, indeed, if I were to avail myself of the advantage which the pulpit gives me in the shape of immunity either from interruption, dissent, or debate, for the purpose of advocating any party issues. My aim now is not partisanship, but patriotism. I desire to see all parties among us purified and elevated; I wish to bring the people to the determination to choose only such men as Jethro has here described—" Men of ability, such as fear God and hate covetousness "—to all posts of office, from the ruler of ten to the ruler of the republic itself; and if that hurts any party, then so much the worse for that party. I am here to expound God's Word in its application to living issues among ourselves; and neither the frown of one party nor the favor of another will keep me from saying what I believe to be right. The true remedy for all our political evils is in the hands of the people themselves; and when they shall determine to act on the principles of Jethro, and carry them out in every election, they will preach a sermon more eloquent and effective for the advancement of truth and righteousness among us than the greatest pulpit orator has ever given.

XI.

SINAI AND THE DECALOGUE.

Exodus xix., 1; xx., 19.

"IN the third month, when the children of Israel were gone forth out of the land of Egypt, the same day came they into the wilderness of Sinai." The place of their encampment is described as "before the Mount," and its identification is one of the most interesting problems of Sinaitic geography. For its settlement, we have to determine also which of the summits in the region is that from which the law was given; and as almost every peak in the range has been advanced to that honor by some enthusiastic traveller, the matter is one which requires patient and minute investigation. A careful study of the sacred narrative itself gives us the following requirements, all of which must be met and satisfied by the real site. We must have, first, a valley sufficient for a camping-ground for the entire Israelitish host.* Then over this valley there must be one summit so conspicuous, and rising so commandingly above all others, as to be called "the Mount."† Moreover, this peak must be everywhere in sight throughout the camp,‡ while at its base it must be hedged in by no natural boundaries; for if it had been so marked, Moses would not have been commanded to set bounds around it.§ Still further,

---

* Exod. xix., 2. † Ibid.
‡ Ibid. xix., 11. § Ibid. xix., 12.

the plain of encampment must be large enough to afford space for the people both to come forth to meet with God, and to remove and stand afar off.*

Now, it happens that in the immediate neighborhood of the mountain range of which Jebel Musa is the highest point there are two plains, either of which has been believed to meet sufficiently the conditions which I have just enumerated, and both of which have had their respective partisans. It is difficult, without an ordnance map, or something equivalent to that, to make the matter perfectly intelligible to an audience; but I will set it before you as clearly as I can. Imagine, then, a mountain block of about three miles in length, lying north-east and south-west, and separated from the surrounding ridges by deep defiles, which here and there expand into valleys of a greater or less breadth. At the south-eastern end, the mountain shoots up to an immense dome-like summit, which is about seven thousand feet above the level of the sea, and which springs from a perpendicular wall of rock that rises sheer from the valley beneath to a height of about two thousand feet. This is Jebel Musa, which is the traditional site of the giving of the law. It was long believed, however, that tradition here, as in so many other cases, was wrong, because it seemed that there was no valley of sufficient magnitude near from which the summit could be seen. But though that was the opinion of so painstaking an investigator as the late Dr. Robinson of this city, more recent explorers have alleged that the Wady Sebaiyeh, stretching away to the south of the Sinaitic range, is extensive enough to fulfil all the conditions of the sacred narrative. One of the earliest modern travellers to visit this site has thus described it: "Here, close at my right, arose almost perpendicularly the holy mountain, its shattered pyramidal

---

* Exod. xix., 17; xx., 18.

peak towering above me some fourteen hundred feet; of a brownish tint, presenting vertical strata of granite, which threw off the rays of the morning sun. Clinging to its base was a range of sharp, upheaving crags, from one to two hundred feet in height, which formed an almost impassable barrier to the mountain itself from the valley beyond. These crags were separated from the mountain by a deep and narrow gorge, yet they must be considered as forming the projecting base of Sinai. Directly in front of me was a level valley, stretching onward to the south for three or four miles, and enclosed on the east, west, and south by low mountains of various altitudes—all much less, however, than that of Sinai."*

This plain, according to Mr. Arthur,† who made actual investigation of it, has ample accommodation for the encampment; and, without any hesitation, he identifies Jebel Musa with Sinai, and puts the encampment in the plain of Sebaiyeh, which is to the south of the range. The other plain, known as Er Rahah, is at the opposite or north-western end of the mountain block, where the bare and granite ridges of Ras Sufsafeh, the Horeb of tradition, rise from the valley to a height of about twelve or fifteen hundred feet. This mountain is very difficult of access; but those who have ascended it, and looked down on the plain beneath, have little hesitation in determining that from its summit the law was given. My own preferences have hitherto been in favor of Sebaiyeh for the encampment, with Jebel Musa as the Mount; but from the statement made by Canon Cook in the "Speaker's Commentary," to the effect that military surveyors have declared that there is no level plain in Se-

---

* M. K. Kellog, quoted in Kitto's "Daily Bible Readings," vol. ii., p. 138.

† See Fairbairn's "Imperial Bible Dictionary," *s. v.* SINAI.

baiyeh on which the Israelites could be assembled, while in Er Rahah, with its branches into Es Sheikh and El Leja, which form the transept to this natural cathedral, there is abundant accommodation for the tribes, and the Sufsafeh summit is everywhere visible, I am constrained, though somewhat reluctantly, to accept the theory of Robinson and his followers.

Either of these situations furnishes an admirable and appropriate temple for the solemn services which the historian here describes; and we may be sure that, on a people accustomed from their infancy to the flat, sandy, and unbroken level of Lower Egypt, the first sight of these thunder-riven peaks, pointing in silence to the sky, must have produced the most marked effect. The majesty of the external scenery prepared them for the revelation to them of the majesty of Jehovah. The vision of the mountains was to them like an appropriate organ prelude, which almost insensibly leads the soul into the presence of its God. "The cliff," to borrow Dean Stanley's words, "rises like a huge altar, and is visible against the sky in lonely grandeur from end to end of the whole plain;" while the valley itself "is the adytum, withdrawn, as if in 'the end of the world,' from all the stir and confusion of earthly things."*

But we have lingered long enough on the mere topography; let us advance to rehearse the events of which this natural temple was the scene. After the encampment had been fairly settled, and, expecting some communication from Jehovah, Moses ascended the Mount, perhaps to the place where he had formerly seen the bush that burned and yet was not consumed. As he was wending his way upward, the Lord called unto him, and said, "Thus shalt thou say to the house of Jacob, and tell the children of Israel: Ye have

---

* "Sinai and Palestine," p. 43.

seen what I did unto the Egyptians, and how I bare you on eagles' wings, and brought you unto myself. Now, therefore, if ye will obey my voice indeed, and keep my covenant, then ye shall be a peculiar treasure unto me above all people: for all the earth is mine; and ye shall be unto me a kingdom of priests, and a holy nation. These are the words which thou shalt speak unto the children of Israel." And very wonderful words they are, constituting the preliminaries of the covenant, and forming what one has suggestively called "the gospel of the Mosaic dispensation." Now was about to be established among the Hebrews that state of things which Josephus has so admirably called a theocracy, in which Jehovah was to be the only king; and though the external system has disappeared, yet, as every Christian has succeeded to the heritage of these promises, spiritually interpreted, it may be well to linger a little over the terms in which they are expressed.

Let us not overlook the fact that this royal relationship is not one of natural right, but rather one of gracious protection. There is a sense in which Jehovah is king of every nation, but this people he took for a peculiar treasure; and while not in the least degree withdrawing his former favor from other communities — for all the earth is his — he yet condescended to enter into special engagements with the house of Jacob. But he would not force his favors on a reluctant or unwilling community; and, recognizing that freedom of choice which is the birthright of every man, he asked them first whether they were prepared to accede to his terms, and would indeed obey his voice and keep his covenant. He who has made the soul respects its rights, and will not force his way into its throne. He stands at the door and knocks, and only when its bolt is undone does he consent to enter; but when he enters, he passes in to reign.

In making this demand on the Israelites, however, he

bases his right not on the common prerogative of Deity, but on the special claims which he had upon them as their Redeemer and Deliverer. He had ransomed them from the power of their oppressors, and had nursed them in the infancy of their national life, guiding them by the pillar of cloud and flame, and providing for them by the gift of the manna and the smiting of the rock. He had broken the power of the Egyptians, and borne his people as on eagles' wings—or, taking the beautiful amplification of this figure made by Moses at a later day, "As an eagle stirreth up her nest, fluttereth over her young, spreadeth abroad her wings, taketh them, beareth them on her wings, so the Lord alone did lead them"*—and it was on this ground that he claimed their special allegiance as his spiritual subjects. "He gave before he demanded; he gave proofs of his love before he asked for obedience; he gave himself to Israel, before he required Israel to give itself to him;"† and his deliverance of them from their captivity, so far from absolving them from their obligation to serve him, only laid them under deeper, because more tender, responsibility.

Then, if they rose to their new relationship, and fulfilled the duties which it involved, there were yet higher honors in store for them; for they should be unto him a kingdom of priests, and a holy nation. As the head of the community, he should be himself the king; but the kingdom would be one of priests. Not yet, indeed, had the family of Aaron been set apart to the priestly office; but in the patriarchal priesthood exercised among them by the heads of their houses, they had already in the midst of them an order which enabled them to understand this promise. They were to be among the nations of the earth what the priest-

---

* Deut. xxxii., 11, 12.
† Kurtz, "History of the Old Covenant," vol. iii., p. 92.

hood is to the community of which it forms a part; that is to say, they were to be the trustees, for humanity at large, of the revelations, promises, and ordinances which God communicated, and they were to keep them for the benefit of all mankind. For a time, indeed, these heavenly communications were to be reserved to themselves; only, however, that they might be the more securely preserved; but at length all restrictions would be broken down, and that which, in its ritual exclusivism, had been confined to them, would, in its spiritual pervasiveness, become the heritage of every true believer who should, like them, enter into covenant with the Lord, not over a merely typical sacrifice, but over the true and real atonement which Christ would make for the sins of men. Thus, in this peculiar promise, which looks at first as if it conferred a patent of protected privilege, we see that the present protection is in order to the future diffusion; and we have an echo of the Abrahamic blessing, "In thee and in thy seed shall all the nations of the earth be blessed." What the Levitical tribe ultimately was among the Israelites themselves, that the Israelites were to be among the nations; and the more faithfully they performed their duties, the richer would be the ultimate blessing to the Gentiles.

The same thought is presented in another form when the Lord adds, "Ye shall be a holy nation." Their outward consecration was to be accompanied with, and to result in, spiritual purity. Their external separation was in order to their inward holiness; and whenever they exalted the former above the latter, they were living beneath their privilege, and losing sight of the mission to which he had called them. He selected them from the nations to be the teacher of the nations; they were set upon a hill that others might learn from them; and the light which was given them, though it was isolated and apart, like that of the lone tower on its island rock, was elevated so as to be seen by every voyager on life's rough sea, for his guidance into safety. But as the light in the lantern shines farthest when the reflector behind it is clearest, so they were to learn that their own prosperity and their usefulness to others depended on the purity of their hearts and lives. God set them apart to show what holiness was; and the effectiveness of that demonstration on the world at large depended on the excellence of the holiness which they manifested. I know not if all this was clearly before the mind either of Moses or any one of the people when first they heard these words; but reading them now, in the light of the history to which they form the introduction, we can see that it was all implied; and it needs no great keenness of insight to perceive the bearing of these principles upon ourselves: for we Christians are now the world's priests, custodiers of those spiritual blessings by which our fellow-men are to be benefited; and only in proportion as we maintain holiness—not of ritualism, but of character—shall we discharge our duties to mankind at large. So, side by side with these promises, at the foundation of the earthly theocracy, we place the words of the Lord Jesus Christ, in his manifesto at the inauguration of the kingdom of which he is the head; and we find in the latter the spiritual interpretation of the former: "Ye are the salt of the earth: but if the salt have lost his savor, wherewith shall it be salted? it is thenceforth good for nothing, but to be cast out, and to be trodden under foot of men. Ye are the light of the world. A city that is set on a hill cannot be hid. Neither do men light a candle, and put it under a bushel, but on a candlestick; and it giveth light unto all that are in the house. Let your light so shine before men, that they may see your good works, and glorify your Father which is in heaven."*

---

* Matt. v., 13-16.

When Moses repeated God's words to the people, on his descent from the Mount, they answered, "All that the Lord hath spoken we will do." Then he returned up the mountain with his report, and received directions against the third day, when the Lord said he would come down upon Mount Sinai "in the sight of all the people." He was ordered to set bounds around the Mount, and straitly to charge the tribes that neither man nor beast should touch it, on the pain of death, until the sound of a trumpet, continuing long, should give permission to those who were called up to ascend. So he again descended: the people, at his command, sanctified themselves for two days, in dread expectancy of the heavenly visitant; and when the third morning dawned, Moses led them forth into the plain "to meet with God." "They stood," says Dean Stanley, "in a vast sanctuary not made with hands—a sanctuary where every outward shape of life, animal or vegetable, such as in Egypt had attracted their wonder and admiration, was withdrawn. Bare and unclothed, the mountains rose around them; their very shapes and colors were such as to carry their thoughts back to the days of the primeval creation, 'from everlasting to everlasting, before the mountains were brought forth, or ever the earth and the world were made.' At last the morning broke, and every eye was fixed on the summit of the height. Was it any earthly form, was it any distinct shape that unveiled itself? There were thunders, there were lightnings, there was the voice of a trumpet exceeding loud; but on the Mount itself there was a thick cloud—darkness and clouds and thick darkness. It was 'the secret place of thunder.'"* Mount Sinai was "altogether on a smoke, because the Lord descended upon it in fire, and the smoke thereof ascended as the smoke of a furnace, and the whole mountain quaked

---

* "Lectures on the History of the Jewish Church," vol. i., p. 130.

greatly." Then, at the loud and long sounding of the trumpet, Moses, called of God, ascended, followed by the eager eyes of the multitude, up into the cloud; only, however, to be sent down again, to take yet stronger precautions lest any one, through ignorance or rashness, might break through the bounds and perish; and it was while the leader and the people stood thus together in a common brotherhood of dread,* that the voice of Jehovah broke over the plain into articulate speech, and, amidst a retinue of attendant angels,† proclaimed those words which men of every succeeding generation have read with awe-struck reverence.

No reader of the Pentateuch can fail to mark the fact that a special importance belongs to these commandments. They were not only the first laws to be promulgated, but they formed the basis of all the rest. They were spoken, as we have seen, directly and immediately by the voice of God; and that, too, amidst the most solemn and impressive symbols of his majesty. The other precepts, bearing on things civil or ceremonial, were communicated through Moses; but "God spake all these words" from out the darkness that covered the Mount.

Again, they were written on two tables of stone, by the very finger of the Almighty; thus indicating that they were designed to have a greater measure of permanence than the statutes and ordinances that were given through Moses, and which were merely inscribed in a book. This, as one has suggestively remarked, was "an emblem of relative perpetuity;" while in the very number of the commandments—ten —which was the symbol of completeness, we have conveyed to us the idea that all duties incumbent upon men, as related to God, on the one hand, or to each other, on the other, can be classified under one or other of these precepts.

---

* Heb. xii., 21.   † Gal. iii., 19; Heb. ii., 2.

Moreover, when the tabernacle was set up, the tables containing this law were put within the ark, which stood between the cherubim, in the very Holy of Holies. They were thus at the very centre of the covenant, and had a place and an importance peculiarly their own; and, while closely related to the system in connection with which they were proclaimed, they yet rose to a sublimity and a spirituality possessed by no portion of that law which was given by Moses.

Foremost among the peculiarities of the Decalogue, we notice the prominence which is given to the supremacy and spirituality of God. The first utterance is still that which was so frequently repeated to Moses when he entered upon his formal controversy with Pharaoh, "I am Jehovah."[*] This lays down the ground on which the obligation to obedience rests in the case of every man. But it was intensified, in the case of the Israelites, by the fact that he had brought them out of the land of Egypt, and out of the house of bondage; and that they might not confound him with any of the deities of the land which they had so lately left, they are straitly enjoined not only to worship no other god, but also to worship him without any visible or emblematic device. The Exodus was thus a divine protest at once against polytheism and idolatry; and we shall fail to recognize one of the greatest purposes which the Lord had in view in the selection of the Jewish people, if we do not take note of this peculiarity. Amidst the deterioration of the race, men were gradually losing sight of the unity and spirituality of God; and so, out of the very hot-bed of idolatry, God brought the Hebrews to this rocky temple, that they might see the storm-robe of his outer majesty, might recognize his unity, and, observing no material image, might lay fast hold on his spirituality. In the course of years, indeed, even the Hebrew

---

[*] See Exod. vi., 1–8.

nation repeatedly lapsed back into the debasing practices of idolatry; but, as often, they were restored by the aid of this dread law; and it was only when, after their long captivity, they had learned these truths too thoroughly ever to forget them again, that the fulness of the time for the appearance of their Messiah was come. Humanly speaking, but for this law, these two truths—the unity and spirituality of God—would have disappeared altogether from among men; and it was to guard these, and all that depended upon them, from destruction, that the Mosaic ritual as a whole, and especially the Decalogue, was given.

Almost equally noticeable, however, is the moral tone of these precepts. They deal not with formal distinctions, or outward services, or temporary and changing relationships, but with fundamental principles. In this they differ from those portions of the Mosaic law which enjoin minute ritual observances, and which might be described as religious rubrics. Concerning this feature, Fairbairn has well remarked that "at such a time, in an age when religion was everywhere running out into shows and ceremonies—under an economy, also, which itself partook so largely of the outward and the symbolical—it surely was a remarkable, as well as an ennobling peculiarity, that this central revelation of truth and duty should have stood so much aloof from the circumstantials, and brought men's hearts so directly into contact with the realities of things."[*]

Then, again, the very order of the precepts is suggestive. First come our duties to God, and then those to our fellowmen. As in the Lord's Prayer we are taught to think first of God's name and kingdom, before we ask anything for ourselves, so in the Decalogue our obligations toward God are first set before us, and then those under which we lie to our

---

[*] Fairbairn's "Imperial Bible Dictionary," art. DECALOGUE.

fellow-men. The earliest thing to be sought by any one is to be right with God, and that will bring him into harmony with men. Religion is the foundation of morality. The first table of the law is the root and trunk of the tree; the second is the outbranching, effloresence, and fruitage thereof. Our neighbor has a God-given right to our love, but before we can acknowledge that right, we must acknowledge the God who gave it; and, though there may be apparent exceptions in the history of individuals, it will be found that all communities which have thrown off allegiance to God have been cruel and oppressive to men; while it is just as true that they who study to obey the first four commandments, will be impelled, as if by some inner necessity, to seek to comply with the other six. They cannot stop with the first table, but they must go on to the second, and the Sabbath law forms the point of transition from the one to the other; for in it, while reserving a day for himself, the Lord teaches all who observe it to have a tender regard for the comfort and rest of others. And in this respect, as furnishing a witness to man's need of periodic relief from labor, and leading all who receive it to think for the welfare of others, as well as for their own, the fourth commandment has an importance which is too seldom recognized. It is the link that binds the love of our neighbor to the love of our God; and if that link should be permitted to be broken, the poor working-man would be the first to feel the oppression which would ensue.

But the order in which the several precepts of both tables follow each other is at once strictly philosophical and richly suggestive. Our duties to God relate first to his being, second to his worship, third to his name, and fourth to his day; while our duties to our fellow-men have their starting-point in the home, and then flow out to our neighbor, having regard first to his life, second to his other self, his wife, third to his property, and fourth to his general standing and position. The law begins with the state of the heart toward God, saying, "Thou shalt have no other gods before me," involving therein all the other precepts regarding God; and it concludes with the state of the heart toward our fellow-man thus, "Thou shalt not covet thy neighbor's house; thou shalt not covet thy neighbor's wife, nor his man-servant, nor his maid-servant, nor his ox, nor his ass, nor anything that is thy neighbor's;" and that involves in it all the other precepts concerning our neighbor. Thus the Decalogue spheres itself into full-rounded perfection, the spiritual nature of the law is vindicated, and the golden circlet that began in love to God is clasped and completed by the love of man.

Finally, we cannot fail to note the negative mould into which the commandments are run. With but two exceptions—indeed, we might truthfully say with but one exception, for the fourth commandment is more apparently than really so—they take the form "Thou shalt not." This, of course, implies also the positive "Thou shalt," in relation to the duty whose violation is forbidden; still, the prohibitory character of the law is incidentally a proof of that inherent depravity in the hearts of men which is so constantly tending toward the commission of sin, and which needs to be not restrained merely, but transformed by the renewing of the mind. Paul affirms, in his letter to the Galatians, that the law was added to the promise "because of transgressions;"[*] and if we have read this history aright, we must have perceived that all the guards and restraints which were enacted by God through Moses were but so many outworks and circumvallations thrown up around the original promise that was given to Abraham, to keep it from being lost, either by the treachery of the garrison within, or the assaults of foes without. They were preservatives to protect the truth, not

---

[*] Gal. iii., 19.

for the Jews only, but for all nations; and the fact that we to-day, after so many hundred years, go back to Sinai for the first principles of morality and religion, and have this law engraven in our Christian churches, is a marvellous attestation of the wisdom of God in the whole matter.

But let us ask ourselves, in conclusion, how we appear when judged by its standard. And that we may come to a thoroughly accurate decision, let us read its precepts in the light of that commentary and exposition of them which Jesus gives in the Sermon on the Mount. You remember how there he draws the distinction between the overt act and the sinful desire, and makes it plain that, unlike the enactments in a human statute-book, these precepts take cognizance of the thoughts and feelings and desires, as well as of the words and actions. This was no new doctrine then for the first time introduced by him. Reformation by him, in this regard, was sought by bringing his hearers back to the original spirituality of the Decalogue. This, as we have seen to-night, was one of its most characteristic features. In the process of years, however, men, in the interpretation of these commandments, had put the sole emphasis on the killing, the stealing, the false witness, the profanity, as external things. But Jesus, in his rendering of them, laid the original stress upon the personal *thou;* and let us see that the killing was not merely that of the hand, but of the heart; the profanity not that of the lip, but of the thought; and the impurity not that of the act, but of the desire. And when we take these commandments thus, in all their length, and breadth, and depth, who is there among us that has not to plead guilty to the charge of disobeying them? When they heard these dreadful words proclaimed out of the thick darkness, the parties to the old covenant trembled, and cried out for a mediator, saying unto Moses, " Speak thou with us, and we will hear; but let not God speak with us, lest we die." And it is when we test ourselves by the standard of this law that we are most thoroughly convinced of sin, and feel most our need of Christ. Blessed be God, from Sinai we can come to Calvary, and there, through the propitiation for sin which Christ has made, we can secure forgiveness and reconciliation. It were a painful thing for me to-night if, after having brought you to the law which condemns, I could not also proclaim to you the Saviour who redeems. Thanks be unto God, it is written that "Christ hath redeemed us from the curse of the law, being made a curse for us, that the blessing of Abraham might come on the Gentiles through Jesus Christ; that we might receive the promise of the spirit through faith." Mark these words, "through faith."* They are all-important. Without faith in him, we are left condemned, and "the wrath of God abideth on us;" but believing in him we have everlasting life, and are among those concerning whom the sacred writer speaks when he says, "Ye are not come unto the Mount that might be touched, and that burned with fire, nor unto blackness, and darkness, and tempest, and the sound of a trumpet, and the voice of words; which voice they that heard entreated that the word should not be spoken to them any more: but ye are come unto Mount Zion, and unto the city of the living God, the heavenly Jerusalem, and to an innumerable company of angels, to the general assembly and church of the first-born, which are written in heaven, and to God the Judge of all, and to the spirits of just men made perfect, and to Jesus the Mediator of the new covenant, and to the blood of sprinkling, that speaketh better things than that of Abel."† Beware, my unconverted hearers, that ye despise not these blessings; but to-night, in sight of all these celestial witnesses, enter, through Jesus, into covenant with Jehovah—that on earth you may enjoy his favor, and in heaven his fellowship.

---

* Gal. iii., 13, 14. † Heb. xii., 18–24.

XII.

THE GOLDEN CALF—AARON'S WEAKNESS.

EXODUS xx., 18; xxiv., 1–18; xxxii.

WHEN the people saw the dreadful accompaniments of Jehovah's presence on the Mount, and heard his voice proclaiming the words of the Ten Commandments, they were filled with terror, and stood afar off, saying the while to Moses, "Speak thou with us, and we will hear; but let not God speak with us, lest we die." Though they were called to become a kingdom of priests, and might have risen to the privilege of direct and immediate fellowship with God, yet their consciousness of guilt would not allow them to venture nigh to him, and they cried for a mediator who should stand between them and him. This suggestion of theirs, as we learn from the account in Deuteronomy,* was approved by the Lord himself; and accordingly, at the request of God, and with the confidence of the people themselves, "Moses drew near to the thick darkness where God was." There he received those commands which constitute what has been called "the civil polity of the Jewish theocracy,"† and which are comprised in the twenty-first, twenty-second, and twenty-third chapters of the Book of Exodus. These will fall to be more fully considered when we come to treat, as we propose to do, in a separate discourse, of the legislation given by Moses. Meanwhile, it may be enough to say that they are arranged apparently in seven groups, each being an expan-

---

* Deut. v., 28. † Murphy, *in loco.*

sion or development of one of the Ten Commandments.*
The first, relating to the duties of masters and servants, is
an appendix to the fifth commandment; the second, dealing
with injuries tending to destroy or endanger life, belongs to
the sixth commandment; the third, treating of property, falls
under the eighth commandment; the fourth, bearing on the
marriage vow, belongs to the seventh commandment; the
fifth, enforcing veracity, is an exposition of the ninth commandment; the sixth, appointing set times for religious festivals, grows out of the fourth commandment; and the seventh, on the acknowledgment and worship of the true God, is
almost equally related to the first and second commandments.

These laws, which, when compared with those of other
contemporary nations, appear to bear the mark of divinity
upon their face, were rehearsed by Moses to the people;
and on their agreeing to obey them, he wrote them in a
book, and then took measures for solemnly engaging the
tribes, by covenant, to keep them. As we learn from the
case of Abraham,† and from the words of Jeremiah,‡ in a
well-known passage, the common form of entering into covenant was over sacrifice; the body of the victim being divided in twain, and the parties to the engagement passing
between the pieces. Something of the same kind seems to
have been done in this instance; for an altar was built, and
twelve pillars, according to the number of the tribes, were
set up, while young men officiated as priests for the occasion, and sacrificed peace-offerings unto the Lord. We do
not read that the carcasses were divided, but the blood was;
for half of it was sprinkled on the altar, and half upon the
people; while between these two sprinklings the book of the
covenant, containing the laws to which I have just referred,

---

* For this arrangement we are mainly indebted to Murphy, as above.
† Gen. xv., 17, 18. ‡ Jer. xxxiv., 18, 19.

was read in the audience of the multitude; and in connection with the whole service, Moses said, "Behold the blood of the covenant, which the Lord hath made with you concerning all these words." Then, to complete this great solemnity, he went up again to the Mount, taking with him his brother Aaron, his nephews Nadab and Abihu, and the seventy official representatives of the tribes, and there they met their God. But the darkness in which the Eternal had shrouded himself had given place to the likeness of "a paved work of a sapphire stone, and as it were the body of heaven in its clearness." No emblems of judgment were seen by them now. He who had before covered himself with clouds, and indicated his presence in tempests, is now arrayed in light. The storm has passed. The calm serenity of the sky now hides him in its peaceful majesty, and nothing comes to create in them either terror or dismay, for "upon the nobles of Israel he laid not his hands." Therefore, with calm composure and with grateful hearts, they sit down before him to keep sacramental feast: "They saw God, and did eat and drink."

The vision of God thus enjoyed could not have been a perception of the divine essence by the bodily eye, for that is an impossibility, neither could it have been the sight of God's glory face to face, for he has said himself, "Thou canst not see my face; for there shall no man see my face and live." Nor was it even up to the level of that which Moses afterward enjoyed, and which the Lord himself has thus described: "And it shall come to pass, while my glory passeth by, that I will put thee in a cleft of the rock, and will cover thee with mine hand, and thou shalt see my back parts, but my face shall not be seen." We must conclude, therefore, that there was among these elders a vivid mental perception of the immediate presence of Jehovah with them, suggested and increased by some symbolical appearance, the nature of which is undescribed, but which they were led by unmistakable indications to associate with him. Whatever it was, however, there was beneath it the "infinite azure" of the sky, and the robe of light was unaccompanied by those elements of terror in which it had formerly been enveloped. In all this, we have clearly set before us the difference between God's manifestation of himself to the impenitent sinner, and to the repentant one who enters into covenant with him over the sacrifice of his Son; for now that they approach him as his covenanted ones, the heads of the people "find his presence no more a source of disturbance and dread, but radiant in all the bright loveliness of supernal glory;" and their feast upon the Mount may, without any great stretch of fancy, be regarded as a foretoken not merely of the happiness of those who are one with God in Christ, but also of the blessedness of that celestial abode, where, in the highest sense of which the words are capable, it will still be true of its inhabitants that they "see God, and do eat and drink."

After this sacred feast was over, Moses, leaving Aaron and Hur to take the superintendence of the people in the valley, approached with Joshua still nearer to the presence-chamber of Jehovah; and at length, leaving his youthful attendant behind him, he went up, on the seventh day, into the cloud that covered the Mount, and there remained alone with God for forty days. We know not all that passed between them on these eventful days, when the favored prophet spoke to God face to face, as a man talketh to his friend; but it was at this time that Moses saw the pattern of the tabernacle, and received instructions concerning its erection, its furniture, and its services. And at the close of their conference, God gave to his servant two tables of stone, "tables of testimony," whereon were the words of the Decalogue, graven with his own hand.

But when he descended from the Mount, a sad scene, for which Jehovah had in part prepared him, and against the consequences of which he had earnestly interceded, met his view. His long absence had utterly unsettled the people, who had learned to look on him as their leader and mediator. A purely spiritual worship—that is to say, a worship which has no outward form—is impossible for any man; but for those who had so lately been slaves in the very metropolis of the world's idolatry, it was more than impossible—it was unintelligible. Therefore they sought some visible emblem of Deity, as well as some outward service of a religious sort; and, at the very moment when God, in consideration of their ignorance and earthiness, was giving to Moses the model of an erection which, while appealing to the eye of sense, should yet suggest great truths to the soul, and so at once accommodate their weakness, and keep it from degenerating into wickedness, the people had rebounded to the grossness of Egyptian idolatry. It seems almost incomprehensible; and yet it may, perhaps, be explained much in the same way as we account for the intemperance of the Corinthians, even at the table of the Lord. These early converts from heathenism had come out of a system in which they showed honor to their gods by becoming intoxicated, and, in their ignorance, they transferred their old superstitions to their Christian worship, so that it became necessary for the future purity of the Lord's house that signal punishment should be visited upon them; and hence, as Paul says, many were weak and sickly among them, and many died. Similarly here, the Hebrews, having, perhaps, some sort of an idea that Moses had gone to receive for them an outward form of worship, were disappointed at his long delay, and, fearing that he might never return, they determined to take the matter into their own hands. In carrying out this design, which was in itself a violation of their covenant, they brought the notions of their old Egyptian neighbors to bear upon what they supposed to be their present necessity, and said to Aaron, "Up, make us gods, which shall go before us; for as for this Moses, we wot not what is become of him." Here was an utter mutiny against Jehovah, and, alas! Aaron was not the man to meet it. Instead of bravely battling with it in its initial stages, he temporized with it, and gave it time to grow, until it assumed such proportions that it was impossible to cope with it. First of all, he tried to enlist their worldliness against their idolatry, by asking them to bring to him their golden ornaments. He thought they would never part with these, and that he would be quite safe in making such a proposal, believing that, when they saw it was to cost all that, they would go no further; but when they laid their jewels at his feet, he found that he was taken in his own snare, and felt compelled to make for them a molten calf, like the Egyptian Apis with which they had been familiar. When they saw it, they were delighted, and said, "These be thy gods, O Israel, which brought thee up out of the land of Egypt!"

This exclamation of theirs indicates that they did not wish to repudiate Jehovah, but simply to worship him under the similitude of the calf; and so their sin was rather a violation of the second commandment than of the first. But it was serious enough, in any case; and Aaron, catching at any straw which might win for him some delay, said, "To-morrow is a feast to the Lord." Thus he postponed the consummation of the wickedness for a few hours, hoping that Moses might meanwhile arrive at the camp; but at last the morning came, and, with all the disgusting rites of heathenism, the people kept their festival. They were in the very midst of their abominable idolatry, when Moses made his appearance; and such was his sense of their sin that he cast from him the tables of stone whereon God had written the Ten Commandments, and "took the calf which they had made, and burned it in the fire, and ground it to powder, and strewed it upon the water, and made the children of Israel drink of it." Then, turning to Aaron, he asked of him an explanation of this great apostasy, and got this "lame and impotent" excuse, "Let not the anger of my lord wax hot: thou knowest the people, that they are set on mischief; for they said unto me, Make us gods, which shall go before us: for as for this Moses, the man that brought us up out of the land of Egypt, we wot not what is become of him. And I said unto them, Whosoever hath any gold, let them break it off. So they gave it me; then I cast it into the fire, and there came out this calf." Alas! this pitiful display made it but too apparent that even his own brother could not be relied on in an emergency; and so, standing in the gate of the camp, Moses cried, "Who is on the Lord's side, let him come unto me." His appeal was answered by the rallying round him of the sons of Levi, whom he ordered to take their swords and execute justice on those who had thus rebelled against their Jehovah-king. And there fell of the people that day about three thousand men.

In reviewing this narrative for practical purposes, I shall to-night restrict myself to the lessons which seem to me to be suggested by the weakness of Aaron—reserving the consideration of the bearing of Moses until I have had the opportunity of bringing before you the whole of the incidents which centre in his intercession for the people and his prayer for himself. This will give distinctness in our view to the individuality of the two brothers, while it will prevent us from presenting a fragmentary or divided account of those facts in the history of Moses which are not merely the most exalted in his career, but also the most sublime in the records of humanity.

Older than Moses by three years, Aaron does not always

appear to advantage in the sacred narrative. This may be partly owing to the pre-eminent greatness of his brother, whose brightness of character outshone the meaner endowments of Aaron, but it is mainly due to his own imperfections. Of ready and eloquent utterance, he seems, like many who have been similarly gifted, to have been of a pliant and flexible disposition. He bent, like the sapling, to almost every breeze; his nature was receptive rather than creative; he took impressions from others, but made little or no impression on them in return; he floated on the current which others formed, but he rarely, if ever, made a torrent which swept all opposition before it. He had little of that formative power which is always the indication of the possession of the highest greatness, and by which the individual moulds and fashions all who come within the range of his influence. He had more of the soft impressiveness of the melted wax than of the hardness of the die that stamps it. Hence he was well enough in time of peace, and when everything was going smoothly; but when a sudden emergency arose, when a mutiny was to be quelled, or, as in the present instance, a fit of idolatrous madness was to be repressed, he proved unequal to the occasion, and was found yielding, against his better judgment, to the demand of the multitude. From a timid and pusillanimous regard to his own safety, he would not oppose the wishes of the people; and so it happened that the spark, which a moment's firmness might have trodden out, became at length a mighty conflagration, in the flames of which some thousands were consumed. It was in his power, had he resisted the demand at the first, to have prevented all this evil; and even if he could not have put down the idolatrous revolt, it was still his duty to have offered to it the most uncompromising opposition. Hence his conduct was not only condemned by Moses, but also in the highest degree displeasing to God;

for in the account in Deuteronomy Moses uses these words: "And the Lord was very angry with Aaron to have destroyed him: and I prayed for Aaron also the same time."[*] Now, as the same "fear of man" which brought a "snare" to Aaron is entangling multitudes among ourselves, and as many who would never think of originating evil are found weakly yielding to it when it is proposed by others, it may be well to make the case of this ancient worthy the germ of a few practical exhortations bearing on this phase of character.

In the first place, then, I would lay it down as a fundamental principle that it is always wrong to do wrong. That may seem a mere truism, and you may be tempted to smile at the silliness of the preacher who thus gravely puts forth so simple a proposition. But think on it for a moment or two, and you may see reason to change your opinion; for you will find that the extenuations or excuses offered by men for their evil deeds commonly amount to this, that in the circumstances in which they were placed there were certain things which made it unavoidable or warrantable for them to sin; that is to say, that, as they were situated, it was not wrong for them to do wrong. Thus, in the instance before us, Aaron does not think for a moment of denying that idolatry is a sin; but the whole drift of his reply to Moses is that his making of the golden calf was, as far as he was concerned, a thing which he could not get rid of. He could not help himself. Abstractly considered, it was certainly improper; but in the state of affairs at the moment, it could not have been avoided; and so he would have Moses believe that it was no fault of his. Nor is this a solitary case of such self-deception. We have another illustration of it in a man of quite different general character from Aaron.

---

[*] Deut. ix., 20.

Herod's whole soul revolted from the crime of putting John the Baptist to death. He knew that it was murder; but because of a rash oath which he had sworn, and because of the men by whom he was surrounded, he tried to persuade himself that it was a thing absolutely unavoidable, or, in other words, that it was not wrong for him to do wrong. But we need not go so many centuries back to seek for cases of this sort. The man who came home intoxicated last night, saying that he could not help it, because he met some friends who insisted on his going with them, and he could not get away; the family who are ruined by reckless extravagance, and declare that they were under the necessity of keeping up appearances; the merchant who, on the eve of bankruptcy, has recourse to dishonorable expedients, because they were required to save himself; the youth who helps himself to his employer's money, because he had to do something to pay his debts—all are in the same category with Aaron here; and, while acknowledging that they have done wrong, do, at the same time, attempt to justify themselves; that is to say, they believe that it was not wrong *for them* to do wrong. Now, if there should be one here under this delusion, I would say to him that morality is not a changing thing, dependent upon fluctuating circumstances. In no possible contingency can that which is wrong become right. Let not your minds be confused by the consideration of mere accidental surroundings. Turn away from all else, and fix your attention on the one thought, "This is wrong;" and therefore it must be wrong in all places, in all cases, and at all times. Then, if you are true to conscience, and to Christ, who is the Lord of conscience, you will exclaim, "How can I do this wickedness and sin against God?"

I am the more particular to put the matter thus, because Satan, like a cunning tempter, invariably strives to divert attention from the main issue, and to fix it upon the supposed advantages that will result from your yielding to his enticement, or on the apparent disadvantages that must follow from the opposite course. But in settling what is your duty, you have nothing to do with consequences. Your sole concern is with what is right; and when that is clearly seen, you are under obligation to do it "in the scorn of consequence." The moment you begin to trouble yourself about what will be the issue, you admit the tempter to a parley; and it will be well if in the end he do not bring you over to his views. Butler was right when he said, "In all common, ordinary cases, we see intuitively, at first view, what is our duty—what is the honest part. That is the ground of the observation that the first thought is often the best. That which is called considering what is our duty in a particular case is very often nothing but endeavoring to explain it away. Thus those courses which, if men would fairly attend to the dictates of their own conscience, they would see to be corruption, excess, oppression, uncharitableness; these are refined upon—things were so and so circumstantiated—great difficulties are raised about fixing bounds and degrees; and thus every moral obligation whatever may be evaded."* It remains, therefore, that, if we would avoid this evil, we must fix our thoughts entirely upon the wrongness of that which we are tempted to do, to the utter exclusion of all other considerations.

But yet, again, we must remember that no one can compel us to sin. Sin is a voluntary thing, and no external force can constrain us to commit it. We cannot do wrong until we choose to do it, and the choosing is a free act of our own. I say a free act—that is, a thing which we might have refrained from if we had pleased. But some one says, "Suppose my life would have been in danger if I had refused;

---

* Sermon on the character of Balaam, in Bishop Butler's works.

what then?" Even in such a case your choice would be voluntary; and your yielding to such a temptation, when translated into words, just means that you prefer the life of the body to the best interests of the soul. No man, no set of circumstances, can compel you to will; that you do always for yourself, and for that you are responsible. Thus, whether we look at the external standard of God's law, or at the internal agent, which is your will, it is undeniable that it is always wrong to do wrong. Treasure up that maxim in your memories. Write it on the tablets of your hearts, yea, on the palms of your hands; and if, by God's help, you seek always to act upon it, you will be kept secure.

But a second thing suggested by this conduct of Aaron is that the difficulty of doing right is always exaggerated by the timid. "The slothful man says there is a lion in the way;" and in general, if a man be minded to evade duty, he conjures up before him all manner of dangers which he must encounter in its performance. Now, even if these were a thousand times more formidable than he imagines them to be, it would still be right for him to face them; since, at whatsoever cost or sacrifice, duty must be done. But the point which I now wish to make is that, generally speaking, it is not nearly so difficult to do duty as the timid man thinks it is. The tempter, indeed, when he seeks to entrap us, would say, "You will lose your life," or "You will be deprived of your situation," or "Your temporal interests will suffer;" but though we should do the will of God even at the risk of all these things, in reality his threats are either wholly false or greatly exaggerated. Take the case of Aaron here; and while I readily admit that, after he had allowed the passion of the people to gather strength, there might have been some personal danger in standing against them, yet a small measure of firmness on his part at the outset would have effectually controlled them. His error, therefore, lay in not nipping the idolatry in the bud. Had he possessed only a small degree of his brother's promptitude and courage, he would have reminded the people of what they had so lately seen; and, satisfactorily accounting for Moses's delay, he would have diverted their minds into some other channel. But he temporized, until the current was too strong for him; and then, when it carried him away, he weakly said that he could not help himself. Or, taking the case of Herod, to which I have also referred, who does not see that if he had only set his oath at defiance, and done what his better nature indicated, the men by whom he was surrounded, instead of blaming, would have applauded, and the public opinion of the country would have sustained him in the act? In general, when the opinion of men is in the case, it will be found that, though at first there may seem to be a sentiment opposed to rectitude, yet that is itself the result, in the people, of their fear of each other; and, if only one be faithful to himself, to truth, and to God, there will not be wanting multitudes to join him and approve. Behold what took place on Mount Carmel when the false prophets and priests of Baal accepted the challenge of Elijah. To human view, at first, the Tishbite was in a minority of one; and if he had quailed, a glorious opportunity would have been lost. But see how, as he stands firm and proves his case, the people, who had been not more afraid of Ahab than of each other, took courage and shouted, "Jehovah he is the God, Jehovah he is the God." If but you give the popular conscience an opportunity to express itself in the first fervor of feeling, before trimming calculations begin to be made, you may always reckon that it will be with you when you stand forth for the right, the manly, and the true. Hence, if with dashing promptitude and Elijah-like energy, you stand up for God *early enough*, you will carry the mass with you. Your protest against wrong will rally them, and your valiant opposition will furnish an occasion for them to emancipate themselves from their slavery one to another. The world's own maxim is, "Grasp the nettle firmly, and it will not sting;" and a deep knowledge of your own heart, or a large experience of the ways of men, will convince you that, if with spirit and energy you do the right thing at the right time, opposition will fall away from before you, and they who threatened to persecute will in the end approve. The way to provoke ridicule or antagonism is to be nervously afraid of it; and men may be excused for trampling on you if you lay yourself crouchingly at their feet. Nor ought we to forget here that God has promised to be with those who stand up bravely for his cause. He who says "Go forward" will divide the sea for us to pass; and not a few who have been anxiously dreading the consequences of their adherence to conscience have had the way opened to them as they advanced; even as the women found the stone rolled from the sepulchre when they reached its portal, and were greeted by the angel of the resurrection when they supposed that they were going to complete a funeral. "When a man's ways please the Lord, he maketh even his enemies to be at peace with him." True, it stands recorded here that "all who will live godly in the world will suffer persecution;" but it is also said, "Be of good cheer, I have overcome the world." "This is the victory that overcometh the world, even our faith;" and the tribulation is always sorer to the craven spirit than it is to him who can dare the world to its face, feeling that the Lord Jesus is at his side. The stern eye of an unflinching man will hold—so it is said—even the lion spell-bound; and courage in the service of God, turning an unyielding eye on Satan, will send him away from us for a season. There may be, there must be, difficulties; but the more you play the man for Christ, the less formidable will all obstacles become.

But I remark, in the third place, as suggested by this case, that the consequences of wrong-doing are always more serious than the wrong-doer at first supposed. Aaron here might think that the making and worshipping of a golden calf would not, in the long run, matter much to the people. True, it was wrong, but Moses would soon be among them again, and he would be able to remedy the evil; so, after all, it was of no great moment. But behold the result in the death of three thousand of the people! Yet it is ever thus. When Satan wishes to impose upon us, he says, "Ye shall not surely die; the case is not so serious as you suppose; and, in any event, the results are nothing when compared with the enjoyment." Thus, when a youth enters upon the path of dishonesty, the tempter whispers to him that he will never be found out; and keeps carefully out of view the prison, the loss of character, and the disgrace for life. And similarly in regard to every sin. He puts before us the maximum of danger which we shall incur in resisting it, and the minimum of evil which will ensue from our commission of it, and thus he intrigues us into it. Dear friends, believe him not. "He is a liar, and the father of it." Every sin has consequences which stretch through eternity; every sin is a hideous and abominable thing to God, fraught with pernicious results to ourselves, and in most cases also to others. When Lot pitched his tent toward Sodom, he little thought that in Sodom itself he should leave all his property, and his whole family, save his two daughters. When Achan hid the wedge of gold and the Babylonish garment in his tent, he never imagined that for his transgression Israel would be worsted before the enemy, and many of the people put to death. Let us not, therefore, imagine that if we commit sin the consequences will be slight; for who are we that the unalterable law of God should be suspended for our deliverance? I say the unalterable law; for with a certainty as great as that fire will always burn, we may be sure that punishment will follow iniquity, either in this life or in that which is to come. Nay, more; as no man liveth unto himself, so no man sinneth to himself, or perishes alone. I can imagine Aaron bitterly upbraiding himself for his weakness when he saw the fatal fruits of it, but then it was too late to repair the wrong. You cannot stay the shell midway in its flight; after it has left the mortar, it goes on to its mark, and there explodes, dealing destruction all around. Just as little can you arrest the consequences of a sin after it has been committed. You may repent of it, you may even be forgiven for it, but still it goes on its deadly and desolating way. It has passed entirely beyond your reach; once done, it cannot be undone. So be it yours to guard against all such after-reproaches, by resolutely refusing, in any circumstances, to commit iniquity yourselves, or to be parties to its commission by others. And to this end let me urge you to keep near to Christ, for it is always easy to be courageous when you are at his side.

XIII.

INTERCESSION.

EXODUS xxxii.–xxxiv.

HE who enters upon a new life, or begins a special enterprise, must lay his account with trial. Some test will meet him on the very threshold of his endeavor, and according as he stands that, his future career will be. If he fail, he will be turned away from the door by which he sought to pass in to his work; but if he be found approved, he will be introduced to yet higher honors than, up till that moment, he had ever thought of. Many illustrations in point might be cited from Scripture. Thus, our first parents were very early confronted with a command by which their allegiance to God was put to the proof. Each new advance made by Abraham toward the attainment of the promise was attended by a new temptation; and after the birth of Isaac came the severest of all, in the shape of the command to offer him in sacrifice. Nay, even the Lord Jesus himself was led straight from the glory of his baptism to the solitude of the wilderness, where he was assailed by the prince of darkness. Modern engineers, after having erected a viaduct, insist upon subjecting it to a severe strain by a formal trial trip, before allowing it to be opened for public traffic; and it would almost seem that God, in employing moral agents for the carrying out of his purposes, secures that they shall be tested by some dreadful ordeal before he fully commits to them the work which he wishes them to perform.

This principle of the divine administration may help us,

perhaps, to understand more fully the incidents connected with the idolatry of Israel at the base of Sinai. The people had come to their testing-place, and now it would be seen whether or not they were possessed of those qualities which would fit them for taking immediate possession of the land which God had designed for them. The absence of Moses was the means of proving what was in their hearts. The proposal made by them to Aaron, that he should make them a god, was the searching acid which revealed the alloy that was in the character even of the future High-priest. The suggestion made to Moses that he should consent to the rejection of the people, and allow himself to be made the progenitor of a great nation, was the strain to which he was subjected.

The people and Aaron failed, and it was only in answer to Moses's intercession that another probation was given them; for, so far as appears, if it had not been for his mediation, the decree which afterward excluded the whole adult generation from Canaan, and which was pronounced at Kadesh-barnea, would have been issued at Sinai. But Moses stood; and through his success not only showed his fitness to be the mediator between the people and God, but also passed up to a clearer vision of Jehovah than he had before enjoyed, and a fuller comprehension of his wonderful name.

To have a clear view of all this, we must go back a little over some of the details which, from one side at least, were considered by us in our last lecture. Nowhere is a sharper contrast brought before us than that which this history presents. In the valley the multitude, as if infected by some epidemic insanity, are preparing for their idolatrous orgies; on the mountain, within the cloud-veil that shrouds its summit, Moses is communing with Jehovah. Below, all is noise, and tumult, and passion; above, all is peace, and contemplation, and fellowship of spirit with spirit: below are sin and shame; above are intercession and forgiveness. Sharp and distinct is the contrast, yet not singular; for often still, while the masses are wild with some new excitement, the Moseses are on the hill-top pleading with God for their pardon and restoration; and when the cloud rises it is seen that they have been the saviors of the community.

After he had seen the pattern of the tabernacle, and taken the two tables of testimony written with the finger of God, Moses was startled by receiving this command, with its accompanying explanation, "Go, get thee down; for thy people, which thou broughtest out of the land of Egypt, have corrupted themselves: they have turned aside quickly out of the way which I commanded them: they have made them a molten calf, and have worshipped it, and have sacrificed thereunto, and said, These be thy gods, O Israel, which have brought thee up out of the land of Egypt. I have seen this people, and, behold, it is a stiff-necked people: Now therefore let me alone, that my wrath may wax hot against them, and that I may consume them: and I will make of thee a great nation."*

This must have come on Moses like a thunder-bolt, and there was much in it to sadden and alarm him; while, from another point of view, there was in it that which might have inflamed selfish ambition to the highest point. On the one hand, it was an apparent renunciation of Israel by Jehovah, for he calls them to Moses "thy people," "this people," "a stiff-necked people;" on the other, it seemed to renew to him individually the promise given to Abraham at an earlier date, "I will make of thee a great nation;" and had he been desirous of personal honor or glory, he would have eagerly caught at such a proposal; but he who had resisted the attraction of the throne of the Pharaohs, offered by his foster-

---

* Exod. xxxii., 7-10.

mother, had long ago flung away all such earthly ambitions, and so such a vision of a great nation from his loins had no charm for him, even when it was put before him by the Lord. He had accepted a mediator's position, and he would not be a traitor to either of the parties for whom he was called to act; therefore, with great boldness, and with noble self-denial, he set himself to plead the people's cause. He reminded the Lord that they were his people, and that he, and not Moses, had brought them out of Egypt; he spoke, also, of the injurious effect which it would have upon the surrounding nations if it should appear that the one God, whose supremacy and omnipotence had been so clearly shown in emancipating the Hebrews from their house of bondage, had led them from slavery only to destruction; he recalled, also, the covenant, confirmed even by an oath, which he had made with Abraham, Isaac, and Israel, saying, "I will multiply your seed as the stars of heaven, and all this land that I have spoken of will I give unto your seed, and they shall inherit it forever." And on these grounds he urged that, in spite of their great sin, the Israelites might be spared. It is thus noteworthy that the intercession of Moses proceeds entirely on a regard for the honor of Jehovah, and that the noble man does not permit himself even to refer to the proposal that he should be made the head of a covenant nation in room of the rejected tribes. Thus triumphantly does he stand the test to which Jehovah subjected him, and we do not wonder that his pleading was successful, for "the Lord repented of the evil which he thought to do unto his people."

But, after this, it is with a feeling of surprise that we read of his apparent vehemence, and of his stern execution of what seems a very severe sentence, when he descended into the valley. Before he came in sight of the camp, he heard the noise of singing; and when he caught a glimpse of the people dancing in their idolatrous worship, he cast the two tables of stone from him, and brake them in pieces. Then, having reproved Aaron, he called for those who were on the Lord's side to show themselves; and when the Levites responded to his appeal, he charged them to fall, sword in hand, upon their brethren, and three thousand were put to death. Now, all this looks, at first, as if Moses had not believed that the sin of the people was forgiven, and almost as if he had been himself moved by uncontrollable indignation. But when we go below the surface, we discover that his motive here, as on the mountain, was a regard at once for the glory of God, and for the highest welfare of the people. He had been true to the people as before God; now he was true to God as before the people; and to prepare their minds and hearts for a right appreciation of the divine pardon, he took means to open their eyes to the magnitude of their guilt. First of all, he broke the tables of testimony; but, though it is said that his anger waxed hot, we must not suppose that this action was due to passion, for Moses was never slow to confess a sin when he had been guilty of it; yet, in the account which he gives of this transaction in Deuteronomy, he speaks of it without any condemnation, and seems to refer to it as a judicial deed. He regarded the law on these two tables not as a burden laid on the people, but as a blessing given to them. It was part of the benefit which they had forfeited by their breaking of the covenant; and he destroyed the stones on which it was written before their eyes, that they might see what an evil thing it was to forsake their God. For the same reason—that they might be impressed with the fact that sin brings in its train not only the loss of good, but also the endurance of penalty—he burned the calf, ground it to powder, and strewed it upon the water, and made them drink of it. Thus they were taught that the sinner must be filled with the fruit of his own doings, and were led to loathe the object which, a little before, they worshipped. Not yet, however, had they been brought to acknowledge their guilt before Jehovah, and to return to him to crave forgiveness; and so he proceeded to still greater lengths, and executed righteous sentence upon them in Jehovah's name.

But here two things must be borne in mind. We must remember, first, that God was the accepted King of the people, and that disobedience to his law was at the same time treason to his authority. These idolaters, therefore, were guilty of that which corresponds to mutiny on board a ship or in an army; and every one knows that in all such cases severity in the outset is the truest clemency in the end. Besides, secondly, we must take note that, before the slaughter of the three thousand, Moses offered an amnesty to all; for when he stood in the gate of the camp and said, "Who is on the Lord's side?" his call was not for those who had never disobeyed God by worshipping the calf, but rather for those who, though they had been guilty of that treason, had now seen the evil of their way, and were willing to return to their allegiance; and if all the tribes had followed the example of the Levites, no man would have been put to death.

So the night closed over this day which had begun with feasting, and had ended in bloodshed; and we may well believe that, during the hours of darkness, there would be great searchings of heart among the people. Now would they begin to see something of the meaning of the words which had rolled over them in the promulgation of the law — "I the Lord thy God am a jealous God;" and when the morning broke, and Moses said unto them, "Ye have sinned a great sin," they were ready to assent to his words; while, when he added, "Now I will go up unto the Lord; peradventure I shall make an atonement for your sin," their hearts eagerly, though silently, appealed to him to do as he had said. Now, if I have succeeded in putting my thought clearly before you, it will be evident to you that, just as Moses was true to the people when he was on the mount, so he was true to God when he was in the valley; and in both places his main solicitude was for the divine honor. He knew that God could never forgive, if, by forgiving, the sanction of his law were to be weakened; and precisely as he insisted on God's faithfulness to his promise when he pleaded with him for the people, so he required that the people should honor the law of God when he pleaded with them for God. He made atonement by insisting on justice; and then, even as the high-priest afterward went within the veil when he had offered sacrifice, so Moses here returned unto the Lord after he had punished these three thousand in the room of the people, and then began to make intercession on behalf of the tribes. And it was this that gave his pleading power; for, as Oosterzee has said,* "What would have been the meaning of such intercession for a race of sinners, if the intercessor had esteemed the sin itself as trivial?" He had honored law, and brought glory to God, while, at the same time, he had led the people to repentance; and so once again he passed in within the cloud to plead on their behalf. Never, surely, was there a more tender appeal. Listen to its pathetic importunity: "Oh, this people have sinned a great sin, and have made them gods of gold. Yet now, if thou wilt forgive their sin—; and if not, blot me, I pray thee, out of thy book which thou hast written." There is the power as of a sob in this broken utterance. It has more of earnestness and sincerity than if it had come with faultless volubility from an eloquent tongue; for often when the heart is fullest, speech is its poorest interpreter. God

---

* "Moses: a Biblical Study," by J. Van Oosterzee, translated by J. Kennedy, B.D., p. 139.

had offered to make of him a great nation, and here is now his answer—"If not, blot me, I pray thee, out of thy book." Of course, he cannot mean what some would make him mean—that, if the people were to be cast away, he desired to be shut out forever from the presence of the Lord. For we have no warrant for believing that those who fell in the wilderness perished everlastingly; and Moses is here referring, not to the life that is to come, but to the life that now is. Just as Paul, at a later date, said, "To me to live is Christ;" so Moses now declares that he values life only for the sake of the people to whose leadership he had been called, and affirms that continued existence on the earth would be a burden to him, and not a blessing, if he were not permitted to conduct them forward to the land of promise. All the loftiest aspirations of his heart, all the joys of his soul, all the things he cared to live for, were bound up in the welfare of those whom he had brought out of bondage; and if now they were to be abandoned by God, then he prayed that he might be taken from the earth. And so we have here, in the prospect of failure, something of the same spirit which, under the idea that he had failed, prompted Elijah, in this same region, to cry, "Take away my life now, for what am I better than my fathers?" while there is, at the same time, much of the self-forgetfulness of Paul, when he said, "I could wish myself anathema for my brethren, my kinsmen according to the flesh." To this appeal the Lord replied, "Whosoever hath sinned against me, him will I blot out of my book;" and the threat of destruction of the people was so far withdrawn that Moses was to conduct them to Canaan, while an angel should go before him.

But these concessions were accompanied with serious drawbacks; for, in the first place, whenever the tribes committed other iniquity, this first apostasy would be remembered against them, according to this word: "Nevertheless, in the day when I visit, I will visit their sin upon them." And we have the full explanation of that threatening at Kadesh Barnea; for, as here they rejected God, so there they rejected the land which God had promised them, and drew down the decree that every one of that adult generation should perish in the wilderness.

Still further, Jehovah, though promising to send his angel with them, declined to dwell any longer in the midst of them; and that as much in mercy to them as in judgment, for thus he speaks, "I will not go up in the midst of thee, for thou art a stiff-necked people, lest I consume thee in the way." This was a terrible blow to them, for it was a virtual revocation of that which was their prime and peculiar distinction; so when the people heard it, "They mourned, and no man put on him his ornaments." They did not wish to be deprived of God; and when they saw that all this was the consequence of their sin, they became convinced of its enormity, and were more deeply penitent than before.

But Moses would not yet give up their cause. The Lord, indeed, had said that he would not dwell among them, so he could no longer meet him as before in the business tent in the centre of the camp; but he would not, on that account, break off, if I may so express it, all negotiations with him. So, taking the tent of meeting, he pitched it outside of the camp; and, as he entered that, the cloudy pillar descended and stood at its door, and the Lord talked with him. He renewed his entreaty with more importunity than ever, and this time on more personal grounds. He had experienced already much of the hardship of leadership among such a people, and if it had been so great with God himself in the midst of them, what would it be with a mere angel there? He did not wish to enter upon the unknown without having God at his side, for no angel, however exalted, could supply his place; therefore he cried, "If thy presence go not with me, carry us not up hence: for wherein shall it be known here that I and thy people have found grace in thy sight? is it not in that thou goest with us? so shall we be separated, I and thy people, from all the people that are upon the face of the earth." This appeal was successful; and then, emboldened by his victory, Moses immediately said, "I beseech thee, show me thy glory." He had been appointed mediator, and, that he might the better execute his office, he wished for a better knowledge of Jehovah. He desired to see what no mortal eye could bear—the unveiled face of the great I AM; but, in mercy to him, this was withheld, and the Lord substituted his goodness for his glory, making the proclamation of his name serve for the manifestation of his essence. He commanded his servant to hew two tables of stone like unto the first, and, taking them with him, to ascend in the morning to the top of the Mount. Then, as he stood in a cleft of the rock, "The Lord descended in the cloud, and stood with him there, and proclaimed the name of the Lord. And the Lord passed by before him, and proclaimed, Jehovah, Jehovah God, merciful and gracious, long-suffering, and abundant in goodness and truth, keeping mercy for thousands, forgiving iniquity and transgression and sin, and that will by no means clear the guilty; visiting the iniquity of the fathers upon the children, and upon the children's children, unto the third and to the fourth generation." Upon this Moses renewed his prayer for the people's forgiveness, and the Lord re-entered into covenant with him in the people's name, recapitulating some of the more important of those injunctions which had been formerly given, and detaining him with him there in holy fellowship for another period of forty days and forty nights.

At the end of that long absence, marked on this occasion with no outbreak of iniquity, he returned to the camp, carrying with him the two new tables of testimony; but as he stood to speak unto the people, they were afraid to look upon him, for the skin of his face shone with dazzling lustre, the reflection of the glory on which he had so long been gazing. At first he was unconscious of its presence, for "he wist not that the skin of his face did shine;" but when his attention was drawn to it, he put a veil over his countenance when he had done speaking to the people, but carefully removed it when he went in to speak with God.

In reviewing this marvellous history, we may best group our remarks round these three centres: its educational purpose, its typical significance, and its practical influence.

Let us consider, first, its educational purpose. One cannot read these chapters without observing the anthropomorphisms in which they abound. Throughout these negotiations, as I have ventured to call them, God speaks and is spoken of as if he were a man. He says, for example, "Let me alone, that my wrath may wax hot against them;" and after promising to send an angel, he consents to accompany Moses himself; while it is recorded concerning him that "he repented of the evil which he thought to do unto his people." Now, superficial readers are apt to take great exception to the narrative on this account. Because, now we have attained to an exalted idea of the spirituality and unchangeableness of God, they affirm that all such representations as are here made are absolutely unworthy of Deity, and they reject them with scorn. But in so doing, they utterly forget that these very anthropomorphisms were, in their day, a portion of the means by which the Jewish people first, and ultimately others, through Jesus Christ, who came as their Messiah, were educated up to the lofty conception of God which we have now obtained. We must not lose sight of the fact that if we are to speak of God at all, we must use human terms regarding him; but these terms are the outgrowth of our own experience, and cannot but have human limitations, so that it is impossible to conceive of God at all except under such conditions. Moreover, God's revelations take their color from the intelligence of the people to whom they are given; and when we reflect upon the ignorance and degradation out of which the Israelites had been brought when they were emancipated from their bondage, we shall not be surprised at the elementary character of the training to which they were subjected. We have seen how hard it was for them to rest in the belief of the truth that God is a spirit. They cried for a material symbol, because they could not rise all at once above the grossness of their old Egyptian surroundings; and in the destruction of the calf, and the chastisement which accompanied its demolition, they had their first severe lesson in theology, and learned to connect Jehovah with no visible similitude.

Nor was this all. They had here their earliest insight into the divine attributes. From our stand-point now we easily understand that all his attributes are permanently present in the Deity. He is not at one time just, and at another merciful; at one time wise, and at another good; but he is always just, merciful, wise, and good. All his perfections are always present and operative in him. We have reached this conception; but the Israelites, up till this time, seem to have had no clear view of any of the perfections of God, and if they were ever to obtain such a view of them, they could do so only through the consecutive presentation of the attributes, one after another, to their minds. It would have been useless to have attempted, in their low state of religious development, to set before them a full-rounded idea of the Deity; so advantage was taken of their sin to show them those attributes consecutively, or one after the other, which we now know to be always simultaneously present and active in him. Thus their sin is represented as provoking his anger, and so they are led to think of his justice.

Again their leader intercedes for them, and prevails, and thereby they are introduced to the knowledge of his mercy; while, midway between the expression of his anger and the manifestation of his mercy, there is the execution of the three thousand in the stead of the people, which made them feel that the mercy of the Lord could never be exercised except in such a way as to uphold his justice. In this way they learned more of God through these events than they had ever known before; and it was not an accident, but indeed the culmination and climax of the whole lesson, when, as he passed by Moses in the cleft of the rock, the Lord proclaimed his name thus as "Jehovah, Jehovah God, merciful and gracious, long-suffering, and abundant in goodness and truth, keeping mercy for thousands, forgiving iniquity and transgression and sin, and that will by no means clear the guilty; visiting the iniquity of the fathers upon the children, and upon the children's children, unto the third and to the fourth generation."

Thus we reach another landing-place in the great staircase up which God was leading his people in that education which was to result in the knowledge of himself. At the burning bush he reveals himself as Jehovah; at Marah as Jehovah-Rophek; at Rephidim in such a way that Moses himself called him Jehovah-Nissi; and now as Jehovah the merciful, yet not clearing the guilty; and in this latter case, as in the others, the revelation was connected with certain incidents in the history of the people themselves. It thus appears that those very things in the narrative which excite the ridicule of modern objectors are seen to have been just so many lessons in the religious primer of the Israelites, through which they were led ultimately to nobler things. Those attributes which at Calvary are seen in simultaneous and harmonious operation working out redemption for mankind sinners, are here consecutively presented—first the justice, and then the mercy—that they might be the better understood by the ignorant people to whom the revelation was given. But it ought never to be forgotten by us that if it had not been for this original presentation of them in their separate manifestation, the world would not have been prepared to understand that marvellous display of their consentaneous operation which the cross of Christ has furnished. And yet it all came through the people's sin! How wonderful it is that God has made the very disobedience of men the occasion of revealing himself to them, so that, as we read this name in connection with the events on Calvary, we can say, "The highest angel never saw so much of God before."

But I direct your attention now to the practical influence of this subject. That connects itself with the statement that "Moses wist not that the skin of his face did shine." He had grown so accustomed to the brightness that he ceased to be conscious of its presence. The highest excellence is that which is least conscious of itself. The very forth-putting of an effort to be great in any direction indicates that we lack that greatness. How true that is in art, for example, every one who has an artist among his friends can tell. The greatest achievements made by the sculptor or the painter have been those in the production of which he has been fullest of his conception, and had least thought of himself. I do not mean to say that the noblest artists have not been indefatigable workers; on the contrary, they have labored with such persevering effort that at last they can produce, almost without the consciousness of exertion, something that will never be forgotten; and their supreme work is that which seems almost to have come to them of itself, so that they were more passive than active in its transmission to their fellows. The best sermons write themselves, and are given to the preacher before they are given by him, so that he cannot think of them as wholly his own. But it is the same in spiritual things. If I am conscious of an effort to be humble, very clearly I have not yet attained to humility; while, on the other hand, the very moment I become conscious that I am humble, I have become proud. And so with every other grace. What a discount you take from a man's character when, after you have said of him he is this, or that, or the other thing that is good, you add, "but he knows it." You might almost as well have taken a sponge and wiped out all that went before. So if you know your excellence, you have not yet reached the highest excellence; there remaineth yet the loftiest and the hardest peak of the mountain to be climbed by you, and that is humility. A beautiful corroboration of this truth is furnished to us by the description which the Lord gives of the awards of judgment. He represents the Judge as saying to those on his right hand, "Come, ye blessed of my Father, inherit the kingdom prepared for you from the foundation of the world," and adding, "for I was an hungered, and ye gave me meat," and so on; but they are taken by surprise at the revelation, and reply, "Lord, when saw we *thee* an hungered, and fed thee?" Now, that is no mere mock humility on their part; it is the real truth. The things done by them of which he makes so much were done unconsciously. Like Moses, they "wist not that the skin of their faces shone." A caviller, indeed, might say that it is a farce to reward men for actions the real value of which they did not know when they were performing them; but when you remember that the highest excellence knows not its own excellence, everything is explained. Let us, therefore, brethren, aim after this sort of perfection. This is the true higher life; and to get it we must be much with God himself upon the Mount.

I have left myself little time to speak of the typical significance of this veiled face of Moses; but that is the less to be regretted, as the subject will come up again in other connections. I may not conclude, however, without directing your attention to the use made of it by Paul in the third chapter of his Second Epistle to the Corinthians. He is speaking of the Christian ministry as contrasted with that of Moses, and, while admitting that the ministry of Moses was glorious, as indicated plainly by the shining of his countenance, he affirms that as the letter surpasses the spirit, as the table of the heart is nobler than any table of stone, as life is better than death, as righteousness exceeds condemnation, as the permanent is superior to the transitory, so the ministry of the new covenant is grander than that of the old. And it is especially in contrasting the transitory with the permanent that he refers to the veiling of Moses's face. The radiance of the old mediator's countenance continued but for a time, and the veil was put on, so Paul argues, to conceal its fading. His glory, therefore, was an interrupted and transitory thing; but that of the Christian minister is continuous and increasing.

Again, he uses this veil to illustrate the blindness of Israel to the meaning of their own law. As they could not recognize the transitoriness of Moses's ministry, so they do not now see the temporary character of the law. It is not perceived by them that the law is vanishing away in Christ; but when they shall turn to the Lord, then the veil shall be taken away, as Moses removed his when he went in to speak to God. Then the light shall be kindled by God's presence, as it was on Moses's face; they shall get through the law to the Spirit, from the law to the Lord who gave it; and, having come under the power of the Spirit, there shall be open vision; so that, "beholding with unveiled face the glory of the Lord as in a mirror, they shall not only recognize him, but be assimilated to him, and be changed into the same image from glory to glory."

In all this, of course, the apostle is using Moses as an illustration of the system which he inaugurated; and while his words throw light on the rejection of Jesus by the Jews, they also remind us that the time is coming when Israel shall turn unto the Lord, and the veil shall be taken away. One cannot study this old Hebrew literature, and discover how much the world has learned from it, without having his heart drawn toward the Jewish race. That religion which is at the root of our prosperity as a people, which is the source of our individual happiness in time, and the inspiration of our hope for eternity, is the outcome and development of theirs. The Lord we love and trust and worship was "made of the seed of Abraham;" and it is unutterably sad to think that, as a race, the Jews have turned against him to whom all their prophets gave witness, and in whom all the shadows of their law had their true substance. Truly, to this day, when Moses is read among them, the veil is upon their heart. But it shall not always be thus; for when the fulness of the Gentiles is come in, then the Jews shall return to their allegiance; and their conversion will be as a new Pentecost to the Christian Church. I think if this truth were more thoroughly understood, and more constantly remembered by us, we would look with more favor on all wise efforts for the conversion of God's ancient people, and would take a deeper interest in everything that concerns their welfare. Too long they were made, as it were, the foot-ball of the nations, and denied the common rights of humanity. But a better day has dawned. Christians are now acting toward them more thoroughly in the spirit of their religion; and soon, perhaps, the cruelties of by-gone generations will be forgotten and forgiven by them, as they take their places among the followers of Jesus. But if that time is ever to come—if that veil is ever to be taken from their hearts, it can only be by our giving them, in our character and deportment toward them, a correct representation of the spirit of

Him who wept over Jerusalem's doom, and who still yearns over his covenanted nation. Therefore, despise them not, ostracize them not; but remember that they are still "beloved for their father's sake," and deal kindly with them out of regard for him who took their nationality upon him when he came to earth.

XIV.

THE TABERNACLE, AND ITS SYMBOLISM.

EXODUS xxv.–xxxi.; xxxv.–xl.

WHEN Moses undertook the religious education of the Hebrews, the problem which he had before him was one too hard for merely human intellect to solve. It was something like this: Given a people who have been accustomed to look upon the grossest idolatry, and have just come from the midst of polytheism, how shall they be instructed in the great truths of the unity, spirituality, holiness, justice, and mercy of Jehovah? under what symbols shall these be set before them, so that they shall be most easily apprehended by them in their present stage of development? and by what forms or restrictions shall these symbols be guarded, so that they shall not aggravate the danger, and foster the very evils which are most to be avoided? Happily, he was not left to grapple with these questions in his own unaided strength. During his first forty-days' fellowship with God upon the Mount, the whole divine plan for the training of the tribes in spiritual knowledge, and for the maintenance of worship among them, was minutely unfolded to him. The immediate realization of that design was interfered with, for a season, by the outbreak of idolatry in the matter of the golden calf; but after the renewal of the covenant, and his return from his second sojourn on the summit of Sinai, it was the first thing that claimed his attention.

The plan, as we have said, was God's; yet we must not fail to observe that it took its shape, in some degree, from the capacity and past history of the people. The terms in which a teacher gives a lesson are conditioned, not only by the nature of the subject which he is handling, but also by the extent of the previous knowledge of his pupils. He must descend to their level, and put his thoughts into such language as they can comprehend; otherwise his instruction will be of no value. In the subsequent history of his scholars, they may outgrow all such necessity, and may be disposed to smile at the expedients to which their teacher had recourse; but they served their purpose at the time, and that vindicates their excellence. The full-grown man laughs at the stepping-stones which were put into the brook for him when he was a little child, for now he can bestride it like a Colossus; but they were very welcome when he needed them. And in the same way we may regard the pictorial and symbolic character of the Mosaic worship as a childish thing which manhood has now put away; yet for such comparative babes in religious knowledge as the Hebrews then were, it was every way admirable. It put the truth into forms of a sort to which they had been in some measure accustomed, and by which they were kept from the materialism of other nations.

They belonged to an age in which symbolism was everywhere employed. They had come from a land in which much of the writing was pictorial; and the nations then, as the recently-discovered monuments attest, were in the habit of putting all religious truths into external emblems. That form, therefore, as being the existing and recognized medium for the communication of such things at the time, was employed by Jehovah. He chose it just as, in giving us a revelation of his will, he chose language, because he found it already in use. But he did with it as in his revelation he has done with human language—he elevated it and refined it, and put such new significance into it, that men, looking at it, can see as marked a difference between the tabernacle of the Hebrews and the temples of the heathen as there is between the Bible and the so-called sacred books of India and China.

The Hebrews of Moses's day were not ready for such a clear statement of the truth about the nature and worship of God as that which Jesus gave to the woman at the well of Sychar. They could not have taken that into their minds; and, even if they could have apprehended it, they could not have retained it. They craved for something external. That eager desire for an embodiment of Deity which, among the heathen, tried to satisfy itself in idolatry, and which has now been met for all men in the Incarnation of God in Christ, was as strong in them as in others. Their lapse into image-worship at the very base of Sinai proves that this was the case; and, therefore, it became necessary to give them an outward symbolism—which should meet the craving of their hearts, and yet not minister to materialism because it had no visible representation of God.

Such a symbolism was set before them in the tabernacle. It was, from first to last, an external emblem of spiritual truth. It spoke to the people in a language that they could and did understand; it preached to them always the same great sermon; and its special typical significance, as pointing to the Christian dispensation, is but the result of its general symbolism, and springs from the fact that it was designed to be emblematic of those abstract principles which have found their perfect concrete expression now in the person and work of the Lord Jesus.

Bearing these things in mind, we shall be the better able to understand the meaning of the Hebrew tabernacle, to the consideration of which I now proceed. The plan after which it was constructed was given to Moses either by the exhibition of a model of it before his eyes, or by the communication to his mind of a clear and perfect idea of it, so that he was able distinctly to apprehend and accurately to reproduce it. The materials for its erection were contributed voluntarily by the people themselves, who manifested extraordinary enthusiasm in the matter, and brought actually more than was required, although the cost of the structure has been estimated as amounting to more than a million and a quarter dollars of our money. The workmanship was superintended and directed by Bezaleel, of the tribe of Judah, and Aholiab, of the tribe of Dan, both of whom were divinely qualified and designated for the service. Under them all the skilled artificers of the host were engaged, and thus the training in various handicrafts which they had received in the land of Egypt was utilized in the service of Jehovah. The curtains of linen and goat's-hair were spun and woven by "wise-hearted" women; and such was the industry with which they all wrought that on the first day of the second year from the date of their emancipation the sacred structure was set up, and its services inaugurated with great splendor and solemnity.

It was placed in the centre of the encampment, and was enclosed within a rectangular court, whose entrance faced the east, and before each side of which, at the distance of two thousand cubits, three tribes had their allotted camping-ground. On the east, facing the entrance, were Zebulon, Judah, and Issachar; and between them and the enclosure were the tents of Moses and Aaron and Aaron's sons; on the north were Asher, Dan, and Naphtali, and between them and the wall of curtains were the children of Merari; on the west were Manasseh, Ephraim, and Benjamin, with the Levitical family of the Gershonites between them and the sacred edifice; on the south were Gad, Reuben, and Simeon, with the Kohathites intervening between them and the southern wall.

The enclosure itself was one hundred cubits long by fifty wide, and was formed by hangings of linen—or, as some think, cotton—fastened to pillars by silver hooks and fillets. The pillars were five cubits in height, and numbered ten for the west end, and twenty for each side; while at the eastern end, in which was the entrance, there were three pillars on each side, leaving a space of twenty cubits, in which were four pillars, whereon was hung a curtain of fine linen, with variegated strips of purple, and blue, and crimson.

As one entered this enclosure, he came first upon the altar of burnt-offering, the fire on which, being supernaturally kindled at the first, was to be perpetually maintained. "It was also a place of constant sacrifice: fresh blood was shed upon it continually, and the smoke of the burning sacrifice ascended up toward heaven without intermission."* A little farther in, beyond this altar, was the laver of brass, cast from the metallic mirrors given by the women, and containing water which was used by the priest for washing his hands and feet as he passed into the sanctuary. Then, at the distance of fifty cubits from the entrance, and precisely midway between the two sides of the court, was the tabernacle proper. This was a rectangular structure, thirty cubits long, by ten in width and ten in height. It was open above, and was composed of planks of acacia-wood, overlaid with gold, which were fixed at the base by tenons fitting into silver sockets, and were kept together by means of bars of acacia-wood passing through rings of gold. The area thus formed was divided into two compartments, the outer one twenty cubits long, and the inner ten. The separation was made by a veil, of the richest material and most beautifully adorned, which was hung upon four pillars of gilt acacia. The entrance into the outer apartment was also through a veil

---

* Eadie's "Cyclopædia," *sub voce* ALTAR.

adorned with needle-work, which was suspended by hooks on five pillars.

I have said that there was no roof; but the absence of that was made up for by a series of coverings, which were thrown over the whole, so as to make a flat surface; though some are of opinion that they were suspended on a ridge-pole, like the canvas of an ordinary tent. The innermost curtain was of fine linen or cotton; the second was of goats'-hair, which was the ordinary tent-fabric of the time; the third was of rams'-skins dyed red; and the fourth was of the skins of the tachash, an animal which has not yet been identified, but which is thought by some to have been a kind of fish—probably the seal—and by others to have been a species of deer. Thus, while the under coverings had a symbolical character, the upper were added to protect the whole fabric from the weather.

In the inner of the two apartments, known as the Most Holy Place, was a chest of acacia-wood, two and a half cubits long by one and a half broad, having a raised ornamental border round the top. It was overlaid with gold, and the lid was made entirely of the precious metal. At each end of the lid, looking toward each other, were two symbolic composite figures of beaten gold, having wings which "stretched forth on high;" and between these wings and over them hovered evermore the mystic cloud, wherein the presence of God was at once revealed and concealed. Within the chest were the two tables of stone which Moses brought with him from the Mount; and, with the exception of a golden pot which contained a specimen of the manna, and the rod of Aaron, of which we shall afterward hear, this ark, with its contents and its cherubic adjuncts, was the only furniture of the Holy of Holies.

In the outer apartment there were three objects of interest. In the centre, and immediately in front of the entrance to the Most Holy Place, was the altar of incense, on which sweet spices were burned daily. On the south side of that altar was the golden lamp-stand, having one main stem, on each side of which were three branches. The lamps were to be lighted in the evening, and kept burning all the night. On the north side of the altar of incense was the table of shewbread, which was made of acacia-wood overlaid with gold, and on which were laid twelve loaves, corresponding to the number of the twelve tribes. These loaves were removed, and fresh ones substituted, every Sabbath; and only the priests might eat of those which had been taken away.

When the tabernacle, of which we have given the briefest possible description, was set up, it was consecrated to God by the anointing of its separate parts and its different articles of furniture with oil specially prepared, according to God's command, for the purpose. In the same way, special attendants were set apart for the stated performance of duties in it and about it. Designed as it was for a travelling people, it was made so that it could be easily taken down, removed, and set up again; and the tribe of Levi, accepted by God in lieu of the first-born who had been spared on the night when they left Egypt, were appointed and consecrated to that work. The Merarites had charge of the boards, bars, and pillars; the Gershonites, of the coverings and hangings; and the Kohathites, of the ark, the table, the candlestick, and the altars and the vessels of the sanctuary. Then, out of the tribe of Levi the family of Aaron were chosen for the priesthood; and special ceremonies, of great meaning and solemnity, were connected with their consecration. It was the duty of the priests to watch over the fire on the altar of burnt-offering, and keep it continually burning; to attend to the lighting and extinguishing of the lamps on the golden lamp-stand; to offer a lamb in sacrifice morning and evening, and two lambs on the Sabbath; to remove the loaves of presentation, and put others in their stead; and to be always at their post, to do the work of sacrifice or offering for any humble penitent or any thankful worshipper who might present himself. Then, over these, the head of the family of Aaron was designated to the office of high-priest, and, with great pomp and ceremony, consecrated to the performance of its duties. A dress of great splendor was prescribed to him. His were the ephod and the breastplate, the Urim and Thummim, and the mitre with its plate of gold, whereon were inscribed the words, "Holiness unto the Lord." And he alone, of all the people, had the right of entrance into the Holy of Holies. Yet not even he could enter when he chose; for only on the great day of annual atonement, when he carried with him the blood of the sin-offering, and sprinkled it upon the lid of the ark, was he permitted to venture within the veil; and even on that occasion minute and particular directions were given him, which he was most sacredly to follow, on the pain of death.

Now, if we carry in our thoughts these particulars, which I have endeavored to make as clear as possible, we shall have little difficulty in discovering the meanings which they symbolically taught. They set before the Hebrews very vividly these two sides of truth—God coming to them, and the manner of their approach to God.

From the divine side, this structure symbolized the coming of God to the people, and his dwelling among them. At its consecration, we are told that "a cloud covered the tent of the congregation, and the glory of the Lord covered the tabernacle;" and in the Holy of Holies, the Shechinah, or mystic cloud, was always hovering between the cherubim over the ark of the covenant. Here, therefore, was the seat and centre of the Jewish theocracy. As the kingdom was visible, so was the palace, and so also was at least the presence of the King. Thus we account for the fact that, when

God commanded Moses to erect it, he said, "Let them make me a sanctuary, that I may dwell among them," and promised regarding it, "I will dwell among the children of Israel, and will be their God."* His symbolic presence was over the ark, wherein were the two tables of stone having the law engraven on them, to indicate that he was in the midst of them, a righteous Lord and Governor. "Justice and judgment" were thus seen to be "the habitation of his throne."

But the palace wherein God dwelt was also the meeting-place between him and the people. It was called "the tent of meeting," for that is the correct translation of the phrase which, in our version, has been invariably rendered "the tabernacle of the congregation;" and it was thus described, not because the people met there with each other, but because it was the locality in which God had covenanted to meet and converse with them. Hence he said to Moses, "There will I meet with thee, and I will commune with thee from above the mercy-seat, from between the cherubim which are upon the ark of the testimony, of all things which I will give thee in commandment to the children of Israel."† Moreover, the blood of expiation sprinkled on the lid of the ark denoted that it was through sacrifice that God was thus gracious to those who had sinned against him. In this way, the grand central truth of the tabernacle symbolism was the gracious presence of God with his people as a righteous governor, whose justice has been upheld by sacrifice, so that his honor is untarnished in the forgiveness of sin. It was, in its own emblematic language, a repetition for all the people, in a standing and permanent form, of the proclamation by the Lord of that name which he had revealed to Moses, when, as he passed by, he said, "Jehovah, Jehovah God, merciful and gracious, long-suffering, and abundant in good-

---

* Exod. xxv., 8; xxix., 45. † Ib. xxix., 43.

ness and truth, keeping mercy for thousands, forgiving iniquity, transgression, and sin, and that will by no means clear the guilty."

But in connection with this revelation of God there were certain other peculiar features of amazing interest. For instance, the spirituality of Deity is admirably suggested by the bright cloud over the ark. There was no manner of similitude permitted; such a thing, indeed, was expressly forbidden. The presence was visible, but the Divine Being was invisible. There was enough of the visible to meet the craving of the soul for something on which the eye could work; and yet that which the eye beheld was itself a veil, within the luminous folds of which the great I AM was hidden from view. Thus there was no encouragement given to image-worship, for the presence was in a form which concealed as well as revealed, and which suggested a spiritual rather than a corporeal Being. We to-day have reached a faith in God which does not need even the visible emblem of a glory-cloud to sustain it; but we should never forget that we are the inheritors in this of an education which could not have attained to such an exalted conception unless in its earlier stages it had been thus assisted.

In the same way it appears to me that the unity of God is throughout this symbolism vividly kept before the mind. Just as the Holy of Holies differed from the shrines of heathen temples in having no image, it was unlike them, also, in conserving the notion of the unity and supremacy of Jehovah. There is but one ark, one altar of incense, and one altar of burnt-offering; and only at this divinely-appointed place were the Hebrews, in all time coming, to offer sacrifices and offerings to God. In one point of view, indeed, this seems to have been, perhaps, the narrowest feature of the Mosaic system; and we congratulate ourselves that now we live in an age when neither to this spot nor to that is acceptable service of God restricted, but the worshipper may worship the Father anywhere, provided he do so in spirit and in truth. Yet, when we look at the subject from another side, we see that even this exclusivism was meant to conserve a great truth; for in the proportion in which a nation multiplies altars, it ultimately multiplies divinities. At first, indeed, the shrines may be erected professedly to the true God; but after awhile local influences and jealousies begin to work, the different "high places" become rivals, and so they put forth exclusive claims, which end in each becoming the altar of a new god. One has only to read the history of the Jews themselves to see how true this assertion is; and a glance at the great centres of heathen worship in India at the present day will convince you that the tendency of the human heart is to have a distinct god for every altar. But all this was guarded against by the provision of only one altar in the tabernacle, and the command that on it alone all sacrifices were to be offered.

Then, to mention no more, what an impressive manifestation of the holiness of God was given by this whole structure, and the services to which it was consecrated. Not only was the tabernacle set up within an enclosure, but its entrance was veiled; and in the innermost apartment, behind another veil, was the presence-cloud of Deity. Thus, though dwelling among the people, he was yet hedged round with such restrictions, and to be approached with such rites, as emphatically suggested his purity. Everything about the tabernacle was set apart by a special consecration unto him. The very furniture was holy; the Levites who carried it from place to place had to bear a sacred character; the priests had to be consecrated to their office with great solemnity. When they went into the sanctuary they had to purify themselves at the brazen laver; and every personal injunction laid upon them was of such a nature as to enforce the command, "Be ye holy, for I am holy." So, also, the high-priest bore upon his mitre the golden plate with the inscription, "Holiness unto the Lord."

But perhaps the most striking enforcement of this attribute of the divine character was given by the cherubim. It is not possible, indeed, now to furnish an accurate description of these composite figures; but, whatever their appearance was, it seems to me to be plain, from the references to them throughout the Scriptures, that they are to be understood as the symbolic guardians of the divine holiness; and the very fact that no detailed account of them is given here indicates that both their likeness and their significance were well known to the people. We first meet them guarding the tree of life in Paradise, and keeping back our fallen parents from its fruit; we next come upon them here, in golden effigy, looking down with satisfaction on the blood-besprinkled mercy-seat; we see them next in Isaiah's vision, and hear the temple echo with their praise, "Holy, holy, holy is the Lord of Hosts;" we find them next in the vision of Ezekiel, in which they are the guardians of the mystic wheels, which are supposed by many to signify the providence of God; and we behold them for the last time in the Apocalypse of John, where we hear them once more singing, "Holy, holy, holy Lord God Almighty;" where, also, there is a throne, with a lamb upon it, as if it had been slain, and beside the throne four-and-twenty elders, representing the tribes of the redeemed. Now, observe how the Apocalypse, with its Paradise regained, stands in contrast to Genesis, with its Paradise lost. In Genesis, the cherubim are warding men away; in the Apocalypse, they are complacent onlookers, while the elders are seated on either side of the throne; and the reason of the difference is that on the throne itself there is the Lamb of God who took away the sins of the world. But just as, in John's vision, the cherubim are satisfied at the reception of the Redeemed, because the Lamb was slain, so here on the ark of the covenant they are complacent on-lookers as God meets and communes with his people through their representative, because his holiness has been conserved by the blood of atonement. Perhaps this lesson was not learned by the people all at once; yet the fact that, in both the visions of Isaiah and John, the cherubic anthem voiced itself in the words, "Holy, holy, holy, Lord," is not without its significance as furnishing the key to the meaning of their symbolism.

But now, looking to the teaching of the tabernacle as to the manner in which the people were to approach God, there are some things of great importance suggested. I have already incidentally referred to certain truths which could not rightly be overlooked when speaking of God's abode among his people; yet if I should touch them from another side, that will only serve to show the importance which they held in the view of the Divine Instructor. Pre-eminent among the lessons, from the human side, which the tabernacle taught, I place the necessity of a Mediator. The people did not come into direct and immediate dealing with Jehovah. Everything was done with him for them through the consecrated priest, and on the great annual day of atonement through the mediation of the high-priest. At the base of Sinai, when they requested Moses to become their mediator, they relinquished the honor which God designed for them when he said, "Ye shall be unto me a kingdom of priests;" and, therefore, when they presented themselves to him, it was through one who was ordained of God to offer their gifts and sacrifices. Their guilt rendered them unfit to come into immediate fellowship with him, and so only through one who was accepted as holy in their stead could they offer praise or make request to him. Moreover, this mediator approached on their behalf always with sacrifice. The fire on the altar of burnt-offering never went out; victims were always upon it, and every priestly duty was performed on the ground of their acceptance. The altar stood at the gate—or at least, nearest the gate of the tabernacle enclosure—to show that expiation was the first great indispensable thing; and every step that was taken by the priest beyond the altar was taken on the ground of the sacrifice that was offered thereon. Then, in the outer sanctuary, the first things that met the eye of the high-priest after he had made atonement, and when he was leaving the Holy of Holies, were the table of shewbread, the altar of incense, and the seven-branched lamp-stand; and these were the appropriate emblems of that constant service which one reconciled to God by the blood of atonement ought to render unto him. The shewbread represents the fruits of diligence in that holy living to which all God's culture of the soul ever tends, even as bread is the ultimate result of the natural husbandry of the agriculturist in the cultivation of his fields; the incense, as many passages of Scripture make evident,* represents the offering of prayer, which is the exhalation of the sweet spices of the heart before God, when they are set on fire with the flame of sincere devotion to his will; the golden lamp-stand represents sanctified character, composed of the interblending of knowledge with holiness,† from which a radiance, sustained by the spirit of God, is emitted, and by which not the Church only, but the world, is to be illuminated. Thus the worshipper, who is represented by the priest, went through the gate of expiation into the chamber of peace, and emerged therefrom into a life of prayer and fruitfulness and radiant holiness, by which God was honored and the community enlightened.

---

* See Psa. cxli., 2; Luke i., 10; Rev. v., 8; viii., 3, 4.
† See Eph. v., 8; Phil. i., 14.

It remains that we look for a few moments now at the typical significance of this remarkable structure. As I said in the outset of my present discourse, the typical teaching rests upon the general symbolism; and as we have now a firm grasp of the latter, it will be comparatively easy for us to rise to the comprehension of the former; while the principles which we have already established will save us alike from that weak and puerile literalism which would make a spiritual meaning out of every loop in the curtains, or every little article of furniture, like the spoons and the snuffers; and from that extreme and prosaic naturalism which will not allow that there was in all this ritual any anticipation or prophecy of the Gospel. The truth lies between these two, and may be expressed thus: As a symbolism, the tabernacle ritualism was a correct representation of the great spiritualities which have their genuine incarnation in Christ; and so it stood as it were midway between the abstract doctrine and the concrete fact. It was the halting-place of the ideal on its way toward the real, and thus its very incompleteness was a pledge and prophecy of the perfection that was to come.

The tabernacle was the dwelling-place of Deity, and the point of meeting between God and his people. Where now in Christianity do we find the substance of which that was the shadow? You have only to put the question, to see what the answer must be. The New Testament tabernacle is the person of our Lord Jesus Christ, in whom dwelleth all the fulness of the Godhead bodily; and in whom, also, God is reconciling the world unto himself, "not imputing unto them their trespasses." Of this tabernacle his flesh is the veil, hiding, as it did so largely, the lustre of his deity; and when that veil was rent in his death he entered into the holy place, having obtained eternal redemption for us. Thus the truth that God dwells with his people, which was in the tabernacle in symbol, was in Christ in reality. His name is "Emanuel—God with us;" and the evangelist, with perhaps a reference to this very symbol, has said, "The Word became flesh, and dwelt"—literally, "tabernacled"—"among us, and we beheld his glory."

Now, having found out the typical meaning of the tabernacle itself, we can be at no loss to see who the mediator is; for Christ is himself called by that name, and his very Incarnation enables him to lay his hand upon both God and man. So, again, we find the expiation in his atoning blood; "For such a high-priest became us, who is holy, harmless, undefiled, separate from sinners, and made higher than the heavens; who needeth not daily, as those high-priests, to offer up sacrifice, first for his own sins, and then for the people's: for this he did once when he offered up himself." Thus, wherever I look in the tabernacle there is something that points me to Christ. The structure, as a whole, is a finger-post directing me to that mystic person in whom "God in very deed dwelt with man upon the earth." Its white-robed priest is the shadow of him who was white in something higher than vestments, being "holy, harmless, undefiled," and whom I recognize as my true High-priest. Its bleeding lamb laid upon the altar is the likeness of that Lamb of God by whose precious blood I have been redeemed from all iniquity; its innermost sanctuary is the type of that heaven into which he has entered to make atonement for my sin, and its outer apartment is the analogue of the present world, in which we are to serve him with the incense of our devotions, the light of our characters, and the fruit of our lives. The incarnation in the person of Christ, the mediation and expiation of his priestly work, and the consequent obligation under which his redeemed people lie to honor him with unceasing service and shining holiness—or, putting it all into four words, INCARNATION, MEDIATION,

EXPIATION, CONSECRATION—these are the things of which the tabernacle, with its furniture, services, and attendants, were the special types; and as thus we have condensed its teachings into their essence, we have come to a larger and more comprehensive view of the doctrines of the Gospel itself, and discover that we have been studying the same truths, only under a different form.

We have been so thoroughly engaged with doctrine to-night that a few practical lessons will be welcome; yet I can do little more than name three.

In the first place, we have here an example of liberality. The people gave until they had brought too much. But the universality of the giving is as striking as the aggregate amount. They all gave something. No class or sex was excluded from the privilege. The rulers brought precious stones; the princes gave the wagons and oxen for the transportation of the fabric; the men gave acacia-wood, and brass, and silver, and gold; and the women contributed their mirrors for the brazen laver. So the tabernacle was raised without debt; and herein there is a lesson to our modern congregations. Commonly, nowadays, men proceed with their building, calculating that the necessary funds will be forthcoming in the end; but here the offering came first, and that ought to be the invariable rule. If the contributions are small, then let the fabric be according to them. It is all very well to have an exquisite baptismal font; but it is better to do with an earthenware one that is paid for, than to go in debt for one of marble. It is better to have a plain, substantial building, with no extravagance about it, but without a debt, than to have the most splendid specimen of Gothic architecture that is overlaid by a mortgage. Observe, I do not say a word against elaboration in church architecture. I do not think anything is too good for the house of God; and it ought not, at least, to be in any way behind the comfort and elegance of the homes of the people who frequent it. But I do say that the church is too good a place to be in debt; and that if these other adornments can be had only by contracting pecuniary obligations of a permanent character, then it is every way better to do without them. The apostolic rule is good for churches as well as individuals—" Owe no man anything, but to love one another;" and even that love we must be always paying. Oh, how many churches in our land to-day would have been happier, more prosperous, and more aggressive, if only they had acted on this principle!

But we have here, secondly, an example of consecrated ability. Bezaleel and Aholiab were, doubtless, men of skill before the Lord inspired them to take the oversight of the erection of the tabernacle; and they, and all those who wrought under them, willingly devoted their genius to the Lord. Now, of course, there was a special divine influence on these two artists; but in a very real sense, it is true of every man of genius that his excellence has been given him by God, and he should seek to consecrate it to God's service. Let us be just, also, and add that, in a large proportion of instances, they have done so. Take the noblest things in poetry, music, architecture, and painting, and you will find that they have been done in the service of God, and have a religious significance. The grandest epic in our language is on a religious theme; and some of our noblest lyrics have come from the harp of a pious heart, swept by the breeze of a holy influence. What are the oratorios of Handel but the consecration of his genius to Jehovah? and the finest specimens of architecture which Europe has to show are its venerable cathedrals, every one of which, in the ideal of its designer, was a sermon in stone. The greatest triumphs of the painter have been in the delineations of sacred subjects; and many among them who have become famous have, like the Fra Angelico, done their work upon their knees. I do not think the average Christian has been at all just to genius in this respect. It has been far too much insinuated that genius is the natural antagonist of religion. But the truth is, that it is designed to be its spiritual ally; and where it has not been so, I fear the Church has itself been too frequently to blame. We are coming round to a better mind upon the subject; and men are learning that painting, sculpture, and architecture may be wedded to the Gospel, as well as poetry and music. Every true product of art, no matter in what department, is a poem; and if we can adopt the lyrics of the singer into our hymnology, why should we not encourage our artists to preach on the canvas and in the marble? Never minister gave a more eloquent sermon than that painted by Holman Hunt in "The Light of the World." And the advantage is on the painter's side in more ways than one; for, while the sermon dies out of recollection, the picture lives. So let us encourage men of genius to consecrate their abilities to God's service; and then, perhaps, the time will come when, in the highest of all senses, "the day of the Lord shall be upon all pleasant pictures." Nothing is so delightful to me as to see a work of art which is the embodiment of a religious idea; and if we were but to encourage our artists to produce such things, our galleries would be educational even in a nobler respect than that of refining the taste, for they would be the repositories of good and striking enforcements of the truth of God.

> "How beautiful is genius when combined
> With holiness! Oh, how divinely sweet
> The tones of earthly harp whose chords are touched
> By the soft hand of piety, and hung
> Upon religious shrine, there vibrating
> With solemn music in the ear of God!"

Finally, we have here an example of thoroughness. Everything was made as near perfection as possible. The loops and hooks of the curtains were attended to with as religious care as the ark of the covenant itself. Nothing was slighted. There was no covering up of bad work with what looked like an ornament, but was really a hypocrisy. The very smallest thing was made as thoroughly according to pattern as the greatest. They were working for God, and they would do it well. The same thing was seen in the Temple in Solomon's time; and those who inspect the mediæval cathedrals give a similar testimony in reference to them; so that Longfellow's words are true when he says,

> "In the elder days of art,
> Builders wrought with greatest care
> Each minute and unseen part,
> For the gods are everywhere."

But in these times a far different spirit seems to be abroad, and men cover over with a fair appearance workmanship which is simply dishonest. The cry is for cheapness, and to meet that, efficiency is neglected; so that here not the workmen alone, but the public as a whole, are to be blamed. Now, the first great requisite in every product of labor is excellence. I care not what a thing may look like; if it be not really that which it is represented to be, it is a fraud, and it is dear at any price. We want to-day more preaching of this gospel of honesty. It is needed all round. You blame those who wish to pass ninety-two cents off for a dollar in the shape of a piece of silver, and I join you in doing so; but what better are you if you sell a counterfeit for a genuine article, or put out of your hands an inferior production that appears for the moment to be all right? Ah! have you forgotten that God is everywhere, and that he sees what is below the surface? Mr. Spurgeon tells of a domestic servant who came to him to speak about joining the Church. After testing her knowledge, and getting at her experience of the great change, he said, "That is all very well; but what evidence have you that you have been really converted?" She replied, after a moment's thought, and with a slight blush upon her cheeks, "Well, sir, I sweep under the mats now." That is to say, she had learned thoroughness. So to-night let each of us go hence and look below the mats in his heart, in his home, in his business, in his public life; and sweep out everything he finds that is unholy, ignoble, dishonorable, and dishonest there. Let us have less of the double standard of profession and practice, and more of the gold coin of genuine sincerity in all the businesses and relationships of life; and we shall show that we have learned something from the workmanship of this old tabernacle.

XV.

THE MOSAIC LEGISLATION.

DEUTERONOMY vi., 1.

AS the laws of Moses were given, for the most part, during the encampment of the tribes at Sinai, this will be the most convenient place for a brief analysis and review of that remarkable system of legislation which gave its distinctive character and influence to the Hebrew nation. At first sight, it might seem that these statutes have little connection with the character of Moses, since they were given to him by Jehovah, and he was only the instrument of communicating them to the people; but such a view is entirely inconsistent with the workings of divine inspiration in other cases, for the Holy Spirit has always spoken through the individuality of the men whom he has chosen as prophets and apostles. We do not hesitate to believe that the natural lyric genius of David is as conspicuous in his Psalms as is the elevating and revealing influence of the supernatural spirit; and we feel no difficulty in tracing the mental ability and peculiarities of Paul in his Epistles, while, at the same time, we cheerfully admit that he wrote the things which the Holy Ghost taught him. In the same way we distinguish between the poetic grandeur of Isaiah and the mystic symbolism of Ezekiel; while the intuitional depth of the Apostle John is easily recognized as different from the practical pungency of James. In all these cases we concede that the personal characteristics of the men underlay the spiritual communications which they made, and qualified and conditioned their utterances. They were the moulds into which the several divine messages were run; and these, when given to the people, took their shape from their individual peculiarities.

But the same thing was true of Moses and his laws; so that, while we constantly see in them the marks of the divine wisdom, we may also obtain from them an insight into his ability as a statesman and legislator. Just as John saw farther into the heart of Christ than any other of the disciples did, and has given us the benefit of his keen-eyed perception in the fourth gospel, so we may not hesitate to conclude that the Mosaic legislation is the result not only of God's revelation to Moses, but also of Moses's ability to take in the meaning of the divine plan, and to reproduce it to the people of his charge. Such a system could not have been given through Aaron, for example, because, great as the high-priest was, he had not those natural aptitudes for such subjects which his brother possessed, and could not have seen all that was visible to him who, for twice forty days, was on the Mount alone with God. Inspiration did not use the prophet or law-giver as a machine, but it employed his powers of apprehension as well as of utterance. Moses was far more to God and to the people than the mere attendant, who passed the word from the one to the other, as the seaman transmits the order from the captain to the helmsman on board ship. He was the interpreter of the one to the other; and because he understood God so well it was that he gave this noble collection of statutes to his fellow-countrymen. Jehovah employed his heart, conscience, judgment, and intelligence, as well as his speech; and so, in the study of the law, we come into contact as really with his human ability as with the divine wisdom. It would be impossible, therefore, to form anything like an accurate conception either of his mental and moral greatness, or of his influence not only on his own age, but on all succeeding generations, without taking into account the legislation which is called by his name.

In reviewing that, however, certain important preliminaries have to be carefully noted.

We must remember, in the first place, that, though given to the people while they were in the wilderness, these laws were adapted and designed for a nation permanently settled in the land of Palestine. The mere proclamation of them, therefore, was an act of faith. Minute and particular enactments regarding the holding of property were given to a homeless and wandering host, who, to human view, were far more likely to sink back into the degradation of the slavery from which they had just escaped, than to advance to the foremost rank among the nations of antiquity. Laws requiring the attendance of all the men three times a year at some central spot were enacted before they had acquired a foot of land that they could call their own, and while yet they were sojourning in one unbroken encampment. In this view of the case, the very reception and promulgation of these precepts by Moses is as great a triumph of faith as was his observance of the Passover on the night of the deliverance from Egypt. I am aware, indeed, that some of our modern destructive critics would have us to believe that this legislation belongs to a much later period of Jewish history, and would put it as far down as the age of Josiah, if not even of Ezra; but surely we have only to look at the character of many of these enactments to be convinced that they could have been published and enforced only in the age in which they are here set. If they came from Moses at all, then, since he died on the eastern side of the Jordan, they must have been promulgated in the desert; and if they were not proclaimed there, to what other period of Jewish history can they be assigned? The age of the Judges was one of alternate servitude and war, altogether unfitted for the publication of such a code; that of the Kings saw a total change in the character of the nation, which was entirely inconsistent with much of the spirit of these laws; and if they be referred to the later portion of the Hebrew history, it is inexplicable that they should contain no remotest allusion to Jerusalem, which was the pride of the people, or to the Temple, which was the glory of all who looked upon its splendor. Moreover, the statutes concerning the allotment of the land are of such a character that, at any later point in the history of the people, they could not have been acted upon without the forcible resumption of all real estate by the State; and the difficulty of carrying any such measure into execution would have been so great that we must have had some account of the revolution which it created. But the absence of any such record is almost equivalent to a demonstration that the law as a whole belongs to the wilderness stage of Hebrew history, to which it makes so many natural and incidental allusions; and so its publication takes its place side by side with Joseph's commandment concerning his bones, as one of the brightest illustrations of the power of faith.

Again, in considering these laws, we must not forget that they were designed for a theocracy. God chose the people for his own, and the people chose God as their king. The fountain of authority, therefore, was his will; and the statutes which he enacted were not merely a law for the Jewish nation, but a part of God's revelation of himself to men. Thus these precepts link themselves on to the great system of prophecy which is comprised in the Old Testament, and form a part of that divine education through which the Jews, and ultimately the world also, were led up to the fuller and more spiritual legislation of the Gospel.

But this theocratic character of the Mosaic law accounts,

not only for its relation to prophecy, but also for many of the statutes which it contains. Sin, where God is the king, becomes also crime; and idolatry, in such circumstances, is not only a moral evil, but a civil treason. In this we have the rationale of the fact that image-worship, blasphemy, and Sabbath-breaking are all punishable with death, while a terrible denunciation is made against the false prophet. In a similar way we explain the existence of the whole Levitical system in this code. The head of the nation was at the same time the head of the Church. The Church and State were not so much united as identical; and the two precepts, "Fear God," and "Honor the king," were virtually synonymous. We cannot, therefore, fairly judge of such legislation from our modern stand-point, neither can we argue from it to a state of things so wholly dissimilar as that which exists among ourselves. We make a distinction—and we rightly make it—between that which is sin, as committed against God, and that which is crime, as committed against the community. But where God was, not in a mere figurative and spiritual sense, but literally and actually the king, that distinction vanished; and things which now we should not think of punishing at all, inasmuch as they lie in that department which is between God and conscience, were, in this code, visited with the severest penalties. It was right and beneficial in a theocracy, but it would be intolerant and fraught with mischief in an ordinary state; and for lack of perceiving this distinction, many great mistakes have been made by those who, in putting religious errorists to death, have imagined that they were doing God service. Idolatry now is a sin against God; but among the Hebrews it was also subversive of the very fundamental principle of the constitution, which was the acceptance of Jehovah as the only king; and therefore it was punished with death, just as, in these days, he would be treated as a traitor who sought to subvert our republic, and set up a throne in the midst of us.

Still further, we must bear in mind that this legislation was grafted on a previously existing state of things, and took its character, in some respects, from customs which were inveterate among the people. Laws, to be obeyed, must be practicable. They must have regard to the history and present condition of the community. They who are to be subject to them must be willing to accept them. Nothing is gained, but much is frequently lost, by legislation that is far in advance of public sentiment; and so, very frequently, the law-giver has to consider, not what is the absolute best, but rather what, in the circumstances, will work best. Solon said that his laws were not by any means the best which he could have made, but that they were the best which he could get the Athenians to accept; and that something of the same sort was present to the mind of Moses, is evident from the words of the Lord Jesus, when, in the matter of divorce, he says, "For the hardness of your heart he wrote you this precept."* It is noticeable, however, that, wherever things in themselves questionable are tolerated, because they were too deeply seated to be removed by an immediate prohibition, the legislation regarding them is of such a character as to mitigate the evils, and prepare the way for their ultimate repression. Thus, in the very instance of divorce referred to by the Saviour, the abuse was in some degree restrained by the necessity which the law enforced of publicly giving the wife that was put away a writing of divorcement; and so a fulcrum was left whereon Christ put his lever when he lifted men up to the great Christian law of marriage. But perhaps a more striking illustration of the peculiarity on which I am now commenting was furnished by

---

* Mark x., 5.

the law in reference to the avenger of blood. Among the Arab tribes, the nearest of kin is bound by a sacred law of honor to put to death the man who has slain his relative. He makes no inquiry. He takes no time for deliberation. It is his duty—so he is taught—to track the man-slayer, and hunt him to his death; and in a rude state of society, such red-handed justice is better than no justice at all. Indeed, we have the testimony of some Eastern travellers to the effect that this institution has contributed, in a greater degree than any other circumstance, to prevent the warlike tribes of Arabia from exterminating one another.* But under such a system it is inevitable that many guilty ones shall escape, and some innocent ones shall be put to death; and so, while continuing the responsibility of the nearest of kin in part, Moses drew a sharp distinction between murder and manslaughter; took the murderer out of the hands of the avenger, and put him into that of the law, requiring that he should be put to death; but prepared six cities of refuge, into one or other of which the man-slayer might flee. Yet he did not make the right of sanctuary inviolable, for it was the duty of the elders of the city to investigate the case; and if they found it murder, they were to give him up; while, if it were death by misadventure, he was to be taken into the city, and kept there until the death of the high-priest. Thus, while nominally maintaining the old custom, its evils were minimized, and a new and important distinction introduced, which has been recognized by all civilized nations since.

Again, in the case of slavery, the same thing is apparent. At the date of the Exodus, this evil was universally prevalent among the nations; and, though the Hebrews had only

---

* See Layard and Burckhardt, as quoted in Fairbairn's "Imperial Bible Dictionary," article BLOOD, AVENGER OF.

recently been themselves emancipated, they were not yet prepared for the enforcement of its entire prohibition. But while in name the thing remained, the Mosaic enactments greatly modified the thing. The free-born Israelite might become a slave, either by his own consent, or as an insolvent debtor, or as a thief unable to make restitution; but in no case could his bondage continue more than seven years. If, at the end of that time, he preferred to remain in service, then he appeared before a magistrate and had his ear bored; but even such voluntary slavery came to an end in the year of Jubilee. No Hebrew could be held to perpetual servitude. Then, the stealing of men from other nations for the purpose of selling them as slaves was punishable with death. It is true that captives taken in war might be kept in bondage; yet care was taken to make their position as comfortable as was compatible with their loss of freedom; and if the death of such a slave was caused by the violence of his master, then the punishment was capital; while if, by the smiting of his master, he lost an eye, or even a tooth, he was to be instantly set free; and many are of opinion, from the absolute and universal nature of the language employed, that all foreign slaves came under the operation of the law of Jubilee, and regained their liberty in the fiftieth year. Besides all this, they shared in the rest of the Sabbath and the great annual festivals; they had a right to everything that grew of itself in the Sabbatical years; and everywhere the Hebrews are enjoined to treat them with special kindness, from the memory of their own Egyptian bondage. There was also a fugitive slave law, but it was of an entirely different kind from that which became so obnoxious in the history of this land. When a servant escaped from his master, it was presumed that he had good reason for running away; and therefore the law had this provision: "Thou shalt not deliver unto his master the servant which is escaped from his master unto thee: he shall dwell with thee, even among you, in that place which he shall choose in one of thy gates, where it liketh him best: thou shalt not oppress him."* "After all," as Milman† has said, "slavery is too harsh a term" to apply to this state of things; and the influence of this legislation may be seen in the fact that it has been made a question whether servitude, even in this modified form of it, existed in Palestine in the days of our Lord. It was to be found, indeed, in its most odious shape in the Roman Empire, in the days of the apostles; but there is nothing in the Gospel narratives to indicate its existence in any sense among the Jews. And if this view be correct, it furnishes ample vindication of the wisdom of the course which Moses followed in his legislation regarding it.

We might illustrate this characteristic of the Hebrew laws, also, in the matter of the *lex talionis*, and in that of the treatment of filial disobedience; but we have said enough to show how hollow must be the argument of those who attempt to sustain polygamy and slavery as Scriptural institutions, simply because they were not abrogated, but only regulated by the Mosaic law. The course of Moses was similar to that followed, at a later date, in reference to Roman slavery by the apostles. They did not enter upon a deliberate struggle with it, determined to crush it at once; for that would have instantly brought upon them the iron hand of imperial despotism. But they contented themselves with disseminating great principles, which would in the end elevate the public conscience to the conviction that it was sinful. And those who would defend either slavery or polygamy as permanent institutions, because the one was tolerated by Moses, and the other was not attacked by the apostles,

---

* Deut. xxiii., 15, 16.   † "History of the Jews," vol. i., p. 215.

are utterly oblivious of the fact that, from the first, society has been passing through a process of moral and spiritual education.* God, in both instances, spoke through his servants to the degree of intelligence then existing; and entering into that, he sought to purify and ennoble it. This is the explanation, which Mozley has so well elaborated in his work on "Ruling Ideas in Early Ages," of all those moral difficulties which arise when, with our New Testament notions which have been developing for nearly nineteen centuries, we study the historical parts of the Old Testament; and when we apply these principles not only to the Hebrew legislation, but also to such cases as those of the command of God to offer up Isaac, and the order to exterminate the Canaanites, the vindication is complete.

Still further, in judging of this code of laws we must have regard to the purpose for which the Hebrew nation was called into existence. The Pentateuch was not designed for a permanent and universal statute-book. The Hebrews were selected that God might train a people to be the ultimate disseminators of his truth throughout the world; and the legislation to which they were subjected, while, as we have seen, it was educational not for them alone, but for all others, was at the same time exclusive. They were hedged off from other nations by religious restrictions, and by enactments which forbade intermarriages with the heathen. If others chose to come and live in their territory, they were to be treated with kindness, but the Israelites were to keep themselves isolated and segregated. Much has been said in ridicule of this by unthinking men, and it cannot be denied that it did tend, through the depravity of the people's hearts, to foster in them ultimately a spirit of pride and vain-

---

* See Fairbairn's "Imperial Bible Dictionary," articles SLAVERY; MARRIAGE; LAW.

glory; yet, if you have regard to the divine plan in the case, you will see at once how easily it can be vindicated. Let me take two well-known institutions among ourselves by way of illustration. We have no standing army, or at least none to speak of; yet, in the exigencies of international relations, it may happen at some time or other that we shall have to go to war. But who then shall organize an army or man a navy for us? The country has answered that question by instituting and maintaining a military and a naval academy for the training of cadets as officers; and it relies that, in the event of their being needed, these competent men will bring to the occasion all the skill they have acquired at West Point and Annapolis. But, in order to give them that skill, they must, while they are in attendance at these institutions, be put under certain restrictions. They are, in a sense, secluded from the rest of the people. They do not mingle with them; they cannot come and go as they will; they are under special law, because they are under special training; and when the training is finished, the restraints are removed, and they will come forth again among the people, competent, in any emergency, to serve the country which has educated them for its defence. You do not complain of exclusiveness in such a case as that. It is imperatively demanded for the education of the young men; and, indeed, a certain degree of the same thing is needed in every school and college in the land. Now, Palestine was the West Point and Annapolis for the world. In that little country God was training up a people out of whom, when the fulness of the time should come, his Gospel cadets should emerge, fitted by all the training of all their national history for going out among the heathen and proclaiming the unsearchable riches of Christ. No doubt you reckon the terms in that old seminary by centuries rather than by months, but the principle is still the same; and our own procedure, in the cases which I have specified, furnishes at once an illustration and vindication of that system of exclusiveness which, by its religious rites and matrimonial restrictions, surrounded Palestine with a wall more impassable than that of China.

But it is more than time now that we turned to the legislation itself; and here, as the statute-book itself is in all your hands, the merest outline must suffice. At the foundation of the civil polity of the Hebrews, we find—three thousand years before the Declaration of Independence, and long before any other earthly nation had reached that broad table-land of liberty—the equality of every man before the law.* The people were represented in a great congregation, but we do not know either how the members of that body were appointed, or what was the proportion of their number to that of the population as a whole. All that appears is that it was a kind of rudimentary parliament, which was summoned on great occasions; for we find mention of it once or twice in the history of Moses,† and at least twice in the history of Joshua, while it recurs again in the histories of Samuel and David. Above this was a council of seventy, called "elders of the people, and officers over them,"‡ which formed a sort of upper house. The duties of these senators are not definitely stated, neither does it appear how they were appointed, though the presumption is that they were heads of houses; but, as they are associated with Moses at the rebellion of Korah, the probability is that they were the privy council, or cabinet of him whom God had for the time designated as the leader of the State. Judges, chosen by the people, but appointed for life, were designated, as we

---

* Lev. xix., 15; xxiv., 22; Deut. i., 17; xvi., 19.
† Num. xiv., 1–10; xvi., 2; Joshua xxiii., 1; xxiv., 1.
‡ Num. xi., 16.

recently saw, at the suggestion of Jethro; and as the jurisdiction was most minutely subdivided, with the right of appeal from the lower to the higher tribunals, there was no danger of delay in the administration of justice; while in important cases the decision of the ablest, wisest, and most experienced men in the nation was secured. Each tribe, again, had a separate autonomy of its own. Its members lived in one territory, had their own chief or sheik, with his counsellors, and governed their own affairs almost like a separate republic. But, lest that independence of the tribes should lead to the alienation of one from another, and the fostering of distinct interests among them, the unity of the nation as a whole was conserved by the religious code, and especially by the ordinance which required that three times in the year all the males should assemble at the place where the tabernacle should be fixed. The value of such a custom for the welding of the people together is apparent from the fact that when Jeroboam, with the ten tribes, separated from the other two, one of the first things which he did was to discourage the people under his rule from going to Jerusalem at the feasts, and to set up for them shrines at Dan and Bethel, the attractions of which might counteract those of the Temple on Moriah.

The only distinction which was made among the people was that between the tribe of Levi and the priests of the family of Aaron, and the rest of the nation; but that was a religious enactment, and did not in the least interfere with the civil liberty of the tribes. The priesthood, indeed, is sometimes spoken of by writers as a hierarchy, but the word, as applied to the sacred ministers of the Jewish religion, is a misnomer. The priests had no *ex officio* duties as civil rulers, like those of the English Bishops in the House of Lords; and care was taken, apparently, to withdraw them from all positions in which they could unduly and injuriously influence the people. "There were no private religious rites in which they were called to officiate. Circumcision was performed without their presence; marriage was a civil contract; from funerals they were interdicted. They were not mingled up with the body of the people; they dwelt in their own separate cities. Their wealth was ample, but not enormous."* Thus, though they were set apart from the people, they were not placed above them, but were, equally with others, amenable to the law; while, as priests, they were put under certain restrictions which affected themselves only.

In the matter of education, the great responsibility was laid by the Hebrew law-giver on the parent. The home was pre-eminently and peculiarly the school. Parents were commanded† to teach their children "when they sat in the house, and when they walked in the way, and when they lay down, and when they rose up." The commemorative festivals, like the Passover, were designed to stimulate the curiosity of the young, and dispose them to ask, "What mean ye by this service?" The very monuments of the land were constructed with an educational object in view;‡ and, as we saw in our last lecture, the tabernacle itself was a standing object-lesson, by which constantly the thoughts of the children would be raised to things spiritual and divine. Then, on each seventh year, at the feast of Tabernacles, the priests were commanded to read the law before all Israel in their hearing.§ Thus the sons of Aaron were, in a sense, also the teachers of the nation; but, in addition to them, a prophetical order was established, of which Moses was himself the first representative, which combined in itself many of the functions discharged among us by the press and the pulpit, and from which, ultimately, those schools of the sons

---

* Milman's "History of the Jews," vol. i., p. 208.
† Deut. vi., 7. ‡ Joshua iv., 5, 6. § Deut. xxxi., 10–13.

of the prophets arose whereby the people were so greatly blessed.

The criminal code of Moses took special cognizance of all injuries to person or to property. No ancient laws set anything like such a high value upon human life as those of the Hebrews did. Man was viewed, from first to last, in this statute-book as made in the image of God; and so, murder being the destruction of God's image, was regarded as a kind of secondary violation of the first commandment, and punished with death. The capital sentence could not be commuted into a fine. There was no redemption. In cases of manslaughter, as we have seen, a refuge was provided, pending investigation; but deliberate murder was always capitally punished; and in one instance, typical, probably, of a class, inexcusable carelessness which caused death was similarly treated. That instance was the following: if an ox gored a man so that he died, the beast was put to death; but if the owner had been warned of the dangerous habit of the animal, and had taken no means to prevent him from doing injury, he, too, was sentenced to death; though it is added, "If there be laid on him a sum of money, then he shall give for the ransom of his life whatsoever shall be laid upon him."* If the dead body of a slain man was found, and no one knew who had slain him, then the elders and judges of the city nearest to the place where it was found were to purge themselves over a heifer that had been sacrificed, and to make such a declaration as implied that they had instituted and finished the strictest inquiry into all the circumstances.† No one can read the section of the law bearing on this case without feeling that, in the absence of such facilities as the press has furnished in modern times, this was the best means of securing publicity and compel-

---

* Exod. xxi., 28–32.   † Deut. xxi., 1–9.

ling investigation; and there is little doubt that we have here the germ which, in our own legislation, has grown up into the coroner's inquest.

A further illustration of the sacredness of human life is found in the enactment that the builder of a house was to make a battlement, or balustrade, to the roof; and probably that was given only as an indication of a whole category of cases, the design being to enforce the principle that all proper precautions should be taken, so that no preventible death might be permitted to occur.

In the matter of property, the provisions of the Mosaic code were unique, and singularly adapted for the maintenance of the liberties and comfort of the people as a whole. The land was regarded as God's, and was divided to the people by lot. Every man thus became a landlord. If he were unfortunate or improvident, he might sell his patrimony, but not forever; for the great principle of the law was the inalienability of estates. At the Jubilee, every field reverted, without repurchase, to its original proprietor. Thus it became impossible for the rich to accumulate all the lands, and the political equality of the people was secured; while, no matter how wasteful individuals might be, they could not perpetuate a race of paupers. The eldest son had a double portion, the rest of the estate being divided equally among the other sons; and though it might have been supposed that, under such a system, the land would become over-populated and infinitesimally subdivided, practically no inconvenience arose.*

Theft was punishable by double or fourfold restitution; and if the man had not the means of making such return,

---

* Houses might be redeemed within a year; but if not so redeemed, they were permanently alienated, except in the case of the houses of the Levites, which might be redeemed at any time.

he might be sold into service for his transgression. A nocturnal robber might be slain as an outlaw.

A beautiful feature of the code was the care which it enjoined for the poor. The gleanings of every harvest-field were left to the fatherless and widow; the reaper might not go over it a second time. If the garment of the poor was taken in pledge, it was to be restored at nightfall; and the wages of the laborer were to be paid him day by day. The house of the poor man was his castle, and it could not be entered for the purpose of seizing that which he had pledged. Nothing absolutely necessary to life was to be taken as security; and not only usury, but all interest whatever, was forbidden for money lent to a Hebrew. And the same thoughtful kindness which dictated these statutes for men had regard also to the lower animals. The ox was not to be muzzled while treading out the corn; the mother-bird was not to be taken with its young; and beasts of unequal strength were not to be yoked together. Thus this code did much to soften the ferocity of manners, and to develop kindness and humanity among the people. The mere rehearsal of its main provisions, necessarily brief as it has been, is its noblest panegyric; and if we were to make ourselves familiar with its details, and compare them with the contemporary enactments of other nations, we should begin to understand how much the world has owed, even in the matter of jurisprudence, to the Hebrew law-giver; for, in the very points in which the best modern legislation has outgrown his system, it has done so only by the ampler development of its principles.

After the full consideration already given to the tabernacle ritual, I need not spend long on the religious and ceremonial departments of the Mosaic system. For me the statutes in these categories range themselves under three divisions. There is, first, that of *Expiation*, which includes the whole rubric of sacrifice, from the daily morning and evening burnt-offering to the elaborate service of the great day of annual atonement. The second is that of *Consecration*, which comprises the manifold purifications of individuals from different sorts of defilement, each of which had some symbolical connection with sin; the distinction between animals as clean or unclean; the holiness of the priests and Levites; and the holiness of the tabernacle and its furniture. The central truth of the old economy was the holiness of God maintained through sacrifice, while sin is forgiven; and the outcome of that was the dedication of the people, purified from sin, to the service of the Lord. The first was set forth in sacrifice, and the second was exhibited in the continued maintenance of their purity by the people through their divers washings, and their scrupulous attention to the kind of food they ate. Then the third division, under which may be ranged many provisions in this sacred code, is *Jubilation*. You cannot read the book of Leviticus without being struck with the number of sacred festivals which they enjoin. There was, first, the weekly Sabbath, which was not by any means the day of gloom which so many falsely associate with what they call the Jewish Sabbath. It was a joyous season, in which the household was glad before the Lord. Of the same sort was the *fête* of the new moon, which was specially brilliant in the seventh month of the year, and was then called the feast of Trumpets. Then there were the Passover, the Pentecost, the feast of Tabernacles, and the feast of the great day of Atonement, all of which were characterized by demonstrations of gladness, and each of which had its own peculiar element of delight. Besides these, every seventh year was one of gladsome rest; and at the end of seven times seven came the fiftieth, or Jubilee, year, whose advent brought with it the welcome sound of release from debt and bondage, and restoration to the lost inheritance, and so crowned the cycle with its coronet of glory and blessedness.

Expiation; Consecration; Jubilation. In what more condensed form could we set forth the three great principles of the Gospel than these? "Behold the Lamb of God, that taketh away the sin of the world;" "The temple of God is holy, which temple are ye;" "Rejoice in the Lord always: and again I say, Rejoice." Thus we condense the Leviticus of the Old Testament into the Gospel of the New; and that is always the noblest life into which these three elements enter in the fullest measure.*

I dare not detain you longer, but will simply leave with you two thoughts which you may elaborate for yourselves, and which seem to me to rise naturally from our consideration of this intensely interesting theme. In the first place, redemption does not absolve us from law, but only brings us under a higher rule. When the Hebrews were led forth from Egypt, they were not set free from all subjection. They only exchanged the iron despotism of Pharaoh, the tyrant, for the loving education of God the Father. In like manner, the sinner when forgiven is not set free from obligation. Nay, rather he is placed under a new law. From his Egypt he too is led to Sinai. Here is the whole philosophy of conversion as unfolded by Paul. "But now being made free from sin, and become servants to God, ye have your fruit unto holiness, and the end everlasting life." The

---

* Those who desire to prosecute the investigation of the interesting subject to which the foregoing lecture is devoted are recommended to study the learned work of Michaelis on the "Laws of Moses," and the "Commentaries on the Laws of the Ancient Hebrews," by E. C. Wines, D.D., LL.D., to both of which, and especially to the latter, I desire to express my personal obligations. The synopsis given by Dean Milman in his "History of the Jews" is a model of elegance, accuracy, and condensation.

law of holiness, therefore, is not made void by our redemption, but becomes only thereby the more sacred in our eyes.

In the second place, redemption makes a brotherhood among the redeemed, and stimulates us to kindness toward those who are as yet enslaved. The Hebrews were forbidden to oppress each other. They were commanded to assist each other in every emergency, because they had all been alike redeemed by God. So Christians should regard each other as brethren for Jesus' sake. And as the Hebrews were enjoined to be tender to the alien from the remembrance of their own Egyptian misery, so our hearts should go out in love and compassion to the ignorant and them who are out of the way. Brotherhood for believers, and compassion for the unconverted, these are for us, in the Church of Christ, the great lessons to be learned from the civil code of the Jews. May God help us to learn them well, and practise them constantly!

In after-days the tribes who were thus exhorted to mutual brotherhood became alienated from each other. Judah vexed Ephraim, and Ephraim envied Judah. More than once, indeed, their swords were turned against each other in fratricidal war; and, alas! the same evils have appeared during the Christian centuries, among those who profess to have been redeemed by the blood of the same Redeemer's cross. Oh! how often the folly of the Crusaders, who spent their energies in quarrelling with each other, instead of in battling with the common enemy, has been repeated by the people of God in their conflicts with the spiritual evils by which they are surrounded. They have expended, in controversy with each other about mint, and anise, and cummin, the strength which ought to have been put forth in seeking to mitigate the miseries of their fellow-men, and to advance the cause of holiness and benevolence. Thus the lack of brotherhood among believers themselves has paralyzed the Church in front of the scepticism and immorality of the world; but when we go back, in simple faith, to the one great fact of our redemption, we shall be both brought into closer fellowship with each other, and stimulated to more tender regard for the salvation of men.

On the wall of the study of that Olney vicarage so long occupied by the good John Newton, these words were inscribed: "Remember that thou wast a bondsman in the land of Egypt, and the Lord thy God delivered thee;" and in the overmastering sense of personal obligation which these words, thus selected as his motto by that earnest man, express, we find the root of his brotherhood to all believers, and his intense passion for the salvation of souls. Let us get back to this same humble, grateful, loving spirit to-night, and we shall go forth with new tenderness to our fellow-Christians, and with new consecration to those works of faith and labors of love by which the world is to be regenerated. God grant us grace to receive this deliverance for ourselves; and then we shall show, in the new life of the Gospel, something higher far than the old brotherhood of the law.

XVI.

FINAL INCIDENTS AT SINAI.

LEVITICUS x., 1-20; xxiv., 10-16; NUMBERS x., 29-32.

THE tabernacle was set up on the first day of the first month; and on the twentieth day of the second month the encampment of the tribes at Sinai was broken up, and the people moved forward to the wilderness of Paran.* Between these two dates many interesting and important events occurred. Indeed, the entire book of Leviticus belongs to this interval; and within these fifty days were given the great rubrics which for so many generations regulated the sacrificial, ceremonial, and festive institutions of the Jewish nation. We cannot attempt to present even an analysis of these enactments, but must restrict our attention to the few incidents of a personal and public character which, after the manner of Moses, he has recorded in connection with his laws.

The first of these is the sad termination of a most solemn and important service. After they had been invested with their appropriate garments, and anointed with the sacred oil, and marked on ear and hand and foot with the blood of sacrifice, Aaron and his sons had remained in a state of probationary separation for seven days at the door of the tabernacle. Then the high-priest was formally inaugurated into his office by the presentation of different kinds of offerings in the manner specified for each, and by being introduced

---

* Exod. xi., 1; Num. x., 11-13.

by Moses into the tabernacle. Thus far everything had gone well, and the approbation of God was evinced by the descent of fire miraculously upon the altar of burnt-offering, which, when the people saw, they "shouted, and fell upon their faces."* But, before the day closed, their joy was turned into mourning; for Nadab and Abihu, the two elder sons of Aaron, who had been with him and the seventy elders at the sacramental feast upon the Mount, were guilty of such irreverence that they were stricken dead in a moment by the lightning-flash of Jehovah's indignation. The particular act of disobedience for which they were thus summarily punished is somewhat involved in obscurity. The record says that they "took either of them his censer, and put fire therein, and put incense thereon, and offered strange fire before the Lord, which he commanded them not."† Now, this may mean either that the fire which they put into their censers had not been taken from the altar of burnt-offering, as the law prescribed; or that the incense which they burned was not that which the Lord had so minutely designated for the purpose; or that, forgetting the specific enactments for their guidance, they had been carried away with the excitement of the occasion, and had gone at a wrong time to offer incense within the holy place. Perhaps the last of these hypotheses is the correct one, for the times appointed for the burning of incense were morning and evening, when the lamps were trimmed and lighted; and, if we are correct in supposing that this judgment occurred on the day of Aaron's installation, then we can see that the morning would be required for the offering of sacrifices; while his vindication of himself to Moses‡ for not eating the sin-offering, shows that the evening had not yet come when his sons were killed. Therefore we may conclude that they took it upon themselves to offer

---

* Lev. ix., 24.   † Ib. x., 1.   ‡ Ib. x., 19.

incense at an unauthorized time, and, erring in that respect, they might not be particular, either, as to the fire they employed; so that we may combine in one, two out of the three possible interpretations of the words, and find in that combination the true description of their conduct.

But how came they to be thus unmindful of the responsibilities of their position? No explanation of their rashness is given in plain statement in the narrative; but the fact that the law forbidding the priests to drink wine when they went into the tabernacle was enacted in immediate connection with the death and burial of these two newly-consecrated priests, leads to the inference that they were under the influence of strong drink when they thus foolhardily intruded into the holy place. Sin-offerings, burnt-offerings, and peace-offerings had been already made that day; and, in connection with these, it is quite possible that they had partaken somewhat freely of the wine which formed one of the constituent parts of at least one of these kinds of oblations. I do not mean to say that they were so inebriated as to be unconscious of what they were doing, but probably they were so excited as to be reckless; and, thus viewed, their case is an illustration of the fact that much evil may be done by those who, though they have been taking wine, are yet a good way from being what would be called intoxicated. The balance of their judgment had been disturbed; their caution had been destroyed; and in the enthusiasm of the moment, when they heard the shout of the people, they rushed on to do that which, if it had not been for the wine, they would never have dreamed of attempting.

It may seem to some that this was a dreadful punishment for such an offence; but we have to take into account, in estimating the severity of this judgment, the purpose which God had in view in the whole tabernacle ritual. His design was to lead the people up to something like an adequate idea of the majesty of his holiness. For this end it was that the symbol of his presence among them was doubly veiled from their view, and that the priests could enter his palace only at certain times and in certain ways. Any infringement of his laws in these respects, therefore, was an insult to his holiness; in particular, the taking of common fire for the purpose of burning incense was a severing of the connection which he had established between the altar of sacrifice and the altar of service; and so the overlooking of such an act would have neutralized the lesson that only through the fire of love, which is kindled in the heart by the acceptance of forgiveness over sacrifice, can we offer to God the incense of holy service. Moreover, this was the first day of the new ritual; and as in a mutiny sternness in the outbreak is truest kindness in the end, so here the marking of this irreverence with such swift and awful judgment was the best possible means of insuring caution in the priesthood of every after-age. We have a similar case in the breach of Uzzah, when David was bringing up the ark; and under the New Testament dispensation we see the operation of the same law in the deaths of Ananias and Sapphira, and especially, perhaps, in those of the Corinthian Christians who had been "drunken" at the table of the Lord. On each of these occasions there was what was virtually a new departure in the progress of men toward the great goal of human perfection; and, therefore, in connection with each of them a solemn and important lesson was given, the effects of which were in the highest degree salutary in all concerned.

But in this case, also, as in that of the Corinthians, the judgment was simply temporal death. Nadab and Abihu had just come out of Egypt, bringing much of their Egyptian error with them; and it is not unlikely that they were trying to wed some of their former notions to their new service, even as the Corinthians supposed that they must keep the feast of Christ as they used to keep those of their old idols. So, as we are not warranted to conclude that these mistaken Christians at Corinth were visited with everlasting punishment, neither are we at liberty to draw such an inference in reference to the sons of Aaron. The mere infliction of temporal death as a penalty did not carry with it, of necessity, the permanent exclusion of the soul from fellowship with God, for Moses himself died on Nebo, as we shall afterward see, in consequence of his sin at Meribah; and, therefore, we must not suppose that because the sons of Aaron were smitten in the act of irreverence they were excluded from the heavenly Canaan.

But, though that was not necessarily involved in their punishment, yet the time, place, and manner of their death were such as must have produced the deepest and most painful impression on the people. On Aaron, especially, the blow must have fallen with terrible severity; and though in the matter of the golden calf we have had occasion to criticise his weakness, yet under this trying ordeal he manifested the calmest self-control. As he contemplated the awful spectacle of his sons stricken together in death, Moses came to him and said, "This is it that the Lord spake, saying, I will be sanctified in them that come nigh me, and before all the people I will be glorified." But no murmuring word escaped the high-priest's lips — he "held his peace." He could not say just then, perhaps, with Job, "Blessed be the name of the Lord;" but he would not say anything derogatory to the honor or the glory of Jehovah. His silence was not that of stubborn stoicism, nor that of unfeeling indifference, but that of patient submission. He felt keenly, for he loved his sons, and had an honest pride in their consecration to the priestly office; but the Lord had done it; and though the circumstances were unusually painful, he quietly acquiesced, not because it was inevitable, but because it was the doing of him whose minister he was. No such wail of agony came from him as that which burst from the broken heart of David when Absalom was slain; and, though he could not sing a hymn of trustful affection, like that which Paul Gerhardt chanted over his dead boy, yet his very silence was the bowing of a soul which said, "The will of the Lord be done." The deepest sympathy is often speechless, and truest resignation is often that which holds its peace. Silence sometimes is a better interpreter of the soul than speech, and he who reads the heart never misunderstands its dumbness. On ordinary occasions, Aaron was of ready utterance, but no address he ever made was so eloquent as this holding of his peace. Truly, he was great in grief; and remembering that, we can afford to pass lightly over his imperfections in other respects. Ye who have wept irrepressible tears over the biers of your children — taken from you not by such a sudden and suggestive visitation of God, but after weeks of illness—may understand how hard it was for Aaron here to control himself, and you will not accuse him of stolidity, but rather think of him as illustrating the poet's words:

> "Pain's furnace heat within me quivers,
>   God's breath upon the flame doth blow;
> And all my heart in anguish shivers
>   And trembles at the fiery glow;
> And yet I whisper, 'As God will!'
> And in his hottest fire stand still."

But the death of his sons was not his only affliction; for the restrictions of his office would not allow him to attend to their remains, and so his nearest relatives who were not priests were called upon to carry forth the corpses from before the sanctuary out of the camp; while he and his surviving sons were forbidden either to uncover their heads or to rend their clothes, and were commanded to go on with the performance of their sacred duties. This they all faithfully observed; but when it came to the eating of the sin-offering in the holy precinct, they had no heart for food; and when Moses blamed not Aaron, but Eleazar and Ithamar for this, the high-priest made reply, "Behold, this day have they offered their sin-offering and their burnt-offering before the Lord; and such things have befallen me: and if I had eaten the sin-offering to-day, should it have been accepted in the sight of the Lord?" and when Moses heard that, he was content. It was an acceptable fast; and in this case the instinct of Aaron's heart was more nearly right than the judgment of Moses's head.

Shortly after this painful chastisement, another incident almost equally distressing occurred. There was in the camp of Dan a woman named Shelomith, who had during the days of their slavery married an Egyptian husband, by whom she had a son. This son, now grown to man's estate, accompanied his mother at the Exodus; and, while the tribes were encamped at Sinai, a dispute arose between him and one of the Israelites, in the course of which he "blasphemed the name,* and cursed." This greatly shocked all who heard the words; but, as no law had as yet been given for such cases, the judges to whom he was brought knew not what to do, and put him in confinement until the mind of the Lord might be shown them. When Moses consulted the oracle, the Lord commanded him to take the guilty one without the camp, and to have him stoned to death by all the members of the congregation—after they had laid their hands upon his head; and it was enacted that every blasphemer should be punished in a similar manner. It is hardly necessary to repeat what we have already said in re-

---

* That is, the sacred and incommunicable name of God (Lev. xxiv., 10–16).

gard to such legislation; but, to prevent misconception, we must remind you that we are dealing with a theocracy, where the distinction between sin and crime did not exist, and where blasphemy, like idolatry, was virtual high-treason. That will account for the severity of the penalty here inflicted on what is now regarded as a sin rather than a crime; while, at the same time, it will explain why it is that we cannot reason from a State in which God was the king to one like ours, where the civil constitution is of the nature of a mutual compact entered into by the citizens themselves. Yet, though blasphemy is not punished among us as it was in the instance to which we are here referring, let no one imagine that it is now any less heinous as a sin in the sight of God than it ever was; for the third commandment is to-day as binding as it was when it first thundered from Sinai in the ears of the multitude; and, though human law takes no cognizance of the evil, we may be sure that the Lord "will not hold him guiltless that taketh his name in vain."

After the erection of the tabernacle, Moses organized the encampment, and gave to each tribe its place, not only in relation to the sacred enclosure, but also on the march; while at the same time he gave orders for the making of the silver trumpets, and explained how they were to be blown, so as to give the different signals for the summoning of the assembly or the princes, or for the making of their journeyings. It is interesting, as indicating the wisdom of Moses, to mark how the different tribes were arranged, so as to prevent as far as possible the outbreak of jealousies and rivalries and animosities between them: for the schism which was made by Jeroboam after the death of Solomon had its roots away back in early divisions; and even in Moses's time the spirit which ripened into that revolt was already at work. Judah and Ephraim were the great rivals, each wishing the sovereignty; and so to them were given the two posts of honor, the one in the front, and the other in the rear, alike in the encampment round the tabernacle and on the march. This kept them always as far apart as possible. Judah led the van; but from Ephraim, Joshua, the military leader, was selected. Judah had in its encampment Issachar and Zebulon, younger sons of the same mother, Leah; while Ephraim had with it Benjamin and Manasseh, both of whom, like Ephraim, were the descendants of Rachel. Reuben was Jacob's eldest son, but his birthright was taken from him; yet, to prevent anything like sullen discontent, his tribe was placed at the head of another division. But even that precaution was not entirely successful; for at the rebellion of Korah the discontented Levites were joined by Dathan, Abiram, and On, all of whom belonged to the tribe of Reuben; and it is a singular coincidence that the Reubenites occupied the south side of the tabernacle, having the Kohathites between them and the sacred tent, so that their proximity to each other gave them ample opportunities for hatching a plot.

The standards of the different encampments are nowhere described in Scripture; but Jewish tradition has given to the four leaders the four cherubic symbols—to Judah the lion, to Reuben the man, to Ephraim the ox, and to Dan the eagle; while the ground on which these symbols were embroidered was of the same color as the precious stone in the breastplate of the high-priest, on which the name of the tribe to which it belonged was engraved.

In connection with the preparations for breaking up the encampment, a census was taken, which gave the number of fighting men at 603,500. The Levites, who numbered 22,000, were adopted by God, and consecrated to him, in lieu of the first-born whom he had spared on the night of the Exodus; but as these last outnumbered the Levites by

273, the surplus was redeemed by the payment of five shekels for each individual to Aaron and his sons.

Before they set out, the Passover was observed for the only time between Egypt and Canaan; the Levites were consecrated; various laws relating to personal and tribal purification were enacted; the beautiful form of priestly benediction was prescribed; and when, at length, the signal was given to march, Moses affectionately entreated his friend and brother-in-law, Hobab, to accompany them in their journeyings. So natural and affecting was the colloquy between them, that we must reproduce it in its original simplicity: "Moses said unto Hobab, the son of Raguel the Midianite, Moses's father-in-law, We are journeying unto the place of which the Lord said, I will give it you: come thou with us, and we will do thee good: for the Lord hath spoken good concerning Israel. And he said unto him, I will not go, but I will depart to mine own land, and to my kindred. And he said, Leave us not, I pray thee; forasmuch as thou knowest how we are to encamp in the wilderness, and thou mayest be to us instead of eyes. And it shall be, if thou go with us, yea, it shall be, that what goodness the Lord shall do unto us, the same will we do unto thee." And he went with them; for in the book of Judges mention is made of his children as dwelling in the land of promise.*

In reviewing the course over which this evening we have come, we find three important practical lessons suggested for our consideration.

There is, first, the danger of tampering with strong drink. As we have seen, we can hardly be wrong in attributing the irreverence of Nadab and Abihu to the influence of wine. And when we read such a law as this, "Do not drink wine, nor strong drink, thou nor thy sons with thee, when ye go

---

* Judg. i., 16.

into the tabernacle of the congregation," we may not forget that all Christians now are priests, and that, as they are always doing service before the Lord, they ought to be specially on their guard against the snare in which Nadab and Abihu were taken. It might be unwarranted, indeed, if we were from such a passage as that to evolve the principle that every Christian should be an abstainer from strong drink; but it is equally unwarranted, on the other side, to seek to restrict it to ministers of religion when they are engaged in the conduct of the sanctuary services: for now the Christian priesthood is as wide as the circle of believers; and the sphere of service is not narrowed within any so-called holy place, but is co-extensive with the area of our daily lives. Therefore, the warning which this law suggests is appropriate, not to clergymen alone, but to all who profess and call themselves Christians. It is, no doubt, a healthy public sentiment among us which requires that ministers of the Gospel should be above suspicion in this respect; but the danger is as great for others as for them, and there is need here for universal caution. The very nature of strong drink is such as to require that we should be on our guard in dealing with it, for its tendency is to dethrone reason; and even when taken in quantities far short of producing absolute drunkenness, it removes the brake from the balance-wheel of judgment, and makes the man reckless, defiant, and self-willed. Nothing is more difficult than to secure an exact definition of intoxication; and scarcely any two men will agree in their testimony as to whether, in certain described circumstances, a person was or was not what we call drunk. Yet I do not think that in modern society generally we are enough alive to the fact that even that which some would call moderation may be the cause of great mischief, by reason of the unnatural excitement which it produces in the system. I have a profound conviction that a very large proportion of so-called accidents, alike on land and on sea, on the railroad and in the workshop, are the result of drinking which is short of intoxication. Enough has been taken to make the man reckless, but not enough to make him stupid. An on-looker would not be warranted to call him drunk; and yet if he had not been "tasting the wine," he would not have been so rash and thoughtless. Thus, one in such a condition goes to attend to an engine or to look after a boiler, and the result is an explosion, which causes the deaths of a score of people and the loss of much valuable property; or a locomotive engineer, in that exhilarated state, perfectly rational to all appearance, but yet inwardly excited and unbalanced, forgets to look for the signal, or does not see that it stands at danger, and so lets the train dash on to ruin; or a merchant, in a similar plight, goes to make his purchases, and buys such materials and at such prices as clearly convince him, when he returns to his home and examines the goods, that his judgment had been blinded, even although nobody would have dared to call him drunk. Now, all such cases are so many parallels to that of Nadab and Abihu as I have this evening described it; and they all go to establish the conclusion that the safest course is to have nothing whatever to do with strong drink as an ordinary beverage.

But the blinding and exciting influence of wine is not its only evil; for it produces a craving for itself, and creates an artificial appetite of the most appalling sort. It is one of the daughters of the horse-leech, which is continually calling, "Give, give!" The oftener you indulge in it, the oftener you want to repeat the folly; until at length, in the case of the drunkard, the physical system becomes so diseased that the taste or smell of the liquor will set the whole man aflame with the desire to have it; and he will go on and on, into the horror of delirium tremens. The beginning is thus like the putting of a train of cars on an inclined plane; and, the end is the catastrophe which occurs when, at the bottom of the slope, they are all piled upon each other in promiscuous and irreparable ruin. Of course you will say that, though this has been the case with hundreds, there is no fear of you; but so all these hundreds said at one stage of their career, and they felt—what you too may feel—that appetite and custom were too many for them in the end—for custom here comes in to intensify the danger. How strange it is that men will always admit that there is peril in strong drink, and yet, in spite of the peril, will put it on their tables, and make it the acknowledged offering of hospitality and the general symbol of good-fellowship! They do not deal thus with other dangerous elements. You would not handle gunpowder so freely in close proximity to fire as you handle strong drink in the immediate neighborhood of your friends and children; yet the danger is probably not greater to property in the one case than it is to character in the other. Therefore, while the drink retains its nature and the custom keeps its hold, it is safest by far for you never to touch it, save under medical supervision. The mere possibility of your being harmed by it, or of your doing harm through it, ought to be enough for you; and so care for others, as well as caution for yourselves, should lead you to abstinence. Nor can I forbear to add that it is in this way that you will best secure the redemption of those who have already fallen. They *must* abstain. There is no middle course possible for them; but their abstinence will be easier and your influence will be stronger if you abstain along with them. When the Lord of all will say to each of us, in reference to those whom intemperance has ruined, "Where is thy brother?" what answer shall we give? We dare not say we are not their keepers, for in the light of the Gospel of Jesus Christ that cannot be maintained; but if we are persisting in the common use as a daily beverage of that which is causing our brethren's destruction, and so maintaining the customs which have wrought their ruin, can we say that we have done all we might have done to help them? And if we cannot, are we guiltless? I judge no man; I simply present these questions for the consideration of every thoughtful hearer. I ask that they may be fairly faced and deliberately answered, lest at length, when we stand before the bar of God, the "Lady's Dream" of the poet may prove the waking reality of our experience, and we may be compelled to say, like her—ah me!

> "The wounds I might have heal'd,
>   The human sorrow and smart;
> And yet it never was in my soul
>   To play so ill a part.
> But evil is wrought by want of thought,
>   As well as want of heart."

But the second lesson suggested by the history over which to-night we have come is the evil of intermarriages between the people of God and those who care not for his name. It is not without deliberate purpose that Moses has here so carefully recorded the fact that the blasphemer's father was an Egyptian; and many passages of ancient Hebrew history emphasize the warning which is thus, by implication, given. But perhaps the most suggestive of them all is that which has been so recently before the attention of all our Sunday-scholars as they have been studying the International series of lessons. Jehoshaphat, the good king of Judah, entered into a political alliance with Ahab and Jezebel, who then occupied the throne of Israel. That led to a marriage between Jehoram, the son of Jehoshaphat, and Athaliah, the daughter of Jezebel, who seems to have had all the unscrupulous cruelty and all the idolatrous fervor for which her mother was so infamous. Her son Ahaziah succeeded his father, but was slain by Jehu; and then, murdering all the seed royal, save one little boy of six years old, who was concealed from her, she made herself the reigning sovereign, and spent six years in introducing Baalism into Jerusalem, and despoiling the Temple of its treasures and its glory. Nay, long after her death the evil leaven appeared again in Joash, the boy-king, whose life had been so signally preserved; and thus the Jezebelism of that fatal intermarriage wrought itself out in cruelty and idolatry from generation to generation. I know that you will say that the effects in modern families cannot be so disastrous as they were in that instance, and that we may not reason from the case of kings to those of persons in common life; but, in reply, I affirm that such a case as that of Jehoram and Athaliah is like the picture in the stereopticon, enlarged and illuminated, so that we may see all the more clearly the character of the consequences which commonly ensue in ordinary households. What the lantern and the lens and the limelight are to the slide, that the royalty of the parties and the fierce and unsparing illumination of inspiration are to the instance which I have cited; and few chapters in history, whether ancient or modern, can furnish such an enforcement of Paul's command, "Be not unequally yoked, believers with unbelievers," as it affords. I say not, indeed, that the issue in every case is blasphemy, idolatry, and moral ruin, for there have been marked exceptions. Ahaz was the wicked son of a good father, and Hezekiah was the good son of a wicked father; therefore we cannot speak unqualifiedly here. But the tendency of all such unions is evil, and the families are too frequently characterized by spiritual indifference. There is a warning against them, so that they who enter into them incur a fearful peril. The Christian rule is, "Only in the Lord;" and they who observe that do thereby make themselves heirs to the promise which Peter declared is to us and to our children. They who are not one in Christ are destitute of the highest happiness of married life; and the children, according to my observation, are often worse than those both of whose parents are indifferent to Christ and his salvation. They are not so always; but there is danger that those who are guilty of Shelomith's thoughtlessness may at length be visited with Shelomith's sorrow; so let all young people prayerfully ponder the apostolic law, and see that they obey it.

Finally, we have in the colloquy between Moses and Hobab a beautiful illustration of the reciprocity of true friendship. Moses and Hobab had learned to love each other during the shepherd sojourn of the former in the land of Midian; and in their recent fellowship in the Sinaitic valley they had grown even more closely into each other. From a mere vague monotheism Hobab had advanced, under Moses's influence, to a fuller knowledge of the personal, living Jehovah, while the advice of Hobab, like that of his father Jethro, may have been valuable to Moses in many secular matters. So they were loath to part; and, therefore, Hobab yielded ultimately to Moses's entreaty to remain beside him. But see the ground on which Moses puts his request. "Thou mayest be to us instead of eyes; and what goodness the Lord shall do unto us, the same will we do unto thee." There was true friendship, consisting in the interchange of mutual help; and we may learn from that, on the one hand, not to look for companions who shall be the mere echoes of ourselves; and, on the other, not to think of getting without giving in such a relationship. "A man that hath friends must show himself friendly," and those are ever the most profitable fellowships in which the weakness of the one party is fortified by the strength of the other. Moses was ears to Hobab to hear what the Lord might say, and to share with him the knowledge which he thus obtained; and Hobab was eyes to Moses, to communicate to him all his familiarity with that trackless desert in which he had lived so long. So they journeyed on, each helping the other; like Peter and John in a later day, and both illustrating the graces of self-sacrifice and fidelity. Moses received the earthly assistance, and sought to reward it by sharing the spiritual blessing; even as Paul tried ever to repay his benefactors by enriching them with the blessings of salvation. Let not this lesson be lost on you young men, who are beginning the journey of life, and looking out for those with whom you may prosecute your pilgrimage, and who may prove helpful to you by the way. Search for such as have a large measure of those qualities in which you are conscious of your own deficiency; and be ready to make return by imparting to them of those things in which you are strong, while they are weak. Let the young seek to share in the experience of the old, and the old refresh themselves with the vivacity of the young. It was a rule with the elder Lord Lytton to have all his friends older than himself until he was forty years of age, but after that to turn and cultivate the younger; and there was great wisdom in his resolution. Remember, however, that no friendship will be truly helpful that leads you away from fellowship with God; and be careful to accept those only who will journey with you "to the place of which the Lord hath said, I will give it you." Make that the test of all your friendships, and you will find at least one Friend that "sticketh closer than a brother."

But how can I conclude without making an appeal to you, who have come in to mingle in our worship for this evening, but have not yet cast in your lot anywhere with the people of God? We would have you come with us. We know whither we are going. We have a good guide; a sure provider; an unfailing protector; and a happy destination. Come with us. You will share all these blessings with us. The Lord, whom we follow, will give you pardon, peace, holiness, heaven. You need all these. You cannot get them elsewhere than in Christ. And the Church of Christ needs you. There is a work waiting for you, which only you can perform. There are spheres of usefulness which only you can fill. You will be to the Church instead of eyes, and will bring reports of misery to be relieved, and ignorance to be instructed, of which otherwise we might not have heard. Do not stand outside criticising any longer. Come in and help us, and you will find then that the Church will strengthen you. She will gird you with her prayers; nourish you with her ordinances; cheer you with her love; and encourage you with her co-operation. "Come with us and we will do you good, for the Lord hath spoken good concerning Israel."

XVII.

MURMURINGS.

NUMBERS xi.

AT length, after a sojourn of all but twelve months* at the base of Sinai, the cloud-pillar ascended from the midst of the camp; and Moses, recognizing the appointed signal for departure, said, "Rise up, Lord, and let thine enemies be scattered; and let them that hate thee flee before thee." As soon as they heard these words, a portion of the Kohathites, bearing the ark of the covenant upon their shoulders, set forward, followed by the tribes of Judah, Issachar, and Zebulon. The Gershonites and the Merarites, with the external parts of the tabernacle, went next; and behind them Reuben, Simeon, and Gad took up their march; while the rest of the Kohathites, carrying the sacred vessels, brought up their rear. Next the tribes of Ephraim, Manasseh, and Benjamin moved into line; and those of Dan, Asher, and Naphtali formed the rear-guard of the host. It must have been an imposing spectacle when the solitudes of those mountain passes were filled by this moving multitude, not one of whom knew precisely where they were to pitch their tents at nightfall, and all of whom depended implicitly for their guidance on the mystic cloud, which hovered on unceasingly before them. On this occasion it took them in the direction of the wilderness of Paran; and after three

---

* The exact time spent in the Sinaitic valley was a year, all but ten days.

days it rested at a place which became memorable in their history, because it was the scene of a double calamity.

When Moses saw the halting of the pillar, he cried, "Return, O Lord, to the many thousands of Israel;" and once again the tabernacle was raised, while the tribes took their appointed stations round it. But with the renewed experience of the difficulties of travel through these rocky and fatiguing wadys, the old spirit of discontent broke out among the people; and their complaints were displeasing unto the Lord. This was a more serious evil now that they had been at Sinai, and seen so much of the greatness and majesty of Jehovah, and had entered into covenant with him, than it had been before; and we cannot but observe that, from this point on, their murmurings were visited with severer chastisements than they had been on the march from Egypt to Sinai. Indeed, at Marah and Sin the Lord had borne with them as one bears with the weakness and ignorance of childhood, for then they had not had much opportunity of knowing him; but now that they had experienced his goodness for a whole year, and had seen and heard so much of his glory, there was no excuse whatever for their discontent, and, therefore, every complaint they made was severely punished. Their sin was no longer one of ignorance, and therefore it could not be overlooked; so, either by lightning or in some other way which clearly connected it with the divine displeasure, a fire was sent upon the outskirts of the camp, and consumed those whose tents were in the neighborhood of its outbreak. It seems to have commenced at one of the extremities of the encampment, and we can easily imagine the panic which it created. They had no facilities for putting out a conflagration; and, if the wind were high, and blowing in an unfavorable direction, the consequences might have been disastrous. In their consternation they cried to Moses, and Moses cried unto the Lord, by whom, in answer to his prayer, the fire was quenched.

But the spirit of mutiny was harder to extinguish than the flames had been, and very soon it broke out anew in a more aggravated form. It may be remembered that on the night of the Exodus a multitude of Egyptians joined themselves to the Hebrews, and went with them into the wilderness. These persons belonged to the lower order of the people; and, having little to lose, we may suppose that they were animated mainly by the love of adventure, or by the desire of change. Some of them, perhaps, were genuine converts, but the majority were idle hangers-on; for the terms by which they are designated literally mean the "riffraff," or "loafers," and their presence was anything but a blessing. Indeed, from the fact that the fire to which we have just referred began in the outskirts of the camp, and was confined to them, some have supposed that it fell not upon the encampment proper, but on the irregular and ill-regulated tents of these lawless stragglers, and have concluded that *they* were the complainers against whom principally it was directed. But, however that may have been, it is certain that, even before they moved from this first station after Sinai, these low-caste Egyptians began to cry out very loudly for flesh to eat. They looked back longingly to that which, when they had it, they cared little for; and talked with gusto of the fish, the cucumbers, the melons, the leeks, and the garlic which they had eaten so freely in their native land — nay, not content with magnifying the excellence of these national dainties, they despised the manna which God had miraculously provided. Their discontent spread like the contagion of an evil disease, and very soon the Israelites also became infected with it; so that throughout the camp the people were weeping, and crying, "Who shall give us flesh to eat?"

Moses was terribly discouraged. On the one hand, he knew that the Lord would be displeased; on the other, he perceived that the disease was likely to be chronic with the people; and as he thought of the difficulties and perplexities attendant on the office of a mediator between the two, he was fairly overwhelmed, and cried to Jehovah in the bitterness of his soul, "I am not able to bear all this people alone, because it is too heavy for me. And if thou deal thus with me, kill me, I pray thee, out of hand, if I have found favor in thy sight; and let me not see my wretchedness." Is this the man that has talked so often face to face with God? Is this the dauntless hero that never quailed before the haughty Pharaoh? Is this the resolute and determined ruler who stood alone against an idolatrous host? Alas, it is even so, and he who has already so often reminded us of Elijah is now, like the Tishbite, praying for death. But let us not judge him harshly whom Jehovah has not condemned. No mere man can be a perfect mediator between God and men. The burden of the people was too heavy for him to bear. He did, indeed, in a sense, carry their sins and bear their sorrows. He did, indeed, in a sense, feel the scorching of that fire which they provoked. But he sank beneath the load. How true it was, as Kurtz has said, that the real mediator was not yet! *He* had not come, who could without a murmur carry the burden of a world's sin. There was only one who could with steady step and unrepining heart, not only bear with, but bear the guilt of men, and *he* was more than *man*. We need not blame Moses, therefore, because he was not Christ; but from the failure of the greatest of mere men here, we may learn to value the mediation of him who "himself bare our sins in his own body *to* the tree," and *on* it, saying the while, "The cup which my Father hath given me, shall I not drink it?"

The Lord had compassion on his servant, and gave him seventy men to help him in his work; qualifying them for the purpose by making them sharers with him in the special graces of the Holy Spirit. He did not take from Moses anything which he possessed, but out of the plenitude of his resources he gave them of the same spirit; and that his discouraged friend might have full assurance of the fact, he called them out before the people and made them stand around the tabernacle, and, while they occupied that prominent position, he talked with them out of the cloud, and the Spirit rested upon them and they prophesied. But two of those who had been designated as Moses's colleagues had from modesty, or from some other cause, remained in the camp; yet upon them also the Spirit came, and, as they prophesied under his influence, Joshua ran to Moses, to complain of the irregularity, and to ask that it might be prohibited, but the noble man replied, "Enviest thou, for my sake? Would God that all the Lord's people were prophets, and that the Lord would put his Spirit upon them." It is an interesting remark of Trench on this incident, that "in the dividing of the Spirit which Moses had upon the seventy elders of Israel, we recognize an earlier, though a weaker Pentecost, in which, however, the later was surely implied; for if from the servant could be imparted of his Spirit, how much more and in what larger measure from the Son. This should be contemplated as a preparatory working in a lower sphere of the same Spirit, which afterward wrought more gloriously in the later and crowning act; as knit to that later by an inner law, as sharer of the same organic life with it."*

But though the Lord was thus gracious to his overburdened servant, he punished severely the discontented people,

---

* Trench, "Hulsean Lectures," p. 74, quoted also by Jamieson *in loc.*

and he did so through giving them that which they desired. For, though the faith even of Moses was staggered at the very mention of it when he intimated his design, he brought, as he had done a year before, flocks of quails over the camp; but this time they were in such abundance that they fell, "as it were a day's journey on this side, and as it were a day's journey on the other side, round about the camp, and as it were two cubits high upon the ground." That does not mean, however, that the dead birds lay upon the ground to the depth of two cubits, for the word "high" is supplied by the authorized version; but that the quails, wearied with their flight, flew about breast-high, and were easily secured by the people. The result may be easily anticipated. After so long abstinence from flesh, this surfeit of animal food bred a pestilence among the people, and many of them died; so that they named the place Kibroth-Hattaavah, the graves of lust, or greediness. Thus these two miracles, the bringing of the quails, and the inflicting of judgment upon the people, were wrought by the divine energy through natural causes; for it is nothing unusual for these birds to appear in such quantities and at such a height from the ground as to be easily secured; and God's wrath aggravated the natural consequences of a surfeit into a special visitation. But now, reviewing this history, let us take with us some of those practical lessons which it so richly suggests.

We may learn, then, in the first place, that those who are merely hangers-on to a church are usually the beginners of mischief among its members. It is not without significance that we are informed in this place that the murmuring of the tribes had its origin in the discontent of the mixed multitude. They did not belong to the chosen race; they had no fixed principles; they left Egypt simply for what they thought they could make by it; and we cannot wonder, therefore, that they were disappointed when for rest they had toil, and for variety of food they had an unchanging diet. There was nothing in them to sustain them under such a trial. They could not fall back upon the spiritual privileges to which Israel had been called, for they did not care for these; neither could they look forward to the land of promise, for it was not promised to them, and therefore we can very well account for their dissatisfaction. But the misfortune was that the proximity of the Hebrews made them also liable to be infected by this fickleness; and thus it came about that what began among the mere outsiders spread ultimately through the camp. The same thing has been seen often since. Judas was no true disciple; yet his remark concerning Mary's use of the ointment, when he said, "To what purpose is this waste? ought not this ointment to have been sold for three hundred pence, and given to the poor?" started off all the other eleven upon the same track; and the heart of the loving woman might have been wounded by their rudeness, or broken by their unfeelingness, if Jesus had not come to the rescue. So, in the community, the men who have no stake in the welfare of the country are always the most dangerous element of the population. They have nothing to lose in any event; and it is just possible that, in the confusion, they may gain a little. Thus they are always ready for either riot or *emeute*. The "mixed multitude" in our cities represents what others call the dangerous classes; and in proportion as their existence is ignored by the respectable portion of the people, and nothing is done for their education or elevation, the danger is aggravated. At every time of crisis this peril comes to the front. We had a specimen of what it might result in during the strikes of last summer; and it becomes us, not only from the higher motive of Christian love, but also from the lower one of patriotic selfishness, to do our utmost for the evangelization of the masses who are our neighbors; for if a fire breaks out among them, it may not be stayed until it has consumed everything that we hold dear. We may apply to them the lines which, with almost prophetic presage, Longfellow wrote, more than thirty years ago, concerning the slave:

> "There is a poor blind Samson in the land,
>   Shorn of his strength, and bound in bonds of steel,
> Who may, in some grim revel, raise his hand
>   And shake the pillars of the common weal,
> Till the vast temple of our liberties
> A shapeless mass of wreck and rubbish lies."

But I did not mean to dwell on that particular illustration of the point which is now before us; I desire, as more befitting this evening and this place, to give prominence to the truth that the dangerous element in all our churches is not so much in their members as in those who keep outside of their pale, and yet, as ordinary hearers, have a kind of identification with them. I admit, of course, that this class is very far from being socially of that low-caste character which belonged to the mixed multitude here. I gladly bear witness, also, that many among them are every way estimable; and, for aught I can see, might as well be in the churches as many of those who are already there. I must emphatically declare, too, that, so far as my individual experience goes, in the churches, both in England and here, with which I have been connected, no element of bitterness has come from them. But still, from an extensive observation of the history of churches, I have come to the conviction that many envyings and divisions, resulting in the breaking up of congregations, and the crippling of ministerial usefulness, have arisen from those who are not pillars within the church, but only buttresses on its outside walls. The pastor may be an eminently spiritually-minded man; but his very faithfulness in the denunciation of fashionable follies may arouse the antagonism of some wealthy hearers who are not church-members, but who, as bearing the purse, have more importance in the church than the holiest office-bearer. They begin to express dissatisfaction; and, as a bad example is easily followed, the rôle is taken up by others, until, with tears in their eyes, the good people say to the minister, "You will have to go; we are deeply grieved about it, but we cannot support you without them; and we hope the Lord will soon open up to you another sphere." The "mixed multitude" fall a-lusting for a pastor who will not wound their consciences; and so a church is sacrificed to their patronage, and a good man is turned adrift, to "wander where he can find a place." But think you God takes no notice of these things? Will not the fire of his justice somehow descend upon the perpetrators of such selfish cruelty? and is it not often seen that the very next man they get becomes the rod, in God's hand, for their chastisement? This is a sore evil under the sun; and I long to see the day when the spiritual element of the Church shall not be at the mercy of those who frequent its courts merely for the status it may give them, or from the intellectual or æsthetic pleasure which they may derive from a preacher who is no more to them than "one who has a pleasant voice, and can play well upon an instrument." Only the Levites should carry the ark, and all outside murmuring should be conclusively put down by those who are within.

We may learn here, in the second place, that murmuring is invariably one-sided. These discontented Egyptians and Israelites did nothing but look back on Egypt; and even when they did that, they saw only the lights, and not the shadows. There is a sense, indeed, in which every one idealizes the past; and sometimes, as we look back, we see a great deal of good that we did not recognize in it when it was present; so that, as the poet says:

> "The past will always win
>   A glory from its being far;
>   And orb into the perfect star
> We saw not when we moved therein."

But that was hardly the case with these murmurers, for they took out the good and left the evil unthought of. It was true that they had their rations regularly; it was true, also, that they had such variety as cucumbers, leeks, onions, and garlic afforded—though, for my part, I do not envy them their diet—but then they had slavery with it all. They had the hard toil of making bricks without straw; they had the bitterness of the bastinado, and the shame and sting of the lash; and if they had wished to make a right estimate of their Egyptian life, they should have taken in both sides of the account.

Again, in their depreciation of their present lot they were equally one-sided. They could see in it nothing but the one fact that they had no flesh to eat. They took no notice of the manna, save to despise it; they said nothing of the water which God had provided for them; they never spoke of the daily miracle that their clothes waxed not old; they made no reference to the constant guidance and presence of Jehovah with them—all they saw just then was that they had no flesh to eat. Now, this was flagrantly unjust; and yet, in condemning that, it is to be feared that we are passing judgment upon ourselves, for if we were fully to reckon up both sides of the account, would there ever be any murmuring among us at all? It may be true that we have sickness, or poverty, or the antagonism of men, or whatever else that is adverse you please to add; but then we have Christ, we have pardon and reconciliation to God here, and we have heaven hereafter; and if we had anything like a right idea of these blessings, the song which began in the minor key of complaint would speedily change into the major key of praise. I cannot read the account of these murmuring Israelites without remembering the answer of a reclaimed and converted man to his wife, who, seeing him give his daughter some money to put into the church collection-box, said to him, "It seems to me that we have lost a great deal by this religion of yours." "Yes," said he, turning round upon her with a sad yet earnest look—"yes! I used to go in rags, and to keep you in them, too, and we have lost our rags; I used to have a cheerless room, without any furniture in it, for a home, and we have lost that, and gained this neat and comfortable dwelling; I was a cruel husband to you, and kept you in want and wretchedness— ay, God forgive me! I have lifted my hand in these old days to strike you—but we have lost all that; I used to feel that the children were in the way, and to grudge them every copper that went for food or raiment, so that they were afraid to come near me lest I should injure them with my violence; but we have lost all that." And when he had gone thus far his wife burst into tears, and said, "Forgive me! there has been no loss; and, if I had seen aright, I might have known it was all gain." So let us kill our disposition to discontentment, by making a fair and faithful balance of both sides of the account; and we shall find that adversity of any kind, with God, is better than prosperity without him, and will not repine at any sacrifice which he demands.

We may learn, in the third place, that God is always considerate of his faithful servants. See how tender he was to Moses here. The great leader is broken in spirit. He has had a tremendous strain on him for the last eighteen months. All the conflict with Pharaoh; all the excitement of the Exodus; all the arrangement of the journeyings to Sinai, had told upon him. Jethro saw the difference in his appearance when he came to Sinai to visit him, and perhaps that was one reason for his suggesting to him to divide his judicial labors among colleagues. But the spiritual elevation of Sinai must also have produced its own effect upon his frame. He could not be so often with God without having his mental powers exhausted. His double sojourn of forty days each time upon the Mount must have worn his system down; and so we cannot wonder that this new epidemic of discontent should have so distressed him. But God knew it all; and, therefore, there is no word of upbraiding addressed by him to his servant. As on a similar occasion he strengthened Elijah by sleep and food, so now he encouraged his friend by giving him the assistance of seventy properly called and qualified men. He saw that he needed human sympathy and support, as well as divine, and therefore he hasted to provide him with them. The throne's glory is a lonely thing, and the leader of a great host like that of Israel must be, from the very nature of the case, a solitary man; so God surrounded Moses with a cordon of kindred spirits, who might act as a breakwater, and keep the waves of trouble and discontent that rose in the camp from dashing upon him. One cannot read of this without being impressed by the tenderness of God; and it is to me a suggestive fact that on almost every occasion on which we are told of his judgment falling upon sinners, we have in the near vicinity some manifestation of gentleness to his friends. Brethren, ye who are trying to serve God with steady, loving loyalty, and whose hearts are despondent because of the difficulties with which you have to contend, I pray you think of his kindness to Moses here, and take new courage. "He stayeth his rough wind, in the day of his east wind." We serve a considerate master. He knoweth our frames, and remembereth that we are dust; and as in each new perplexity he appeared to Paul, and said "Fear not," so we may be sure that he will somehow sustain us, either by bestowing his grace upon us, or by furnishing us with some human helpers whose counsel may guide us, and whose love may cheer us.

We may learn, in the fourth place, that the truly great man is never envious of others. When Joshua saw Eldad and Medad prophesying in the camp, he thought it was a grievous irregularity. But Moses knew that God's Spirit could make no mistakes, and that if these men were under His influence, they were really on his side; so he would not have them silenced, but said, "Would God that all the Lord's people were prophets." Now here is a lesson for us all, and especially for ministers of the Gospel. How hard it is to rejoice in the excellence of another, especially if he be in the same line with ourselves? And yet the disparagement of the gifts of another is really an indication of our consciousness of the weakness of our own. It is a pitiful thing to hear ministers of all others depreciating each other; and when an earnest man is publishing the Gospel, though he follows not with us, it is a paltry thing to think of forbidding him, even if, in a country like our own, it were possible to do anything of the kind. When Paul heard that the Corinthians were quarrelling over the men who had preached to them, he let them know that he regarded their conduct as very reprehensible, and he showed them that every true minister belongs to all Christ's people alike, for he said, "All things are yours, whether Paul, or Apollos, or Cephas;" and if we had his spirit, we would rejoice in all the good which every preacher, no matter whether he be ordained or not, is enabled to accomplish. Even when men thought to spite the apostle by preaching, his only remark was, "What of it? nevertheless, Christ is preached, and therein do I rejoice, yea, and will rejoice." O for more of this spirit among us all, that we may be all for the Lord Jesus, and none of us for ourselves! But, alas! this is the loftiest attainment of Christian excellence; for the highest and the hardest cliff to climb on the mountain of holiness is humility.

We may learn, in the fifth place, that we can set no limits to the resources of God. When the Lord said to Moses that the people should eat flesh for a whole month, the leader was startled for a moment into unbelief, and said, "The people among whom I am are six hundred thousand footmen; and thou hast said, I will give them flesh, that they may eat a whole month. Shall the flocks and the herds be slain for them, to suffice them? or shall all the fish of the sea be gathered together for them, to suffice them? And the Lord answered Moses, "Is the Lord's hand waxed short? thou shalt see now whether my word shall come to pass unto thee or not." We rather wonder at this unbelief of Moses, after what he had already seen; but we have a similar spirit in Andrew, when, putting the five loaves and two fishes into the Saviour's hand, he said, "What are these among so many?" Moses soon saw what the Lord could do, and Andrew helped to gather baskets of fragments, each of which held more food than what had been served at first for five thousand men. So, often in the history of the Church it has been proved that God's hand is not shortened, and if we will only set out to do anything earnestly for him, we may be honored to do something great in the advancement of his kingdom; and, no matter what it requires, we may be at least sure of this, that he will keep his word.

Finally, we may learn from this history that it is not good for us to get everything we desire. When the flesh came to the Israelites it caused pestilence and death; and on a similar occasion, unless, indeed, the reference be to this very narrative, the Psalmist says, "He gave them their request, but sent leanness into their soul."* So again, when the tribes

---

* Psa. cv., 15.

desired a king, he gave them Saul, that through the infliction of that monarch's tyranny they might be convinced of the wickedness of their wish. Thus we may learn that if God denies us our request, it may be because the granting of it would cause us misery rather than happiness. Surely, it is better to do without that which we long for, and have marrow and fatness in our hearts, than to get it, and leanness of soul with it. Prayers born out of murmuring are always dangerous. Rachel cried for children, yet she had no joy in them, and had to call the latest born Benoni—"the son of my sorrow." When, therefore, we are in a discontented mood, let us take care what we cry for, lest God give it to us, and thereby punish us. And when the petition which we offer in simple faith seems to be denied, let us take even the denial for a favor, for "we know not what we ask," and we may well trust that he who gave his son to die for us, will in every respect consult for our highest good. Even one of the world's own poets has said—

> "We, ignorant of ourselves,
> Beg often our own harms, which the wise powers
> Deny us for our good; so find we profit
> By losing of our prayers."

And surely we who have learned to say "our Father" at the lips of Jesus may learn also, from his example, to append to all our petitions, "Nevertheless, not as I will, but as thou wilt."

XVIII.

MIRIAM AND AARON'S SEDITION.

NUMBERS xii., 1-16.

FROM Kibroth-Hattaavah the tribes advanced, still in the direction of the wilderness of Paran, to a station named Hazeroth, where a new and sorer trial came on Moses. Hitherto the murmurers against him had been restricted to the mixed multitude, and to the masses of the Hebrews who had little personal intercourse with him, and were important rather because of their numbers than because of their character or position in the encampment; but now the members of his own family began to speak against him, and Miriam and Aaron combined to set his authority at defiance. This must have been a terrible blow to Moses, for Miriam was very dear to him. He had often heard her tell the story of her faithful watch over him as he lay, a helpless babe, in his bulrush ark by the river's brink; and the prominent place which she took in leading the responsive chorus when he sang his song of triumph on the Red Sea shore, betokened that she was of one heart with him, alike in piety and patriotism. That she should turn against him, therefore, would be a positive grief to him; while the adherence of Aaron to her mutiny would be an aggravation of the affliction; for, though the high-priest had some weaknesses and faults, he had been, in the main, a true brother. Shoulder to shoulder Moses and he had stood all through that long and terrible encounter with Pharaoh—strong not only in their faith in Jehovah, but also in their fidelity to each other; and though, in the matter of the golden calf, Aaron had disappointed Moses, and forfeited his right to unabated confidence in a time of crisis, yet he was still a tower of strength to his brother; and, at such seasons of peril as that through which they had passed at Kibroth, it was something for Moses to have one with whom he could unbend, and on whose perfect sympathy and co-operation he could, in some degree, depend. But now that solace too is taken from him, and Aaron has become a negative quantity in the equation of the camp; not merely a non-assistant, but, for the time at least, a positive antagonist.

How shall we account for this? Miriam seems to have been the prime mover in the matter; and, from the words that passed between her and Aaron to this effect, "Hath the Lord, indeed, spoken only by Moses? hath he not spoken also by us?" it is evident that envy was at the root of their estrangement. They were displeased at the fact that Moses had more importance in the camp than that which they possessed. They belonged to the same family as he did; they were both older than he; they had both been chosen as the vehicles of divine instruction, as well as he; and they could not brook that he should stand at such a height above them. They thought themselves as good as he was, and they wanted to have a public recognition of their equality.

Now, there were some things connected with Moses, on the one hand, and with themselves, on the other, which made their guilt in this matter peculiarly aggravated. For Moses had not courted pre-eminence. The leadership with which he had been invested was not of his own seeking. If any man could say that greatness had been thrust upon him, that man surely was Moses. His fault had been rather in the direction of declining responsibility, than in that of assuming prerogative; and the use which he had made of his position was not such as to secure his own aggrandizement, but rather such as to promote the highest welfare of the nation. He had carried on his administration not for the profit of Moses, but for the glory of Jehovah, and for the good of the people. No man in the entire encampment worked so assiduously and incessantly as he. The superintendence of everything had devolved upon him; he carried on his heart the care of all the tribes; and he was not thinking either of his own interest or of his own honor, but only of the interest of the Hebrews, and the honor of their God. No mere man was ever more unselfish in his administration of a great office than was Moses; and, with the consciousness of his own utter disinterestedness within his breast, it must have been peculiarly trying to him to hear those to whom he was most nearly related, and who ought to have known him best, accuse him of taking too much upon him. If they thought so meanly of him, what must others say regarding him? If they rebelled against him, the mixed multitude might well be excused for their repinings.

Thus inexcusable, so far as the conduct of Moses himself was in the case, the reproaches of Aaron and Miriam were equally unjustifiable by any consideration of their own position; for what had either of them of honor or of influence which was not due to the accident of their relationship to Moses? Miriam might have been known for her strength of mind and general excellence of character among the slave population of Egypt, and Aaron might have risen to some paltry officership over the brickmakers; but if it had not been for the fact that Moses was their brother, neither of them would have come into prominence in the Exodus, or would have achieved a permanent and independent renown. Moreover, it is not to be forgotten that, by his investiture with the office of the priesthood, Aaron had received an honor which, in its own sphere, was peerless and pre-eminent. Why, then, should he be discontented? Having obtained so much, wherefore should he murmur that he had no more? Was it that already, so soon after his assumption of the ephod and the mitre, that spirit of arrogant intolerance which has always been associated with the priesthood had begun to work in him, and he was impatient of any influence in the camp which should seem to be even on a level with his own? Was this the beginning of that jealousy of the prophetic office which was so frequently manifested in the after-history of Israel by the priestly caste? and are we to regard these two brothers as the representatives of that ritualistic pretensiveness, on the one hand, and that determined assertion of the supremacy of truth, on the other, which have been continually striving with each other for the mastery in all the religious history of the human race? Is it but another form of the same conflict which emerged, at a later day, between Peter and Paul at Antioch?—a collision of the same sort as that which convulsed Europe when Leo the priest anathematized Luther the prophet, and sought occasion for the condemnation too, in a similar complaint, of the woman whom he had married? We cannot tell; but the fact is not without its significance that this mutiny occurred after, and not before, the inauguration of Aaron into the high-priest's office.

However we may account for the envy which Miriam and Aaron felt, there can be no difference of opinion as to the meanness of the spirit which they manifested in veiling their jealousy of Moses himself under an attack upon his wife. They spake against him, "because of the Ethiopian woman whom he had married: for he had married an Ethiopian woman." They grudged him his greatness, and showed that they did so by putting a slight upon his wife. But who was this Ethiopian woman? Some suppose that she was a second wife, whom Moses, after Zipporah's death, had married, perhaps without waiting for the elapsing of a decent interval, and certainly without consulting his near relatives about the wisdom of the step which he was about to take. Much may be said in favor of that opinion; and, considering the very free criticisms on second marriages which are indulged in, not by relatives alone, but by all and sundry; considering, also, the family quarrels which such alliances have often caused in modern times, we cannot suppose that there is any improbability in such a view of the case. But, in the absence of any mention of the death of Zipporah—not to speak of the improbability of her death, and the marriage of Moses to another, as all having occurred in the brief interval between the arrival of Jethro at the camp and the coming of the tribes to Hazeroth—I prefer to believe that the allusion is to Zipporah herself, who is called a Cushite, "not as being of the children of Cush, but as belonging to a country which had received from them its name."* And if this solution of the question be adopted, it will help us to understand how Miriam, taking occasion from female jealousy, won Aaron over to her side, and they united in their desire to humiliate and annoy their brother.

Zipporah had been brought to Sinai only a few months before. Up till then Miriam had never met her; and when she did come, Miriam would subject her to that sort of microscopic scrutiny to which one woman can subject another, while yet she seems to be all the time intent on some quite different business. The result of that investigation would be prejudicially affected by the fact that Zipporah was a foreigner. Further intercourse might reveal, what we learned for ourselves from that singular controversy over the circumcision of her younger son at the caravansary, that she was not very earnest in her religious life, or very reverent in her conjugal subjection. This would produce a certain re-

---

* Kitto's "Daily Bible Illustrations," vol. ii., p. 184.

straint in Miriam's manner toward her; and as Zipporah would naturally resent such treatment, the breach between them, without a word of reproach from either side, would grow daily wider. Meanwhile the post of female priority in the camp, which had been heretofore freely yielded to Miriam as the sister, is naturally and inevitably transferred to Zipporah the wife. It could not be otherwise; and if Miriam had allowed herself to think rationally for a moment, she would have seen that it ought not to have been otherwise. But it is a dreadfully hard thing to give up that precedence which we have formerly enjoyed, and which another has now come to claim; and Miriam did not enjoy seeing Zipporah in the place she used to fill, the rather, perhaps, as she was conscious that she was better able to perform its duties than Zipporah ever would be. Then we must not forget that Jethro's advice was taken in the appointment of the judges, and that Hobab, when he was about to depart, had been pressed by Moses to remain with them, on the ground that he could render to them all incalculable services. Brooding over all these things in her moody and discontented frame of mind, we can easily understand how Miriam came to think that these "Cushites," as she called the Midianites in a kind of scorn, were getting too much of Moses's attention, and exercising too great an influence over Moses's mind. "You and I," we can conceive of her saying in her private colloquy to Aaron, "are nobodies now. Our new relations are all in the ascendent. I wonder whatever Moses saw in her! and as for her giving herself such airs because she is his wife, she ought to remember that there are others here as good as he, for if the Lord has spoken by him, he has spoken also by us."

This spirit in his sister ought at once to have been rebuked by Aaron, but instead of reproving it, he encouraged it, and joined Miriam in making a representation to Moses on the subject. We wonder that Moses did not immediately pour out on them a torrent of sanctified indignation. We could have forgiven him, if he had showed them unceremoniously to the tent-door, and ordered them to attend to their own affairs. But he was too deeply wounded to be violent. A little thing might have irritated him. But this was too serious to allow of any manifestation of anger. He was too sad to scold. They had struck at Zipporah, but they had struck through him, and the fact that the blow came from their hands intensified its severity. He loved them very truly. His intercession on a memorable occasion had saved Aaron's life, and his greatest delight had been to minister to their happiness as together they sought to serve the Lord. But now that they should murmur against him, and that they should cloak their envy of his pre-eminence under an attack on one who was dear to him as his own soul, and whose happiness was of far more importance to him than his own, this was an affliction indeed. It was too great to be spoken of. He would not trust himself to say to Aaron and Miriam what he thought of their conduct. Far less would he report any of their envious talk to Zipporah, for that would have tended to make further friendship between her and Miriam impossible. So, with that meekness which, though he had been at first deficient in it, had now come to be the distinctive feature of his character, he held his peace.

But the Lord was his vindicator; for, calling the three out to the tabernacle, he came down in the pillar of the cloud and stood in the door of the tabernacle, and, having separated Aaron and Miriam from Moses, he said unto them, "Hear now my words: If there be a prophet among you, I the Lord will make myself known unto him in a vision, and will speak unto him in a dream. My servant Moses is not so, who is faithful in all mine house. With him will I speak mouth to mouth, even apparently, and not in dark speeches;

and the similitude of the Lord shall he behold: wherefore then were ye not afraid to speak against my servant Moses?" Thus, instead of countenancing the idea that they were all on an equality, Jehovah distinctly maintains the supremacy of Moses, and traces that to his own sovereign appointment. It was true that the prophets among them spoke as the Lord had instructed them, but there were particularly three things in which the pre-eminence of Moses was conspicuous. That which was exceptional and ecstatic with them was ordinary, and on the level of his common experience with him. The prophets needed a special preparation for the reception of God's communications. They needed, as Kurtz has expressed it, " to pass out of the sphere of the senses, and that of intelligent consciousness, into a state of supersensual perception."* The Lord made himself known to them in visions and dreams. But he spoke to Moses in his ordinary every-day condition. The great law-giver received the divine communications not when he was in a trance, or when he was asleep, but in his usual intelligent consciousness; and so it came to pass that the partial obscurity which was necessarily connected with the revelations that came through others, was conspicuously absent in those which were made by Moses. Again, Moses saw the similitude of Jehovah; and although this cannot mean that he beheld the unveiled glory of the Lord, it must denote that there was before him some visible and objective reality, which symbolized for him the presence of Jehovah, and from which, as from the mouth of a confidential friend, he received, not in dark and mysterious utterances, but in plain and unmistakable terms, the messages which he was to convey to his fellow-men. There was thus a difference, if not in the kind of inspiration which he enjoyed, at least in the nature of the revelations which

---

* "History of the Old Covenant," vol. iii., p. 242.

were made to him; for, as the mind of a man takes clearly in that which is only as a wonder or a dream to a child, so Moses distinctly perceived that which to other prophets was little better than a vague and incoherent vision. Moreover, with his function of prophet there was combined the authority of ruler. He was not only a messenger to the people, but he was God's servant over them. He was the steward over all God's house, and here special emphasis must be laid upon the *all.* The department of Aaron was restricted to the tabernacle and its service; but that of Moses took in both the civil and sacred categories. Aaron had no right to interfere with things outside of his office, but Moses was over all the departments alike, and priests as well as princes were to receive the law at his lips. For in his administration of his government, so far from having taken too much upon him, he had been strictly faithful, and had been as jealous for the good of the people as for the glory of God.

Thus not only was there no excuse for any envy of Moses on the part of Aaron and Miriam, but it was a flagrant sin, not against Moses merely, but against God; and, in this aspect, it drew down severe punishment. For when the cloud separated from the tabernacle, it left behind the evidence of Jehovah's indignation in the leprosy, which overspread the body of Miriam, and made her white as snow. Possibly she had indulged in biting sarcasm on the personal appearance of Zipporah; perhaps, also, she had plumed herself on her own stately beauty. We cannot tell; but on her form and features came that ghastly and repulsive malady, which made its victim loathsome; and, under the law of which Aaron was the officer, it fell to him to make a formal inspection of the case, and to declare that she was leprous. So they were both humiliated; Miriam in the defacement of that personal attractiveness to which no woman ever is indifferent, and Aaron in being compelled to utter the words which condemned her to isolation without the camp. This brought them both to penitence. Miriam, indeed, was too much distressed to speak; but Aaron interceded for her with Moses, and Moses interceded for her with God. But the offence could not be condoned without some satisfaction, and the Lord replied to Moses somehow after this fashion: "If her earthly father had shown himself to be displeased with her conduct, by doing something to her which could be speedily removed, she would still have felt so ashamed as to have hid herself from public view for a season; so now that the mark of her heavenly Father's indignation is upon her for her great offence, let her, for very shame, remain apart for seven days, and after that let her be received again." So for a whole week the people were detained waiting for Miriam; and thus again the hands of Moses were established by the vindication of his God.

Let us linger a little longer, to glean the lessons in which this chapter is so rich.

We may learn, then, in the first place, that the noblest disinterestedness will not preserve us from the shafts of envy. As we read this history, we can see that the service of Moses was rendered all for love, and nothing for reward. He did not want honor; he did not care for power; he was not covetous of this world's goods. All he desired was the welfare of his countrymen, and their prosperous settlement in the land which God had covenanted to give them. He was the most heavily-burdened man in the encampment, and was literally only the highest among them, because he was the servant of all. One would have thought, therefore, that he might have escaped reproach; and doubtless he would have done so if his amiability had been of that willowy sort that bends before every blast, and seeks to ingratiate itself with everybody. But Moses was true to God; and his love to the people was so intelligent that it would not let him keep silence when he saw them entering upon courses which were fraught with peril. Hence he faithfully reproved them, just because he had a tender regard for them; but they, measuring him by themselves, imagined that his rebukes were mere matters of personal pique, and sprung from wounded dignity, or a desire to show his superiority; and therefore they spoke against him. They grudged him his position. They thought he was using it for paltry purposes of individual aggrandizement, and so they cried him down. Now, if this were the treatment to which Moses was subjected, we need not be surprised if similar feelings should be cherished by some toward ourselves. The poet has said, in regard to another virtue than that of disinterestedness, "Be thou as chaste as ice, as pure as snow, thou shalt not escape calumny;" and, no matter how unselfish we are, we may lay our account with some envenomed attacks which shall plausibly accuse us of seeking our own things, and not the things that are Jesus Christ's. Nay, the more conspicuous we are for devotion to the public good, we may be only thereby the more distinctly marked as a target for the world's scorn. "I am weary of hearing always of Aristides as the Just," was the expression of one who plotted for that patriot's banishment; and if a man's character be in itself a protest against abounding corruption, he will soon be assailed by some one in the very things in which he is most eminent. The world's plan is to throw mud enough, in the sure confidence that some of it will stick; and its votaries keep on telling lies, because they know that a falsehood will travel a hundred miles while the truth is drawing on its boots. It is very hard, when one has taken a certain course which happens, for the moment, to be unpopular—say, for example, with workingmen, and has taken it because, seeing farther than they can or will do, he perceives that it is for their highest interest—I say it is very hard, in such a case, that the men whose good he has at heart should turn upon him, and accuse him of seeking his own benefit at their expense, and traduce him as a traitor to the trust which has been committed to his hands; but it is enough for the servant that he be as his Lord, and the day of the crucifixion was not the last on which, by the mob, Barabbas has been preferred to Christ. What then? Shall we give over laboring for the welfare of our race, and say, with Moses at Kibroth, "Kill me, I pray thee, out of hand;" or, with Elijah under the juniper-tree, "O Lord, take away my life now, for what am I better than my fathers?"—nay; for that would be to yield entirely to the enemy. Let us stay and keep the ground, and stand bravely out for the right, the true, and the good. If we are what we ought to be, we work not for thanks, nor for the appreciation of men, nor for popularity with the people, but for Christ; and if he did not shrink from the cross for us, why should we flee from the post of duty at which he has placed us? Has he not said, "Woe unto you, when all men shall speak well of you?" so let us take the envy of men as the indication that a divine beatitude is near, and let us work away as he shall strengthen us. Oh, ye public servants! whether in the Church or in the State, who are discharging your duties as before God, and have within you the consciousness of rectitude and entire unselfishness, take heart again when you see how Moses was assailed. And you, ye mischief-makers and self-seekers, who, because you cannot get your axes ground for nothing at the public whetstone, keep forever yelping like curs at the heels of those whose nobleness you cannot comprehend, beware lest ere long the plague of Kibroth or the leprosy of Miriam come upon you; for you are companions in the guilt of their ingratitude.

In the second place, this envy of disinterested greatness may show itself in the most unexpected quarters. I have named Miriam but now side by side with the mixed multitude; and yet I almost feel as if I owed her an apology for so doing, for, in truth, in the best parts of her nature, she had not much in common with them. She was, in the main, a good woman; and Aaron, in spite of some little weaknesses, was a good man. They were not perfect, and neither was Moses; but we might have supposed that they were both above such littleness as is here recorded of them. Yet, that it is recorded of *them* is the great point of the narrative; for while I was speaking, the other night, of the murmuring of the mixed multitude, I could see that you joined in my condemnation of them, and said within your hearts, "Yea, verily, they were a scurvy crew — a mean, contemptible, and discontented set;" but you never thought of yourselves. Now, however, that Miriam and Aaron are infected with the same disease, we cannot help bringing the matter home to our own hearts. This is a different thing from the heartlessness of a mob breaking a great statesman's windows; this is the sin of one who stood, socially, in the same plane with him whom she reviled, and who, to do her simple justice, was also a good woman. This, therefore, bids us look at our own souls; for if Aaron and Miriam were capable of such envy, we may not think that we are immaculate. It asks the minister to examine himself, and see whether he has not been guilty of depreciating a brother's gifts, because he looked upon him as a rival rather than as a fellow-laborer; it bids the merchant search through the recesses of his heart, if haply the terms in which he refers to a neighbor, or the tales he tells of him, be not due to the fact that, either in business or in society, he has been somehow preferred before him; it beseeches the lady, who is engaged in whispering the most ill-natured gossip against another in her circle, to inquire and see whether the *animus* of her deed be not the avenging of some fancied slight, or the desire to protest against an honor which has been done to the object of what Thackeray — I think it is — has called "her due Christian animosity!" Ah! are we not all in danger here? As long as we can patronize one who is below us, we can generously appreciate his excellence; but when he comes to be on a level with us, we begin to question the accuracy of our estimate; and when he shoots above us, we are sure we have been wrong, and we advertise everybody of our mistake. But it is the consciousness of our own inferiority that makes us envious of the superiority of another — nay, more, it is because we are thinking of our own position more than of the cause with which we ought to be identified, that we allow ourselves to murmur against another. How well it would be if we repelled all temptations to envy, as John silenced those who tried to set him against Jesus; for, as Bishop Hall has said, "That man hath true light who can be content to be a candle before the sun of others."

We may see, in the third place, the utter meanness of the weapons which envy is content to employ. Miriam and Aaron must needs expostulate with Moses about his wife; but they had nothing whatever to do with his domestic matters. The privacy of his tent ought to have been sacred, even in their eyes; and all such intrusiveness is an abomination in my sight. Zipporah was Moses's wife; she was his, as a wife, and not theirs. They might have their own views about her as their sister; yet Moses did not marry to please them, but to secure a helpmeet for himself. She was not the public property of the camp, that they might talk of her wherever they went; and if Moses was satisfied, that was enough. Perhaps she was not, in every respect, a model; but, from my observation in similar cases, it is my opinion that there was no ground whatever for any accusations against her. Still, even if there had been, that was no business of theirs; and regard for Moses ought to have kept them silent. A man's house is his castle. No personal malice should enter into it with its attack; and no mean report should be received from the eavesdroppers who have first misunderstood, and then misrepresented. If a man's public life has been blamable, then let him be arraigned; but let no Paul Pry interviewer cross his threshold to get hold of family secrets, or descend into the area to hear some hireling's moralizings. If a minister is unfaithful to his duty, let him be put upon his defence; but let no whisperer say, "His wife! his wife!" At least until such times as congregations are prepared to pay a separate salary to the pastor's partner, as a female missionary among them, let them keep their tongues off her. I insist upon it that, in business, in politics, in religion, and, may I add also, in newspaper reporting, domestic privacy shall be respected. Even the bees, when put into a glass hive, go to work at the very first to make the glass opaque, for they will not have their secrets made common property; and surely we busy human beings may sometimes be allowed to be by ourselves. The man who goes into a house to use what he sees there as an envious weapon against the inmates of it is a spy, and should be treated as a common outlaw.

In the fourth place, we may learn that the assaults of envy are always best met by a silent appeal to Heaven. Moses uttered no word of reproach. But God called the complainers before him, and both vindicated his servant and punished them. And it is somewhat remarkable that the highest testimony to the official pre-eminence of Moses came in consequence of this assault upon him. Therefore let the victims of unjust assault take comfort, for God will be their defence. But let the envious ones take heed, for God hears their words, and he will one day confront them with his judgment. He may do that long before the day of final assize. He may meet them in his providence, and give them to understand that they who touch his faithful servants are touching the apple of his eye; nay, he may bring such trouble upon them that they will be glad to accept of the intercession of those whom they have maligned. They who speak falsely have not only the man concerning whom the lie is told against them, but they have God against them; for he is the foe of every falsehood, and his omnipotence will one day make its falsity apparent, and punish the malice which concocted it. Therefore men may well be "afraid to speak against" those whom God has authenticated, for he has other ways than that of leprosy of punishing the sedition of such as rise up against his servants. You remember the weird poem in which Coleridge has told the story of the man who shot the albatross, and how the bird was hung around his neck, and he was pursued by a phantom ship, and led through uttermost misery. Friends, let me assure you that to wing an arrow of malicious falsehood at the heart of a man who is faithfully seeking to serve his generation by the will of God, is to shoot the albatross; and, sooner or later, they who do it shall be followed by the phantom ship of retribution with its ghastly crew, and there will be no escape from its horror blacker than "an orphan's curse," until love return into their hearts, and they repair in supplication unto God—for so they realize the poet's description:

> "The self-same moment I could pray;
> And from my neck so free
> The albatross fell off, and sank
> Like lead into the sea."

So let us to-night come again to the mercy-seat; let the guilty among us confess our envy, repent of our sin, and seek its forgiveness: thus our hearts will be filled with peace, and will be so enriched with the love of God that jealousy and falsehood shall not be able to find an entrance into them.

XIX.

THE REPORT OF THE SPIES.

NUMBERS xiii., xiv.

THE wilderness of Paran, into which, after leaving Hazeroth, the tribes of Israel advanced, included about a third of the peninsula between Egypt and Canaan. It was bounded on the north by the frontier of Canaan, on the west by the River of Egypt, on the south by the Desert et-Tih, and on the east by the valley of the Arabah, which divided it from the mountains of Edom. Kadesh, in which they were now encamped, was eleven days' journey from Sinai,* and seems to have been situated in the Arabah, about ten miles north of Mount Hor, at a place now known as Ain-el-Weibeh. They had thus reached the southern boundary of Palestine, and Moses said unto them, "Ye are come unto the mountain of the Amorites, which the Lord our God doth give unto us. Behold, the Lord thy God hath set the land before thee: go up and possess it, as the Lord God of thy fathers hath said unto thee; fear not, neither be discouraged."† But they were unwilling to face the hardships which seemed to be involved in obeying that command, and so, veiling their cowardice under a desire to have some reliable information regarding the country, they proposed that men should be sent out to search the land, and bring back a report as to its products and its accessibility. It is not, indeed, affirmed in the narrative given in the Book of Num-

---

* Deut. i., 2. † Ib. i., 20, 21.

bers, that the suggestion to send spies originated with the people; but such an assertion is plainly made by Moses in the account which is preserved in the Book of Deuteronomy, and I am anxious to give it prominence now because it furnishes the explanation of all that came after. The mission of the spies originated in unbelief and craven-heartedness. The mere proposal to inspect the land betrayed that there was in the hearts of those who made it a suspicion that the country would not be found to be so good as it had been represented. The intimation that the commissioners might be able to guide them as to the best way of entering the country was a slight upon the pillar of cloud and flame, by which they had heretofore been conducted. And the whole project was a device to gain time, and to postpone the conflict through which alone they could obtain possession of the heritage which God had designated for them. They did not wish, just then, to exert themselves in any measure, and they adopted this expedient in order, for the moment, to evade all effort.

Seeing that this was their disposition, the Lord determined to unmask it, and to show them whereunto it would grow. He therefore acceded to their proposal; and twelve men, one from each tribe, were designated as inspectors to go up through the Negeb, or territory to the south of Palestine, and search the land, and to bring back an account, which should tell what it was like; whether its inhabitants were many or few, strong or weak, and whether they dwelt in cities or in tents; what was the quality of its soil, and the nature of its climate; and what was the character of its productions. Among the men appointed for this purpose were Joshua, whose name seems, in connection with his mission on this occasion, to have been changed from Hoshea into Joshua; and Caleb, who, though mentioned as belonging to the tribe of Judah, appears from sundry peculiar references made to him in other passages, to have been not a Hebrew by birth, but rather an alien who had come from the Kenizzites to connect himself with the worshippers of the true God, and had been formally associated with the family of Hezron.* The others were apparently men of no great faith or force of character, and only too correctly represented the prevailing spirit of the Hebrews.

Entering Palestine by way of the Negeb, these spies traversed its entire length to Rehob, in the vicinity of the place where the mountain-ranges of Lebanon and Antilibanus approach each other. They came back by Hebron, one of the oldest cities of the world, and dear to them from its associations with Abraham, who dwelt as a stranger in its neighborhood, and whose ashes rested in that Machpelah cave which was his only earnest of the Promised Land. There they saw the gigantic race of the Anakim, whose appearance filled them with dismay; and in the valley of Eshcol, which was close to Hebron, they found—for it was the vintage-time, and the district was covered, as it still is, with vineyards—a branch with a cluster of grapes so large and luscious that they determined to take it with them as an indication of the fertility of the soil.

They were absent from Kadesh forty days; and as they were seen approaching the camp, two of them bearing on a pole between them the vine-branch, with its heavy fruitage, great excitement must have been created among the people. But in answer to the inquiries with which they were met, ten of the spies spoke most discouragingly. They admitted that the land was good, and that its excellence had not been misrepresented, for it did flow with milk and honey. But they alleged that its inhabitants were numerous and fierce; that its cities were strongly fortified; and that, be-

---

* See Smith's "Dictionary," article CALEB.

fore they could possess it, they would have to conquer the Amalekites, the Hittites, the Jebusites, the Amorites, and, above all, the children of Anak, whose lofty stature seems to have filled their imaginations with a vague and indefinable alarm. When the people heard these things, they were grievously disheartened; and, though Caleb and Joshua did what they could to reassure them, "the congregation lifted up their voice and cried" the whole night long.

In the morning their disappointment ripened into a mutiny, more pronounced than any which had yet appeared among them. They looked back wistfully to their old slave-pens in Egypt, and they accused the Lord of bringing them out of their bondage that they might fall by the swords of the Canaanites. With strange inconsistency, the fear of death in the future made them wish that they had been dead already; and they actually proposed to elect another leader who should conduct them back to the land of the Pharaohs.

The effect of all this on Moses and Aaron was tremendous. They were literally struck dumb with amazement and humiliation, and could do nothing but prostrate themselves in silent entreaty before God in the presence of the mutineers. But nothing, apparently, could bring the people to a better mind; for when Caleb and Joshua again stood forth, and declared their belief that the presence of Jehovah with them would make them stronger than the mightiest of their adversaries, "the whole congregation bade stone them with stones." Thus the cup of their iniquities became full, and the time of their probation came to a close. "At Sinai they had rejected Jehovah, who led them out of Egypt, and had desired a god such as they formerly possessed in Egypt; at Kadesh they rejected the land of Jehovah, the land of promise, and wished to return to Egypt."* This brought

---

* Kurtz, as above, vol. iii., p. 152.

their day of visitation to an end; for now Jehovah declares that he will smite them with pestilence, and destroy them as one man, and offers to make of Moses a great nation in their room.

But, true to his mediatorial character, Moses puts the offer away from him; reminds the Lord of his promises; dwells upon the effect that would be produced on the Egyptians and other idolaters if it should be made to appear that he was not able to take his chosen people into the covenanted land; and, recalling that name which he had himself heard proclaimed as he stood in the cleft of the rock, he pleads its significance with him, and implores that the iniquity of the tribes may be forgiven. This prayer was answered, yet only so far as a regard for the honor of Jehovah and the best interests of the people permitted it to be answered. The nation, as such, would be preserved, but the individuals would suffer for their guilt. All of those who had attained the age of twenty years at the date of the Exodus would be excluded from Canaan, and would, according to their own hasty prayer, die in the wilderness. The tribe of Levi, from which no representative had been taken, and which had not been numbered with the others, seems to have been exempted from this doom; but in the other tribes there were no exceptions, save Caleb and Joshua, who had proved their fidelity, even at the risk of their lives. And as the spies had been absent searching the land for forty days, so the people would be detained in the desert forty years, that they might understand what a serious thing it is to murmur against the Lord. Moreover, lest they should imagine that there was no meaning in this solemn threatening, the ten spies, whose unbelief had been the match that lighted the flame of revolt, were immediately smitten by the plague.

This made a very solemn impression upon the tribes. They saw now how much they had forfeited. They discovered that, even when they were at the very gate of possession, they had been sent back into the wilderness of wandering; and now, when it was too late, they would strive to repair the mischief which they had done. In spite of the warnings of Moses, they became as eager to advance as they had been before to return to Egypt; and they actually presumed to attack the Amalekites, and were smitten and discomfited for their pains.

Very suggestive is this ancient history in lessons for the life of to-day. Let us try to gather them for ourselves, and take them with us for our guidance and instruction.

We may learn, then, in the first place, that God's promises will always bear investigation. It was a spirit of unbelief that led to the proposal that spies should be sent to search out the land; but, though they went with a foregone desire to find an excuse for declining to go up to its possession, they could not say, and they did not say, that the Lord had misrepresented the case. His words are always true; and when, in spiritual things, he promises the sinner pardon, peace, purity, and heaven, we may rely implicitly on his assurance. It is true that none of us has entered heaven; but Jesus, who has gone on in advance to take possession of it in his people's name, has sent back an Eshcol cluster of its vintage, that we may know something of what we should expect. He has given us "the earnest of the Spirit in our hearts." The knowledge of God which we possess here will be the foundation of our knowledge there; the happiness which we enjoy here will be the germ of our felicity there; and the holiness which he has imparted to us here will be the bud of that which shall expand into the flower of heaven's own purity. The believer already has everlasting life; for the regeneration which he has here experienced needs but to be expanded and elevated and sublimated, to become the life of heaven. I do not mean that there is anything in our present possession that can give us an adequate idea of the glories of our celestial inheritance. It was, at the best, but a poor notion which the tribes could form of Canaan as they looked upon that grape-cluster, but it showed them something of it; and in like manner, though the earnest of the Spirit is the same in kind with the full fruition of glory, it is no adequate measure of its degree. Life is the same in kind in the infant "puling and whining in its nurse's arms," that it is in the philosopher; light is the same in kind in the first faint streak of dawn that dapples the eastern horizon, that it is in the clear, cloudless brilliance of the summer noon; but how different in degree! Similar will be the difference between the experience of the ransomed saint in heaven and that of the believer who is still upon the earth. The child who stands at the source of a river which he can bestride with his tiny legs like a Colossus, has no conception of the magnitude of the same river when it reaches the ocean, with a breadth and depth ample enough to bear the navy of an empire on its bosom; and so our Christian experiences, exalted as we sometimes think them to be, give us but a very imperfect notion of the bliss of Heaven.

But the important point lies here. Such as they are, these experiences have come down from Heaven into our hearts, and they are an assurance to us that the Promised Land will yet be ours. Thus, what this Eshcol branch was to the men of Israel, the indwelling of God's holy spirit is to every believer. It is an attestation and confirmation of Jehovah's word to him; it is the seal of God himself to the truthfulness of his promise that he shall yet enter into Heaven's own rest; and, amidst all the assaults of scepticism and all the sneers of ridicule, he can fall back upon his own consciousness, and say, "I know that there is a heaven before me, for I have some of it already in my heart." This is that experimental evidence which is ever the innermost citadel of Christian apologetics. It does not depend on logic, and so it cannot be refuted by logic; it does not rest on criticism, and so it cannot be shaken by the captious objections made by supercilious scholars to this and the other book of Holy Scripture; it has not been given by the world, and so by the world it cannot be taken away; it is not an experiment, but it is an experience, and so it is utterly impregnable. Happy is the man who, in this time of sifting and debate, has his mind and heart thus securely garrisoned by the peace of God! "No weapon that is formed against him shall prosper, and every tongue that shall rise against him in judgment he shall condemn."

But, from its very nature, this indwelling Spirit is, in the fullest sense, a confirmation only to him who is already a believer; yet there are first-fruits of another kind which may serve also for a sign to him that believeth not. Of this sort is that cluster of graces which, under the one name of the fruit of the Spirit, Paul has enumerated thus in his Epistle to the Galatians: "The fruit of the Spirit is love, joy, peace, long-suffering, gentleness, goodness, faith, meekness, temperance;"* and where these virtues, not in isolated graces, but as a united company, appear in a man, they are an assurance to those who look upon them, if they care to think the matter out, that God's Word is true, and that there is a heaven in store for them that love him. You may find individual virtues in men who yet are strangers to God and to his salvation, but you never find the aggregation of this cluster save on a branch that is in living union to the true Vine; and when that aggregation appears in a man who was once noted for characteristics entirely inconsistent with such a combination of excellences, there is a clear and irrefutable

---

* Gal. v., 22, 23.

The Report of the Spies.

testimony to the truth of God's words, and the reality of his salvation. Every new convert, therefore, who has given up the works of the flesh, and is bringing forth this fruit of the Spirit, is as real a verification of the truth of the Gospel as this bunch of grapes was of the accuracy of God's description of the Promised Land. Now, these are not rare among us. Men, indeed, continually cast up to us the inconsistencies of so-called Christians; but that is about as honest as it would be to judge of an apple-tree from the few worm-eaten specimens that have fallen from it, while no note is taken of the ruddy, ripening multitudes that bend down its branches with their weight. We admit that there are inconsistent men who call themselves Christians; we do not deny that, absolutely, there may be many hypocrites among those who have named the name of Christ; but we affirm that, relatively, the proportion of such persons to genuine believers in the Church is but like that of the bird-pecked fruit that is lying on the ground to the mellow harvest that is yet upon the tree; and in every true Christian you have an Eshcol branch, whose grape-cluster is an evidence not only of the genuineness of his piety, but also of the true heavenly life of the vine to which he is united. Thus every faithful follower of Christ is a living volume of apologetics, and the trophies of the Redeemer's power are the best evidences of the Redeemer's truth. There is not a person now within these walls who does not know some one individual concerning whom he can say, "Yes, he *is* a Christian; and if all were like him, I would believe the Gospel's truth." That individual is to you the Eshcol by which you may know, if you will, the reality of spiritual things. Out of your own mouth will God judge you, and he will say, "You did recognize my hand in your friend's character; why would you not make trial of its efficacy in your own?"

But, we may be reminded, in the second place, that there

are Anakim to be encountered in the conquest of every promised land. God had not hidden the fact that the Canaanites were in the land, from the knowledge of the Hebrews. Their encounter with Amalek, at Rephidim, had taught them what they might expect, while, at the same time, it had shown them that he that was with them was greater than all they that were against them. Now, in the same way Christ has said, "If any man will come after me, let him take up his cross daily and follow me," and has urged us to count the cost before we commence to raise our tower, lest at length they that pass by mock us, saying, "This man began to build, but was not able to finish." So he would prepare us for self-denial, hardship, and long-continued struggle; but we must not suppose that in all this the Gospel is an exception to the general law. No Canaan of success, in any pursuit, can be gained save by the conquest of the Anakim. He who would rise to a position of eminence in the department of literature, for example, must learn to "scorn delights, and live laborious days." He must deny himself many pleasures in which others allow themselves to indulge, and must keep himself, in a sense, secluded from the world, living in his library and at his desk. The man of business who would climb the steep that leads to wealth, must pursue a similar course. He cannot leave his place; he keeps himself chained to the oar; he knows that nothing will avail but work, work—hard and continuous work; for so only can he conquer those influences that stand in the way of his attainment of his object. It is the same with the artist; and, on a lower platform, with the athlete. All of them have to go into training; and, in every pursuit, a campaign, with its perils and fatigues, comes before a victory. We cannot complain, therefore, if the same law holds in the spiritual life. Rather, we must cheerfully recognize the fact that pre-eminence in holiness, and the attainment of an abundant entrance into the everlasting kingdom of our Lord and Saviour, can be gained alone through earnest, self-denying, and incessant labor. The first stage of Christian experience is one of joy and peace; and, in the consciousness that his sins are forgiven, the believer can do nothing but sing. By-and-by, however, he discovers that, though he has been delivered from the guilt of sin, he has not yet been emancipated from its power. He learns that sin pardoned is one thing, and that sin subdued is quite another thing; and when he enters upon the conflict which that discovery has rendered inevitable, he begins to perceive that his adversaries are "great and tall as the Anakim," and that he must fight if he would reign. Well for him, then, if he do not turn and flee; well for him, then, if he be not like those whom the Saviour has described, who "hear the word, and anon with joy receive it, yet have not root in themselves, but dure for awhile, for when persecution ariseth because of the word, by-and-by, they are offended."

These giants with whom we have to contend are mainly in ourselves, in the shape of evil principles and sins that most easily beset us; and it is only through self-conquest that we can pass to any external victory. David showed that he was prepared to meet Goliath when he held himself in under the stinging taunts of his brother Eliab; and the adversaries that are without us can be easily subdued when we have first overcome ourselves. This, no doubt, is a serious task. It is not a thing of a day. We cannot vault by one spasmodic leap up to the height of holiness, any more than the Israelites could all at once obtain possession of the land of promise. "By little and little" it has to be done. It needs prayer, and watchfulness, and constancy; and if we decline to enter upon the conflict, we shall fall short of the inheritance. Not without special significance, therefore, has the inspired writer said, in reference to this very chapter of ancient history, "Let us labor, therefore, to enter into that rest, lest any man fall after the same example of unbelief."* The faith and the labor thus go together: where the faith is deficient, there will be no labor; and where there is no labor, we make it evident that there is no faith. Be not deterred, therefore, by the Anakim. You have met them before. They are on the confines of every land of promise; and, as with other adversaries, you will discover that they cease to be formidable when you resolve to overcome them.

We may learn, in the third place, that the true believer is always able to conquer his spiritual adversaries, with the help of God. Caleb and Joshua were permitted, at length, to enter Canaan; and, to show you that the son of Jephunneh was not dealing in mere braggadocio when he said to the angry congregation, "If the Lord delight in us, then he will bring us into this land; and the Lord is with us, fear them not"—let me anticipate the history by more than forty years, and read to you a brief section from the Book of Joshua:† "Then the children of Judah came unto Joshua in Gilgal: and Caleb the son of Jephunneh the Kenizzite said unto him, Thou knowest the thing that the Lord said unto Moses the man of God concerning me and thee in Kadesh-barnea. Forty years old was I when Moses the servant of the Lord sent me from Kadesh-barnea to espy out the land; and I brought him word again as it was in mine heart. Nevertheless, my brethren that went up with me made the heart of the people melt: but I wholly followed the Lord my God. And Moses sware on that day, saying, Surely the land whereon thy feet have trodden shall be thine inheritance, and thy children's forever, because thou hast wholly followed the Lord my God. And now, behold, the Lord hath kept me alive, as he said, these forty and five years, even since the

---

* Heb. iv., 11. † Josh. xiv., 6-12.

Lord spake this word unto Moses, while the children of Israel wandered in the wilderness: and now, lo, I am this day fourscore and five years old. As yet I am as strong this day as I was in the day that Moses sent me: as my strength was then, even so is my strength now, for war, both to go out, and to come in. Now therefore give me this mountain, whereof the Lord spake in that day; for thou heardest in that day how the Anakim were there, and that the cities were great and fenced: if so be the Lord will be with me, then I shall be able to drive them out, as the Lord said." So this "Great-heart" had been all these years intent on choosing as his own the very locality which had so filled the rest of the spies with fear. He had declared that God would enable them to overcome the Anakim, and now he will go to prove it; and he did prove it, for in the next chapter* we read, "And Caleb drove thence the three sons of Anak, Sheshai, and Ahiman, and Talmai, the children of Anak." Brave old man! if the other ten spies had been like thee and Joshua, they had not drawn upon the people the forfeiture of their inheritance.

Now, as Caleb succeeded by God's help in conquering Hebron and driving out the Anakim, so, if we resolutely set ourselves to battle with self and sin, we too shall conquer in the might of the Most High. It is not a question of feebleness, but of faith. Whether the work we set before us be our own sanctification, or the evangelization of the city, or the conversion of the world through the missionary enterprise, the principle is still the same. We can do all things through Christ strengthening us; and if we attempt great things, trusting in him, we may expect to do great things, not otherwise. Ah! if there were only more Calebs among us, what might we not accomplish for God and truth and

---

* Josh. xv., 14.

purity in the world! For it was not Caleb that did all this, but God through Caleb; and God is to-day as omnipotent as ever. It was because Caleb knew that he was only, as it were, the conducting wire, through which the might of God was brought to bear upon his adversaries, that he was so bold; and if we but remembered that God is working in us and through us, we would set no limit to our ambition in his service. It seemed rash for David to go with his sling against the mailed Goliath, but then he went "in the name of the Lord God of Israel," and that proved that his daring was not recklessness, but faith. For what is faith? Is it not the attempt at that which is humanly impossible, but which becomes possible through the co-working energy of God? Oh for more of that faith among us, and then the giant evils of our days will fall before the youthful Davids; and the fenced Hebrons, wherein dwell securely all dealers in corruption and iniquity, will be stormed and taken by the Calebs who "fully follow the Lord their God."

Finally, we may learn from this history that there is a point beyond which it is no longer possible to repair the follies of the past. God had borne long and often with these Israelites. They had rebelled, as it is said, ten times; and as ten is the number that denotes completion, that may mean that they had filled up the measure of God's forbearance, so that now he declares in judicial sentence that they shall not enter into the land of promise. They who will not when they may, shall not when they will. Hence, when afterward they made the attempt to attack the Amalekites, they were driven back in ignominious defeat. Now, let no one suppose that, simply because it is recorded in this book, this is an unusual thing. On the contrary, it is only one instance of a common and universal law. You see it in every department and pursuit of life. Up to a certain limit, it seems to be in a man's power, if he choose, to make up for the past; but beyond that limit it is no longer possible, whether he choose or not. So universal is this principle of the divine administration, that the great poet who belongs to the race, rather than to any nation, and whose knowledge of human life seems to have been encyclopædic, has said:

> "There is a tide in the affairs of men,
> Which, taken at the flood, leads on to fortune;
> Omitted, all the voyage of their life
> Is bound in shallows, and in miseries."

Now, when we look at the matter thus, we see at once that the doctrine of a single probation for men is in perfect analogy with the course of God's ordinary providence; and so, while we cannot explain the rationale of it, we can understand that the province of religion forms no exception to God's ordinary law. And to-night, in the midst of all the excitement and discussion which the revival of this question has created, I desire to give emphasis to the truth that the change in the hearts of the Israelites when they expressed their willingness to go up did not lift from them God's judicial embargo. They seemed to repent, and yet now their repentance was vain. But this was, in relation to the land of promise, the analogue of the case of those described over and over again by the Saviour. Listen to these words, "Strive to enter in at the strait gate: for many, I say unto you, will seek to enter in, and shall not be able when once the master of the house is risen up, and hath shut to the door, and ye begin to stand without, and to knock at the door, saying, Lord, Lord, open unto us; and he shall answer and say unto you, I know you not whence ye are;" and these, "Many will say to me in that day, Lord, Lord, have we not prophesied in thy name? and in thy name have cast out devils? and in thy name done many wonderful works? And then will I profess unto them, I never knew you; depart from me, ye that work iniquity;" and these, in the parable of the virgins, which, you remember, is side by side with the account of the last judgment, "Afterward came also the other virgins, saying, Lord, Lord, open to us. But he answered and said, Verily I say unto you, I know you not." Now, no one of these condemned here at Kadesh entered the land of promise. The door was shut on them; the exclusion was final. Equally, no one of those referred to by Christ shall enter Heaven—the exclusion is final; and when to that you add the immortality of the soul, to which nature and revelation alike bear witness, then you have the everlasting exclusion of a living being from Heaven, and that is everlasting punishment. When the probation ends, it ends forever, and is never reopened. That is the lesson of the history that has been before us to-night; and that lesson, applied to the relation between time and eternity, leads to the awful conclusion that the lost are eternally lost; and that even if they seem to cry for salvation, it is denied them. This is not a matter of Greek etymology. It is not to be settled by the meaning of the word αἰώνιος. You have to take into account the principle of God's entire administration, and those terrible sayings of the Lord Jesus, a specimen of which I have quoted; and when you do that, you cannot get rid of it. He that is too late at the marriage, never again has the door open while the feast lasts. But the feast is everlasting life, and what is exclusion from that, while it lasts, but everlasting punishment? I beseech you, therefore, brethren, that you do not allow yourselves to be beguiled into the belief that there will be a state of probation after death, or that there is any hope of repairing the first exclusion from the heavenly land. Now is the accepted time; now is the day of salvation; therefore improve the present opportunity, and press on toward the mark for the prize of the high calling in Christ Jesus: for if you allow yourselves to lose that prize, it is lost forever.

XX.

THE KORAHITIC CONSPIRACY.

NUMBERS xvi., xvii.

THE prohibition of the adult portion of the tribes from entering the Promised Land was followed, after some little interval, by a rebellion more deliberate in its character, and more terrible, at least in its immediate results, than any of those which Moses had to meet. We may best bring out the circumstances of the case if we consider the causes which led to this mutiny, the spirit by which it was animated, the manner in which it was quelled, and the means which were taken to prevent a recurrence of the outbreak.

The ringleader was Korah, a Levite, belonging to the family of Izhar, who seems to have been moved throughout by jealousy and ambition. It will be remembered that the family of Amram, to which Moses and Aaron belonged, was not the eldest branch of the tribe of Levi, and that Levi was not the first-born of Jacob. Now, the patriarchal custom was that the pre-eminence and priesthood should belong to the oldest representative of the oldest family in the tribe; and as that had been set aside in favor of Aaron, Korah could see no reason why, if it were not to be given to the eldest Gershonite, it might not have been given to himself just as well as to Aaron. Thus the preference of Aaron to himself excited jealousy, which by-and-by ripened into revolt.

But it would have been madness in him to think of rebelling single-handed and alone, and therefore he set himself to enlist others with him in his insurrection. He began with his nearest neighbors; for, as his tent was on the south side of the tabernacle, the camp of Reuben was immediately behind him, at the distance of only one thousand cubits, and he used this proximity so well that three of the leading Reubenites were induced to join him. He did not, indeed, make known to them his ultimate intentions; but sought only to get their assistance in overthrowing Moses and Aaron, and reserved the unmasking of his own purpose for the time when a new choice for the priesthood would have to be made. He knew that the Reubenites were sensitive on the matter of primogeniture, for their father had been the first-born of Jacob, and yet, in the organization of the nation, no place of importance had been given to them. The priesthood had been given to Levi; the leadership had been, as they might allege, appropriated by Moses, who was also a Levite; and the foremost banner in the line of march was borne by Judah. Thus Reuben seemed to be slighted, and Korah made the most of this apparent neglect. He was not speaking, so he would have them believe, as a Levite, but as an Israelite; he did not want anything for himself, but he could not reconcile it to his conscience to see the tribe of the first-born ignored. It was true that, if they gained their pre-eminence, he would lose something of the prestige which was connected now with being a Levite, but that was nothing to him; he desired only to see justice done, and the primacy belonged of right to them.

In this way we may suppose that the ears of the princes of Reuben were gained; and the Reubenites, in their turn, veiling their personal designs, would foment discontent among the other tribes, on the general ground that Moses and Aaron "took too much upon them." Thus the spirit of insubordination spread, until, on its first manifestation, apparently at one of the meetings of the congregation, or house of representatives, no fewer than two hundred and fifty of the members of that body, men of renown among the people, stood forth upon the side of the mutineers.

Korah kept his own ambition in abeyance, and stirred up dissatisfaction among the Reubenites on the score of their right of primogeniture, in order that he might secure their assistance. The Reubenites, saying nothing to the other members of the congregation concerning their designs, enlarged upon the arrogance of Moses and his brother. The one object with both was to get rid of the leadership of Moses and the priesthood of Aaron; then, when that had been accomplished, the Reubenites would make a bid for the political presidency, and Korah would strive to gain the priesthood. Thus the conspirators, to use Dr. Kitto's expressive phrase, were playing "a very deep game." Korah was making tools of the princes of the Reubenites, and the Reubenites were making tools of the lords of the congregation. This is the reason why the ground of complaint against the two brothers is so general: "Ye take too much upon you, seeing all the congregation are holy, every one of them, and the Lord is among them: wherefore then lift ye up yourselves above the congregation of the Lord?" The immediate object was to depose the sons of Amram, and therefore the vaguest accusation was made against them; but if they had succeeded in that object, then the rival ambitions would have manifested themselves, and they who had agreed in tearing down might not have been of one mind in the effort at reconstruction. If I may take an illustration from contemporary history, perhaps the condition of France during the last autumn* may help us to understand the situation. Two parties were then in league in that country against the Republic. On the one hand, the Imperialists wished to bring back the Napoleonic dynasty; and, on the

---

* That of 1877.

other, the Legitimatists desired to restore the Bourbons. Each of them had their own ulterior ends in view; but they united to attempt the destruction of the Republic, and trusted to the chapter of accidents to determine how they should proceed after that should be accomplished. In the merciful providence of God, however, they were both defeated. So here, Korah for his own purposes, and the Reubenites for theirs, stirred up the two hundred and fifty princes of the assembly on the common ground of dissatisfaction with the existing state of things, and postponed the attainment of their personal ends until they had effectually put out of the way those who were the great obstacles to their ultimate success.

But the spirit by which these ringleaders were animated was infinitely worse than that of the political bargain-maker; for Moses was no politician, and Aaron was no scheming and arrogant prelate. Neither of these brothers had been desirous of office, and the places which they filled had not been taken by them of their own motive. Moses had been almost pushed into his priority by the hand of God. He had not seized upon authority as a usurper. He had been called to his post by Jehovah, who had given him credentials in the shape of miracles and signs, such as no impostor could fabricate, and no enemy could gainsay. In like manner, Aaron had not taken his office upon himself; he, too, had been "called of God," who had commanded him to be consecrated by peculiar services to his work. Thus the brothers held their places by divine right, and therefore rebellion against their selection for these places was rebellion against Jehovah. As in the army, mutiny against an officer lawfully exercising his authority is mutiny against the Government whose commission he holds; so here, the rejection of Moses as leader, and of Aaron as priest, was at the same time the rejection of God, who had appointed them to their respective offices. It was a disregarding of the clearly expressed and frequently indicated will of God, and therefore it was treason against the head of that theocratic system of government which at Sinai they had so solemnly accepted. If, as in a modern State like our own, the people had been the fountain-head of authority, then it might have been warrantable enough for them to seek to bring about a change of administration, provided there had been good ground for their dissatisfaction with Moses and Aaron, and they had endeavored to affect an alteration in a constitutional manner. There is no sin in attempting, in an honest way, and without cabal, to unseat an unpopular governor and bring in another; but in the Hebrew commonwealth God was politically supreme. The authority of the government in it came from above, and not from beneath. It was the prerogative of Jehovah to appoint his priest, and to designate his magisterial representative. The people, according to their own covenant obligations, had no option but to accept them both. They had been taken out from the nations, and elected to certain great privileges; and in connection with their acceptance of that position they had taken Jehovah to be their King. But his royalty was not a merely nominal thing; it was a reality. It placed them under his authority; it bound them to respect his laws, to obey his legate, and to approach him in worship through his appointed priest. Therefore, this conspiracy to overthrow Moses and depose Aaron was worse than any political plot, because it was rebellion against God, who was not only the fountain of law among the people, but also the object of their worship.

That I am not wrong in thus characterizing the spirit shown by the rebels, will appear from the manner in which their outbreak was met by Moses. When he heard their words, he fell on his face in mingled humiliation and supplication; and, after a few minutes spent thus in silent prayer, he rose and said, "Even to-morrow the Lord will shew who are his, and who is holy; and will cause him to come near unto him: even him whom he hath chosen will he cause to come near unto him. This do; take you censers, Korah, and all his company; and put fire therein, and put incense in them before the Lord to-morrow: and it shall be that the man whom the Lord doth choose, he shall be holy: ye take too much upon you, ye sons of Levi." In vindicating their position, the mutineers had quoted the words of God's promise to the people which Moses had repeated to them before the covenant of Sinai, namely, "Ye shall be unto me a kingdom of priests, and a holy nation." Thus they put forth the universal priesthood of the community as against the special priesthood of the house of Aaron; but they forgot that they had themselves deliberately declined to accept that position, and had cried passionately for a mediator. They forgot, also, that, in answer to that supplication, Moses became the day's-man between them and Jehovah, and that, at the command of God, he had given them Aaron to be their priest. They could not now, therefore, go back and begin anew. They had received a solemn lesson in the matter of the Promised Land which might have taught them, if they had been willing to learn, how a lost opportunity never comes back again. But it was not a personal matter between Moses and them; it was rather a controversy between them and God, and therefore, most appropriately, Moses leaves it to the arbitrament of God. If they will be priests, then let them take censers, and as priests offer incense unto the Lord. If he accepts them, well—there is an end of the matter; but if he rejects them, then his rejection is destruction. Nothing could be fairer or more straightforward than such a course, for it proposed to submit the whole controversy for adjustment to Jehovah; but at the same time nothing could be more solemn, for if they were in the wrong, they were only courting their punishment by accepting such a proposition.

Moses saw all that it involved, and in mercy to them he sought to prevail upon them to back down. Like a wise diplomatist, skilled in the knowledge of human nature, he took the two wings of the conspirators apart, and dealt with each separately. With Korah and the Levites that sympathized with him, he dwelt upon the honor which God had conferred upon them in giving them a place near himself in the service of the tabernacle; and exposed the ingratitude of their hearts, in that, so far from appreciating what they had, they hankered after that which was given to another. Not content with the privileges that belonged to the Levites, they were coveting also the honors of the priesthood. Because God had given them so much, they murmured against him because he had not given them more; yes, against him, for Aaron was only his minister, and held his office by his appointment. Having thus expostulated with Korah, with however but little effect, he sent for Dathan and Abiram from the camp of Reuben; and as On is not mentioned in the summons, and does not appear afterward in the narrative, the presumption is that he had already seen the error and the danger of his ways, and had withdrawn from the conspiracy. But there was no relenting in the heart of Dathan or Abiram. On the contrary, they flatly refused to obey the command of Moses, and sent back an answer of the most impertinent sort, as flippant as it was unjust. They accused Moses of making himself a prince over them; they alleged that he had not fulfilled his oft-repeated promise to lead them to a land flowing with milk and honey; they insinuated that the good land was really that which they had left, and they were not willing to give him another opportunity of throwing dust in their eyes, by appearing before him. "Wilt thou put out the eyes of these men? We will not come up." This reply moved the meek Moses so terribly that he was very wroth; and after his manner when he was excited, he spoke in broken and fragmentary utterances, each of which was like the explosion of a torpedo, and some of which were the only references which he had as yet permitted himself to make to his own administration.

When the morrow came, Korah and his company, two hundred and fifty in number, took their censers, with fire and incense, and stood in the door of the tabernacle, where also were Moses and Aaron similarly provided with censers. There, too, were all the members of the representative body which is called the congregation, that they might be witnesses of everything that took place. While they stood, the glory of the Lord appeared unto them, and a voice from it came out addressed to Moses and Aaron, and saying, "Separate yourselves from among this congregation, that I may consume them in a moment." When he heard that, the magnanimity of Moses returned, and, remembering his mediatorial responsibility, he made intercession for the people—Aaron joining him with a fervent heart—and said, "O God, the God of the spirits of all flesh, shall one man sin, and wilt thou be wroth with all the congregation?" This prayer prevailed so far, that the congregation, as a whole, was not consigned to death; but after a separation had been made between the multitude and the tents of Dathan and Abiram, and while the mutineers stood with their wives and children, apparently in dogged defiance, in the doors of their habitations, Moses said, "Hereby ye shall know that the Lord hath sent me to do all these works; for I have not done them of mine own mind. If these men die the common death of all men, or if they be visited after the visitation of all men, then the Lord hath not sent me. But if the Lord make a new thing, and the earth open her mouth and swallow them up, with all that appertain unto them, and they go down alive into the pit, then ye shall understand that these men have provoked the Lord." While he was yet speaking, the earth opened and swallowed up alive the men of Reuben; and at the same time there came a fire from the Lord and consumed the two hundred and fifty men that offered incense. But the sons of Korah, as we learn from a subsequent chapter,* were not destroyed with their father, and we may therefore infer that they did not share his guilt; while the fact that the families of the Reubenites perished with their heads, may be held as indicating that they all joined in the revolt.

We cannot forget here that the Korahites afterward rose to great honor in the service of the sanctuary. The prophet Samuel† belonged to the family, and its representatives in David's time had an important place in conducting "the service of song in the house of the Lord." Ten of the Psalms bear their names in the inscriptions, and some of these are remarkable for the depth of their experience and the fervor of their feeling. It is not unlikely, therefore, that the fearful infliction of judgment on the head of their house, as recorded in this chapter, may have operated with wholesome effect upon the survivors, and so may have contributed to the production of that excellence for which in later times the members of this family were distinguished.

But sympathy with the mutiny was not confined to those who had suffered the miraculous infliction of punishment at the hands of God; for the next day all the congregation murmured against Moses and Aaron, saying, "Ye have killed the people of the Lord." It seems as if these Israelites will never learn to distinguish between Moses and Jehovah. They are continually blaming Moses for that which God has done; and so they are constantly guilty of doing God dishonor, and of treating his servant with injustice. But no

---

* Num. xxvi., 11.   † 1 Chron. vi., 22-28.

people can do such things with impunity; and even as they are murmuring now the glory-cloud on the tabernacle indicates that some communication of the Divine will is about to be made concerning them. When Moses and Aaron went forward to receive it, they heard these awful words—"Get you up from among this congregation, that I may consume them in a moment." But not yet will Moses abdicate his mediatorial office, for once again he stands forth as intercessor; and knowing that a plague had begun among the people, he sent forth Aaron with his censer, filled with fire from the altar, and covered with incense, to make an atonement for the people: and as he stood between the living and the dead the plague was stayed; not, however, before fourteen thousand and seven hundred persons had perished from its ravages.

Thus, by the destructive results that followed the attempt of Korah and his company to intrude into the priest's office and burn incense before the Lord—as contrasted with the beneficent effects of Aaron's approach with his censer unto Jehovah when the plague was stayed—the divine and indefeasible right of Aaron to the priesthood is conclusively established.

But it was needful that some permanent evidence of this divine vindication should be preserved, and that was secured in two ways by Moses, according to the commandment of the Lord. In the first place, the brazen censers used by the two hundred and fifty mutineers were gathered up by Eleazer, the son of Aaron, and made into broad plates for a covering of the altar, and there they remained, to be "a memorial unto the children of Israel that no stranger, which is not of the seed of Aaron, come near to offer incense before the Lord." But, to make assurance doubly sure, another miraculous testimony was borne to Aaron. Twelve almond rods or staves were taken, one for each tribe, and on each was written the name of the representative of the tribe to which it belonged, just as the name of Aaron was written on that which stood for Levi. These rods, thus marked, were laid up before the ark; and in the morning that of the man whom God had chosen was found with buds, and blossoms, and ripe almonds upon it. The rod thus distinguished was that which bore the name of Aaron, and it was laid up before the testimony, to be kept for a token against the rebels; so that, if possible, all murmuring should cease among the people, and there should be no more necessity for such severe judicial inflictions.

This miracle of the blossoming rod was a sign as well as a wonder; and, in our appreciation of its importance as a witness to Aaron's priesthood, we must not lose sight of its spiritual significance. The staves had in them no natural ability to bring forth buds, blossoms, and fruit. In this respect that of Aaron was no exception to the others; but God, by his power, brought out of it these beautiful things. Now, in the same way, the several patriarchs of the tribes, and Aaron among them, had no natural qualifications or gifts for the priesthood; but God gave to the son of Amram that of which he was originally destitute, and, by his grace, fitted him for the office to which he called him, so that he bore fruit which was well pleasing in Jehovah's sight. Thus the priesthood did not depend upon primogeniture, or upon natural endowments; it was itself the gift of God, and where he bestowed it, the evidence of its divine origin was seen in the holy beauty of him who had received its unction.

Now, in seeking to turn this history to account under the altered circumstances of the Gospel dispensation, we may give the clearest and most easily remembered presentation of the truths which it suggests by classing them under the two heads of doctrinal and practical.

The doctrinal connect themselves with the priesthood of

our Lord Jesus Christ, of whom Aaron was at once the precursor and the type. It is true, indeed, that in the relation of his priesthood to the other offices with which he is invested, as well as in the perpetuity of its continuance, Christ had his fullest prefiguration in the mysterious Melchisedec, to whom Abraham gave tithes of all his spoils; but, as the author of the Epistle to the Hebrews reminds us, there were many things in the Aaronic priesthood which clearly pointed to that of the Messiah. In particular, he teaches us that there was a foreshadowing of the sacerdotal pre-eminence of Jesus in the divine appointment of Aaron; and an illustration of his work in the sacrifices presented, and the intercession made by the Jewish high-priest. Thus he says, "No man taketh this honor unto himself, but he that is called of God, as was Aaron; so also Christ glorified not himself to be made a high-priest, but he that said unto him, Thou art my son, to-day have I begotten thee."* Just as, therefore, the divine appointment of Aaron to his office was manifested by the acceptance of his incense, and by the blossoming of his rod, so the author of the Epistle to the Hebrews intimates that, by many infallible signs, the designation of Jesus as a high-priest by God has been plainly proved to mankind. Among these we might enumerate the scene at his baptism, when the Holy Ghost, of which the sacred oil was only the symbol, anointed him for the work which he came to earth to perform; and when, almost in the words of the second Psalm, the voice from the excellent glory proclaimed, "This is my beloved son, in whom I am well pleased." In a similar way, on the Mountain of Transfiguration, the same testimony from Heaven was borne to him; but the most striking and convincing proof of all is that which is furnished by his resurrection from the dead. It is to this that Paul refers

---

* Heb. v., 4.

when, in the beginning of his letter to the Romans, speaking of Jesus, he says, "He was made of the seed of David according to the flesh; and declared to be the Son of God with power, according to the Spirit of holiness, by the resurrection from the dead."* Thus the empty tomb of Joseph, and the witness borne by many to the fact that Jesus rose from it on the morning of the third day, is as clear a demonstration of the divine appointment of Jesus to the office of a priest, as the brazen plates of the Korahitic mutineers on the altar were to that of Aaron and his sons. Nay, more; as the almond-rod of Aaron, with its fruit in the three stages of bud, and blossom, and ripened almonds, remained before the ark of testimony, to be for coming generations an evidence that the son of Amram had been chosen to make atonement for the people, so the incidents of the day of Pentecost continue embalmed in the imperishable amber of the New Testament, as a proof for all succeeding ages in the history of the human race of the divine origin, the true reality, and the sure efficacy of the priesthood of Jesus. For, as a mere man, the son of Mary was a root out of a dry ground. There was no form or comeliness in him that men should desire him. There was not in his humanity, innocent as it was, any more life-giving potency for the race than there is in any other man. But here, on the day of Pentecost, we find that dry rod putting forth evidences of vitality. We see on it the bud of the awakened sinner, the blossom of the sincere penitent, and the full-formed almond in the preacher of the day and his noble companions, who stood forth to call men to the enjoyment of salvation through faith in him. No human causes will account for the phenomena which that day presented. They were not the results of intemperance, or excitement, or fanaticism, or super-

---

* Rom. i., 3, 4.

stition; they can be truly traced only to the outpouring of the Spirit of God, and that was itself the first great result on earth of the priestly presentation of his sacrifice for us by the Lord Jesus within the veil. In these three thousand conversions, then, we have God's own endorsement of the divine right of the priesthood of Christ; but these were only the first of a series, the last members of which are the converts of to-day; and so every new instance of regeneration that occurs before our eyes is a new attestation of the truth that we have "a great High-priest that is passed into the heavens, Jesus the Son of God."

Still further, when we see Aaron here standing, censer in hand, between the living and the dead, for the staying of the plague which had broken out in the camp of Israel, we are reminded of the pleadings of our great High-priest, "who is even at the right hand of God, who also maketh intercession for us." When the stroke of divine justice is about to fall upon the barren tree, it is he who says, "Lord, let it alone this year also;" when the Roman soldiers were nailing him to the cross, it was he who held the flaming sword of justice back with the prayer, "Father, forgive them; for they know not what they do;" and it is of him the inspired penman has written these memorable words: "Wherefore he is able also to save them to the uttermost that come unto God by him, seeing he ever liveth to make intercession for them."*
Impenitent sinner, will you remember that you owe the continuance of all your blessings to the pleading of that very Priest whom you are now despising? Behold him yonder, standing, censer in hand, before the throne! Hear him say, "Give him this year also;" and as your heart is moved with gratitude for his intervention, oh, beware of presuming on his forbearance! For if you are not led by his goodness

---

* Heb. vii., 25.

unto repentance, the day will come when even he will say, "Cut him down; why cumbereth he the ground?" Anxious sinner, will you bear in mind that by his intercession he is able to save to the uttermost those who come unto God by him? "To the uttermost," whether of guilt or of misery; therefore, he is able to save you. But "them that come unto God by him;" therefore, you must go to God by him, for otherwise there is no deliverance for you. Burdened, tried, and weary Christian! will you never forget that one is pleading for you who knows your case, and will come ere long to your relief? Recall that dreadful night in the experience of the first disciples when, in the effort to cross the lake churned into foaming waves by the storm, they rowed on and on till the fourth watch, toiling apparently without result. But there was One, unseen by them, upon the mountain-side, who was bowed in prayer on their behalf; and at length he came to them, encompassed with a garment that turned the night almost into day, and girded with a power which stilled the angry sea to peace. So, unseen by you, the same High-priest is interceding for you within the veil; and soon—sooner, haply, than you wot of—he will come to you with help.

But, reminded as we are by this narrative of the divine appointment and prevailing atonement of our great High-priest, we must not forget the warning which is here suggested of the guilt and danger of those who would either usurp or destroy his priesthood. If I have rightly read the motives of Korah here, he desired the priesthood for himself, and so wished to depose Aaron. Now, this may suggest to us the conduct of those who, not content with the honor of the Gospel ministry, which is the noblest office any man can hold on earth, desire to mount into that of the priesthood, and claim to stand between God and the worshippers in a certain mediatorial capacity, and offer sacrifice on their behalf. I am far, indeed, from alleging, or even insinuating, that they who adopt such a course are intentionally wanting in reverence for Jesus, or are deliberately disloyal to him. On the contrary, many among them seem to love him with an ardent and almost passionate devotion. Yet the tendency of their doctrine is to take away from the matchless glory of his priesthood. For if in any sense his sacrifice needs to be repeated, then in that sense it must have been imperfect when he offered it at first, and he was wrong when he said, "It is finished!" If in any sense we need another priest to whom to make confession, and from whom to receive absolution, then in that sense Jesus Christ is not a perfect priest for us; and thus, whether they own it to themselves or not, nay, whether they are conscious of it themselves or not, they who would make the Christian ministry a priesthood for the offering of objective sacrifice are undermining the priesthood of Christ, and following "the gainsaying of Korah." We can confess sin really only to him; we can have true absolution only from him; and they who come to a fellow-man for the performance of the duty of confession, or for the reception of the blessing of absolution, are robbing Jesus of his priestly honor, and virtually denying the perfection of his sacerdotal work.

But, on the other hand, and at the other extreme, the same sin is committed by those who explain away his priesthood altogether. Dathan and Abiram said, "All the congregation are holy, every one of them:" we are a nation of priests, and we have, therefore, no need of a special priest at all. So there are those among us who allege that Christians are all priests alike, and that there was no atoning or sacerdotal efficacy in the work of Christ at all. Now, this is one of those pestilent half-truths which, in their results, are always more injurious than unmitigated errors. It is true, as Peter says, that we are "a royal priesthood, a holy nation, a peculiar people; that we should show forth the praises of him who hath called us out of darkness into his marvellous light." It is true that as priests we may all come to God with spiritual sacrifices, such as prayer and praise and benevolence, and that we are to offer our bodies "living sacrifices unto him." But then, how has this been brought about? The New Testament answers that it has been accomplished for us by the sacrifice of himself upon the cross for us by our great High-priest. Without his high-priesthood, our common and ordinary priesthood had not been; and as, in the old tabernacle, the priest took the fire for his censer from the altar of sacrifice, so the incense which we offer in our praises and prayers must be kindled in our hearts with a live coal taken from the altar of the cross whereon Christ, as High-priest, has made atonement for us. If the Lord Jesus did not offer himself a real sacrifice in our behalf, and make a real atonement for our sins, then he was no high-priest, and our praises and prayers are but like the smoke of the incense of Nadab and Abihu when they offered strange fire before the Lord. Think not, therefore, that you here to-night have nothing to do with this old story; for if you repudiate Christ's death as a sacrifice for sin, if you fritter away the crucifixion into a martyrdom, if you deny the necessity for atonement of any sort, then are you kindred spirits with Dathan and Abiram, who maintained that all priesthood was unnecessary. So the middle ground between sacerdotalism on the one hand, and repudiation of sacrifice on the other, is the only safe ground on which to stand. We magnify the high-priesthood of Christ as that of him who offered the one true sacrifice for human sin, and makes the only efficient intercession; but we maintain also the universal priesthood of believers as ordained of God for the presentation of spiritual offerings. By the one we secure the peerless pre-eminence of Jesus, by the other we conserve the liberty and equality of believers; and the denial of either will issue in disaster. The repudiation of the latter will entail upon us the despotism of priestcraft; the rejection of the former will reduce us to a system of the merest naturalism, and give us a gospel without the cross—"another gospel which is not another."

The practical lessons connect themselves with the bearing of Moses and the fate of the conspirators. In the bearing of Moses there is much to awaken our admiration and incite us to imitation. I will not affirm, indeed, that on this occasion there was in our hero no irritation of feeling or bitterness of heart. Moses was human, and in his haste he may have spoken here, as at Meribah, unadvisedly with his lips. But here it was to God he spoke, and not to the people; and in that, at least, we may securely follow him when we are in similar circumstances. Devotion was his safety-valve. He went to God with everything, and he waited for God's vindication. He was conscious of integrity. He could take God to witness that "he had not taken an ass from one of them, or injured any of them." And strong in the knowledge of his own rectitude, he left the whole matter in God's hands. So if we are in the right, and men assail us, let us calmly appeal to God, and bide his time. If we are in the wrong, the noblest thing to do is to acknowledge our error and repent. But if we are right, let us stand still; for when we stand on truth, the world will ultimately come round to us. It may be hard to do all this, but it will become easy when we think of him who, "when he was reviled, reviled not again; when he suffered, he threatened not; but committed himself to him that judgeth righteously." God's government is, in the long run, on the side of truth; and though he may not always appear to vindicate us so speedily as here he vindicated Moses, yet the day will come when he will "bring forth our righteousness as the light, and our judgment as the noonday."

Finally, from the fate of the conspirators we may learn that selfish ambition is courting its own destruction. Korah and his company, with the princes of Reuben, sought only their own aggrandizement, and they gained a violent death. There was but a night here between the manifestation of the evil and its punishment. But sometimes in the providence of God a long interval elapses, and men are tempted to think that success has crowned the schemes of grasping avarice and unscrupulous dishonesty. Yet at length the Nemesis arrives, and it is all the more dreadful because of the delay. Read the histories of those who have waded through blood to their greatness, and have made every interest bend to their ambition, and you will marvel at the manner in which retribution has come upon them. Still, let us not imagine that this holds only in the lives of emperors and the histories of empires. It is just as true of selfishness in politics and in business. The plotter always in the end outwits himself. The only safe ambition is that which Christ enjoins: "Whosoever will be chief among you, let him be your servant: even as the Son of man came not to be ministered unto, but to minister, and to give his life a ransom for many." That is an ambition that sheds no blood, and sacrifices no interests but its own. That is an ambition which blesses humanity and glorifies God. There may be a cross in its path, but the cross is the last step in the ascent that leads to a throne. Moses proved his right to be chief by his continuous self-sacrifice; and so his name to-day ranks next to that of Him whose glory he foreshadows; while Korah, who sought his own interests, lost both these and his good name—so that he stands here a beacon to warn us of the certain destruction that awaits all mere worldly ambition. "He that loveth his life shall lose it; and he that hateth his life in this world shall keep it unto life eternal."

XXI.

THE SIN OF MOSES, AND THE DEATH OF AARON.

NUMBERS xx., 1-29.

BETWEEN the incidents reviewed by us in our last lecture and those which we are now to consider, an interval of thirty-eight years elapsed. During all that time the Hebrews had been wandering in the wilderness, having their head-quarters at the place where the tabernacle happened to be at the time; but probably themselves broken up into separate companies, which scattered themselves over the wilderness of Paran, and led a nomadic life with the flocks and herds. The common idea, indeed, is that they retained their compact unity throughout, and moved all together when they moved at all; but the peculiar phraseology of the verse which introduces this new section of the history—"Then came the children of Israel, even the whole congregation, into the desert of Zin in the first month"—seems to describe a reassembling of the tribes after some such temporary dispersion as that which we have hinted at. The fortieth year of their desert life had now commenced; and, expecting some immediate and important developments, or summoned in some special manner by Moses, the people came and re-formed their encampment at the place to which the spies had brought their report, and from which, therefore, it was most natural that they should make their advance into the land of promise.

The great outstanding features of the camp were the same

as they had been eight-and-thirty years before, but many changes had occurred among the tribes themselves. Those who were old men and women at the date of the Exodus had now been gathered to their fathers; such as had reached middle life when the desert march was begun had also passed away; and, with the exception of Moses, Caleb, Joshua, and the heads of the Levitical households, there were few, if any, out of the two millions of the Israelites who had passed the age of threescore years. Between Moses and the people generally two entire generations had dropped out; and those who had been his coadjutors when he left Egypt were no longer in the land of the living. We can imagine, therefore, that a sense of loneliness would come over his heart; and it is not improbable that this was the occasion on which he composed that plaintive yet trustful and consolatory psalm,* which has come down to us through three millenniums, contrasting for us the eternity of God with the brief earthly life of man, and teaching us to find our solace, amidst the vicissitudes of the world, in that continuous providence whose "increasing purpose," as it runs through the ages, transfigures the "work" of the fathers into the "glory" of their children, and out of days of affliction and years of evil still brings gladness at the last.

These feelings would be deepened in his breast by the death of Miriam, which took place soon after the return of the people to Kadesh; and, as they buried her remains in the neighborhood, there were no sincerer mourners beside the grave than the brothers with whom she had been so long and, in the main, so lovingly associated. Looking back from that point to the first dawning of mental consciousness when he found himself listening to his sister's song, or playing gleefully at her feet, Moses would feel anew the truth

---

* Psalm xc.

which he has expressed in the psalm before referred to, "We spend our years as a tale that is told;" and as he remembered all he owed to Miriam, and thought of the good influence which, for the most part, she had exercised on those around her, all her faults would be forgiven, and all her failings forgotten, in the sense of loss which stole into his spirit.

But little time was allowed him for the luxury of sorrow; for, though the people generally must have sympathized with him in his bereavement, yet their solicitude for him was soon swallowed up in their anxiety for themselves. There was no water for them to drink; and, in the blind unreasonableness of their suffering, they repeated the sin of their fathers, and blamed Moses and Aaron for their misery. With that perversity which seems always to have possessed them, and which led them to look backward rather than forward, they envied those who had died, and they complained that they had been brought out of Egypt upon false pretences. Thus the same spirit of discontentment and unbelief which had been so severely punished in the parents seemed to be springing up in the children, and Moses was at his wits' end. But he went to his old refuge, and, appealing to God, received directions as to how he was to proceed. He was commanded to take his rod and speak to the neighboring rock before the eyes of the assembly, and was assured that an abundant stream of water would immediately gush forth for their supply. But the self-control of Moses gave way before the perversity of the people; so that, instead of speaking to the rock, he spoke to them—and that, too, in words of anger—while he smote the rock with blows which manifested a spirit of vindictiveness strangely out of harmony with his later disposition, and calculated to bring dishonor on the name of the Master whom he served. Such an evil—though it were in Moses, the saintliest of all the

The Sin of Moses, and the Death of Aaron. 361

people—could not go unchastised; and therefore, though the water came just the same as if he had done everything as he had been commanded, the Lord said to him, and to Aaron, who was a consenting party to the sin, "Because ye believed me not, to sanctify me in the eyes of the children of Israel, therefore ye shall not bring this congregation into the land which I have given them." Thus the sin of Moses is not to be gauged simply by the facts that he smote the rock instead of speaking to it, and that he scolded the people for their murmurings, and seemed to indicate that the miracle was as much his as God's. It is to be judged of by the spirit out of which these things themselves did spring. His sin was unbelief in God; his petulance of temper, and hastiness, alike of act and speech, grew out of his temporary distrust of God. The murmuring of the people shook, for the moment, his confidence in Jehovah, and that having given way, his self-control went with it as a thing of course. Now, this unbelief was, for the time, so great that he gave up all hope of reaching the Land of Promise; and so he put himself in precisely the same category with those who "entered not in because of unbelief," and was visited with the same punishment. I think we can easily understand the case. For eight-and-thirty years he had been looking forward to the time when he and the people should enter the land of the covenant; and now, after all that has happened, they manifest the same old mutinous spirit as their fathers had shown, and he sees nothing before them but a prolongation of the ban which had kept them so long in the wilderness. It seems to him useless to strive longer against their perversity; he gives up all expectation, for the time at least, of ever settling them in their promised inheritance; God's covenant is forgotten in the presence of the people's disaffection; and even as he lifts his rod to strike the rock, he is thinking less of Jehovah than of them, and saying within himself, "If this is to be their spirit, then we may as well give up the hope of Canaan." Thus the sight of their discontentment affects him as the sight of the Anakim affected the majority of the spies: it makes him doubt the possibility of their ever acquiring possession of the goodly land; it makes him forget the promise, "Certainly I will be with thee;" and, therefore, having become a partaker in their sin, he is a partaker also in their punishment. It was a terrible disappointment to him; and again and again he appealed to God for a reversal of the sentence, until at length he was met with a peremptory command, "Let it suffice thee; speak no more unto me of this matter."* Ere long, too, the irrevocable nature of the decree was impressed upon him by the death of Aaron, which took place amidst circumstances of deep solemnity, and in a manner which clearly connected it with the hand of God.

From Kadesh, wishing to cultivate friendly feeling with the Edomites, who were descendants of Esau, Moses sent messengers to their king, asking permission to pass through his territory. While these messengers were absent, and calculating, perhaps, on obtaining the favor which they asked, Moses and the people marched up the valley of Arabah, encountering on their way, and defeating, the army of Arad, one of the Canaanitish kings, and pitching their camp at length at the foot of Mount Hor.

This somewhat remarkable mountain, now called Jebel Nebi Haroun, or the Mount of Aaron the prophet, is in Arabia Petræa, on the borders of Idumea, about midway between the most northern point of the Red Sea and the most southern point of the Dead Sea. In its immediate vicinity are the ruins of Petra, the famous city of the Rock. The ascent is steep and toilsome. Its summit is about five thou-

---

* Deut. iii., 26.

sand feet above the level of the Mediterranean, and consists of two peaks, which give it a castellated appearance. On the loftier of these there is a mosque built, over what is said to be the tomb of Aaron, and from the flat roof of this building the traveller's eye may wander over the last prospect looked upon by the first Jewish high-priest. It is thus described by Dean Stanley: "He looked over the valley of the Arabah, countersected by its hundred watercourses, and beyond, over the white mountains of the wilderness they had so long traversed; and at the northern edge of it there must have been visible the heights through which the Israelites had vainly attempted to force their way into the Promised Land. This was the western view. Close around him, on the east, were the rugged mountains of Edom, and far along the horizon the white downs of Mount Seir. A dreary moment and a dreary scene—such, at any rate, it must have seemed to the aged priest."* Another says, "There is no part of the landscape which the eye wanders over with more curiosity and delight than the crags of Mount Hor itself, which stand up on every side in the most rugged and fantastic forms; sometimes strangely piled one on the other, and sometimes as strangely yawning in clefts of a frightful depth."†

As the people were encamped in full view of this peculiar mountain, the command came from Jehovah which designated it as the scene of Aaron's death. Observe, as we pass, the kind consideration for Moses which was shown by God, in the manner in which the communication was made. On other occasions injunctions which had reference to Aaron were given to Moses alone, and were by him transmitted to his brother. But now, when the message is one of

---

* Stanley's "Sinai and Palestine," p. 87.
† Irby and Mangles, quoted in Alexander's "Kitto," s. v. HOR.

death, which it would have given exquisite pain to Moses to repeat, God gives it to them both at once, and says to them, "Aaron shall be gathered unto his people: for he shall not enter into the land which I have given unto the children of Israel, because ye rebelled against my word at the water of Meribah." What feelings in the hearts of these two brothers would be stirred up by these words? Their long companionship in these wilderness wanderings; their former association in Egypt, when together they contended with the tyrannic Pharaoh, and the tender recollections of boyhood, when they met and amused themselves from time to time in the home of Amram, would crowd upon their memories, and thoughts too deep for utterance would fill their minds. Nay, more, the consciousness on the part of Moses that he was the main transgressor at the rock would add poignancy to the grief he felt, and we may well believe that they sought relief each in the silent and loving embrace of the other. But not long time could be given to such natural emotion, for the command of God must be obeyed. Accordingly, in the sight of all the people, Aaron, in his full pontifical attire, as if he were going to officiate on a high and sacred festival, steps forth, and with Moses on one side, and his son Eleazar on the other, he sets out for the summit of the mountain. As they move up its steep and rugged slopes, they are followed by the eager eyes of the people, on whose behalf he had gone so often with the blood of atonement within the veil. What earnest converse has he now with Moses concerning the world beyond? What faithful exhortations does he address to Eleazar as to his conduct in that office on which he is so soon to enter? What deep consciousness of unworthiness and sin would burden his heart? What calm trustfulness in the God of the mercy-seat would cheer and sustain his spirit? And now they have reached the summit, on which he pauses a moment to take his last look

The Sin of Moses, and the Death of Aaron. 365

of earth. There at his feet are the "goodly tents" of Israel, and over the people once again he pronounces his priestly benediction. There is the tabernacle in whose service he had found at once his labor and his joy; yonder, away before him, is the wilderness through which he had wandered under the guidance of the mystic pillar for so many years; and far off to the right are the hills beyond which Canaan lies—but that Canaan is not for him. Yet there is no murmur. Once again it may be written, "And Aaron held his peace." But now he strips off his official robes, and sees them put upon his son. Then he bravely and quietly lies down to die, and even as Moses and Eleazar look at him his spirit has departed, and he is on earth no more.

Thus sublimely died the brother and companion of Israel's great leader. He had not, in the highest degree, the qualities of insight, promptitude, energy, and firmness for which Moses was pre-eminent; but he excelled his brother in the passive virtues of patience and endurance. Under the stunning blow which deprived him of two of his sons in a moment, no word of reproach escaped his lips; while on the occasion of the Korahitic rebellion he waited, with a quiet and becoming dignity, until his pre-eminence had been established, and then he used his priesthood in making intercession for the plague-stricken multitudes. But his character shines most brightly at "the evening time;" and to him we may apply the poet's words, "Nothing in his life became him like the leaving it." We forget his faults as we see him ascending so quietly the hill on which he is to be gathered to his people. The clouds which at intervals, in the long day of his life, had obscured his sun, have now all cleared away; and, as it set behind the castellated summit of Mount Hor, it threw thereon a golden glory, which lingers on it still! Three went up, but only two came down—Moses with a keener sense of loneliness than ever, and Eleazar mourning his father's absence, all the more because of the added responsibility of his new position. For thirty days the people halted in sorrow for their loss, and then the pillar rose from above the tabernacle, and led them on and out toward the country of their hope. Everything went on as it had done before; but Aaron was not there!

In turning this narrative to profitable account for our modern Christian life, I restrict myself to three particulars. Let us learn, then, in the first place, that faith in God is the regulating grace of the Christian character. So long as that is preserved, it will keep all other principles of our nature in restraint; but when that is lost, the brake is removed from the wheel, and everything goes wrong. The prophet has written, "He that believeth shall not make haste." His faith enables him to act with deliberation, and he does nothing unadvisedly; but when he sinks into despair he is apt to become reckless, and allows himself to speak and act in such a manner as to bring reproach upon himself and dishonor upon God. The loss of faith leads to panic, and panic is utterly inconsistent with self-control. We have a remarkable illustration of the truth of these remarks in the history of David; for it was when, losing hold of God's promise to him, he sank into unbelieving despondency, saying, "I shall now perish one day by the hand of Saul," that he fled to the court of Achish, and became entangled in those subterfuges and deceits which culminated in the burning of Ziklag and the mutiny of his men; and if we have given a correct analysis of the conduct of Moses here at Meribah, we have a manifestation of the same truth in that. Now, the importance of this principle can hardly be over-estimated; for, on the one hand, it shows us how we may attain to that rule over our own spirits which is a greater glory to a man than the taking of a city is to a warrior; and, on the other, it gives a very serious aspect indeed to those ebullitions of temper, and selfishness, and self-will which we are all too prone to regard as of little moment. If we wish to overcome ourselves, then the victory is to be won through faith in God. Mere watchfulness will not suffice; but we must cultivate that confidence in God which believes that all things work together for good to them who love him; which realizes the universality of his providential administration as including the minutest as well as the vastest concerns of life; and which has the unwavering assurance that we shall enter at last upon our heavenly inheritance. Watchfulness is like the boy who knows no better than to be continually setting the hands of the clock which is standing still; but the cultivation of faith winds up the spring, and sets and keeps everything in proper motion thereby. Therefore, if you want to control self, seek faith in the nearness, the faithfulness, and the universality of the providence of God. You will not be provoked by the stupidity of a servant or the occurrence of a preventible calamity, or the perversity of those with whom you come into contact, so long as you can say, "This also cometh from the Lord, who is wonderful in counsel, and excellent in working." The grasping selfishness or unreasonable fault-finding, or plotting cunning of those with whom, for the time, you may have to deal, will not throw you off your balance, or tempt you to speak unadvisedly with your lips, so long as you can remember that you are journeying to heaven, and that the meeting of these difficulties is a part of the training through which God is bringing you, for the purpose of preparing you for its enjoyment. "He will keep him in perfect peace whose mind is stayed on him." Therefore, if we wish to preserve our equanimity of temper and disposition, let us stay our minds on God. Looking to him will always keep us right. If I wish to walk in a straight line across a pathless field, I fix my eye on some prominent object on the farther side of it, and go steadily toward that, looking neither to the right hand nor the left. If I desire to keep my head from reeling as I cross the narrow bridge that spans a deep ravine, I fix my gaze on some rock upon the other shore, and go forward; but so sure as I look down, I begin to tremble, and my panic may be my destruction. Similarly, in the trackless mazes of life, and in the dizzy paths of business, our only safety is in looking to God in Christ. We shall never go wrong while we keep him in view; but when we lose sight of him our danger begins, and we grow reckless.

Then, on the other side of the subject, see what the root of our explosiveness of temper and rashness of conduct is! There is no sin for which we are more ready to excuse ourselves than irritability. We speak apologetically of that "rash humor which our mothers gave us," and persuade ourselves that testiness and haste of speech are very venial things. Now, I will not deny that temperament has something to do with them; but faith can overmaster temperament, as even the case of Moses here illustrates, for meekness was not one of his original characteristics; and, therefore, in every instance I am bold to say that the loss of self-control has its origin in lack of faith, for the time being, in God. We bear a great calamity with composure, because we see God's hand in that; but when it comes to the upsetting of a tea-urn, or the breaking of a valuable ornament by an inexperienced servant, we act as if there was no providence in that, and we are guilty, like Moses here, of speaking unadvisedly with our lips. The leader who is calm in a great crisis, is thrown off his guard by a little breach of discipline; and the Christian who can stand in quiet composure beside the grave of a child, is excited into terrible anger by the removal of an article from its right place on his desk. He thinks it is temperament; but he ought to learn that it is lack of faith in

God, and he should be on his guard lest it shut him out from some promised land of usefulness, into which he would otherwise have entered.

But, in the second place, we see here how important it is to be always ready for death. The death of Aaron was not altogether without warning, but in some sense it may be regarded as sudden. There were no premonitions of it in his bodily frame, else he could not have ascended Mount Hor; and when God's command came, it might take him, and probably did take him, by surprise. Yet he was not appalled, for he believed God, and that kept him in perfect peace. "What, sir," said a domestic servant, who was sweeping her door-step, to the young Spencer, of Liverpool, as he was hastening by, "is your opinion of sudden death?" He paused a moment; then saying, "Sudden death to the Christian is sudden glory," he hurried on; and in less than an hour afterward he was drowned while bathing in the Mersey. The coincidence was remarked on at the time; and the truth that underlies the words was the consolation of his sorrowing congregation, as they missed him from the midst of them. A great change has come over the minds of Christians on this subject in later years. The petition of the Litany, "From battle, from murder, and from sudden death, good Lord, deliver us," is not now regarded as so appropriate as it was once; and many who would be far from agreeing to the other changes which it introduces, would prefer the amended reading of the Liturgy of the old King's Chapel of Boston in this place—"From battle, from murder, and from death unprepared, good Lord, deliver us." We are coming now to the opinion which, strangely enough, the great dramatist has put into the mouth of Hamlet, in reference to the time and manner of death, when he says, "There's a special providence in the falling of a sparrow: if it be now, 'tis not to come; if it be not to come, it will be now; if it be not now, yet it will come; the readiness is all!" The pith of the matter lies there—"the readiness is all;" and the only readiness is that which Paul has described, when he says, "For to me to live is Christ, and to die is gain." Life is the solemn thing, therefore; and if only that be right, we may leave the ordering of our death to Him whose providence is in the fall of a sparrow. That was a beautiful answer given by John Wesley to a lady, when, being asked by her how he would spend the intervening time if he certainly knew that he was to die at twelve o'clock the next night, he replied, "How, madam? Why, just as I intend to spend it now. I should preach this evening at Gloucester, and again at five to-morrow morning; after that I should ride to Tewkesbury, preach in the afternoon, and meet the societies in the evening. I should then repair to friend Martin's house, who expects to entertain me, converse and pray with the family as usual, retire to my room at ten o'clock, commend myself to my Heavenly Father, lie down to rest, and wake up in glory." Here is the secret of an active life, which shall not have its interest lessened by any longing to die, or its enjoyment marred by any fear of death. Let us serve God, through faith in Christ, in all our engagements. These may not be apparently so spiritual as those of Aaron in the tabernacle, or of Wesley in the pulpit. They may be simply petty household cares or common business transactions; they may be laborious, and to a degree distracting; but if they be duties manifestly set before us, and if they be performed cheerfully, as unto the Lord and not to men, they may be so sanctified by the Word of God and prayer that the spirit, while busily occupied on earth, may be in holy harmony with heaven; and death, when it comes, shall only lift us into a higher kind of that enjoyment which is our delight on earth. Let us aim after this "readiness;" for it will give new zest to our present existence, and put for us new interest into the life beyond, when we are able to say, "To me to live is Christ, and to die is gain."

But, in the third place, here we may learn the place and power of the individual in the onward progress of human society. Aaron gives his vestments to Eleazar before he dies, and so the priestly work is perpetuated, though he no longer performs it. On one side of it, this is melancholy enough; and it would almost seem as if no one man was of any great service in carrying forward the work of God upon the earth. We are accustomed to say that nobody is indispensable, and there is a sense in which that is true. The death of Aaron does not stop the tabernacle service; and, as we shall by-and-by see, the death of Moses does not keep Israel from entering upon Canaan. So it is good for us sometimes to remember that God and the world can do without us. The king dies; but with the announcement of his demise, the herald proclaims his successor, and says, "Long live the king!" Ministers and people die, but the Church abides, and carries still forward its beneficent work. That is all true, and it is as consolatory to society as it is humbling to the individual. But there is another side to the subject, which must in nowise be forgotten, for the progress of the ages is made through the deposit left by each successive generation of individual men. Our possessions to-day in life are not all the fruits of our personal efforts. We are the heirs of all the preceding generations; and if we act well our part, we shall leave something additional of our own behind us, which shall enrich those who shall come after us. Geologists tell us that, through long millenniums, this earth was in process of preparation for the dwelling-place of man. One species of vegetation after another came, and left its deposit; one kind of animals after another appeared, and left their bones to petrify. Thus stratum after stratum rose, until at length our planet was furnished for the abode of the human race. Now, just so it has been with the successive generations of men themselves. They have not been simple repetitions of each other, as the generations of the lower animals have been; but each, as it has passed away, has left something behind it as a legacy to its successors. You see how true this is in literature; for we are to-day the heirs of all that is worth preserving in the English language, from the days of Chaucer to our own. You know how true this is, also, in science; for the discoveries of the philosophers of the past have made a vantage-ground from which their followers have risen, in this age, to results of which the former never dreamed. But it is true, also, in moral and spiritual things. The children of Israel conquered Canaan without Moses. That is, doubtless, the case; but do not forget that, if he had not led them out of Egypt, and governed them for forty years, they would not have been in circumstances to cross the Jordan under Joshua. The tabernacle service went on without Aaron. That is true; yet if Aaron had not gone before him, Eleazar would not have entered upon such a sphere of usefulness as that which now opened up before him. If there had been no Bacon, there might have been no Newton; and if there had been no Newton, our modern philosophers would not have been what they are. So in Christian history. If there had been no reformers, there would have been no Puritans; and if there had been no Puritans, there would have been no Pilgrims; and if there had been no Pilgrims, there would have been no such churches as we have to-day in our land, conducting missionary operations both at home and abroad.

What, then, is the lesson of all this? You already anticipate the answer: it is that each of us shall strive to do his utmost in the work to which God has called him, so that we may leave a higher platform for those who shall come after us. It seems humble to say that God can do without us;

but though that is true, let us not forget that when he can do without us, he will do without us. So long as we are here, however, we are required by him for something. Let us therefore find out what that is, and do it; and while we do it, let us pray that God may establish it so that it may remain to bless posterity. The little coral insect beneath the waves builds its tiny cell, and dies; another comes, and builds on that, and dies; and so on and up it grows, until first a reef, and then an island, and then an archipelago of islands rises up above the waters. So, my brethren, let us do our work, that others entering on it may carry it forward through after generations. Thus shall the work of the fathers become the glory of their children; and in the end, when the mystery of God shall be finished, we shall see in its completed beauty and proportion the great fabric into which we put our little all; and we shall rejoice at once in the skill of the architect and the diligence of the successive builders.

XXII.

THE BRAZEN SERPENT.

NUMBERS xxi.

THE courteous request addressed by Moses to the King of Edom for liberty to pass through his dominions was bluntly and defiantly refused. This compelled the tribes to turn back, and go down the entire length of the valley of the Arabah, until they reached a point a few hours distant from the shore of the gulf of Akabah, where the Wady Ithm furnished an opening through which they marched round the southern border of the land of Edom, and went up on the eastern side of Mount Seir, taking a north-easterly direction, and following very much the line of route taken in modern times by pilgrims between Mecca and Damascus. The first part of this journey must have been exceedingly depressing. They had been, as it were, on the very threshold of the door into Canaan, but by the rudeness of Edom they were turned away; and as they went down with their faces toward the Red Sea, it would seem to them that every step they took was increasing the distance between them and the land to which they had looked so long as their goal. Besides, the valley through which they marched is one of the most disagreeable to be met with even in that dreary land. Dr. Robinson writes thus concerning it: "We were now up on the plain, or rather the rolling desert of the Arabah; the surface was in general loose gravel and stones, everywhere furrowed and torn with the beds of torrents; a more frightful desert it had hardly been our lot to behold. Now and then a lone shrub of the ghudah was almost the only trace of vegetation."* The heat, however, is even more terrible than the desolation; for almost all travellers bear testimony to the discomforts that are connected with traversing a district where the sirocco seems to blow incessantly.† It is not wonderful, therefore, that "the soul of the people was much discouraged because of the way;" but it is somewhat surprising that after all their experience of God's care over them, and provision for them, they should have allowed their despondency to pass into dissatisfaction with Jehovah, and murmuring against Moses. The very manna which had sustained them so long has become to them an evil; "Our soul," they cry, "loatheth this light bread;" and though Egypt must have seemed a long, long way behind them, they still harp upon its material comfort, and express regret that they had ever left its borders.

This new sin brought with it a new penalty; for "the Lord sent fiery serpents among the people," and many of them died. The district in the immediate neighborhood of the head of the gulf of Akabah is still said to be infested with snakes. Burckhardt tells his readers that on the shore of a bay in this vicinity he found everywhere the impression of the passage of serpents crossing each other in many directions, and then continues, "Ayd told me that the serpents were very common in these parts; that the fishermen were much afraid of them, and extinguished their fires in the evening before they went to sleep, because the light was known to attract them."‡ But, though it is thus probable that serpents were already in the neighborhood of the encampment, it must not be supposed that there was no divine agency, or

---

* "Biblical Researches," vol. ii., p. 121.

† See Smith's "Dictionary of the Bible," article ARABAH.

‡ See Kitto's "Bible Illustrations," Morning Series, Nineteenth Week, Third Day.

moral purpose connected with their attacking the Israelites at this time. It is quite likely that the people had been under special providential protection during all their wanderings, and that at this point, as a punishment for their murmuring, that protection was judicially withdrawn. In any case, God availed himself of the presence of these snakes, to use them as the means for bringing the Israelites to a sense of their iniquity. And they were not long in coming round; for, under the burning inflammation produced by the venomous bites of these fiery reptiles, they cried to Moses, saying, "We have sinned, for we have spoken against the Lord, and against thee; pray unto the Lord, that he take away the serpents from us." Then, true to his mediatorial character, Moses made intercession, the result of which cannot be more clearly or succinctly described than in the words of the narrative itself: "And the Lord said unto Moses, Make thee a fiery serpent, and set it upon a pole: and it shall come to pass, that every one that is bitten, when he looketh upon it, shall live. And Moses made a serpent of brass, and put it upon a pole; and it came to pass, that if a serpent had bitten any man, when he beheld the serpent of brass, he lived." Yet the healing power was not in the glittering symbol, but in the Lord himself; and so when, hundreds of years after, in the days of Hezekiah the king, that which had been preserved as a memorial of God's power and love, was itself worshipped as an idol, the good monarch destroyed it before the eyes of its devotees, and called it Nehushtan, a piece of brass.*

It has been a matter of speculation with many how it came that, though the second commandment forbade the making of the likeness of anything, Moses should have been enjoined to make a brazen serpent; and some have replied

---

* 2 Kings xviii., 4.

that the origin of the symbolism here employed is to be found in the history of the Fall; while others would have us believe that it was designed to meet the moral and intellectual development of the people to whom it was first manifested, and was chosen because in Egypt they had learned to look upon the serpent as the emblem of the power to heal. But to me it rather seems that it was selected and appointed by God as the means of healing now, in order that it might, in the fulness of time, clearly illustrate the way of salvation by Jesus Christ, and help us, on whom the ends of the world are come, to identify the Saviour, and understand the nature of that faith by which alone we can be benefited through him. This is one of the miracles which are foreshadows, and so to say parables, of that great supernatural healing which comes to men's souls through faith in the uplifted Christ; and in the conversation of our Lord with Nicodemus, we have at once the explanation and the vindication of the symbolism which Moses was commanded to employ.

From the way of the Red Sea, the tribes passed up on the eastern side of Mount Seir, through Oboth, Ije-abarim, Zared, and on to the borders of Moab. Thence they went to Beer, where, through their own exertions, God gave them water. The song composed by some one of their poets, to commemorate the digging of the well, is here preserved, and is a curious and interesting specimen of that rhythmic cadence of echoing parallelisms which is so characteristic of the Hebrew lyric. From Beer they journeyed on through various stations, which cannot now be precisely identified, until they came to the mountain of Pisgah, whence they had their first view of the valley of the Jordan and the land of promise.

But before they could reach that point, and indeed in the course of those journeyings which we have but now summarized, they had been compelled to encounter two very formidable enemies. The first was the army of the Amorites, under Sihon their king, who, not content with refusing to permit them to pass through his territories, came out and attacked them in the wilderness of Jahaz. The result was a signal victory for the Hebrews, who took all his territory, and all the cities and villages thereof. This deliverance, commemorated by a song, here incorporated in the narrative, and taken, as it seems, from the Book of the Wars of the Lord, was highly prized by the people; for it is frequently mentioned, and always with gratitude, in their later literature.

After the defeat of the Amorites, Moses and the people approached the kingdom of Bashan, whose monarch, apparently without provocation, and moved by pure animosity to the Hebrews, came forth to fight against them at Edrei. He too was defeated and slain. Had he remained in his own land, the Israelites would not have attacked him; and even if they had, he might have laughed them to scorn, seeing that the strongholds of Bashan, now known as the Lejah, are almost impregnable. Our friend, Dr. W. H. Thomson, has thus described it: "It consists of an extensive and rich plain, capable of sustaining a large population, but surrounded by a complete wall of volcanic rocks, so closely heaped together as to have been aptly compared to the waves of a great sea instantaneously petrified. Here, amidst the thickets of scrub-oak and in numerous caves formed by the tilted rocks, some 2000 Druses took refuge in 1838, and compelled Mohammed Ali to sacrifice 30,000 of his soldiers to bring them to terms. In the precarious and constantly hostile state of the ancient world, such a country would afford peculiar advantages to its inhabitants to maintain their independence. It had also the effect of rendering anything like general law or government impossible, except after long struggles, and then for brief intervals, during the sway of some great foreign empire. Each city or district, though flourishing in itself by reason of its rich soil, was yet at war with its neighbors. Hence, though the land is now covered with the ruins of those times, yet in most cases these remains indicate the work of a people whose thoughts were almost wholly bent on fortifying themselves. Their massive houses were literally so many private castles, with stone doors, stone windows, and stone ceilings; so that whole towns may be entered and occupied now, the houses erected centuries ago still standing as they were built."*

Og himself was one of the last of the giant race inhabiting this region, and doubtless relied on his own personal prowess and on the bravery of his army; but his forces were utterly routed, and the only relic of him is thus referred to in the Book of Deuteronomy, " Behold, his bedstead was a bedstead of iron; is it not in Rabbath of the children of Ammon? nine cubits was the length thereof, and four cubits the breadth of it, after the cubit of a man."† Dr. Kitto supposes that the reference is to a bedstead, properly so called, after the Oriental pattern, and made of iron, owing to the great weight of the giant; but others are of opinion that the allusion is to a sarcophagus, made of the black basalt of the district, which is frequently called iron. In either case, the dimensions would be somewhat in excess of those of the man himself, so that his stature may be set down as about nine feet.

Thus the first battles of the Israelites were fought in self-defence; and in the acquirement of those territories which afterward became the property of Reuben, Gad, and half the tribe of Manasseh, they had the earnest of the success which awaited them on the other side of the Jordan.

In seeking to turn this narrative to good practical account, I would direct your attention, first, to the danger of

---

* " First Statement of the American Palestine Explor. Society," p. 26.
† Deut. iii., 11.

giving way to despondency. The Israelites, as they turned southward from Mount Hor through the hot and dusty Arabah, were very naturally discouraged; and if they had turned to God in simple, yearning weakness, as a weary child seeks to be comforted by its mother, all would have been well; for he would have soothed them by his grace, and guided their thoughts in the direction of the great mercies which they were continually receiving. But, instead of doing that, they brooded over their discouragement until it became rebellion; and so that which through prayer might have been turned into praise, was by moody and unbelieving misery nursed into a kind of mutiny. Now, in all this we see the peril which constantly attends spiritual despondency. There are many causes for such a state of soul. Some of them may be purely physical, some of them may be connected with the condition of our temporal affairs, and some of them may be associated with disappointment—as when we see a blessing, which we seemed to be on the very eve of securing, snatched away from us, and we are sent down some dreary waste of difficulty, that appears only to be leading us farther and farther into misery.

But, natural as, in such circumstances, despondency may be, and much as we may be disposed to sympathize with him who is, for the time, its victim, we must not lose sight of the danger in which he stands; for the longer he is in this condition, the more prone he is to begin to murmur against God. That which at first is only passive unbelief, develops ultimately into active disobedience, and he who is discouraged is apt very soon to become rebellious. This is a truth which we too frequently lose sight of. We speak of despondency as a misfortune, but we rarely, if ever, regard it as perilous; and, in urging the weeping one to rise above his trouble, we do not set before him with sufficient distinctness the danger of his condition. Immoderate grief over bereavement, undue depression over temporal misfortunes, extreme sensitiveness to the assaults which men may make upon us while we are seeking to follow Christ, morbid regret at the disappointment of our hopes of serving God in some peculiar way on which our hearts are set, and exaggerated ideas of the evil which will ensue from the refusal of some Edomite to do that which would have been of great benefit to us, that which would have cost him nothing, and which we had courteously requested at his hands—all these are at the next station on the line toward rebellion against God, and ought to be checked at once, before they lead to more serious consequences.

A friend of mine, some years ago, received a letter from a missionary on the west coast of Africa, in which, as a curiosity, some serpent-eggs were contained. He laid them carefully aside, thinking to preserve them as they were; but one day, when he went to show them to a visitor, he discovered, to his dismay, that the heat of the drawer had hatched them into serpents, and there was a heap of crawling things before his eyes. So despondency is a serpent's egg, which, if we are not careful, will hatch in our hearts into a serpent itself, and poison us with its venomous bite. It has the germ of serious and aggravated sin within it, and we must seek very speedily to overmaster it; nor need we have much difficulty in rising above it, for we have only to remember and believe that God is on our side, and all discouragement will disappear. What though the Arabah be dreary, and the way be long, God is in the camp. He has fed us with his manna, he has guided us by the pillar of his providence, he has redeemed us by the sacrifice of his own Son, and he has pledged himself to bring us at last into his heavenly home.

Why, then, should we be discouraged? Let us take both sides of the account into consideration; and when we are reckoning up the disagreeables, let us not rise until we have put over against these the unnumbered and invaluable blessings of our daily lot; and then, though we have begun in despondency, we will end in triumph, and sing the old, familiar strain, "Why art thou cast down, O my soul? and why art thou disquieted within me? Hope in God, for I shall yet praise him, who is the health of my countenance and my God." It is hard, when we have reached what we thought to be the end of a long lane, to be turned back, and sent away round; and there are many among us in these days who have had just such an experience—some in business, and some in spiritual pilgrimage—yet forget not, I pray you, that, with God beside you, and so long as you have faith in him, nothing can be really against you. Hold on, therefore, in patience and in trustfulness—the day of your redemption draweth nigh; and oh! let not your despondency ripen into complaint, for that will only increase your guilt, and ultimately also aggravate your misery.

But, in the second place, let me give emphasis to the typical significance of the method which, in obedience to God's command, Moses adopted for the healing of the people.

Here was, first of all, a disease. The Israelites were bitten by serpents, and the consequence was that the poison thereby injected into their systems speedily affected their whole bodies, and caused death. Now, alike in its origin and nature, the malady of sin is well illustrated by a serpent's bite. Have we not been taught to trace the entrance of evil into the world to the agency of Satan, who, because he veiled himself on that occasion under the form of a serpent, has come to be called among us "the old serpent?" And has not the moral poison of evil affected our entire natures? Our souls, indeed, have all their original powers; but, alas! these have all come under the deflecting and perverting influence of sin. Our perceptions are biassed; our judgments are one-sided; our memories do not care to retain God in their grasp; our consciences are blunted, and take little or no knowledge of the evil we commit—nay, they are like a compass that has been somehow tampered with, and gives an erroneous indication; they put light for darkness, and darkness for light—sweet for bitter, and bitter for sweet; our affections are set on things which have been described by one of the apostles in this descending climax, "earthly, sensual, devilish."

Thus the derangement made in our spiritual natures by the presence of sin is like that produced in the body by a serpent's bite; and, unless a cure be effected, the death of the soul must be the result. The death of the soul—ah! who can tell all that is implied in that? It is not the loss of being, but the loss of well-being, and that forever; and if we were but as sensible of our malady as these Israelites were of the disease that was burning up their bodies, we would cry out in an agony of earnestness for deliverance.

But let us not forget to look at the cure which was here effected. The instrument through which it was wrought was a serpent of brass, elevated on a pole or flag-staff, in a conspicuous position in the camp. Of course there was nothing in that, in itself considered, to produce a cure. The healing power came from God. This was recognized even by the Jews themselves; for the author of the apocryphal Book of Wisdom, commenting on this history, has said, "Thy wrath endured not forever; but they were troubled for a small season, that they might be admonished, having a sign of salvation to put them in remembrance of the commandment of thy law; for he that turned himself toward it was not saved by the thing that he saw, but by thee, that art the Saviour of all." So, also, the author of the Targum of Jonathan must have similarly understood the promise to the bitten one; for he adds to the proclamation, "If he shall have directed his heart unto the name of the word of the Lord." Their case was so serious that there was no help for them but in God; and it is just the same with the sinner—he is helpless and hopeless, if God will not deliver him.

But this instrument of salvation was a brazen serpent; and probably Alford has given the true parallelism here when he says, in his comment on the Saviour's words to Nicodemus, "The brazen serpent, made in the likeness of the serpents which had bitten them, represented to them the poison which had gone through their frames; and it was hung up there on the banner-staff as a trophy, to show that for the poison there was healing, that the plague had been overcome. In it there was no poison—only the likeness of it. Now, was not our Lord Jesus made in the likeness of sinful flesh?* Was he not made sin for us, who knew no sin? Did not he, on his cross, make an open show of it, and triumph over the enemy, so that it was as if the enemy himself had been nailed to it?"†

Thus the "lifting up" of the serpent on the pole is the prefiguration of that lifting up of Christ when he was crucified for the sins of men. But we must not suppose that, because there was no inherent efficacy in the serpent of brass to heal the bitten ones, therefore there is no intrinsic value or influence in Christ's death upon the cross. The one was shadow, but the other was substance; and the power of the former, such as it was, was due only to its connection with the latter. There was an inherent efficacy in the death of Christ; for has not Paul said, "What the law could not do, in that it was weak through the flesh, God sending his own Son in the likeness of sinful flesh (accomplished), and for sin condemned sin in the flesh?"‡

---

* Rom. viii., 3.
† Alford's "Greek Testament," on John iii., 14, 15.
‡ Rom. viii., 3.

The bitten Israelites were healed by looking to the serpent of brass; so the sinner is saved by believing in Jesus. Faith is the soul's eye, by which it "takes in" that on which it is turned. Hence the prophet says, in Jehovah's name, "Look unto me, and be ye saved, all the ends of the earth: for I am God, and there is none else;"* and, from the side of human experience, the Psalmist sings, "They looked unto him, and were lightened: and their faces were not ashamed."†

Two things are specially taught us by this emblem of faith. The first is, that the object of faith is not anything in ourselves. That on which one looks is external to him that looks on it; and so, if we are ever to be saved from sin, we must not seek to build on anything within us, but turn in faith to the Saviour without us. So long as we look in, we can see nothing to give us hope or happiness; but when we look to Jesus, we behold in him a deliverer, and see in his righteousness a foundation on which we may securely rest. Thus there is no merit in faith. It is not I who deserve credit for the delight which I have in looking upon an exquisite picture, but rather the artist whose work the picture is; and, in like manner, it is not the sinner who deserves honor for his salvation, but rather the Christ through looking to whom he has obtained it. "It is of faith, that it might be by grace." The eye is that which "takes in" the realities of the external world, and faith is that which "takes in" the truth about Christ. It is the receptive faculty of the soul; and when by it we receive and rest upon Christ for our salvation, our act corresponds in spirit to the look of the outward eye which was turned by the suffering Israelite on the uplifted serpent.

Observe, I said, when we receive and rest on Christ; and

---

* Isa. xlv., 22. † Psa. xxxiv., 5.

this resting is the second thing taught us by this emblem of faith. "I will look to you, then, to arrange all that," said one friend to another, at the close of a business conference; and that trustfulness which he expressed in the honor of his friend is of the same kind as the restful confidence which the believer has in his Lord. In precisely the same sense he "looks" to Jesus, not with expectancy only, but with firm assurance that he is all that he declares himself to be, and will do for him all that he has promised to accomplish; and with that look come peace, and joy, and love, and life.

But who may look? Moses was commanded to proclaim "That every one that is bitten, when he looketh upon it, shall live;" and as the herald passed along, what a scene the camp would present! There you might see the man all but dead, raising himself upon his arm, and straining his glazed eyes if haply he might behold the glittering symbol; yonder another, wiping away his tears of anguish to look upon the glorious object; and yonder still, a mother with her child, eagerly pointing to the flag-staff, if perchance she may fix her loved one's gaze upon the mystic healer. But no one would be tempted to ask, will it heal me? for he would reason thus: it will cure any bitten one that looks, and fherefore me. So Jesus Christ has been lifted up, that whosoever believeth in him might not perish, but have everlasting life; and there is no need for any one to ask, "Will he save me?" The proclamation runs, "whosoever believeth;" and therefore it is for you if you will believe. Instead, therefore, of asking, "Will he save me?" the question rather is, "Will you look or not?" The "whosoever" includes you, beyond all the possibility of doubt; but how is it with the "whosoever believeth?" Does that describe you? and if not, why not? Ah! my fellow-sinner, how near has salvation thus been brought to you? "There is life for a look at the crucified one;" there is everlasting life for "whosoever believeth."

"And it came to pass, that if a serpent had bitten any man, when he beheld the serpent of brass, he lived." No one looked in vain; and in like manner, the Gospel of Christ is "the power of God unto salvation to every one that believeth." No one has ever come to Jesus and gone away unblessed; and in the place of woe at last there shall not be found a single soul to say, "I looked to Christ, and he would not or could not save me." "He is able to save to the uttermost them that come unto God by him;" and so, if any one in this assembly goes away unsaved, I take him to record that it is not because there is no Saviour, or because the way of salvation has not been simply and plainly set before him; but it is because he will not come unto Christ that he may have life.

XXIII.

BALAAM.

NUMBERS xxii.–xxv.; xxxi., 8.

AFTER their conquest of the Amorites, the Hebrews found a camping-ground in "the plains of Moab," a strip of land about four miles in width, on the eastern bank of the Jordan, and extending from the northern end of the Dead Sea to the river Jabbok. Originally, this territory belonged to the Moabites, but it had been taken from them by the Amorites; and thus it had come into the possession of the Israelites when they subdued Sihon, while it retained the name of its first owners. It was bounded on the east by the mountains of Abarim; and immediately opposite to it, on the western bank of the Jordan, stood the city of Jericho. The tribes were thus at length on the very threshold of that land to which they had so many years looked forward as "the Sabbath and port" of their wanderings; and it might have been expected that they would have hastened forward to enter upon its conquest. But their unexpected acquisition of the country of the Amorites required that they should take some measures for its protection; and some important religious services demanded their attention before they were permitted to advance into the fields of Canaan. During this delay they were exposed to a new danger, the singularity of which combines with the strangeness of the character and position of him who was especially prominent in connection with it, to invest it with a peculiar interest.

We may, perhaps, reach the most satisfactory conclusions

regarding it by giving first a simple epitome of the narrative, and following that with a brief discussion of the questions which it suggests, and a practical analysis of the character which it portrays.

The destruction of the Amorites by the children of Israel filled the hearts of the Moabites with dismay. Had they known, indeed, that Moses had been commanded[*] not to attack them, they need not have been so greatly alarmed; but when they saw that their powerful neighbors had been discomfited, they were sore afraid. So Balak, their king, entered into an alliance with the elders, or sheiks, of the Midianites, who were leading a nomad life in his neighborhood; and their united forces occupied a strong position on the heights of Abarim. They were eager to destroy the newcomers; but, with the fate of Sihon and his army before them, and having heard the report of the calamities that had fallen on the Egyptians for their oppression of the Hebrews, they felt that it would be useless to attack such enemies with ordinary weapons. Accordingly, after the manner of the heathen of that age, they resolved, if possible, to steal from them the protection of their God by putting them under his ban, or curse. With this object in view, Balak sent messengers to Pethor, in Mesopotamia, to invite Balaam, a famous soothsayer who resided there, to come to Moab and pronounce a malediction over the host of Israel.

When the messengers arrived, with the rewards of divination in their hands, Balaam detained them for a night, that he might consult his oracle; and in the morning he made reply, "Get you into your land: for the Lord refuseth to give me leave to go with you." But when they returned with this answer, Balak felt that there was that in it which indicated that Balaam had a desire to come; and, thinking that

---

[*] Deut. ii., 9.

he was only hanging back for a larger reward, the Moabitish king sent a more imposing embassage with more alluring proposals, saying, "Let nothing, I pray thee, hinder thee from coming unto me: for I will promote thee unto very great honor, and I will do whatsoever thou sayest unto me." Balaam, however, still held out, and at first repeated, with even stronger emphasis than before, his refusal to go with the messengers; but, having detained them, as on the former occasion, for a night, the Lord appeared to him, and permitted him, in judgment rather than in approval, to accompany the men, with the caution that he was to say nothing which he had not received. On his way to Moab, a last and solemn appeal to his conscience was made by the appearance of an angel, whose presence was miraculously revealed to him in connection with the speaking of the ass on which he rode. But, though he offered then and there to turn and go back to his home, the Lord saw that his obedience was that of constraint, and not of voluntary and wholehearted choice; and so permitted him to go.

When he reached Moab, he was received in great state by Balak, who took him to the high places of Baal, whence he could see the utmost part of the people; and, after seven oxen and seven rams had been offered on seven altars, he received a message for his employer. But, lo! it was a message of blessing, and not of cursing; a message, too, expressed in language of unwonted sublimity and force. Balak was amazed; and, thinking that the sight of the whole encampment had unduly impressed Balaam, he took him to a place whence only a small part of Israel could be seen. But there also, after the offering of sacrifice, a similar communication was given; so that the King of Moab began to fear that he had lifted a stone by which his own head was to be broken. He had wished a curse, but now he would be content if only Balaam would say nothing; so he made this request to him, "Neither curse them at all, nor bless them at all;" and he took him to still another place. But there also a blessing came out more emphatic and sublime than ever; and then the king's anger could not be restrained, for "he smote his hands together: and Balak said unto Balaam, I called thee to curse mine enemies, and, behold, thou hast altogether blessed them these three times. Therefore now flee thou to thy place: I thought to promote thee unto great honor; but, lo, the Lord hath kept thee back from honor." But Balaam would not be corrupted; and ere he left the monarch's presence, he was prompted by the Divine Spirit to advertise him what Israel should do unto Moab in the latter days. With this message he quitted the court of Balak; and if we had heard no more of him, we might have gone away with the impression that Balaam was a man of unbending rectitude and conscientiousness.

But there is a darker record behind, which we are left in a large degree to fill in for ourselves from suggestive hints here and there let fall by the sacred writers. When Balak gave up negotiations with Balaam, it would seem that the sheiks of Midian, heretofore in the background, went into consultation with him. And at his suggestion the women of Midian were used as temptresses to seduce the children of Israel to commit abominable iniquity.* "They called the people unto the sacrifices of their gods: and the people did eat, and bowed down to their gods,"† serving them with those impure and adulterous rites which were so often connected with Baal worship among the Eastern nations, and the service of Venus among the idolaters of the West. The results of this were, first, a terrible infliction of judicial punishment at the hands of Moses, who said, "Take all the heads of the people, and hang them up before the Lord

---

* Num. xxxi., 16; Rev. ii., 14. † Num. xxv., 2.

against the sun, that the fierce anger of the Lord may be turned away from Israel;"* and, second, a fearful plague which swept away twenty-four thousand of the people, and which was stayed only by the red-handed interposition of Phinehas the high-priest, who slew two of the transgressors in the very act of their iniquity.† Then, to chastise the Midianites for their agency in this vile apostasy, an army composed of twelve thousand men, one thousand from each tribe, was sent against them, "and they warred against the Midianites, as the Lord commanded Moses; and they slew all the males. And they slew the kings of Midian, beside the rest of them that were slain; namely, Evi, and Rekem, and Zur, and Hur, and Reba, five kings of Midian: Balaam also the son of Beor they slew with the sword."‡ Thus, by the method of indirectness, Balaam sought to accomplish that, from the direct denunciation of which in the name of the Lord, he had so resolutely held himself. And he who had pronounced the grandest blessings on the nation of Israel was slain as one of its most insidious enemies.

Such is a brief and comprehensive summary of this marvellous episode in the history of Israel. Many questions arise out of it which are much more easily asked than answered, and most of them connect themselves with the position and character of Balaam. Was he a genuine prophet? or a mere heathen soothsayer? Some have without qualification adopted the former alternative; and others, with equal confidence, have accepted the latter. But it is not possible for me to rest in either of these opinions. On the one hand, it is evident that he possessed some knowledge of the true God. Dwelling as he did in that country whence Abram emigrated, and where Nahor, and that branch of Terah's family remained, he may have gathered some tradi-

---

* Num. xxv., 4.   † Ibid. xxv., 6–9.   ‡ Ibid. xxxi., 7, 8.

tional ideas of Jehovah from those among whom he lived; while the marvels of the Exodus, reports of which had spread abroad among the nations, may have led him to clearer views of the unity and supremacy of God than had been attained by the multitude. He saw that there is a clear distinction between the life and death of the righteous and those of the wicked;* he would not allow it to be supposed that Jehovah is changeful and capricious as a man, to be influenced by momentary considerations of favor or of anger;† he sought his direction before he entered upon the enterprise to which Balak summoned him;‡ and his prophecies, as any one who reads them will be immediately convinced of, were the utterances of a genuine divine inspiration.§ Their poetry is not more remarkable than their prescience; for, while indicating that Israel would be taken captive by Assyria, they intimate also that another power should arise, which, coming in ships from the West, would subjugate Assyria: moreover, in words of rapt sublimity, preceded by a personal lament which trembles with the pathos of despair, he gives a forecast of Messiah's advent, the lingering echoes of which, hundreds of years after his day, led the Magi to the cradle of the Christ—"I shall see him, but not now: I shall behold him, but not nigh: there shall come a Star out of Jacob, and a Sceptre shall rise out of Israel, and shall smite the corners of Moab, and destroy all the children of Sheth." Without controversy, therefore, he was a prophet.

But then, on the other hand, he retained, either as matters of sincere conviction or for the purpose of making gain, many of the heathen practices connected with divination. He was so much in advance of his generation as to see and

---

* Num. xxiii., 10. † Ibid. xxiii., 19. ‡ Ibid. xxii., 8.
§ Ibid. xxii., 7-10, 18-24; xxiii., 3-9, 15-24.

know more than the average of his neighbors comprehended, and he was mercenary enough to make a merchandise of that knowledge, under color of practising augury or magic. Thus, in the Old Testament History he occupies a position similar to that of Simon Magus in the New. He recognized the glory of Jehovah very much as Simon acknowledged the wonder-working power of Jesus through his apostles; but, alas, like him too, he was attracted to the truth more by the profit which he thought he might derive from it, than by the spiritual effects which it was calculated to produce upon his own heart. Thus he was both a divinely inspired prophet and a heathen soothsayer.* "He stood," as Kurtz, following Hengstenberg, has admirably put it, "with one foot upon the soil of heathen magic and soothsaying, and with the other upon the soil of Jehovistic religion and prophecy."† In him heathenism and revelation touched each other; the truth and the error met and grappled, and the summons of Balak was the crisis of his career, wherein, by his own choice, it was to be determined whether he would come forth entirely into the light, or go back again into the darkness.

It is this fact which makes his history so fraught with instruction to every reader. There came to him—as, sooner or later, there comes to every one who is confronted with God's truth—a fork in his pathway, at which he was required to make a definite and decided preference of one or other of two courses; and then it was discovered that, by the habit of his life in turning his knowledge into gold, he had already committed himself to the wrong side, so that he went forward to his destruction. He tried as long as he could to retain his hold both on Balak and on Jehovah; but he ended by breaking with Jehovah, and so his name stands

---

* Compare 2 Pet. ii., 16, with Josh. xiii., 22.
† Kurtz's "Old Covenant," vol. iii., p. 343.

upon the page of sacred history as a beacon-light to every after-generation; and his course is, perhaps, the most striking illustration afforded by the annals of humanity of the truth of the Saviour's words, "No man can serve two masters: for either he will hate the one, and love the other; or else he will hold to the one, and despise the other. Ye cannot serve God and mammon."*

Now, if we have been correct in thus describing the position of Balaam, little or no difficulty will be felt concerning the miracle of the ass speaking, which has provoked so much ridicule among the adversaries of the Scriptures, and which, I fear, is about the only incident in all this singular history with which they are acquainted. We cannot accept the theory of those who maintain that the whole scene in which the ass played so unwonted a part was a vision; for, if that view be adopted, it will be impossible to retain our faith in any objective miracle whatever. We are shut up, therefore, to the acceptance, in its literal sense, of the narrative of which this singular episode forms a part; and, in the peculiar position occupied by Balaam, which we have just described, we find sufficient occasion for the miracle.

It was one of those meeting-places of truth with error which—as in Egypt, in Babylon, in Antioch, in Ephesus, in Corinth—were always signalized by supernatural works; and, just as in Egypt Pharaoh was met and conquered by God on his own ground, so here the soothsayer was outdone even in his own domain. Often before Balaam may have startled those who came to him for counsel by making a living human voice come apparently from a dead image, or from an irrational animal; and now God comes to him through the utterances of his own ass. "Indeed," to quote the words of a modern commentator, "to an augur priding

---

* Matt. vi., 24.

himself on his skill in interpreting the cries and movements of animals, no more startling warning could be given than one so real as this, yet conveyed through the medium of his own art ; and, to a seer pretending to superhuman wisdom, no more humiliating rebuke can be imagined than to teach him by the mouth of his own ass."* Besides, as he was setting out to go to Balak, with a desire to say, if he could or dared, that which was not in accordance with the will of God, it was important to remind him, by the miracle to which we are referring, that the power of thought and speech were entirely under the divine control. And, on the whole, the devout reader of this history will be led to acknowledge, with Bishop Newton and Van Oosterzee, that "the greatest wonder in this case is, not that an animal should have spoken, but rather that a man who but runs away, like an irrational animal, to utter words of cursing, is led to bless like an angel of peace."†

Passing now to the analysis, for practical purposes, of the character of Balaam, we must be on our guard against imagining that he was so peculiarly bad that his guilt is impossible except in connection with the singular circumstances in which he was placed. It has fared with him, as with Judas and one or two others who are so unqualifiedly condemned in the Scriptures, that ordinary readers are disposed to put them in a category by themselves, and to thank God that they are not in the same class. But though, with Bishop Newton, we may call him "a strange mixture of a man," yet the strangeness does not consist so much in the uncommonness of the combination of opposites which we find in him

---

* "Speaker's Commentary," *in loc*. While quoting and appropriating these words, however, I cannot adopt entirely the view given by the writer in the rest of the note.

† "Dissertations on the Prophecies," by Thomas Newton, D.D., p. 62 ; "Moses : a Biblical Study," by J. Van Oosterzee, p. 247.

as in the degree to which, by the intensity of the influences that were at work upon him, that combination was developed. His case, in its elements, is simply one of practical inconsistency; and its value as a warning arises from the fact that, owing to the force of the agencies in operation, we are shown, in a short time and in a terrible manner, what is in every case the inevitable issue of such a course.

It is said that sometimes, under the pressure of severe anguish, a man's hair may turn from raven blackness to snowy whiteness in a single night, but that was only when there had been already in him constitutional tendencies in that direction; and so I think that there have been instances in which, under great testing influences, a character which, up till that time, had a fair appearance, has all at once developed its real self, and has stood forth in hideous distinctness, an object of common execration; but the evil had been already latent in it. In saying this, however, I am not vindicating the Balaams, for every man is responsible for the character which he chooses to form. Still less am I throwing the blame upon their circumstances, for these were really opportunities such as, if they had been rightly improved, would have made their subjects not the warnings, but the exemplars of humanity. I am only giving emphasis to the fundamental principle that morality is a thing of quality rather than of magnitude, in order that we may all realize that there may be in ourselves the elements of Balaam's character, though we may not have had the opportunity of manifesting them to the same degree.

Let me point out to you two great inconsistencies by which this man was distinguished, and then let me endeavor to account for their existence.

Observe, then, in the first place, that he knew what was right, and yet did what was wrong. His was not a sin of ignorance. His intellectual, nay, more, his moral convictions were correct. He knew what he should do, and there was in him also a feeling of obligation to do it. Many eminent commentators believe that the words recorded by Micah, "He hath showed thee, O man, what is good; and what doth the Lord require of thee, but to do justly, and to love mercy, and to walk humbly with thy God?"* were part of Balaam's answer to Balak referred to by that prophet; and if that view be correct, then we have from his lips a definition of human duty which is at once clear, comprehensive, and accurate. Yet over against that we have conduct which was neither just, merciful, nor godly, in leading Israel to sin.

Again, it was he who declared that "God is not a man, that he should lie; neither the son of man, that he should repent;" while, by his repeated yieldings to Balak's entreaties, he acted just as if he supposed it to be possible to change the purpose of God in reference to Israel.

Once more, it was he who said, with a clear perception of the blessedness of the death of the righteous, and its connection with a righteous life, "Let me die the death of the righteous, and let my last end be like his;" yet "he loved the wages of iniquity," and died in the ranks of Jehovah's enemies. Thus, knowing and feeling are different from being and doing. But it is not alone in Balaam that this difference is apparent. In him, indeed, the sentence may be seen printed, so to say, in the largest type; but it is visible, in smaller characters, in many others. A well-known Roman poet represents one of his characters as saying, "I see and approve of the better course; I follow the worse." Paul has spoken of some who, "knowing the judgment of God, that they who do these things are worthy of death, not only do the same, but have pleasure in them that do them;" and Jesus himself tells of the servant who "knew his Lord's

---

* Mic. vi., 8.

will, and did it not." Nor need we look very far for the modern counterpart of these descriptions. Does not this phase of Balaam's character, indeed, come very near ourselves? Does it not hold up to us the mirror in which we may behold our own image? Is there no one here who is intellectually convinced of the existence of a future life, and yet lives precisely as if there was no such thing as retribution? no one who has been warned by his own conscience as really and powerfully as Balaam was by the angel, and yet, alas, as vainly? no one who clearly understands what the issues of his conduct must be, and yet persists in it unto the bitter end? no one who acknowledges in his conscience the right of the Lord Jesus to his allegiance, and yet in his life repudiates the authority which intellectually he dares not deny? My hearers, let us not deceive ourselves where it is of supreme importance that we should be right. He who knows what his duty is, and yet deliberately sets himself either to evade it or compromise with it, or to go against it, has within him the essential elements of that character which in Balaam was so fully and so fatally developed.

But I find in this man another inconsistency; for his conscience was remarkably sensitive in one respect, and yet unscrupulous in another. He could not bring himself to utter as God's word that which was not really given him by God. He said, "If Balak would give me his house full of silver and gold, I cannot go beyond the word of the Lord my God, to do less or more." That was noble. That had the true ring in it. That sounds almost like Peter's "half-battle" words, "we ought to obey God rather than man." And it will not do to say that he was supernaturally restrained, for there is nothing of that in the narrative. It was a matter of personal purpose with him. He shrunk from the daring impiety of prophesying lies in the name of the Lord. Yet, though he would not allow himself to do that, he had no scruple about giving abominable advice to the Midianites, by the following of which they seduced the Israelites to the vilest sin, and drew down upon them a terrible infliction. He was afraid to sin in one way; yet he did not fear to suggest a sinful course of another sort to others. Nor, alas! is this apparent anomaly uncommon. The Pharisees would not defile themselves by going into Pilate's house, but they could see no evil in their determination to put Jesus to death. What a strange faculty is conscience! and how it may be educated to strain out a gnat, while it swallows a camel without compunction! It may keep a man from going in the teeth of God's prohibition, and yet it may be for the time perfectly peaceful, while the same end is attained in a roundabout way. Afraid of the penalty of human law, one may keep a statute in the letter, while breaking it in the spirit. He may say to some less scrupulous instrument, "It will not do for me to appear in the matter, but if you manage it, I will see that you are taken care of."

You remember how, in one of the great dramatist's wonderful productions, King John would not let himself murder the young prince, but hired others to do it for him, and soothed his conscience with this soporific, "How oft the sight of means to do ill deeds makes ill deeds done;" forgetting that such a thing is true only when one desires that the ill deeds should be done. And in common life, though the deed may not be exactly murder, there are multitudes who, while they are restrained from doing it themselves, have no objection to incite others to its commission. They would not defy the Almighty to his face, but they will try to outwit him, while they appear to be regarding his prohibition. They will try to outwit God; ah, what irony has unwittingly escaped me! as if he did not know the secrets of their hearts, and their hidden plottings with their rougher instruments. As if, too, he would not hold the instigator and the actor as both guilty, and the instigator as the guiltier of the two. Still such is their plan; and in every heart in which such a plan is formed in reference to any matter, however small it may be, whether in family jealousy, or business rivalry, or political animosity, there is in embryo the character of Balaam, which will ere long ripen to its doom.

But how are we to account for this moral perversion? How came it that Balaam acted so inconsistently with his knowledge and convictions, and succeeded for the time, as we may say, in juggling with his conscience? The answer is not hard to find. He loved money. His heart was set on gold. He had allowed the passion of covetousness to become the ruling principle of his nature. During his former life he had made a gain of his knowledge, and had nourished his avarice to such a degree that now, when the dazzling offers of Balak were placed before him, he was carried away with its overmastering power to do that which in his inmost heart he knew to be wrong. There was a time when his convictions might have controlled it, but now it was predominant, and so it bore him on through that course which the apostle has called "the madness of the prophet."

I have somewhere read of one who, having found a young leopard, petted it, and trained it to be his daily companion in his chamber. It grew up to maturity, but still it was kept beside him, and men wondered at his foolhardiness in permitting it to go unchained. But he would not be advised. One day, however, as it licked his hand with its rough tongue, it ruffled the skin, and tasted his blood; and then all the savage nature of the brute came out, and there was a fearful struggle between them, from which he escaped only by destroying it. So it was, in some respects, in this case. Balaam had nurtured his covetousness into strength; and now, at the offer of Balak's rewards, its full force came out; but, instead of fighting with it and slaying it, he yielded to it, and was destroyed. Had he always steadily resisted the craving for money for its own sake, then the overtures of the King of Moab would have been no temptation to him at all; but after he had allowed that evil passion to become dominant, you can easily understand how, for it, he went against his moral convictions, and silenced his conscientious scruples on one point, by an apparent deference to them in another. Thus his fear of God kept him from showing his enmity to Israel in a plain and direct way, while his love of reward determined him to seek Israel's undoing by roundabout means. His covetousness led him to receive Balak's messengers, and lodge them, under color of deliberating about a duty which he saw only too clearly, and which he only deliberated how he might evade; it impelled him to go with the ambassadors, even against the warning of God; and it led him finally, when all other hope of getting the wages of unrighteousness had been abandoned, to suggest that the women of Midian might do more to ruin Israel by their allurements than he could accomplish by his divinations, or than the warriors of Moab could effect with their swords. Thus his passion held and kept the helm of his soul. It might tack now in one direction, and now in another, to satisfy some scruple, but still it beat ever up toward the attainment of the object by the gaining of which he would secure Balak's gifts.

What a terrible passion is this of covetousness! and how dangerous it is, especially to those who wish to preserve a fair appearance! For in men's estimation it is, at least in its beginnings, a respectable thing. One cannot become a drunkard or an adulterer without losing his position in society; but this covetousness, gratified but a little, will help him into the best circles; and thus it happens that few passions have wrought so much havoc among the members of the Church, and even among the ministers of religion, as this. Nor is its respectability its only danger, for in the minds of many it is associated only with large sums of money; whereas in reality it may be as strong in the heart of him whose dealings are carried on in cents as in that of one whose transactions are concerned with hundreds of thousands of dollars. The poor man thinks that this, at least, is an evil which he is in no danger of falling before; and so, all unconsciously to himself, by his avaricious disposition in small matters, he may be fostering that very principle which, when the testing hour arrives, shall work his ruin. No one of us, therefore, whether rich or poor, whether minister or layman, has a right to say that there is no fear of him in this matter; for if the love of money takes possession of the heart, it will blind the eyes, and harden the conscience, and become a root of evil, so that, as Paul has expressed it, "we shall fall into temptation and a snare, and into many foolish and hurtful lusts that war against the soul."

But what is true of covetousness is true also of every evil principle, so that we may generalize the lesson here, and say that if the heart be fixed on any object as its god, other than the God and Father of our Lord Jesus Christ, we may expect in the end, whatever may be our knowledge, and whatever our scruples in other respects, that we shall act against our convictions, and make shipwreck not only of the faith, but also of ourselves, "without possibility of salvage."

Take here, for example, the love of display. See how, in those who can afford it, there are plannings and schemings of the most contemptible sort, with the constant ambition to outshine all rivals. See, too, how, in those who cannot afford it, all manner of expedients will be resorted to, and honesty itself ignored in the determination at all hazards to keep up appearances, and put a neighbor into the shade. On other points the conscience may be scrupulously correct; and in respect to other people the judgment may be sound. You could not get them to profane the Sabbath, perhaps; and no stronger condemnation of other forms of sin can be heard than that which comes from their lips; but in respect to this matter, and in reference to themselves, all is perverted. They will do anything rather than step down to a lower level, and bring their positions into harmony with their means. They think they cannot dig. They are ashamed to beg, and therefore, like the steward in the parable, they steal. Oh, the miseries, the envyings, the triflings with conscience, and the effacings of moral distinctions, the private pilferings and public dishonesties that have been caused by this one thing! Yet men will tell us that Balaam is an uncommon and incomprehensible character!

And, to take only another instance, behold how morally degraded the appetite of the drunkard makes him! He is scrupulous in some respects. There is a restraint upon him such that he will not think of cursing those whom God hath blessed. Yet for that selfish gratification of his, which is itself a dethronement of reason, the claims of conjugal affection, domestic happiness, and religious profession will all be set aside; and though he knows better than another can tell him that death, both temporal and eternal, is in the cup, he will drain it to the dregs.

You see, thus, what a fearful thing it is to allow any one evil principle to become predominant in us; and if we would keep ourselves from Balaam's inconsistency and doom, we must never permit anything to come between our hearts and God. When we divide our allegiance between God and another, we are already guilty of high-treason against Jehovah, and our destruction is at hand. The only passion which it is safe to have as the "ruling passion" of our hearts is the love of Christ; for if we enthrone him in our affections, he will keep us holy; our impulses will be thoroughly in harmony with our convictions; and we shall be gratifying our desires most fully, just when we are living most after his example and for his glory. Mark, I said the love of Christ; not the fear of him. Balaam was afraid of Jehovah, and that terror kept him from attempting to curse Israel in his name; but it was not strong enough to keep him from seeking their ruin through other forms of sin. Had he loved God instead of Gold, it would have been a different case, and all the allurements that could have been set before him would have been impotent to draw him into evil. It was because he feared God, and did not love him, that he manifested that vacillation between God and Mammon by which he was characterized. Fear may keep the man from some forms of evil, and may lead him, when he seeks others, to take a roundabout road to them; but it will not prompt to wholehearted and entire allegiance. The servant who feared his Lord did not consume his talent in riotous living—so much of restraint as that the dread of his Master had put upon him—but it did not keep him from burying it in the earth, and it did not impel him to "occupy" it to the full.

Wherever, therefore, a soul is simply afraid of Christ, there will be a similar result. There will be a similar refraining from doing some things out of regard to God's law, while at the same time the heart will seek in other and circuitous methods to obtain its own sinful desires; and the end will be a similar catastrophe. "Cast ye the unprofitable servant into outer darkness: there shall be weeping and gnashing of teeth." But let the love of Jesus become the master-principle of our hearts, and there will be no halting or irresolution; no parleying with temptation; no seeking to explain away our duty under color of deliberating to discover what it is; no looking one way and walking another; but with undivided souls, and with enthusiastic devotion, we shall do only and always the will of Him who loved us, and gave himself for us.

Thus, through the mazy labyrinth of this strange character, I lead you up once more to the cross of Christ; and if you would save yourselves from Balaam's infamy and Balaam's doom, let me beseech you to receive Jesus into your hearts, and to make his love the ruling passion of your lives. Then, instead of seeking to combine two incompatible services, your soul will be concentrated on one thing, and your history will illustrate the words of Paul—" For the love of Christ constraineth us; because we thus judge, that if one died for all, then were all dead: and that he died for all, that they which live should not henceforth live unto themselves, but unto him which died for them, and rose again."

But, long as I have dwelt on this history, I dare not conclude without making one remark suggested by the Israelitish side of the case. No curse can come upon us save through our own sin. All Balak's efforts could not harm the Hebrews; but when they fell into idolatry and impurity, God's punishment came down upon their heads. So let us keep ourselves calm under the enmities of earth. No matter how our adversaries may plot, or how ingeniously they may plan our ruin, they cannot hurt us while we are true to God. Sin is the only curse, and that is a voluntary thing, depending on ourselves. You remember how, appealing to the last lingering embers of patriotism in modern Greece, the English poet says:

> "'Twere long to tell, and sad to trace,
> Each step from splendor to disgrace;
> Enough, no foreign foe could quell
> Thy soul, till from itself it fell.
> Yes! self-abasement paved the way
> To villain bonds and despot sway."

But that is just as true, in spiritual matters, of the individual, and just as applicable to him. No man is really cursed, until he curses himself by yielding to sin; and our enemies are powerless to harm us, until we ourselves become their allies in the commission of iniquity.

How full of comfort, and yet how full of warning is the thought! The Christian's graces are his armor also; and it is only when he falls from grace and consents to sin, that he becomes disarmed and is an easy prey to his enemies. They that seek our undoing have no better allies than our sins, and our surest defence is in our loyalty to God. Keep thyself pure, therefore, and thou mayst laugh to scorn the Balaks that are seeking to curse thee from the hills of Moab; but if thou permittest thyself to sin, thine own act has doomed thee to a punishment heavier by far than any earthly adversary could have brought upon thee.

XXIV.

DEUTERONOMY.

Deuteronomy i.-xxx.

THE territory taken from the Amorites on the eastern side of the Jordan was peculiarly a grazing district. It was natural, therefore, that the men of Reuben and Gad, whose wealth consisted mainly in cattle, should desire it for their permanent abode; but when they applied for it to Moses, Eleazar, and the princes of the congregation, they were met with scathing reproof. Moses at first believed that their object was purely a selfish one. He supposed that they meant to settle down there and then, and go no farther; leaving their brethren, who had assisted in the conquest of Gilead for them, to go forward and fight their battles with the Canaanites as best they might by themselves. Such a course, he felt sure, would issue in the discouragement of the other tribes, and in the indefinite postponement of their settlement in the Land of Promise. This led him to speak to them in the sternest tone, "Shall your brethren go to war, and shall ye sit here?" and to warn them against incurring the fate of those who had been cut off in the wilderness, "Behold, ye are risen up in your fathers' stead, an increase of sinful men to augment yet the fierce anger of the Lord toward Israel."

It does not clearly appear whether or not the Reubenites and the Gadites had any such intentions as Moses imputed to them, though it is probable that the sagacious leader saw something in them which furnished good ground for his suspicions; but if they had been forming any such design, this indignant remonstrance was all that was needed to lead to its abandonment; for when they heard it, they proposed to leave their cattle in sheepfolds, and their families in cities under the care of the aged, while the men of war among them would go over ready armed with their brethren, taking the hazards of the campaign along with them, and only returning to their households when "the children of Israel had inherited every man his inheritance." This put the matter on a proper footing; and, therefore, after solemnly reminding them that if they refused to keep their compact they would be guilty of sin against the Lord, and their sin would surely find them out, Moses consented to their request, and gave to them "the kingdom of Sihon, king of the Amorites, and the kingdom of Og, king of Bashan, the land, with the cities thereof in the coasts, even the cities of the country round about." With these two tribes he joined a portion of the tribe of Manasseh, because the children of Machir and the children of Jair belonging to that tribe had largely contributed by their personal prowess to the conquest of a great part of Gilead. This was done by Moses, both as a matter of simple justice to these brave men, and as an incitement of the other nine tribes to show similar valor when they should cross the Jordan for the assault of the Canaanites.*

And now the time of Moses's departure was drawing nigh. Twice already during this fortieth year after the Exodus the shadow of bereavement had fallen darkly upon him. In the first month, before the tribes left Kadesh, his sister Miriam had passed away; and in the fifth month his brother Aaron had died on the top of Mount Hor. The former of these events, coming, as it did, in what we may call the course of

---

* Num. xxxii., 1-42.

nature, might affect him simply with a sense of personal loss. But the latter had been judicially connected with that sin at Meribah, in which he, and not Aaron, had been the principal agent, and its occurrence would sound to him as the warning of his own approaching dissolution. His exclusion from the earthly Canaan was a bitter disappointment to him; and, as it would seem, he had repeatedly begged of God that he might be allowed to go over "and see the good land that is beyond Jordan, that goodly mountain, and Lebanon." But when the answer came, "Let it suffice thee; speak no more unto me of this matter," he bent his will to that of God;* and, therefore, when, shortly before the war with the Midianites, referred to in my last discourse, the Lord told him that he should be gathered unto his people on Mount Abarim, as Aaron had been on Mount Hor, he was not taken by surprise. No murmur escaped his lips; no expression of sorrow for himself was indulged in by him. His whole concern was for the people whom he had so long and so faithfully led, and he entreated that the Lord, the God of the spirits of all flesh, might set a man over the congregation, to go out and in before them, that they might not be as sheep without a shepherd. This request was met by the command to take Joshua, whom we have met already on three several occasions as his minister, and to set him apart as his successor before the high-priest and before the people.† And so, having been freed from all anxiety on the score of the leadership of the tribes, he made haste to put everything else in order, in anticipation of his death. How diligently he labored with that end in view will appear from the fact that the entire Book of Deuteronomy belongs to the closing days of the great law-giver's life.

According to the third verse of that book, he began the

---

* Deut. iii., 23–26. † Num. xxvii., 15–23.

discourses which it contains on the first day of the eleventh month of the fortieth year of the wanderings. But from a reference in the Book of Joshua* we find that the Israelites under Joshua kept the passover in Gilgal on the fourteenth day of the first month of the following year. Four days before that, or on the tenth day of the first month, they had crossed the Jordan.† Previous to their crossing, they had spent three days in making preparations, and in waiting for the return of the spies from Jericho.‡ This brings us to the seventh day of the first month. But before this they had mourned thirty days for the death of Moses. Thus the death of Moses must be put not later than the seventh day of the twelfth month; and therefore the entire series of addresses which form the Book of Deuteronomy must have been delivered in the short interval between the first day of the eleventh month and the seventh day of the twelfth month,§ or in the brief space of thirty-seven days. A fact like that is in itself an evidence of the depth and fervor of Moses's interest in the people of his charge, and at the same time an incidental corroboration of the statement that his bodily vigor and mental energy were not in the least impaired by his advanced age. Here is a book equal in size to the entire collection of the predictions of some of the larger prophets, dealing, too, with minute and intricate details, and delivered orally to the representatives of the people, by a man

---

* Josh. v., 10.   † Ibid. iv., 19.   ‡ Ibid. i., 11; ii., 22.

§ Mr. Espin, in his admirable introduction to Deuteronomy in the "Speaker's Commentary," vol. i., p. 791, has fallen into a singular mistake of a month in his reckoning from the above passages, making thirty days from the tenth of the first month lead back to the tenth of the eleventh month, instead of the twelfth. He has forgotten, also, to allow for the three days at Shittim before the crossing of Jordan; and so he restricts Deuteronomy to the first ten days of the eleventh month, instead of to the thirty-seven days following the first of the eleventh month.

one hundred and twenty years old, within little more than a month. Surely we may venture to say that such a work, having in it no symptoms of senility or weakness, is, inspiration altogether apart, sufficient to stamp its author as one of the greatest men whom the world has produced.

You will not expect that, in a series of discourses like that which is now drawing to a close, I should enter upon a microscopic analysis of the work which I have thus incidentally characterized. Nevertheless, as in the course of modern controversy, the battle between rationalism and faith for the Old Testament has largely narrowed into a discussion over the Book of Deuteronomy—even as for the New Testament, the key of the position has come to be the Gospel by John—it would betray a sense of weakness or a cowardice, which I am far from feeling, if I did not spend a little time in putting before you the present state of the question, and estimating the weight of the arguments which have been advanced against the commonly received opinions regarding it.

Before doing so, however, it may be well to give a summary of the contents of the book itself. It consists of three discourses, to which are added three appendices, in the shape of the Song of Moses, the blessings pronounced by him on the tribes, and the narrative of the time, place, and manner of his death. The first address, extending to the fortieth verse of the fourth chapter, is mainly introductory, and consists of a recapitulation, for the purposes of warning and instruction, of the more important incidents in the history of the people, from the time of the breaking up of the encampment at Horeb until their arrival in the plains of Moab.

The second, and longest address, begins with the fifth chapter, and continues to the end of the twenty-sixth. It contains a practical exposition, with certain modifications and additions, of the law which had been given from Mount Sinai. But it is not a mere recapitulation; for throughout the tone is that, not of the statute-book, but of the teacher, who is at the same time the father of his people; and in every appeal there is the heart-throb of tenderest affection. His solicitude for the welfare of Israel is equalled only by his jealousy for the honor of Jehovah. He stands once more as the mediator between the Lord and them; and urges them by every consideration of love, and loyalty, and regard for their supreme welfare, to be faithful to his commands.

The third address begins with the twenty-seventh chapter, and continues to the end of the thirtieth. It is almost exclusively occupied with the giving of directions for the renewal of the covenant by the people at an appointed place in the valley of Shechem, after they had crossed the Jordan; and with an enumeration of the blessings which would follow their obedience of God's law, and of the curses that would fall upon them if they forsook his covenant and violated his injunctions. The blessings are exceedingly rich; but with a too sure forecast of the unfaithfulness of the people, the law-giver dwells longest on the curses, if by any means through this use of the terror of the Lord he might persuade them to be true to his covenant. As Dean Milman has said: "The sublimity of his denunciations surpasses anything in the oratory or the poetry of the whole world. Nature is exhausted in furnishing terrific images; nothing, except the real horrors of Jewish history, the miseries of their sieges, the cruelty, the contempt, the oppressions, the persecutions, which for ages this scattered and despised nation have endured, can approach the tremendous maledictions which warned them against the violation of their law."*

---

* "History of the Jews" (latest edition), vol. i., p. 256.

Thus, though called by its Greek name Deuteronomy—the second law—this book is not a mere rehearsal of statutes moral, religious, and civil. Its aim throughout is hortatory. It is the law, so to say, homiletically expounded, with such amplification of its principles and modification of its requirements as were called for by the new circumstances of the people. Those now before him were not the men to whom at Sinai the law had been proclaimed. A new generation had arisen since then; and as large portions of the statute-book had lain in abeyance during the journey through the wilderness, it became necessary that those parts of it bearing on the people generally should be clearly set before them. As Mr. Espin has said: "He speaks to hearers neither wholly ignorant of the law, nor yet fully versed in it. Much is assumed and taken for granted; again, on other matters, he goes into detail, knowing that instruction in them was needed. Sometimes, too, opportunity is taken of promulgating regulations which are supplementary or auxiliary to those of the preceding books; some few modifications suggested by longer experience or altered circumstances are now made, and the whole Mosaic system is completed by the addition of several enactments of a social, civil, and political nature."*

But through all and over all the moral purpose of the speaker is maintained. In his other writings, Moses is, for the most part, a historian or a legislator; in this he is pre-eminently a prophet, whose spiritual intuition pierces to the true meaning of the law, and interprets it as love; and whose inspired prescience foretells not only the future destiny of the Jews, but also the appearance of another prophet like unto himself, in being the author of a new economy, whom we recognize in the Messiah of the Gospel. In this charac-

---

* "Speaker's Commentary," vol. i., p. 791.

ter he rises to a sublimity not surpassed either by Isaiah or Jeremiah, and delivers some of the most remarkable predictions which the Word of God contains.

Specially noteworthy here, however, is his insight into the character of the Jews, and his presage of the dangers which lay before them. On the one hand, he guards them against idolatry, and on the other, against self-glorification; and it is remarkable that the first of these was the constant besetment of the people before the captivity, and the second their peculiar characteristic after it. From all these dangers he sees no safeguard but in the spiritual devotion of the people to Jehovah; and so it comes to pass that in this book, almost side by side with ritual enactments, we have a glorification of love as the comprehensive summary of the law, and an exhortation to circumcise the foreskin of the heart, as the grand essential thing in the sight of God. Thus he was at once the anticipator and forerunner of the Christian apostle, who wrote, " He is not a Jew which is one outwardly; and circumcision is that of the heart, in the spirit, and not in the letter; whose praise is not of man, but of God;" and who affirmed that " love is the fulfilling of the law."

But now, that higher criticism, from which nothing escapes, steps in and says, with a confidence which is apt to answer all the purposes of argument, that Moses did not write this book. It does not seem to weigh with those who make that affirmation, that if Deuteronomy was not written by Moses, it must have been written by some one who represented himself to be Moses, or personated him; and they see no moral incongruity between the doing of such an action and the insisting on that truth in the inward parts to which I have but now alluded. They appear to think that it is a perfectly natural thing for the highest morality to be enforced by one who, even at the very moment, is himself guilty of deceit. Therefore we must descend from this lofty region, that is so far above them, and we must seek to meet them on their own ground.

If Moses did not write Deuteronomy, then let us ask when and by whom it was written? And the moment we put that question, the greatest controversy arises; for, in fact, the antagonists of this book are agreed in nothing save in the opinion that Moses was not its author. Some will have it that it was composed during the Captivity; others, that it belongs to the time of the later kings. One eminent critic* dates it in the reign of Manasseh, and ascribes it to a writer in Egypt. Another believes it was composed in the days of Hezekiah; and others hold that it belongs to the age of David and Solomon; while a favorite idea with many used to be that the book which Hilkiah said he found in the Temple during the reign of Josiah was no other than the Book of Deuteronomy; which he or some person known to him had actually written, and which he pretended to find in the Temple for the purpose of securing its reception by the king and the people.

Now, if truth be one and error be manifold, it is apparent that we have here much of the manifoldness that is said to be characteristic of error. These various theories have been adopted almost at random, and on the most arbitrary principles, and they might well be left to neutralize each other by what Dean Milman has somewhat caustically called "mutual slaughter."† But as an illustration of the false and capricious proceedings of this school of critics, we may analyze the view of those who hold that Deuteronomy belongs to the age of Josiah, and was written by those who professed to have found the book of the law in the Temple.‡ They accept the history so far as to believe that

---

* Ewald. † "History of the Jews," vol. i., p. 178.
‡ 2 Chron. xxxiv., 14–33.

Hilkiah brought out a book; but they choose to disbelieve it when it says that it was the book of the law which had been long laid up in the Temple, and affirm that Hilkiah wrote it himself.

Now, on what ground is this discrimination made? We have as much reason for believing the historian when he says that the book was found, as when he says that Hilkiah brought out the book. The two statements rest precisely on the same authority; and if it were not to bolster up a preconceived theory, no such distinction would ever have been made between them. Moreover, the story is told simply and without parade; and all who are familiar with the history of the Scottish Regalia, as written by Sir Walter Scott, will acknowledge that, in an age like that of Manasseh, when persecution raged, it was quite probable that the book, which the law required to be laid up in the ark, should have been hidden for safety by those whose hearts were then trembling for the cause of Jehovah. It is equally probable that the secret of its hiding-place may have died with those who knew it at the first, and that in the repairing of the Temple it had been accidentally stumbled on by the workmen, who brought it, as of right, to the high-priest.

There is nothing improbable or unnatural in all this. But what an array of improbabilities we encounter on the other hypothesis! If that be true, then a great moral and spiritual revival throughout the land had its origin in a fraud. But we are wrong, we should not have said revival; for, if that hypothesis be true, this was the inauguration of the law which goes by Moses's name. But by what authority could such a system of enactments have been forced upon the people then? We can understand the enactment of these statutes through Moses, and their acceptance by the people, if they were promulgated at the Exodus, and in connection with the marvels of Sinai; but that, centuries after, any monarch, however popular, could have procured the acceptance of these precepts, is utterly inconceivable by us. Besides, how shall we account for the knowledge of that law, which is clearly implied by the history of Israel, in the interval between Moses and Josiah?

In the life of Samuel, in the history of David, especially, perhaps in the record of the building of the Temple by Solomon, we have many passages which imply that *in their respective days* the books of Moses were in existence. There is the same evidence of their existence in the times of Joash and Hezekiah; so that if this book found by Hilkiah was a forgery by him, we must suppose that he virtually rewrote the history of his nation in order to make that accord with his first fraud. The very utterance of such an idea is an exposure of its absurdity. The simplest theory of the history is that it is true. That is the key which will be found most easily to unlock all difficulties; every other will break in the lock.

It will be said, indeed, that surely much ignorance of the law must have existed, else such a revival of religion as the Chronicles describes would not have been produced by the discovery of the book in which it is written. But the analogy of the Reformation in Luther's time will help us to understand how it all came about. Manasseh had almost stamped out all knowledge of God's truth. Education, never, in Judea, at all to be compared with our modern standard, must then have been neglected, and religion, at least the religion of Jehovah, was persecuted. Hence, all interested in it would keep out of the way; and just as Luther's finding of the Bible in the convent library was the germ of the Reformation, so the finding of this book in the Temple was the beginning of the last revival of religion that preceded the captivity of the Jews.

We cannot, therefore, admit that any weight is to be

given to the opinion of those who have asserted that the book said to have been found by Hilkiah was then for the first time written. It deals arbitrarily with the narrative; it is attended with the greatest improbability in itself; its acceptance would require us to believe that much of the history of Israel had been fraudulently manipulated in the interests, professedly, of truth; and the idea that now for the first time the law of Moses was proclaimed and accepted by the people is so wild as to be felt by every candid reader to be practically inadmissible. Then, on the other side, there are naturalness, probability, and truth-likeness; for we have scenes in the later history of other nations which are in many respects similar to that which is here described. So, without hesitation, we dismiss, as utterly untenable, all the negative criticism which has sought to find a foothold on Hilkiah's discovery of the book. We agree with those who believe that this book was either the original autograph of Moses, or the official Temple copy of the law; and we hold with Canon Cook that "fraud or mistake might as easily have imposed a new Bible on the Christian world in the sixteenth century, as a new law on the Jews in the reign of Josiah."*

It would be easy to point out in a similar way the baselessness of the several opinions which I have enumerated; and the result would be to emphasize the statement of Milman, when he says, "Read the Book of Deuteronomy, and fairly estimate the difficulties which occur; . . . then read it again, and endeavor to assign it to any other period in the Jewish annals, and judge whether difficulties do not accumulate twenty-fold."†

But what are the reasons which have induced these critics

---

* "Speaker's Commentary," vol. iii., p. 127.
† "History of the Jews," vol. i., p. 253.

to affirm that Moses was not its author? Let us take a few, and estimate their force. First of all, it is affirmed that there are various notes of manners and places introduced which evidently belong to a later date. Of this sort are the references to the Emims, the Horims, the Avims, and Hermon;* but these have all the look of parenthetic glosses, introduced for the purpose of elucidation, by a later editor, probably by Ezra, or by some one before his time; and the authorship of the book as a whole is not to be invalidated by them, any more than it is by the admission of the fact that the closing chapter, describing the death of Moses, was written by Joshua, or by some one equally well acquainted with the facts. These are but in the place of foot-notes to a modern volume; and we know that such additions from the hand of an editor furnish no ground for disputing the authorship of the work itself.

Again, it is affirmed that because Deuteronomy contains allusions to the appointment of a king, it could not have been written until after the beginning of the Jewish monarchy; that because the descriptions of royal extravagance present features which are appropriate to Solomon, therefore it must have been produced after his day; and that because in the curses mention is made of the Captivity, therefore it must have been composed after the people had been carried away into Babylon.

Now, all these assertions spring from the adoption of a foregone conclusion. Those who make them have adopted the opinion that prophecy is impossible; and just as Renan places the Gospel by Luke at a date later than the destruction of Jerusalem, because it contains a prediction of that event, so others would reject the Mosaic authorship of Deuteronomy because of the prophecies it records. The point

---

* See Deut. ii., 10-12, 22, 23; iii., 9.

thus raised, however, belongs not to criticism, but philosophy; and if the view of these authors is correct, then the supernatural becomes impossible, and the Bible ceases to be anything different from an ordinary book. Before a question of such magnitude as that, all discussions concerning mere date and authorship dwindle into insignificance; and we have to go much farther back, and begin with the personal existence of God, in order to debate it fully. Evidently we cannot do that here; but it is enough to point out that such arguments as those which I have enumerated would, if sustained, deprive us of the Word of God as a whole; and, fairly pushed to their legitimate conclusions, would land us in the dreary region of atheism.

Again, it is alleged that the style of the book is different from that of those by which it is preceded, and in particular that there are so many resemblances between it and the writings of Jeremiah, as to suggest the probability that it was either written by that prophet, or by some one who belonged to the same age; but, so far as the difference of style between Deuteronomy and the other books of the Pentateuch is concerned, that is sufficiently accounted for by the different circumstances of the author. The spoken style is always distinct from the written; and he who addresses his fellow-men for a practical and hortatory purpose will naturally adopt a different method from that of the statute-book or the historical register. At the same time, it is not to be forgotten that there are not infrequent parallelisms between it and its predecessors;* while all the classes of idiom, whether in vocabulary or grammar, which have been accounted peculiar to the Pentateuch, are found in Deuteronomy.† Then, as regards the similarity of Jeremiah's prophe-

---

* Compare Deut. xxviii. with Lev. xxvi.
† "Speaker's Commentary," *ubi supra.*

cies to some portions of Deuteronomy, we admit the fact, but we deny the inference drawn from it. The resemblances are both numerous and striking, but they are easily accounted for on quite another hypothesis.

Remember that Jeremiah was a contemporary of Hilkiah, who found the book of the law in the Temple in the days of Josiah, and that he was, perhaps, the nephew of Shallum, the husband of that prophetess Huldah† to whom the king applied for counsel as to what he was to do in the matter of the law, and you will see in these facts a sufficient explanation of the hold which the Book of Deuteronomy had taken upon him. It came to him with all the freshness of a new discovery. Its special application to the times in which he lived would be apparent to him on a first perusal, and so he would go back upon it again and again, until it literally possessed him, and became part and parcel of himself. Thus the resemblance of his style to that of Deuteronomy is a legitimate effect of the finding of the book by Hilkiah, and of the interpretation given to it by the occurrences of his own times, and is only what might have been expected in the circumstances.

Once more, it is affirmed that there is such a difference between the allusions to the priests contained in Deuteronomy and those made to them in Numbers and Leviticus, that it is hardly conceivable that these books all came from the same hand. In the middle books of the Pentateuch the priests are carefully distinguished from the Levites; while in Deuteronomy it is alleged that no such hierarchical division is found, but the Levites only are mentioned. This, however, is not absolutely true; for when Moses speaks of the death of Aaron,† he says also, "Eleazar his son min-

---

* Compare Jer. xxii., 7, with 2 Kings xxii., 14.
† Deut. x., 6.

istered in the priest's office in his stead;" and a verse or two subsequently* he refers to the separation of the tribe of Levi to other purposes than those of the priesthood. In the eighteenth chapter, also, there is a passage in which the priest is clearly distinguished from the Levite.† These two cases are sufficient to overthrow the theory of those who imagine that the Deuteronomist, as they call him, knew nothing of the hierarchy. But we are willing to admit that, in the vast majority of instances, the Lord's ministers are all included under the one word, "Levites;" and we find the satisfactory explanation in Mr. Espin's words: "Moses, in Deuteronomy, is not prescribing the several functions and privileges of the various orders of clergy, as he has to do in the preceding books, he is addressing the people; and when he has occasion to mention the clergy, it is only in a general way, in reference broadly to their relation and duties toward the body of the nation. Hence he, for the time, very naturally disregards the difference of orders among the clergy which was not to his purpose, and ascribes priestly and Levitical functions indifferently to the tribe of Levi, to which, as the priests were of course Levites, these functions really belonged. . . . The discrepancies, therefore, between Deuteronomy and the earlier books are, in this particular, superficial only. They are at once explained by the familiar consideration that he who speaks to a large and mixed audience will take care, if he knows his business, to shun irrelevant details and distinctions."‡

Finally, it is urged that Deuteronomy contains certain deviations from the earlier narratives, in the way of additions to them or variations from them, and therefore it could not

---

* Deut. x., 8. † Ibid. xviii., 3, 6 ; see also xviii., 1.
‡ "Speaker's Commentary," vol. i., p. 798. See this same point thoroughly and very satisfactorily treated in "The Levitical Priests," by S. J. Curtis.

have come from the pen of their author. But to this it is replied that, on the admission of some of the critics themselves, there is nothing in Deuteronomy which positively contradicts anything in the earlier books. And as for the variations or deviations, their very existence is a proof that the book did not come from an impostor. For that sort of discrepancy is the very thing that a deceiver would most rigorously avoid; and nobody but the original law-giver himself would attempt to treat the subject in the same free and independent manner.

It would serve no good purpose to enter upon a minute examination of the alleged discrepancies between Deuteronomy and the earlier books. They are in their nature similar to those which are to be found on a comparison of the four Gospels with each other. And when they are examined in a spirit of fairness, comprehensiveness, and common-sense, and not after the fashion of an attorney who strains every point to make out a case, they may be either satisfactorily explained, or quietly left until God in his providence shall give more light. Even those of them for which no solution is apparent are not sufficient to counterbalance the weight of evidence on the other side, and it is easier to believe that some mistake may in some unexplained way have crept in regarding them, than it is to hold that the Book of Deuteronomy was foisted upon the Jews at a late period of their history, by one who sought the reformation of the people by a pious fraud.*

Moreover, we must not forget that the book is quoted both by Peter and Paul as the production of Moses, and

---

* Those who wish to examine this matter for themselves may find these so-called discrepancies fairly faced and candidly considered, by the commentator in the "Speaker's Commentary," vol. i.; by Dr. W. I. Alexander, in the *Sunday Magazine*, for 1870-71; and by Dr. Murphy, in the *British and Foreign Evangelical Review* for Jan., 1878.

has at least the endorsement of its inspiration by Christ, who quoted from it as from the Word of God in his conflict with the Tempter. It may be said, indeed, that the question of inspiration is quite distinct from authorship; and in the case of such a writing as the Epistle to the Hebrews that may be frankly admitted, because there the writer does not speak so as to reveal his personality. But in' the Book of Deuteronomy the speaker claims to be Moses throughout (with the solitary exception of the final chapter), and so the attestation of its inspiration becomes thereby also the confirmation of its authorship.

It is alleged, however, that our Lord and his apostles spoke in harmony with the belief of their times, though they were themselves ignorant of the real authorship of the book. But while we may admit that some things were not known to Jesus Christ as the Son of man, yet, as Mr. Espin forcibly reminds us, we must not overlook the distinction between ignorance and error; and we are sure that he does not speak too strongly when he says that, "To assert that He who is the truth believed Deuteronomy to be the work of Moses, and quoted it expressly as such, though it was in fact a forgery introduced into the world seven or eight centuries after the Exodus, is in effect, though not in intention, to impeach the perfection and sinlessness of his nature, and seems thus to gainsay the first principles of Christianity."*

But you ask me why I have been so particular to put this matter before you; and my reply is, in the first place, because I wished to give you a specimen of the way in which the "higher critics," as they are styled, deal with such questions in their works on the Bible. They affect to tell oracularly, from the style of a book, whether its author lived six or thirteen centuries before the Christian era. Now such

---

* "Speaker's Commentary," vol. i., p. 800.

a claim is preposterous. A few years ago, in London, there was a great controversy in the columns of the *Times* over a recently discovered poem which was supposed to be the production of John Milton. Great authorities were ranged on each side, and the same expressions were regarded by some as Miltonic, and by others as a clear proof that Milton had nothing to do with the production.

Now we may surely say that if, two hundred years after the death of one of the greatest English poets, men who were well acquainted with his writings could not agree upon the question whether or not he was the author of certain newly discovered lines, it is in the highest degree presumptuous for critics living thirty-three centuries after the death of Moses to declare on mere internal evidence that the Book of Deuteronomy was not written by him, but must have been composed only twenty-five centuries ago. I make no pretensions to superior Hebrew scholarship, yet I do not hesitate to say that the claims of the higher criticism in this regard are simply ridiculous; and just because they are so confidently made, often too with the coolest *näivete*, it is right that they should be exposed. Moreover, it is important to remark that their allegations are for the most part unproved assertions. Take, for example, here the case of Dr. Robertson Smith, which has made so much stir during the past year in the Free Church of Scotland; and we have in his article on the Bible the following sentences: "But even so, it is difficult to suppose that the legislative part of Deuteronomy is as old as Moses. If the law of the kingdom in Deut. xvii. was known in the time of the Judges, it is impossible to comprehend Judg. viii., 23, and above all 1 Sam. viii., 7." That is his assertion. But he does not attempt to show how the comprehension of these passages in Samuel and Judges is impossible on the theory that the law of the kingdom was existing. He expects his readers will take the statement on his authority, without ever investigating the passages.

But we have had too much experience of what I may call the fallacy of references to be caught thus. We look up the passages, and we are so dull as not to see the impossibility of comprehending them, and at the same time holding the Mosaic authorship of Deuteronomy. Here they are: "And Gideon said unto them, I will not rule over you, neither shall my son rule over you: the Lord shall rule over you." "And the Lord said unto Samuel, Hearken unto the voice of the people in all that they say unto thee: for they have not rejected thee, but they have rejected me, that I should not reign over them."

Now, to our uncritical judgment, these passages are thoroughly compatible with the law of the kingdom in Deuteronomy. That law was an accommodation to the foreseen deterioration of the character of the people of Israel. The ideal of the Jewish state was a theocracy. But that, as Moses, guided by God, foresaw, would be difficult to maintain amidst the influences from surrounding nations to which they were exposed, and so provision is made for a kingdom. Still, it is clearly implied that the setting up of a kingdom would be an evidence of spiritual declension in the people; and it was because both Gideon and Samuel saw that the people were yielding to evil influence that they protested against their conduct. Nay, more, it was for the same reason that God gave them Saul as a king, "in his anger." So the reconciling principle is here, the people would be better without a king; but if they were determined to have a king, then he should be appointed thus and so. Now, that is a fair specimen of the manner in which the higher critics work. They make an assertion as if it were axiomatic or incontrovertible, and, without seeking to prove it, they draw an inference from it. The error in their conclusion is really taken for granted in the unproved allegation of their premise ; and a reference to a passage which, candidly interpreted, goes against their own views, is all the authority they condescend to furnish. That is not argument—that is dogmatism ; and yet I deliberately say that it is a fair specimen of their work.

But my second reason for bringing all this forward is, because Christianity itself is at stake in this controversy. Christianity is the development of Judaism ; and if the divine origin of Judaism is successfully assailed, that of Christianity cannot be maintained. The Old and New Testaments stand or fall together. The deity of Christ cannot be upheld if the divine legation of Moses is overthrown. You may as well imagine that you can blow up the basement of a house without injury to the inmates of the parlor, as suppose that you can demolish the divine origin of Judaism without overturning also that of Christianity. Moses wrote of Christ, and Christ authenticated Moses. They are inextricably and inseparably connected ; and I know few more dangerous symptoms in the present day than the prevalent disposition, even among Christian people, to depreciate the Old Testament. To counteract that it is that I have spent so much of my time in these recent years on the exposition of Old Testament history ; and to protest against that it is that I have devoted this discourse to the Mosaic authorship of Deuteronomy. When we have discovered the practical value of the Old Testament in its bearing on our daily lives, we shall not be willing to let it be regarded as of no account.

And now, having brought to a conclusion this rapid survey of the arguments in defence of the Mosaic authorship of Deuteronomy, I ask your indulgence for but a few moments longer, while I seek to give distinctness to two important features by which the book is characterized. The first is its prophetic character. We have already seen that here, more than in any portion of the Pentateuch, Moses rises from the historian and legislator into the prophet, and emphasizes that "love" which is "the fulfilling of the law." But taking the term prophet in its more restricted signification, as meaning one who foretells future events, it is in Deuteronomy also that the fitness of the application of the title in that sense to Moses is especially vindicated. The Saviour said to the Jews of his day, "Had ye believed Moses, ye would have believed me, for he wrote of me;"* and as we know from Stephen,† one of the passages in which he thus testified to the Messiah is the following: "The Lord thy God will raise up unto thee a Prophet from the midst of thee, of thy brethren, like unto me; unto him ye shall hearken."‡ Now, though this prediction had its partial verifications in the rise of the separate prophets in the history of Israel, its terms are satisfied in none of these, for only in Jesus Christ, the "one mediator between God and men," the "mediator of the new covenant,"§ do we find the counterpart of Moses, who was yet greater and more glorious than he. The pith of the prophecy lies in the words, "like unto me;" and the likeness is not moral but official. It is true, indeed, that as far as Moses transcended other prophets, Christ transcended Moses, in point of character and relationship to Jehovah. The Lord said concerning Moses, "If there be a prophet among you, I the Lord will make myself known unto him in a vision, and will speak unto him in a dream. My servant Moses is not so, who is faithful in all my house. With him will I speak mouth to mouth, even apparently, and not in dark speeches; and the similitude of the Lord shall he behold."‖ But of Jesus he said, "This is my beloved Son, in whom I am well pleased."¶ Thus in dignity of nature and

---

* John v., 46. † Acts vii., 37. ‡ Deut. xviii., 15.
§ 1 Tim. ii., 5; Heb. ix., 15; xii., 24. ‖ Num. xii., 6–8.
¶ Matt. iii., 17.

excellence of character there was more than a likeness to Moses in Jesus. There was superiority over him; for Moses was a servant, but Christ is the Son. But in official position there is a perfect similarity. For as Moses was the mediator between the nation of Israel and Jehovah, so Christ is the mediator between God and men;* as Moses was the introducer of a new economy, so Jesus was the inaugurator of a new dispensation; as Moses was the intercessor for the people, so Jesus is "able to save to the uttermost all that come unto God by him, seeing he ever liveth to make intercession for them."† Thus he crowns the prophecy of his whole typical system with this personal description of his coming Lord, and furnishes us with a mark by which we are enabled to identify in Jesus of Nazareth the Messiah promised to the fathers. Nay, more, the very founder of the Jewish system does thus, in his final address to the people whom he had emancipated, foreshadow the temporary character of the whole ritual with which his name is associated, and turn their eyes in expectancy toward one who has to lead them to heights of privilege, loftier far than those to which with him they had ascended.‡

But it is, perhaps, in his description of the future history of the people whom he had, under God, welded into a nation, that his prophetic character comes in this book most conspicuously out. Read the twenty-eighth chapter. Compare with that the Annals of Josephus, and the history of the Jewish people from the destruction of Jerusalem down to the present day, and you will find a marvellous correspondence between the two! The prophecy—for although it is hypothetical and conditioned on certain actions of the people themselves, it is nevertheless, in the true sense of the word, a prediction—is a forecast epitome of the history; the

---

* 1 Tim. ii., 5. † Heb. vii., 25. ‡ See below, p. 466.

history is but an expansion of the prophecy. For each chapter in the annals of the people you may find an appropriate and descriptive heading in one of the verses of the prophecy; and as to-day we look upon the descendants of Abraham among us, and observe how, living beside us, they are yet perfectly distinct from us, we see before us a living testimony that this book is from God. This must be felt even by those who deny its Mosaic authorship; for, whoever wrote it, there is the clearest evidence that it existed centuries before the destruction of the Jewish state by the Romans. There is, therefore, no possibility of gainsaying the argument that is founded on the fulfilment of this series of predictions. On the one hand, it is clearly established that the prophecy was in writing, as we have it, centuries before it was fulfilled; on the other, the events by which it was fulfilled are as certain as any which history has recorded. These are facts as really as any established by science. What is the inevitable inference? Plainly that we have here something miraculous. But strong as the argument is, even though the Mosaic authorship be given up—and that we have shown good reason for refusing to do—it is even stronger when we regard the prophecy as the utterance of Moses. Here is an arch spanning the whole historic age of the world, with one abutment resting on the epoch of the Exodus and another resting on our own times. Who built that arch? Where shall we find the human prescience that can thus bridge over the gulf of three thousand years? Must we not come to the conclusion, as we gaze upon it, that its architect was none other than He who reared the majestic dome of the heavens, and hung the earth itself in space?

But in connection with this prophecy, also, another characteristic feature of Deuteronomy comes specially into prominence. I allude to its practical bearing on the history and destiny of nations. Bacon has said, in one of his essays,

"Prosperity is the blessing of the Old Testament; adversity is the blessing of the New."* But, though that may be accepted as a general statement—liable, of course, to exceptions—for individuals, it is not true of nations. For individuals there is a future personal existence in another state, in which the compensations for adversity may be given—or rather, to put it more accurately, in which the ripened blessing, of which adversity is the acrid and immature berry, will be enjoyed by the soul—but for nations in the aggregate there is no such future state. Men will be dealt with as individuals in the retribution of eternity. There is no such judgment of nations. On them retribution falls in the course of their history here on earth. And so, in regard to them, it holds true, under the new dispensation as under the old, that their present prosperity depends on their character and conduct. God punishes national crimes by temporal judgments, and rewards national virtue by temporal blessings. This is true even of nations which are ruled by absolute monarchs; how much more evidently so it is of a nation like our own, in which the people are sovereign. If we permit our legislators to frame dishonest laws, to break treaties which have been solemnly made, to oppress the aboriginal tribes who have been dispossessed by the advancing tide of population, to deal unjustly with any section of the community, we may expect that before long the result shall be adversity, in some form or other, which shall be so closely connected with the sin as to be seen to be its punishment; but if we seek to do justly by all, and to have mercy for them that are oppressed; if we faithfully adhere to the principles laid down in our national Constitution, and seek to advance the interests of truth, and righteousness, and humanity—not within our own borders only, but wherever our influence has

---

* Bacon's Essays, with annotations by Richard Whateley, D.D., p. 90.

weight—then we may rely that God will favor us with all the blessings which Israel forfeited. Thus patriotism as well as piety impels us to seek to purify our political life, and to secure as our legislators men who have no interests to advance but those of the community, no rule to follow but that of righteousness, and no reward to seek but the approbation of conscience and of God. Other nations than the Jews have been rejected because of their unfaithfulness. The whole track of history is marked with the ruins of empires which, having been founded in injustice, or perpetuated by wrong, were ultimately destroyed. Assyria, Babylon, Persia, Greece, Rome—where are they now? and why did they go down? The Book of Deuteronomy, faithfully studied, will give us the right answer; while at the same time it unmistakably indicates the lesson for ourselves. May God help us to lay that lesson to heart!

XXV.

DEATH AND BURIAL OF MOSES.

Deuteronomy xxxiv., 1-12.

AFTER he had delivered to the people those addresses of which the main part of the Book of Deuteronomy consists, Moses, at the command of God, presented himself with Joshua in the tabernacle of the congregation. Then, as on former occasions of special importance, the cloudy pillar descended and stood over the door of the tent of meeting, while Jehovah gave from it to Joshua this solemn yet reassuring charge: "Be strong and of a good courage: for thou shalt bring the children of Israel into the land which I sware unto them: and I will be with thee."* After this, having written out, in a separate roll, the words which he had spoken to the assembly at its formal convocation, Moses gave the book to the Levites, with instructions to put it in the side of the ark of the covenant, there to be a perpetual witness of the engagements into which the people had freely and deliberately entered. This done, he gathered all the elders and officers of the tribes, and "spake in their ears" that stirring psalm in which the shout of thanksgiving and the song of joy alternate with a roll of terror which sounds as if the thunder of Sinai were reverberating anew.

For poetic sublimity, for devout piety, for holy expostulation, and for solemn warning, this farewell ode has never been surpassed; and it furnishes an incidental proof of the

---

* Deut. xxxi., 23.

fact that, unlike most other men, Moses continued, to the very end of his long life, to grow in those qualities of imagination and fiery enthusiasm which are usually regarded as the special characteristics of youth. It has nothing in it of the pensive sadness which forms the undertone of the ninetieth psalm, and out of which, like a bird darting up above the mist that fills an Alpine valley, his faith rises only after what seems to be a long and labored effort. Rather, it is akin, in some of its strains, to his song upon the Red Sea shore; while in its exquisitely beautiful reference to the eagle with her young, as well as in the frequent allusions which it makes to the rock-like majesty, stability, and strength of God, it connects itself with his meditations and observations while, as a shepherd, he followed Jethro's flocks in the desert of Midian.

There is in it thus a wondrous combination of the strength of manhood with the experience of old age, and of the imaginative force of youth with the wisdom which increasing years supply. Nor is this all: there is in it a marvellous interblending of the various relationships in which Moses stood at once to God and to the people. He praises Jehovah with the fervor of a seraph, and he pleads with the people with the tenderness of a father. He deals with national subjects in the spirit of a statesman, and warns of coming doom with the sternness of a prophet. Now the strains are soft and low, as if they came from the chords of an Æolian harp stirred by the breeze of a gentle summer eve; anon they are loud and stormful, as if some gust of passionate intensity had come sweeping over his spirit: now they are luminous with the recollection of God's mercies, and again they are lowering, as if laden with the electric burden of God's coming wrath. Of course, in all he spake as he was moved by the Holy Ghost; but, as the Spirit used not the vocal organs only, but the soul of the man, this ode conclusively proves that if Moses had not been the grandest law-giver and statesman of his nation, and even of the world, he might have been one of the noblest poets. It shows, too, that there was in him the exceedingly rare alliance of a mind which was alive to the importance of the minutest details of legislation, with a soul whose wings could soar into the loftiest regions of thought and feeling. With undimmed eye he looked on more trying light than that of the common sunshine, and with unabated force he ascended, even at the age of sixscore years, a more ethereal height than that of Pisgah; so that, if this ode had been found elsewhere than in the Bible, mere literary critics would have risen into ecstasies over its exquisite manifestation of beauty in the lap of terror.

But, noble as the psalm contained in the thirty-second chapter of Deuteronomy is, I am not sure if it be not surpassed by the blessing of the tribes which is preserved in the thirty-third. In form and structure, this last resembles Jacob's benediction of his sons upon his death-bed; yet it rises as far above that as the character of Moses transcends that of the supplanter. It is a mingling of precept, of prophecy, and of prayer; each clause in it being packed with meaning and lustrous with beauty, while here and there we come upon phrases which make us start with a strange joy, because we recognize in them autobiographic references to his own personal history. How touching his benediction of his own tribe of Levi, in which, by mere suggestion, he contrasts their faithfulness with his own sin! What could be finer, too, than his delicate reference to the first meeting between himself and Jehovah, in the words occurring in the blessing of Joseph, "The good-will of him that dwelt in the bush?" Nor can we help seeing the testimony of his own past experience in the prophecy which he gives to Asher, when he says, "As thy days, so shall thy strength be." And if you wish to learn how much the character of the prophet had to do with the texture of his prophecy while yet he spake by inspiration of God, then contrast the blessing uttered by Balaam over the people whom he so wished to curse* with these last recorded utterances of Moses, "There is none like unto the God of Jeshurun, who rideth upon the heaven in thy help, and in his excellency on the sky. The eternal God is thy refuge, and underneath are the everlasting arms: and he shall thrust out the enemy from before thee; and shall say, Destroy them. Israel then shall dwell in safety alone: the fountain of Jacob shall be upon a land of corn and wine; also his heavens shall drop down dew. Happy art thou, O Israel: who is like unto thee, O people saved by the Lord, the shield of thy help, and who is the sword of thy excellency! and thine enemies shall be found liars unto thee; and thou shalt tread upon their high places."†

But now, having set his house in order, there is nothing more for Moses to do but to die; and his death was in keeping with the majesty of his life. The Lord said unto him, "Get thee up into this mountain Abarim, unto Mount Nebo, which is in the land of Moab, that is over against Jericho; and behold the land of Canaan, which I give unto the children of Israel for a possession: and die in the mount whither thou goest up, and be gathered unto thy people." Though born on the flat Egyptian plain, Moses had, for at least two-thirds of his life, been familiar with mountains. Amidst the solitudes of Horeb he had received his commission from Him whose glory burned in the unconsumed bush. Often he had ascended the rocky sides of Sinai to commune with the Eternal, and in one of its cave-like clefts he had stood while,

---

* Num. xxiii., 8–10, 19–24; xxiv., 5–9, 16–24.
† Deut. xxxiii., 26–29.

as his glory passed by, Jehovah proclaimed to him his name. Not many months ago he had climbed to the summit of the castellated Hor, and seen his brother Aaron calmly "unclothed," that he might be "clothed upon with his house which was from heaven." But much and strangely as he had felt on all these other occasions, his emotions now were entirely different from anything he had experienced before. He had not "passed this way heretofore." There was that immediately before him of which he had no experience. He could form no conception of what it was like. He was to take a step out into the unknown. He was to leave the body, and the lower sphere of earth. He was to lay down the charge which he had carried for forty years, and go— whither? He knew not. He only knew that God was there, in a yet more glorious and more comforting sense than he is here, and than he had met him on the earth; and in that assurance he was calm. There is no record of individual leave-takings; for in nothing does the Bible more sublimely differ from ordinary biographies than in the almost utter absence of death-bed experiences or last utterances from its pages. But, withdrawing from the camp, perhaps in a quiet and undemonstrative manner, he took his way alone up to the range of Abarim and the Pisgah summit, which travellers have tried to identify with Jebel Neba, that is over against Jericho. And who may attempt to describe his feelings as he gazed out upon the land which he might look upon but might not enter, while the Lord stood by him to point out to him the many localities which he had written of in his "book of origins," but which he saw now for the first time? At his feet, flowing along the edge of the plains of Moab, was the Jordan, hastening to lose itself in the waters of the Dead Sea; to the right, his eye took in the land of Gilead, until it ended far away in the north; to the left, the grassy fields of Beersheba shaded off into the brown barrenness of the Egyptian desert; while directly in front of him lay all the land of Judah, with the distant hills of Naphtali on the northern horizon, and the "utmost sea" in the far west. "From Jezreel, with its waving corn, to Eshcol, with its luxuriant vines; from Bashan, with its kine, to Carmel, with its rocks dropping honey; from Lebanon, with its rampart of snow, south again to the dim edge of the desert;"* the prospect was before him. As he gazed upon it, the words fell upon his ears, "This is the land which I sware unto Abraham, unto Isaac, and unto Jacob, saying, I will give it unto thy seed: I have caused thee to see it with thine eyes;" and then, not in sternness, nor in anger, but in utmost love, like a mother lifting her boy into her arms, the Lord added, "but thou shalt not go over thither;" and in a moment, in the twinkling of an eye, the soul of Moses had passed within the veil, and was at home with God.

But even the dust of his people is precious in the sight of the Lord; and the body of that honored saint must not be left to become the prey of the vulture, nor his bones to lie whitening on the mountain. So God buried him, and, as Thomas Fuller quaintly says, "buried also his grave," so that "no man knoweth his sepulchre unto this day." What a death! what a burial! How peaceful the one, how unostentatious the other! He died "by the word of the Lord," or, as the word literally is, "by the mouth of the Lord;" and we do not wonder that the Jewish Rabbis understand it to mean "by the kiss of the Lord." As the father kisses his boy when he lifts him to his knee, so death came to Moses as a token of his Lord's affection. And in that lonely burial, whose sublimity touches even the most cursory reader of the narrative, what a rebuke is addressed to those who seek to

---

* "Moses, the Man of God," by James Hamilton, D.D., p. 369.

hide the solemnity of death beneath floral offerings and military processions, or who vainly attempt to perpetuate the memory of an uneventful life by monumental marble. How can I forbear from quoting in this connection the well-known lines?

> "——When the warrior dieth,
>   His comrades in the war,
> With arms reversed, and muffled drum,
>   Follow the funeral car.
> They show the banners taken,
>   They tell his battles won,
> And after him lead the masterless steed,
>   While peals the minute-gun.
>
> "Amid the noblest of the land,
>   Men lay the *sage* to rest;
> And give the *bard* an honored place,
>   With costly marble drest,
> In the great minster transept,
>   Where lights like glories fall,
> And the sweet choir sings, and the organ rings,
>   Along the emblazoned wall.
>
> "This was the bravest warrior
>   That ever buckled sword;
> This the most gifted poet
>   That ever breathed a word;
> And never earth's philosopher
>   Traced, with his golden pen,
> On the deathless page truth half so sage,
>   As he wrote down for men.
>
> "And had HE not high honor?
>   The hill-side for his pall,
> To lie in state while angels wait,
>   With stars for tapers tall;
> And the dark rock-pines, like tossing plumes,
>   Over his bier to wave;
> And God's own hand, in that lonely land,
>   To lay him in the grave."

But though his grave was hid from the knowledge of men, perhaps, as some have hinted, as a safeguard to keep the people from giving it a superstitious sanctity, yet when God wanted it, he knew where to find it; and the passage in Jude, which every reader feels to be so singular in its reference to a dispute between Michael and the devil over the body of Moses, may really allude to the resurrection of Moses, in order that, with Elijah, he might stand in glorified humanity beside Jesus on the Mountain of Transfiguration. And if this be so, it is interesting to note that thus, not through Jordan, but over it by way of heaven, he actually at length did pass into Canaan, and stood upon the dewy Hermon.

Thus died this many-sided man—as many another hero has died—within sight of that which through life he had been straining after; but without reaching it. Yet his life was not therefore a failure. On the contrary, he had made it possible for Joshua to succeed; while in his own character, the consideration of which we must reserve for a final discourse, he achieved the grandest success; so that, take him all in all, he stands before us the noblest of Old Testament worthies, and the peer, if not, in some respects, even the superior, of Paul himself. As the carpenter in "Adam Bede" said, "He carried a hard business well through." And we may add that he did so because the Lord carried him. The Transfiguration mountain has for us now taken all sadness from the contemplation of the death on Pisgah. We shed no tears over a grave which is now empty; but we do not wonder that "the children of Israel wept for Moses in the plains of Moab thirty days." They might well weep, for he had done much for them; and perhaps they had never so appreciated his value as they did now that he was no more among them. Nor could they forget that, if they had not provoked him to anger by their murmuring, they might have had him still among them. There are few tears so scalding as those which disobedient sons drop upon a father's grave; and there might be not a little of similar poignancy in the grief of the Israelites over Moses's death. But the past can neither be recalled nor atoned for by weeping. What remains is, that we amend the future; and it says much for the genuineness of the people's sorrow that they "hearkened unto Joshua," and did not harass and afflict him with their mutinies and their idolatries as they had Moses.

But seeking now for the practical lessons with which this chapter of history is fraught, let us remark, in the first place, that even the good man's life may be shortened by his own sin. Hear what God said to his servant: "Be gathered unto thy people; as Aaron thy brother died in Mount Hor, and was gathered unto his people: because ye trespassed against me among the children of Israel at the waters of Meribah-kadesh, in the wilderness of Zin; because ye sanctified me not in the midst of the children of Israel."* Now, it is true that, as he has elsewhere said,† "The Lord was wroth with him, for the people's sakes." His design was to impress their hearts with the evil nature of sin, from the fact that such an apparently small offence in one so excellent and exalted as Moses entailed on him such a bitter disappointment; and, as I have already hinted, some of the most pungent elements in their mourning over his loss may have been owing to their consciousness that he was, in some sort, suffering vicariously for themselves.

But, while all this must be admitted, we shall lose one of the most pointed lessons of this event if we fail to take note of the fact that untimely death may be the result of special sin. We can all understand how this can be the case when even a good man, moved by a zeal which is not tempered with discretion, forgets the laws of health, and works in such

---

* Deut. xxxii., 50, 51.   † Ibid., iii., 26.

a way as to bring upon himself premature disease of brain or heart, by which he is prostrated long before he reaches the limit of threescore years and ten. Such a one forgets himself in another sense than Moses did when he lost his self-command; and, though we may loosely speak of him as a martyr to the cause in which he labored, we are compelled to admit that he sinned against those physical laws which, in their own place, are as imperious as the moral code itself, and thus entailed upon himself exclusion from his promised land, while no Pisgah prospect of its nearness supported him in his dying hours. This is especially the temptation of the times in which we live. Amidst the hurry and rush of our modern business, with our railroads, and telegraphs, and steam-navigation, we are all too apt to be borne along with the current; and ever and anon we are startled by the hopeless breakdown of some able and energetic leader in the very mid-time of his days; while, in the Church as in the world, men of influence and energy burn themselves out by the intensity of their devotion to their work. Now and then, indeed, a word of warning will be uttered by loving friends and earnest fellow-laborers, but it is silenced by the assertion that "it is better to wear out than rust out;" and the issue, as might have been foreseen, is a sudden collapse, or a premature grave. It is time, therefore, to call a halt. Such self-consuming toil is not only unnecessary, but it is positively sinful. We have no right to kill ourselves, and call it zeal; and perhaps, if we were to get at the root of the evil in each case, we should find it not in public spirit, but in personal ambition. Such a prodigality of vitality is not sacrifice, but suicide; and it ought to be distinctly understood that overwork is wickedness, the guilt of which will keep us forever on the eastern side of our Jordan.

But there is still another aspect of this subject which must not be lost sight of, though we cannot fully investigate it without going into those departments of the divine administration which lie beyond our ken. It is possible that for personal sin, not in the physical but in the moral sphere, a man may die before his time. We recognize the truth of this assertion in the case of the ungodly, but it holds also in those who must be described as servants of the Lord; and if we could see below the surface, we might discover that those deaths which are so often described by us as mysterious dispensations of Providence have no more of mystery about them than this of Moses, but have occurred when they did because of some sin with which the individuals were chargeable. This is a somewhat awful thought, and the mere enunciation of it is all that is required to point the warning which it suggests. David was not permitted to build the Temple, because he had been a man of war from his youth; and the disappointments which have clouded many death-beds may have been similarly connected with the characters of the antecedent lives. It was after he had been indulging in the practice of deceit that the Psalmist wrote, "What man is he that desireth life, and loveth many days, that he may see good? Keep thy tongue from evil, and thy lips from speaking guile. Depart from evil, and do good; seek peace, and pursue it;"* and perhaps the experiences through which he had just passed had given him a glimpse of the truth on which I am now insisting. In any case, it may be well for us to remember that our sins may shorten our lives, and shut us out of the earthly Canaan which we so much wished to possess.

Nor must it be forgotten that the deaths of public men, who, like Moses, are the servants of the Lord, and who, like him, too, seem to be taken away at the very moment when they were about to reach the goal of their endeavors, may

---

* Psa. xxxiv., 12-14.

be designed by God for the instruction and improvement of the people at large, that they may be thrown back more thoroughly upon himself, and may be kept from putting the servant into the throne which the master alone must occupy. We must learn to depend upon Jehovah. We must trust neither in princes nor in the sons of men. We must rely on him whose gift the Moseses and the Joshuas are, and console ourselves with the contrast which Peter has appropriated from Isaiah, "All flesh is as grass, and all the glory of man as the flower of grass. The grass withereth, and the flower thereof falleth away: but the word of the Lord endureth forever."*

But we are reminded by this chapter, in the second place, of the loneliness of the dying. No one accompanied Moses to the summit of Pisgah. He had to confront the last messenger, so far as human fellowship was concerned, all alone. From the first, indeed, he had been isolated from those around him. During his Egyptian education he must have felt, even when moving among his fellow-students at Heliopolis, that he lived apart. His early training in the home of Amram lifted him above the moral and spiritual atmosphere which they breathed. When, again, he assayed to deliver Israel, he was once more a lonely man; for his Hebrew brethren would not understand his overtures, but thrust him away, so that he went into the desert of Midian. A similar solitariness must have environed him in the household of Jethro. We have seen that even his wife Zipporah was not, in the highest sense, his companion; and when he became the leader of Israel, his very exaltation set him apart. Only one can stand upon a pinnacle, and the loftier the pinnacle is, the lonelier he must be; so that we cannot wonder that neither Aaron, nor Miriam, nor any of the elders of the

---

* Isa. xl., 7, 8; 1 Pet. i., 24, 25.

people, was, in the fullest sense, a confidential friend to him. Moreover, as the years revolved, those whom he knew in the various official positions in the camp dropped at his side; and even before he set out for Pisgah, he stood alone, the sole survivor of his generation. Solitude, therefore, was no new thing to him; although never, perhaps, had he realized it so keenly as now. Away from children, and nephews, and dependents, with no human friend to close his eyes, he lay down and died; having in this respect, as his nearest likeness, that African traveller who knelt on the floor of his grass-covered hut, far away from his daughter and his kinsmen, to answer the summons of his Lord. But, though few are thus segregated from their kindred at that last hour, yet, in a very true sense, every man is alone when he dies. You are no doubt familiar with the touching lines of Keble:

> "Why should we faint and fear to live alone?
> Since all alone, so Heaven has will'd, we die;
> Nor even the tenderest heart, and next our own,
> Knows half the reasons why we smile and sigh:
> Each in his hidden sphere of joy or woe,
> Our hermit spirits dwell, and range apart;
> Our eyes see all around, in gloom or glow,
> Hues of their own, fresh borrow'd from the heart."

Thus, even of the lowliest among us, it is true that we live alone; but we become more conscious of the solitude as death approaches: for we must meet that, as far as human fellowship is concerned, by ourselves. No one can pass within the veil along with us; and no mortal can give us of his help while we make the transition. This is true of each of us, just as really as it was of Moses. Our friends may wipe the damp from our brow, and ease our pillow, and whisper to us words of consolation. They may pray for us too, and beseech that God may "shield us in the last alarms;" but they cannot give us their faith, or animate us with their hope, or inspire us with their courage. Each dies upon a mountain-top alone. But when friends are powerless, God may be at our side, and he will be there, if in our lives we have served him, and in our deaths we cling to him. Oh my hearers, will you think of this? Your friends have done much for you, and been much with you in the past, but they cannot die for you, and they cannot die with you. That is an experience through which you must go without them; and there is only one whose aid will be available at that supreme moment. He is the Alpha and the Omega, who knows what death is, and who will come to meet you from the other side, when weeping children must part from you on this. No man was with Moses; but he was not alone after all, for God was with him; and may the same God be with us!

> "Hold thou thy cross before my closing eyes!
> Shine through the gloom! and light me to the skies!
> Heaven's morning breaks, and earth's vain shadows flee.
> In life! in death! O Lord, abide with me!"

In the third place, we may, nay, we must, take note of God's goodness to his dying servant. He took him to a natural observatory, and let him see the land of promise. Thus death was for him minimized of its terror, and he was permitted to know that his life-work would not be lost. So, often, when his servants pass away, God gives them glimpses, not of the earthly Canaan, but of the heavenly, granting them in this an advantage greater than Moses enjoyed; for he saw the land which yet he must not enter, while they have visions of the heaven into which they are about to pass. "At evening time it shall be light." How many of those whom we have accompanied to the very threshold of the world beyond have been thus blessed! and as we heard their sayings, or read them as recorded by those who treasured them as their richest legacy, we were prone to say, "Let me die the death of the righteous, and let my last end be like his!"

But never let us forget that such a life as Moses lived must precede such a death as Moses died. And so it is not the death, but the life, that demands our care. It is ours to live the life, and we may leave God to order the death. Moses did not darken that last year of his labor with any melancholy forebodings of his coming death. He was not harassed and distracted by gloomy fears. He was not constantly asking whether he could meet the great transition without a quiver, or whether his experiences would be those of terror rather than of triumph. No, he simply went on doing his daily duties, if anything a little more diligently than ever, just as the traveller quickens his step when he sees the sun hastening to his setting. He kept the even tenor of his way precisely as he had done before the warning was given him, and just as he would have done if no warning of a special sort had been received by him; and he left all the rest to God. Now that is the way to live, and that is the way to die. Let us follow that rule, filling every day with God's service in the service of our generation, and at the last we shall either get Pisgah, or something which will more than compensate for its absence; and, better than Pisgah, we shall get heaven, and be at home with Christ.

Finally, we must not fail to note God's goodness to his bereaved people. Before Moses goes, Joshua has already received his charge. They missed their great leader indeed. It would have said little either for him or for them, if that had not been the case. They mourned his absence. It was not with him as it has been with some, alike in the family, the Church, and the State, whose deaths have been felt by all concerned to be a relief. They could not so regard the dissolution of Moses; but God would not let them sink into despair; and though Joshua could not have done what Moses did, and was far from being the equal of his master, yet he could and did take up his master's unfinished work, and carried it through, at once to the glory of God, and the settlement of the people. So Aaron died, but the priesthood remained, and not one sacrifice the less was offered on the tabernacle altar. Elijah's mantle fell upon Elisha; and just as Stephen ascends in the fiery chariot of martyrdom, Saul, who also is called "Paul," stands forth to take up the work which the earnest deacon had inaugurated. Thus it always is; for Christ has said that the gates of hell—that is, of hades, or the unseen world—shall not prevail against his Church.

Last summer, as I visited Westminster Abbey, and sought out the monuments which, since my coming to this country, have been added to that marble-chiselled history of the English people, my eye was arrested by a beautiful tablet, having on it medallion portraits of the brothers John and Charles Wesley; and, after I had expressed my gratification to my companion at finding such a memorial in such a place, I was delighted with the simple beauty and consoling truth of the inscription in these words: "God buries the worker, but carries on the work." For, after all, the work is God's, not ours. That is our inspiration in taking it up, and our comfort in laying it down. When Jabez Bunting, one of the greatest of Wesley's disciples in England, died, a minister of the Methodist denomination, in preaching his funeral sermon, closed a glowing peroration by saying, "When Bunting died, the sun of Methodism set." A plain man in the audience, carried away by his feelings, immediately shouted, "Glory be to God! that's a lie!" and though the interjection was more forcible than polite, and was, in fact, considering the time and the place, impertinent, still there was more truth in it than in the preacher's words; for, so far as Methodism is work for Christ, its permanence depends on him, and not on individual men. And the same is true of all branches of the living Church. The cathedral does not remain unfinished because the workmen die, or even because the architect may pass away. Others enter upon their labors; and so, though it may take two generations to complete it, the day comes at length when the pealing organ sounds through its long-drawn aisles, and thronging worshippers crowd its marble pavement. So, from generation to generation, the spiritual Church is rising up toward its perfection; and though one after another the workmen pass away, the fabric remains, and the great Master-builder carries on the undertaking. Be it ours, my hearers, to build in our portion in a solid and substantial manner, so that they who come after us may be at once thankful for our thoroughness, and inspired by our example.

XXVI.

CHARACTERISTICS OF MOSES.

DEUTERONOMY xxxiv., 10-12.

THE life of Moses divides itself naturally into three equal periods of forty years. The first was spent in Egypt, at the court of Pharaoh; the second in the wilderness of Midian, with the family of Jethro; the third in the work of the Exodus, the encampment at Sinai, and the wanderings of the tribes. It is remarkable, however, that the narratives over which we have come cover only a very small portion of this lengthened career. We have a glimpse of him in his infancy, when the king's daughter opened the bulrush ark on the brink of the Nile, and saw a weeping babe; we behold him again, in his fortieth year, chivalrously, though rashly, standing up in vindication of an oppressed Israelite, and striving, ineffectually, to prevent strife between those who were brethren to each other as well as to himself; and just as he is entering the asylum of the desert, we behold him taking again the side of the weak and the injured, by driving away the ill-mannered shepherds who trampled upon and insulted the defencelessness of woman. Then for forty years more he is lost to sight, until, confronted with the vision at the burning bush, he is sent back to Egypt as the deliverer of his people. The events connected with his mission to Pharaoh, and preparatory to the Exodus, filled probably little more than six months. The first year from the Exodus ended while the Hebrews were at Sinai; and the close of the second finds them at Kadesh, under the ban of exclusion from the land of promise until forty years should be accomplished from the date of their leaving their house of bondage. Here, again, there is a hiatus of seven-and-thirty years, during which we have no record of Moses or of the tribes, save the formal and not perfectly clear enumeration of the stations at which, from time to time, they encamped. But in the beginning of the fortieth year the history is resumed, and we can trace the progress of the march from Kadesh to Mount Hor, down through the Arabah, and round the southern end of Mount Seir, up its eastern side, and on through conflict with the Amorites and the Bashanites, until the people rested in the plains of Moab. In reality, therefore, though we have been engaged on a life which lasted for a hundred and twenty years, the incidents which have passed under our review did not themselves, when put together, fill a larger space than about three years and six months. We see him for a moment as a child; then, for a little season, in his fortieth year; again, when he has reached fourscore, we are his companions for a little over two years; and, finally, we are permitted to associate with him for the last twelve months of his course. That is all; three years and a half—therein like another three years and a half in a yet greater life—out of a hundred and twenty.

How small the proportion of that which is recorded to that which is unwritten! And, indeed, when we come to think it out, how little of a man's real life can ever be written! Of the noblest of all lives, which could have furnished materials for numberless volumes, we have but four brief memoirs, none of them so large as many a modern pamphlet; and the grandest biography which the Old Testament contains might, when separated from the statute-book with which it is associated, be comprised in little more than a few pages of an ordinary book. At first view this is greatly disappointing! When we remember that we have more of Luther's Table-Talk in bulk than we have of the sayings and writings of Paul; when we reflect that the hero-worship of James Boswell has given us as many volumes regarding Samuel Johnson as we have tracts regarding the Lord Jesus; when we think that those who swept up the literary crumbs which fell from Goethe and Coleridge have preserved as many of their utterances as would form books larger than the Pentateuch, we are almost tempted to ask why nobody was permitted to do a similar work for Paul or Moses, or the Saviour, to whom we owe so much. Above all, when we take up the memoir which such a one as Lockhart wrote of Sir Walter Scott, or which it seems now to be the custom for some friend to write of any man who has made a name for himself in science, literature, politics, or ecclesiastial affairs, and see how its subject is traced up to his earliest ancestors, and down through boyhood, student-life, and public labor to the time of his death, we marvel that we should have so much about our little more than average contemporaries, and so little about those great sovereigns of the past, who still rule our spirits, not from their urns, but from their living thrones on high.

But the comfort comes when we take time to consider that by-and-by these modern biographies will disappear, while that of Moses, or of Paul, or of Christ, brief as each is, will last. Very soon few will care to inquire, even, regarding those whose memoirs have been such a world of trouble to their biographers. A few lines in a cyclopædia will comprise all that is worth preserving of them; and after the lapse of half a century more or less, even that will be dropped out, so that only here and there some literary resurrectionist will know of their existence. But these remain, and are the common reading of the common people. Does any one know what becomes of the shoals of memoirs that are continually emerging from the press? In a few years they are out of print. You cannot get a copy anywhere. They disappear as completely as if they had never been; and thus, as the very monuments erected in our cemeteries ultimately crumble into decay, so the biographies which love has written perish from the sight and memory of men. But time, which has swept away, and is now sweeping away, so much monumental literature, has only washed into brightness the record of such a life as that which we have been considering; and it stands out, fragmentary, as in some respects it is, from among other records, with an individuality as distinct, and a grandeur as great, and an endurance as indestructible, as those of the Pyramids and of the Sphynx from among the relics of past ages.

But, though so much is omitted in the narrative, it must not be supposed that what is passed over is of no importance. On the contrary, these omitted intervals were the times of discipline and preparation for the doing of the work which is actually chronicled; and if they had not been filled with their appropriate labor and meditation, there would have been nothing in the life worth recording at all. It seems to me, therefore, that no one can study the history of Moses, as we have been trying to do, without learning that the head-springs of true greatness and efficiency lie far away up out of the sight of one's fellows, and are to be filled and fed by lonely studyings and solitary musings, communings with one's own heart, with God, with nature, and with all those questions which any education worthy of the name suggests. The noblest life is thus the outcome of that of which no biographer can take cognizance. It is true of it, as the Psalmist says of the body, that it is "made in secret;" and the consolation of each earnest worker is that, though for the time he may seem to himself to be groping blindly like one in the dark, God has been superintending and shaping all, so that at length he can say, "Thine eyes did see it, while yet imperfect; and in thy book it was all written, what days it should be fashioned, while as yet there was none of it."

How clearly does all this appear in Moses! Each of the two former sections of his life gave its own contribution to the last, with its glorious time of harvest and achievement. He who was to be victor over Pharaoh and the emancipator of the Israelites, was trained in the very military school which he was to oppose. Humanly speaking, he could never have so dealt with Pharaoh if he had not enjoyed his Egyptian advantages. As William the Silent was educated in the closet of Charles V., and at the court of Philip II. into the liberator of the United Provinces, and thus turned to account, in the emancipation of his fellow-countrymen, the lessons in diplomacy and military tactics which he had learned from the oppressor himself, so Moses, under God, made his learning in all the wisdom of the Egyptians subservient to the great work of his life. Nay, as he was to stand before the nations, the grand champion for spiritual monotheism, in the face of idolatry, materialism, and polytheism, he was first initiated in the system which he was to oppose. Just as Saul of Tarsus was prepared, by his education in the school of Gamaliel, for understanding the real symbolism of Judaism—and thereby advancing the simplicity and spirituality of the Gospel—so Moses was enabled by his Egyptian learning to penetrate to the heart of the religious symbolism of his time; and thus at length he became the instrument of producing an external system in which the eye was made to minister to the understanding, while yet there was no sculptured image of Jehovah to ally it with the idolatries of the nations.

Again, the most cursory reader of the history can perceive that his sojourn in Midian, apart altogether from the spiritual training which his personal fellowship with God in its secluded wilderness furnished, was valuable to him, as giving him that familiarity with tent-life in the desert, and that acquaintance with the geography of the desert itself, which were so needful to him in his leading the tribes through it to the land of promise. Thus, even as the river Nile itself is fed by those great lakes in Central Africa whereon no white man's eye had looked until Livingstone, and Baker, and Cameron, and Stanley traced them out, so those inundations of spiritual power, which in Moses swept all before them, have their source in the hidden Nyanzas and Tanganyikas of long preparation and personal seclusion, over which his narrative has drawn an impenetrable veil. These eighty years of preparation, though little is said about them, were not lost; for, when he came to his life-work, that lifted into itself and utilized everything that had gone before. As the eloquent Bishop Wilberforce has said, "The sage, learned in all Egyptian lore; the great soul, mighty in word and deed; the deep philosophic intellect, furnished with all transmitted wisdom, trained in all school subtleties, practised by the oft-handling of State affairs, ripened into mellowness by solitude, nature, and self-converse — these remained; but on them all had passed a mighty change, . . . transmuting the earthly into the heavenly, raising the intellectual into the spiritual, making the man of power into the man of God, the noble, philosophic patriot into the prophet of the Lord."*

But, passing now from the record to the man, we begin our analysis of his greatness with the briefest reference to his intellectual qualities. We remember, of course, that he wrote by divine inspiration; but it is not to be forgotten that the Spirit of God employed the mental powers of those through whom he made his communications to mankind. He used them, not as mere machines, but so wrought in them and through them that, while the history or prophecy

---

* "Heroes of Hebrew History," pp. 110, 111.

which each gave is all that he meant it to be, it is, at the same time, stamped with the individuality of each, and bears upon it the marks of his mental peculiarities. One can see at a glance a difference between the poetic sublimity of Isaiah and the Doric simplicity of Amos; and it is easy to distinguish the intellectual qualities of Paul from those of John, as these appear in their respective epistles.

It must not be supposed, therefore, that we ignore the agency of the Holy Ghost in the production of the Pentateuch, while we direct attention to the marks which it bears of Moses's intellectual pre-eminence. There are about the narratives of Genesis, and the historical portions of the other books which came from his pen, a simple strength and a quiet power which indicate that he was a man of mental force. Even if we adopt the view of those who believe that he made use of documents which he found already in existence, we shall be compelled to admit that in their arrangement and adaptation, as well as in the impartation to the finished whole of that rounded completeness with which it is distinguished, we have something more than mere editorial skill. There is no straining after effect. No attempt is made to gild that which is already gold. The narrative is left to speak for itself; and the author never for a moment stands aside to draw attention either to himself or to the wonderful events which he is recording. He has to deal with such lofty themes as the creation, the fall, the flood, the call of Abraham, and the early history of the patriarchs of his nation; yet throughout there is a quiet naturalness which contrasts most suggestively with the sacred books of other nations, and which, as it seems to me, can be accounted for only by his own familiarity with God's wondrous works; for I cannot suppose that the composition of the Book of Genesis belongs to the earlier years of Moses's life. To me it rather seems that we must put it in those later years between Sinai and Pisgah, of which no record has by him been preserved. He speaks of God's creating might like one who is not surprised thereat. He has no tone of wonder in giving the narrative of the flood. The call of Abraham does not startle him by its singularity, and he does not marvel at the friendship subsisting between the Father of the faithful and his covenant God. No exclamation of wonder escapes from him as he tells of Jacob's vision at Bethel, or of the mysterious wrestling with the angel at Peniel; nor does he stay to moralize over the destruction of the cities of the plain.

Now all this is not a mere literary excellence; it is the result of his own personal experience in communion with God. The vision of Horeb helped him to understand the command which Abram heard in the far land of Ur. Sinai destroyed in him the possibility of being astonished at the burning of Sodom; and his own vision in the cleft of the rock made the scene at Peniel seem perfectly natural in his eyes. Thus, his personal fellowship with God blended with his mental greatness, and gave to it that princely supremacy whereby it dealt with the loftiest things in the simplest and quietest manner.

The feeble writer betrays his weakness by his fondness for epithets, and his ceaseless strivings after climactic elaboration. But in Moses his own marvellous history conspired with his intellectual strength to produce a work wherein the loftiest speculations of men are surpassed, while yet the style is marked with the ease which only perfect acquaintance with the subject can confer. Nor must we fail to note the perfection of historical imagination with which these records are distinguished. He puts us into the midst of the scenes which he describes. We look with Abraham over the fields toward the plain of Jordan, and go out with Isaac to meditate at even-tide. Jacob's life at Padan-aram is as real to us as if we had ourselves been in the encampment at the time; and the story of Joseph and his brethren is as vivid and pathetic to us as if it told of incidents that occurred but yesterday. Now to produce such impressions is one of the highest literary achievements; and even if he had older documents to work upon, the result proves that he did for these documents what Shakspeare did for the stories on which he grafted some of his most marvellous productions. Do not misunderstand me: the Spirit of God was in him and with him when he did all that; but it was done by the Spirit of God through his natural powers, and so it proves that these were of the highest order.

We must not linger thus, however, on that which was merely intellectual, for his crowning excellences were the spiritual graces with which he was adorned. And among these, as the root from which all the rest did spring, I mention first his faith. "He endured," says the inspired penman, "as seeing him who is invisible." He had a vivid and constant sense of the presence of God, and a correct estimate of the relative importance of things seen and temporal, as compared with those which are unseen and eternal. This kept him from contamination during his early education, and while yet he was in the palace of the Pharaohs; and when the day came when he must take the one side or the other in that conflict which has continued through all the ages, he did not hesitate or attempt to temporize, but "esteemed the reproach of Christ greater riches than the treasures in Egypt." Never more alluring prospects opened up before any man than those which the world held out to him. The throne of the greatest monarchy of his age was within his reach. All that wealth could procure, or pleasure bestow, or the greatest earthly power command, was easily at his call. But the glory of these things paled in his view before the more excellent character of those invisible honors which God set before him; and so, without a sigh of regret or a thought of sacrifice, he turned his back upon a position which he could occupy only by proving false to his countrymen and disloyal to his Lord. This faith sustained him in the solitudes of Midian, and animated him amidst all the conflict attendant on the Exodus, and all the difficulties that confronted him in the wilderness. At first, indeed, he seemed reluctant to accept the great responsibility which God almost thrust upon him; but from the moment when he heard the promise, "certainly I will be with thee," on till the day when he set out for Pisgah, he was seldom visited with misgiving. His intercourse with God was of the closest and most confidential character. Jehovah, to him, was no mere abstraction, of whom he might have spoken as "the Infinite," or "the Absolute;" but he was a living person, as real to him as was his brother Aaron, and more helpful to him than any human friend could be. This faith gave him courage in the hour of danger, and calmness in the time of trial. Whether he was called to go in before the angry Pharaoh, or to face the mutiny of the murmuring tribes, he was equally sustained by the sight of the invisible God; and when at length he passed in within the veil, he went only into a higher and closer fellowship with one whom he had long known and loved.

Oh for more of this same principle in us! Give us clear-visioned perception of unseen things such as he possessed, and we too might take our places beside the Emancipators of the world, and become something like worthy followers of him who, in the synagogue of Nazareth, appropriated to himself the prophet's words, "The Spirit of the Lord God is upon me; because the Lord hath anointed me to preach good tidings unto the meek; he hath sent me to bind up the broken-hearted, to proclaim liberty to the captives, and the opening of the prison to them that are bound; to proclaim the acceptable year of the Lord, and the day of vengeance of our God; to comfort all that mourn."

Closely allied with this strong faith, we find the prayerfulness of Moses. In every time of emergency his immediate resort was to Jehovah. His cry was not that of superstition, still less was it that of an experimenter, who wished to test whether there was any value in prayer at all or not; but it was the appeal of one who knew that he was speaking to a real, living, loving person, omnipotently able to help, and pledged also to render assistance. He did not send up his petition and stand aside, like the mocking ones at the cross of Christ, saying, "Let be; let us see whether God will come to save." Rather his prayer was an entreaty addressed to one whom he had often proved, on whose affection he knew he could rely, and by whose fellowship he had frequently been refreshed. He was not speaking to a stranger. He was not like one of those needy ones among us, who, having heard of the benevolence of some prominent citizen, writes to him on the mere speculation of receiving assistance. But he was like a son making application to his father; and so he never pleaded in vain.

We hear a great deal in these days of the power of prayer; and, when we rightly understand the subject, it is hardly possible to over-estimate its importance. But we must not imagine that every request professedly addressed to God is a prayer; and perhaps our failure to receive answers to our petitions may be largely explained by the distinction which I have just now drawn. True prayer is that which, as in the case of Moses, springs out of faith in God—not that which is offered by one who would make the receiving or not receiving of an answer a test whether there be any God or not; and those supplications which are offered by men who, like Abraham or Moses, are the friends of God, and appeal to him as their friend, never come back unacknowledged. When we pray "as seeing him who is invisible," we never pray in vain; for then we have in our hands a wonder-working rod of mightier potency than that with which Moses made a pathway through the sea.

Nor, in speaking of the qualities of Moses, must we forget his humility. He never put himself in the foreground. Even at the bush his modesty ran almost into a sinful excess, as he repeatedly put from him the honor to which God was calling him. He coveted no distinction, and sought no prominence; his greatness came to him, he did not go after it. Not as the result of his own ambitious schemings did he become the leader and the law-giver of the people. These honors were conferred on him unsought; and when they were given to him, he did not use them for his own aggrandizement.

Humility, wherever genuine, is allied with disinterestedness; and so it is hardly possible to speak of the one without taking cognizance also of the other. And when we speak of Moses's disinterestedness, what a field opens up before us! He gave up his own ease and comfort, to secure the emancipation of his people; and, while laboring night and day for them, he had no thought whatever of his own interests. His office brought him no emolument. He was greatest of all, because he was the servant of all; and though, by the command of God, Aaron was made high-priest, no other member of his family was pushed by him into prominence. He never thought of plotting to secure some lucrative employment for his sons; and at the end of his administration he might have said with Samuel, "Behold, here I am: witness against me before the Lord; whose ox have I taken? or whose ass have I taken? or whom have I defrauded? whom have I oppressed? or of whose hand have I received any bribe, to blind mine eyes therewith?"

But even as Paul, when pursuing a similar course, was attacked with calumny, so Moses had to meet ungrateful mutiny; and instead of denouncing that as a base return for all services, he calmly appealed from it to God. History is loud in her praises of those public-spirited patriots who have rendered most eminent services to the countries which they loved, and yet have died leaving no fortune behind them; nor, judging from the rarity of such cases in our own day and in our own land, does it seem that her approbation is unworthily bestowed — but where shall we find equal disinterestedness to that which Moses manifested? Without earthly reward of any sort, so far as we can see, he lived for forty years, not to serve himself, but to serve the tribes; and he did so out of regard to Jehovah. Even when he had it in his offer to be made himself the founder of a great nation if he would give up pleading their cause, he nobly refused to turn against them; and he grounded his refusal on his solicitude for the honor of the Lord himself. So we find that his piety was the source of his disinterested patriotism; and when our legislative chambers shall be filled with men who have some higher regard for the God of Israel than to use his name for the mere pointing of an irreverent jest, we may expect to see similar unselfishness among our statesmen—but not till then.

Leaving other features out of view, I must add a word or two about the meekness, or, as it might, perhaps, be better rendered, the "much endurance," of Moses. Surely we have been impressed with this characteristic of the man of God, as we have followed, Sabbath by Sabbath, the record of his doings. Never was there an undertaking more arduous than that on which he was commissioned; and it would be hard to find a more comprehensive summary of its difficulties than that given in the following words by the eloquent prelate from whom I have already quoted: "To lead forth a mob of slaves, debased as only slavery can debase humanity, sunk below the dead level of pagan Egyptian civilization; to form them into a daring army, a free commonwealth, and a believing Church; to be exposed to all the ready and violent vicissitudes of their desires, and hopes, and fears, and so to have to suffer their manners in the wilderness; to have them upbraid him for their very deliverance when their sensual natures lusted after the flesh-pots of Egypt; to have them talk of stoning him when the wells were dry; to have them dispute with him for his command, and rebel against his rule; to have them break their covenant with Jehovah, and turn to the sacred calf of their old Egyptian oppressors — all this was such a burden as was never laid on any other."* Yet only on one occasion did there come from him anything like complaint; and even then it would seem that God acknowledged the justness of his plea, for he suggested immediate measures for his servant's relief.

Now, at first thought, we may imagine that such noble endurance is discouraging to us, inasmuch as it may seem utterly hopeless for us to attain it. But, so far from that being the case, I venture to say that there is no biography in the Bible so full of cheer to us in this very particular as that which we have been studying; for, if we have read his history aright, Moses was not, at the outset of his career, distinguished either for his patience or his self-control. There were about him, apparently, an impetuosity of temper and a rashness of disposition which had in them little promise of his later excellence. We hear the vehemence of his nature in the very tone of his appeal to the two Israelites whose strife he tried to terminate. There was undeniable haste in the blow which killed the Egyptian who was maltreating the Hebrew; and though we admire the chivalry of his inter-

---

* "Heroes of Hebrew History," p. 119.

ference on behalf of Jethro's daughters, we cannot but remark on its impulsive character, and notice the fact that it was lacking in caution.

So, again, we read of his leaving Pharaoh in a great anger; and in general, concerning his early days, we may affirm that he was not distinguished for the possession of self-control; when he beheld the idolatry of the Israelites as he descended from Sinai, "his anger waxed hot." Yet this was the man in whom at length was formed that much-enduring character which has received the impartial eulogy of the Book of God. So let no one despair of attaining excellence even in the very quality in which he is by nature most deficient; and in particular, let us never again speak of hastiness of temper as an incurable evil. It is a thing not to be regarded as a misfortune, and accepted as such, but to be fought with and overcome; and, blessed be God, it may be overcome through constant faith in and fellowship with him. Still, though, in this aspect of the case, the history of Moses is full of comfort, we may not forget that it is also fraught with warning; for it teaches us that we must not allow ourselves to think that, in respect to our besetments, we are ever out of danger. Moses might have supposed that he had entirely subdued that impetuous fieriness of temper with which in former days he had to contend, and might be giving no heed to that which had been in earlier times a weakness, but had now become a strength, when, lo! at Meribah, it rose again in its might, "so that he spake unadvisedly with his lips." Thus hopeful conflict and constant vigilance are the lessons of this aspect of his character.

And now we must tear ourselves away from that fascinating and instructive study, which has filled the Sabbath evenings of our ecclesiastical year. We have learned much of Moses, and therefore we have learned so much the more of

Christ; for Moses spake of the Messiah, and is in himself one of the most suggestive types of Christ to be found in the Old Testament. The great deliverer was to be "like unto him;" and in many respects we can clearly trace the parallel. As Moses, in the early part of his career, refused the Egyptian monarchy, because it could be gained by him only by disloyalty to God, so Jesus turned away from the kingdoms of the world and the glory of them, because they were offered on condition that he would fall down and worship Satan. As Moses became the emancipator of his people from their house of bondage, so Jesus lived and died that he might save his people from their sins; as Moses, penetrating to the soul of the symbolism of idolatry, introduced a new dispensation wherein symbolism was allied to spirituality of worship, so Jesus, seizing the spirituality of the Mosaic system, freed it from its national restrictions, and ushered in the day when neither at Jerusalem nor at Gerizim would men seek to localize the service of Jehovah, but the true worshipper would worship the Father anywhere, believing that the character of the worship is of infinitely higher importance than the place where it is offered; as Moses was pre-eminently a law-giver, so Jesus speaks with authority, and has, in his Sermon on the Mount, laid down a code which not only expounds, but expands and glorifies, or, in one word, fulfils the precepts of the Decalogue; as Moses was a prophet, speaking to the people in the stead of God, so Jesus is the great prophet of his Church; as Moses stood the mediator of a covenant between God and Israel, representing God to the people, and representing the people to God, interceding for them when they sinned, while at the same time he admitted and condemned their guilt, so Jesus is the mediator of the new covenant, standing between God and man, and bridging, by his atonement and intercession, the gulf between the two. We cannot wonder, therefore, that, in the vision of the Apocalypse, they who have gotten the victory over the beast and his image are represented as singing "the song of Moses the servant of God, and the song of the Lamb."

But though the two are thus combined, the one rises above and surpasses the other. For "Moses was faithful as a servant, but Christ as a son." The servant passeth away, but the son abideth ever. From that "lonely grave in Moab's land" Moses came not again to the tribes that mourned upon the plain; but out of the tomb of Joseph Jesus rose, and now, in a higher sense than any other, he lives for us; so that we can say, "He is able to save unto the uttermost all that come unto God by him, seeing he ever liveth to make intercession for them." The much-enduring Moses, who bore so bravely the burden of his people's infirmities, is excelled by him who never faltered beneath the crushing load of the world's guilt; and, meek as the son of Amram was, we must not forget that there is no Meribah spot on the bright disk of the Sun of Righteousness. Thus "that which was made glorious hath no glory in this respect, by reason of the glory that excelleth."

Yet, though he is far beneath the Son of God, Moses stands peerless and pre-eminent among the sons of men; and having followed his footsteps in the chapters of his recorded life, we can endorse the words of one of the noblest of the Fathers: "This Moses, humble in refusing so great a service; resigned in undertaking, faithful in discharging, unwearied in fulfilling it; vigilant in governing his people, resolute in correcting them; ardent in loving them, and patient in bearing with them; the intercessor for them with the God whom they provoked, this Moses—such and so great a man—we love, and admire, and, so far as may be, imitate."*

---

* Augustine, quoted by Isaac Williams, in "Characters of the Old

God buried Moses. It was fitting, therefore, that he too should write his epitaph. Here it is, given by his inspiration, and, though written only in a book, having a permanence as great as if it had been graven with an iron pen in the rock forever :* "And there arose not a prophet since in Israel like unto Moses, whom the Lord knew face to face, in all the signs and the wonders which the Lord sent him to do in the land of Egypt, to Pharaoh, and to all his servants, and to all his land, and in all that mighty hand, and in all the great terror which Moses showed in the sight of all Israel."

Testament," pp. 84, 85, and by Bishop Wilberforce, in "Heroes of Hebrew History," p. 130.

* "Moses and his Times," by Thornley Smith, p. 294.

INDEX.

AARON, age of, 41; fluency of, 53; given to Moses as assistant, 53; meets Moses on his return from Midian, 66; supports Moses on the rock at Rephidim, 154; left with Hur in charge of the people, 201; weakness of, in the matter of the golden calf, 205, 215; inaugurated as high-priest, 274; resignation of, under severe bereavement, 278; joins Miriam in murmuring against Moses, 307-309; rod of, laid up before the Lord, 349; priesthood of, vindicated, 349; death of, 364; character of, 204, 365.

Abihu, sin of, 275; punishment of, 277; lessons from the guilt and doom of, 283.

Ability, example of, consecrated, 249.

Abiram, takes part with Korah in conspiracy, 345; punishment of, 346.

Abyssinia, British Expedition to, referred to, 162.

Addison, Joseph, hymn by, quoted from, 22.

Ain-el-Weibeh, 323.

Akabah, Gulf of, 375.

Alexander, Joseph A., D.D., lines by, 75.

Alexander, Mrs., lines by, 440.

Alexander, W. L., D.D., Kitto's "Cyclopædia" edited by, quoted from or referred to, 41, 87, 90, 363; article by, on Deuteronomy, in *Sunday Magazine*, referred to, 424.

Alford, Dean, "The Greek Testament," by, quoted from, 384.

Alush, 149.

Amalekites, the, attack the Hebrews at Rephidim, and are defeated, 153.

Ambition, selfish, courts its own destruction, 357.

American Palestine Exploration Society, first statement of, quoted, 378.

Amorites, army of the, encountered by the Hebrews, 377.

Amram, genealogy of, 11; faith of, 13.

Anakim, the, account of, by the spies, 323; have to be encountered in the conquest of every promised land, 332; can be overcome by faith and courage, 334.

Annapolis, academy at, used as an illustration, 263.

Anthropomorphisms of the Mosaic narrative accounted for, 224.
Aperiu, meaning of, 10.
Ark of bulrushes, how made, 14.
Ark of the covenant in tabernacle, 237.
Art in relation to religion, 249.
Asher, place of tribe of, in line of march, 292; blessing of, 436.
Attributes of God, how the Hebrews were educated into the knowledge of the, 225.
Augustine, quotation from, 467.

BACON's Essays quoted from, 432.
Balaam, story of, 389–392; position and character of, 392; test applied to, 394; practical inconsistencies of, 397; covetousness, 401.
Balak, King of Moab, negotiations with Balaam, 389.
Banner, a symbol of decision, 157; mark of distinction, 159; of joy, 160; of protection, 162.
Baptism unto Moses, meaning of, 119.
Bashan, description of, 378.
Benjamin, place of tribe of, on the march, 292.
Bezaleel and Aholiab, examples of consecrated ability, 249.
Bir Musa, 150.
Blessing of Joseph and Asher, 436.
Blood-revenge, law regulating, 259.
Bondage of sin, the, illustrated by the slavery of the Hebrews, 18.
Book, finding of the, by Hilkiah, not the origin of Deuteronomy, 417–419.
Books, how first made, 15.
Boswell's "Life of Johnson" referred to, 453.
Brazen serpent, set up, 376; typical teaching of the, 382–387; destroyed by Hezekiah, 376.
Brotherhood enforced by redemption, 272.
Bush, the burning, vision of, 46; significance of, 47; revelation made to Moses at, 48.
Butler, Bishop, quotation from, 208.

CALEB sent as one of the spies, 324; nationality of, 325; stands with Joshua against the report of the other spies, 326; courage of, in old age, 334, 335.
Censers of the mutineers used for a covering of the altar, 348.
Census of the people at Sinai, 282; of the Levites, 282.
Chabas, the Egyptologist, quoted from, 10.
Cherubim, meaning of the, 243.

INDEX. 471

Christ, reproach of, preferred by Moses, 39; discourse of, on the manna, 139; discourse of, on the brazen serpent, 387; parallel between, and Moses, 430, 466.

Christian life, the, begins in the acceptance of deliverance through sacrifice, 106; is a perpetual feast, 107; should be characterized by sincerity and truth, 108; is not free from hardship, 142; is not all hardship, 143; true theory of the, 146.

Colenso, Bishop, objection to the Passover edict considered, 96.

Coleridge, S. T., quotation from, 322; Table-Talk of, 453.

Commandments, Ten, importance of the, 191; peculiarities of the, 192-196; interpreted by Jesus, 196.

"Commentary, Critical, Experimental, and Practical," by Jamieson, Fausset, and Brown, quoted from or referred to, 10, 16, 296.

Conflict with God always disastrous to his adversary, 94.

Consecration typically taught in the tabernacle, 248; and enforced in the ceremonial laws, 270.

Contentment and holy ambition harmonized, 56.

Courage, distinguished from recklessness, 125.

Covetousness, danger of, 402.

Criminal code, the Hebrew, 267.

Crosby, Rev. Howard, D.D., quoted from, 17.

Curse comes through sin, 406.

Curtis, Rev. Professor S. J., D.D., "The Levitical Priests" by, referred to, 423.

DAN, place of the tribe of, on march, 292.

Darkness, plague of, 83.

Dathan joins Korah in conspiracy, 345; punishment of, 347.

Decalogue, importance of the, 191; peculiarities of the, 192-196.

Declaration of Independence, the, anticipated in the law of Moses, 264.

Deliverance prompts to song, 125; increases obligation, 131.

Desire, gratification of, not always a blessing, 348.

Despondency, danger of, 380.

Deuteronomy, Book of, contents of, 412-415; period covered by, 411; theories about date and authorship of, 416; objections to Mosaic authorship of, considered, 420-425; characteristcs of, 428; prophecies in, 429-431; practical bearing of, on nations of to-day, 431; psalm of Moses in, 436-437.

Devotion, a safety-valve, 356.

Disinterestedness, will not save from envy, 316; is allied with humility, 462; required in modern political life, 180.

Display, love of, a dangerous thing, 403.
Division of labor recommended, 176.
Divorce, law of, referred to, 258.
Domestic responsibility not destroyed by public duties, 173.
Drunkard, the, moral degradation of, 404.
Dying, the, loneliness of, 445.

EADIE, John, D.D., LL.D., "Biblical Cyclopædia" of, quoted from, 236.
Earnest of the Spirit, 328.
Education, provision for, among the Hebrews, 266.
Education of the Hebrews through the history and the law, 224, 232.
Egypt, place of, in history, 7 ; contest of Moses with, 78.
Egyptians, the, education of, described, 25–28 ; written characters of, 25 ; knowledge of the arts and science among, 26–28.
Eldad and Medad, prophesying of, 296, 304.
Elim, encampment at, 132, 143.
Emancipation does not put an end to hardship, 141 ; does not exempt from obligation, 271.
Encampment of the tribes arranged, 281.
"Encyclopædia Britannica" referred to, 25, 26, 42.
Envy, absence of, in the really great man, 304 ; may show itself in the most unexpected quarter, 318 ; is willing to use the meanest weapons, 320 ; is best met by an appeal to Heaven, 321.
Ephraim, tribe of, the place of, in encampment, 281 ; on march, 292.
Exclusion of the lost from heaven final, 338.
Expiation typically taught in tabernacle ritual, 248, 269.
Everlasting punishment, doctrine of, 337, 338.

FACE, the, of Moses, shining of, 224 ; use made by Paul of this passage of the history, 228–231.
Fairbairn's "Imperial Bible Dictionary," quoted from, or referred to, 43, 114, 150, 184, 193, 259, 262.
Faith, distinguished from presumption, 125 ; the regulating grace of the Christian character, 366 ; object of, not in ourselves, 385 ; no merit in, 385 ; is the rest of the soul, 386 ; illustrated in the life of Moses, 36–38, 459.
Fear alone will not bring permanent repentance, 91 ; will not keep from sin, 405.
Feast of the elders on Mount Sinai, 201.
Feasts of the Jews, purpose of, 265, 270.
First-born, death of the, 83.

INDEX. 473

Forbearance of God, the, has a limit, 75, 336.
Fra Angelico, reference to, 250.
Friendship, true, illustrated in Jethro and Moses, 170; reciprocity of, in Hobab and Moses, 289.
Frogs, plague of the, 81.

GAD, position of tribe of, on march, 292; tribe of, ask inheritance with Reuben on the east of Jordan, 408.
Genesis, composition of the Book of, 456.
Gershonites, place of, in the march, 292.
Gnats, plague of the, 82.
God the guide of his people, 123; reveals himself to us in connection with our troubles, 131; dwelling of, with his people symbolized by the Shechinah, 239; spirituality of, suggested by the Shechinah, 241; unity of, taught by the tabernacle, 242; holiness of, taught by the tabernacle, 242; always considerate of his faithful servants, 302; no limit to the resources of, 305; promises of, will always bear investigation, 328; forbearance of, has its limits, 75, 336; goodness of, to Moses at death, 447; goodness of, to his bereaved people, 448.
Goethe, Table-Talk of, referred to, 453.
Guidance, how to obtain, 123.
Gustavus Adolphus referred to, 155.

HAIL, plague of the, 82.
Hamilton, Rev. James, D.D., "Moses the Man of God," quoted from, or referred to, 29, 30, 439.
Handel, oratorios of, referred to, 249.
Hardening of Pharaoh's heart, 65.
Havelock, General, referred to, 54, 155.
Hazeroth, 307.
Hebrews, the, things needed by, for their unification into a nation, 7; position of, in Egypt in the days of Joseph and after, 8; number of, at birth of Moses, 9; oppression of, by the King of Egypt, 9; slavery of, an illustration of the bondage of sin, 18; borrowing by, from the Egyptians explained, 62; reception of Moses and Aaron by, 67; oppression of, by the Pharaoh of the Exodus, 68; despondency of, when their oppression was increased, 68; escape of, from Egypt unaccountable, except in connection with Divine agency, 77; position of, on the night of the Passover, 95; obedience of, to the ordinance of the Passover, 99; departure of, from Rameses, 111; halting of, at Succoth, 111; route of, 112; encampment of, at Ethan, 113; led by pillar of cloud, 113; at

Pihahiroth, 114; pursued by Pharaoh, 115; pass through the Red Sea 116; murmuring of, at Marah, 129; encampment in wilderness of Sin, 133; murmuring of, at Sin, 134; come to Rephidim, 149; attacked by Amalekites, 153; enter into covenant with God at Sinai, 186–189; relapse into idolatry, 202; test of, at Sinai, 215; ultimate conversion of, to Christ, 230; educated by the symbolism of the tabernacle, 232; liberality of, in erection of the tabernacle, 248; educated for the world's benefit, 262; civil polity of, 264, 266; order of encampment of, 281; order of tribes on march, 292; murmuring of, at Paran, 293; mutiny of, at Kadesh, 326; punishment of, 327; murmuring of, at Kadesh again, 360; friendly message of the Edomites, 362; in the Arabah valley, 374; bitten by serpents, 376; defeat the Amorites, 378; encamp in the plains of Moab, 388; mourn for the death of Moses, 441.

Heliopolis, Temple of the Sun at, 25; obelisk at, 25.
Higher criticism, claims of the, 425.
Hobab, relation of, to Moses, 43; invited to accompany Moses, 283.
Holiness of God taught by the tabernacle, 242.
Hood, Thomas, lines from, 287.
Hor, Mount, 362.
Howarah identified with Marah, 130.
Hunt, W. H., referred to, 250.
Hur supports Moses on the rock at Rephidim, 152; left with Aaron in charge of the people, 201.
Husbands, duties of, at home, 174.
Hymnology, enriched by gratitude, 126; of life, 127.
Hypocrisy, evils of, 109.

IMPATIENCE condemned, 54.
Incarnation typically taught in the tabernacle, 247.
Individual, place and power of the, in the progress of the Church, 371.
Inspiration, relation of, to the ability of Moses, 254, 456, 457.
Intemperance, warning against, 283.
Intermarriages between the people of God and the ungodly, 287.
Irritability of temper, how to restrain, 367; sin of, 368.
Issachar, position of the tribe of, on the march, 292.

Jebel Musa, 183, 184.
Jebel Nebi Haroun, 362.
Jehovah, significance of the name of, 50; contrasted with other names of God, 69; proclaims his name to Moses, 226.

Jehovah-Nissi, 157.

Jehovah-Rophek, 131.

Jesus, the Lord, authenticated Moses, 425, 428; parallel between, and Moses, 430, 466.

Jethro, names of, explained and harmonized, 43; character of, 44, 170; sends Moses to Egypt in peace, 64; brings Zipporah to Moses at Sinai, 168; gives Moses wise advice, 172.

Jochebed, genealogy of, 11; faith of, 13; engaged by Pharaoh's daughter to nurse her own son, 16; name of, 50.

Johnson, Samuel, memoir of, referred to, 453.

Josephus, story from, concerning youth of Moses, 29.

Joshua, leads the people against Amalek, 154; minister of Moses on Sinai, 201; complains of Eldad and Medad prophesying, 296; sent as one of the spies, 324; stands with Caleb against the report of the other spies, 326; succeeds Moses, 410, 448.

Jubilation provided for in ceremonial law, 270.

Judah, position of the tribe of, in the camp and on the march, 282, 292.

Judges, appointment of the, 172, 264.

KADESH, position of, 323; assembling of the tribes at, 358.

Keble, Rev. John, lines of, 446.

"Keil and Delitzsch on the Pentateuch," quoted from, or referred to, 66, 139, 155.

Kibbroth-Hattaavah, 297.

Kitto, Rev. John, D.D., "Daily Bible Illustrations," quoted from, or referred to, 10, 134, 184, 311, 341, 371, 379.

Knox, John, referred to, 54.

Kohathites, position of, on the march, 292.

Korah, conspiracy of, with Dathan and Abiram, 341; punishment of, 346; sons of, not included in their father's punishment, 347.

Korahites, position of, in the camp, 282.

Kurtz, J. H., D.D., "The History of the Old Covenant" by, quoted from, or referred to, 295, 314, 326, 394.

LABOR, division of, necessary to health, 176.

Lady, Egyptian, bathing of an, 16.

Lange's "Commentary on Exodus" referred to, 30.

Law of blood-revenge referred to, 259.

Law of divorce referred to, 258.

Law, tables of, broken by Moses, 218.

Laws of Moses adapted for a nation permanently settled in Palestine,

255; designed for a theocracy, 256; conditioned by the character and customs of the people, 258; regarding crimes, 267; regarding property, 268; regarding the poor, 269; religious and ceremonial, 269–272.
Lenormant, François, "Manual of the Ancient History of the East" quoted from, 29.
Levites, position of, among the people, 265; census of, 282.
Leviticus, Book of, 274.
Lex talionis, 261.
Liberality, example of, given by the people, 248.
Life, a good man's, may be shortened by his own sin, 443.
Life, the unwritten of, 453; relation of the, to that which is recorded, 454.
Liturgy of King's Chapel, Boston, referred to, 369.
Lockhart's "Life of Sir Walter Scott" referred to, 453.
Locusts, plague of the, 53.
Loneliness of the dying, 445.
Longfellow, H. W., quoted from, 56, 163, 251, 299.
Love and faith the true roots of repentance, 92; and of holiness, 405.
Luther, Table-Talk of, referred to, 453.

MAGICIANS, Egyptian, works of, not miraculous, 86.
Manasseh, place of the tribe of, on the march, 292; half tribe of, receive inheritance on the east of Jordan, 409.
Manna, given, 135; a double supply collected on the sixth day, 136; none furnished on the Sabbath, 136; design of the, 137; relation of the, to the natural product of the locality, 138; discourse of Christ concerning, 139.
Marah, murmuring of the people at, 129.
Maurice, Rev. F. D., "The Patriarchs and Law-givers of the Old Testament," quoted from, 51.
Medad and Eldad, prophesying of, 296, 304.
Mediation of Moses, 199, 216, 295, 327, 430, 466.
Mediation typically taught in the tabernacle, 247.
Merarites, place of, on the march, 292.
Michaelis, J. D., on the "Laws of Moses," referred to, 271.
Midian described, 41.
Milman, Henry H., D.D., "The History of the Jews" by, quoted from, 261, 266, 271, 413, 416, 419.
Miriam, watching the bulrush ark, 15; leads the answering chorus on the Red Sea shore, 122; joins Aaron in murmuring against Moses, 307; punishment of, 315; intercession of Moses for, 316; death of, 359.

INDEX. 477

Moab, plains of, encampment in, 388.
Moabites, terror of, at the approach of the Hebrews, 389.
Monuments, Egyptian, preservation of, 24.
Monuments of a nation an epitome of its history, 102.
Mosaic dispensation, gospel of the, 186.
Moses, parents of, 11; birth of, 12; concealment of, 12; laid on the bank of the Nile, 15; found by Pharaoh's daughter, 16; meaning of the name of, 17; taken home by Pharaoh's daughter, 24; education of, among the Egyptians, 25–28; story concerning, from Josephus, 29; parallel between, and William the Silent, 30, 455; kills an Egyptian, 30; rebukes a Hebrew, 31; flees to Midian, 31; choice of, analyzed and applied, 33–35; faith of, 35–38; arrival of, in Midian, 41; defends the daughters of Jethro, 42; marriage of, to Zipporah, 42; sons of, 44; influence of solitude on, 45; vision of the burning bush given to, 46; call of, by Jehovah, 49; response of, 50–52; signs given to, 51; slowness of speech of, 52; promise of God to, 60; commission of, 61; leaves Midian, 64; mysterious incident at the inn, in connection with circumcision of child of, 66; meeting with Aaron, 66; first interview with the Hebrews, 67; agency of, in the production of the ten plagues, 85; issues the ordinance of the Passover, 98; divides the Red Sea by his rod, 118; song of, 121; people murmur against, at Marah, 129; at Rephidim, 151; at Paran, 295; at Kadesh, 326; heals the waters of Marah, 130; hardships of his leadership, 144, 460, 461; smites the rock of Rephidim, 151; receives Jethro and Zipporah, 168; adopts the advice of Jethro, 172; ascends Mount Sinai, 185; receives the civil polity of the Jewish theocracy, 198; mediator of the covenant, 199; in the mount with God, 201; descent from the mount, 216; intercedes for the people, 217, 220; punishes the people, 218; prayer to God for his presence, 222; asks that he may see God's glory, 223; shining of the face of, 224, 228; receives the plan of the tabernacle, 235; legislation of, 253; relation of his ability to the reception by him of the laws from God, 254; discouraged, 295; freedom from envy in, 304; assailed by Miriam and Aaron, 307; unselfishness of, 309; vindicated by God, 313; pre-eminence above the prophets, 314; sends the spies to Canaan, 323; effect of report of spies on, 326; intercession of, for the people, 327; meets the conspiracy of Korah, Dathan, and Abiram, 339–343; writes the ninetieth psalm, 359; sin of, at the rock, 360–361; punishment of, 362; time required for addresses by, in the Book of Deuteronomy, 411; psalm of, 434; blessing of the tribes by, 436; commanded to go to Pisgah, 437; death of, 439; burial of, 440; life of, divided into three parts,

451; characteristics of, 456–465; parallel between, and Christ, 430, 466; epitaph of, 468.
Mozley, Rev. J. B., D.D., "Ruling Ideas in the Early Ages," referred to, 262.
Murmuring, one-sidedness of, 300.
Murmuring of the tribes in Egypt, 68; at Marah, 129; at Rephidim, 151; at Paran, 295; at Kadesh, 326; at Kadesh again, 361.
Murphy, Rev. James G., D.D., "Commentary on Exodus," quoted from, 166, 198, 199; article by, in *British and Foreign Evangelical Review*, referred to, 424.
Murrain of cattle, plague of, 82.
Must, the irrepressible, the secret of true excellence, 57.

NADAB, sin of, 275; punishment of, 276; lessons from, 283.
Naphtali, place of tribe of, on the march, 292.
Negeb, or South Country, 324.
Newton, Rev. John, quotation from, 138; anecdote of, 273.
Newton, Rt. Rev. Thomas, D.D., "Dissertations on the Prophecies," quoted from, 396.
Nile, the, Moses exposed on the bank of, 15; turned into blood, 81.

OBEDIENCE the gate-way into authority, 71.
Og, bedstead of, 379.
Overwork, dangers of, 442, 443; how to be avoided, 176.

PALMER, E. H., "Desert of the Exodus," referred to, 130.
Papyrus described, 14.
Paran, wilderness of, 292, 323, 358.
Parents, responsibility of, among the Hebrews, 266.
Parliament, rudimentary, among the Hebrews, 264.
Passover, ordinance of the, 98; night of the, 99–101; feast of the, 101; purpose of the, 102; typical significance of, 104–110; compared by Paul to the Christian life, 105.
Pharaoh, the, of the oppression, decree of, regarding Hebrew infants, 10.
Pharaoh the, of the Exodus, hardening of the heart of, 65; oppresses the Hebrews, 68; conflict between, and Moses, 77–94; pursues the Hebrews, 115; host of, drowned, 119.
Pihahiroth, site of, 113–115.
Pillar of cloud and fire, 113.
Pisgah, view from, 438, 439.

INDEX.

Plagues, the ten, 77 ; purpose of, 79, 90 ; miraculously inflicted, 84 ; climactic in succession, 88 ; results of, 89.
Pleasures of sin analyzed, 38.
Polity, civil, of the Hebrews, 198, 264.
Pollok, Robert, quotation from, 250.
Priesthood, the, position of, among the Hebrews, 265 ; of Aaron vindicated, 349 ; of Christ, 350.
Property, laws regulating, among the Hebrews, 268.
Providence of God illustrated in the birth and preservation of Moses, 19.
Psalm, ninetieth, when written, 359.
Public duties do not absolve from domestic responsibilities, 173.
Public men, qualities to be sought in, 178-181.

QUAILS furnished for the people, 134, 297.

RAMESES, King, 10.
Rameses, departure of the Hebrews from, 111.
Ras Sufsafeh, probable site of the giving of the law, 184, 185.
Readiness for death, importance of, 369.
Redemption does not absolve from law, 271 ; makes a brotherhood among the redeemed, 272.
Red Sea, where crossed by the Hebrews, 113.
Repentance which springs from fear always transient, 91.
Rephidim, site of, 149.
Resignation of Aaron under bereavement, 278.
Retribution on Egypt for oppressing the Hebrews, 120.
Reuben, position of the tribe of, in the camp, 282, 292 ; princes of the tribe of, join Korah in his conspiracy, 340 ; tribe of, ask inheritance on the east of Jordan, and receive it on certain conditions, 408, 409.
Right, the, not so difficult to do as the timid imagine, 209.
Robinson, Rev. Edward, D.D., "Researches in Palestine," quoted from, 374.

SABBATH, the, observed before the people came to Sinai, 136 ; position of law for, in the Decalogue, 194.
Scott, Sir Walter, lines from, 113 ; life of, by Lockhart, referred to, 453.
Serpent, the, idolatrous place of, among the Egyptians, 52.
Serpent, the brazen, made and set up, 376 ; typical meaning of, 382-387.
Serpents, commonness of, in the neighborhood of the Gulf of Akabah, 375 ; attack the Hebrews, 376.
Seventy, council of, 264 ; assistants to Moses appointed, 296.

Shakspeare quoted from, or referred to, 316, 337, 369, 400, 459.
Sharpe, Samuel, "History of Egypt," quoted from, or referred to, 25.
Shelomith, son of, his blasphemy and punishment, 280.
Shur, wilderness of, 128.
Simeon, tribe of, place of the, on the line of march, 292.
Sin, bondage of, illustrated by Egyptian slavery, 18; pleasures of, analyzed, 38; consequences of, cannot be arrested, 212.
Sin, wilderness of, 133.
Sinai, Mount, geographical questions connected with, 182-185; ascended by Moses, 185, 201, 223; law given from, 190; final incidents at, 274-283; duration of encampment at, 292.
Slavery, law regulating, among the Hebrews, 260.
Smith's "Dictionary of the Bible," quoted from, or referred to, 14, 325.
Smith, Rev. Thornley, "Moses and his Times," quoted from, 28, 468.
Solon, reference to, 258.
Song an appropriate expression of gratitude, 125.
Song of Moses, 121; of Miriam, 122.
"Speaker's Commentary," quoted from, or referred to, 63, 78, 132, 166, 396, 411, 414, 419, 421, 423, 424, 425.
Spencer of Liverpool, saying of, 369.
Spies, the sending of, first suggested by the people, 323; route of, 325; return of, 326.
Spirit, the earnest of, 328; fruit of, 330.
Spirituality of God taught by the tabernacle, 241.
Spurgeon, C. H., anecdote from, 251.
Standards of the four camps, 282.
Stanley, Dean, "History of the Jewish Church," quoted from, 50, 111, 190. "Sinai and Palestine," quoted from, 185, 363.
Strong drink, danger of tampering with, 283, 404.
Succoth, halting of the Hebrews at, 111.
Sudden death, prayer for deliverance from, criticised, 369.

TABERNACLE, the, plan of, furnished to Moses, 225; contributors to, in work and materials, 235; place of, in the encampment, 235; description of, 236, 238; attendants on, 238; symbolical meaning, 239-245; typical teaching, 246-248.
Table-Talk of Luther, Goethe, and Coleridge, referred to, 453.
Ten Commandments, the, importance of, 191; peculiarities of, 192; moral tone of, 193; order of, 193; negative character of, 195; expounded by Christ, 196.

Ten plagues, the, 77; purpose of, 79, 90; miraculously inflicted, 84; climactic succession of, 88; results of, 89.
Tennyson, Alfred, quoted from, 45, 301.
Testaments, Old and New, stand or fall together, 428.
Theban tomb, painting on, illustrating the making of brick, description of, 9.
Theocracy, the, establishment of, 186; position of the people under, 219, 343; effect of, on the laws, 256.
Thomson, Dr. W. H., quoted from, 378.

UNBELIEF rooted in the heart more frequently than in the head, 93.
Unconsciousness, element of, in character, 227.
Unity of God taught by the tabernacle, 241.

VAN OOSTERZEE, J., "Moses a Biblical Study," quoted from, or referred to, 220, 376.
Veil on the face of Moses, reference to, by Paul, 229.
Vicars, Hedley, decision of, 159.
Volume, etymology of, 15.

WADY Amarah, 130.
Wady Charibeh, 150.
Wady Er Rahah, 184, 185.
Wady Feiran, 150.
Wady Ghurundel, 132.
Wady Ithm, 374.
Wady Mughara, 132.
Wady Nasb, 132.
Wady Sebaiyeh, 183, 184.
Wady Useit, 132.
Wesley, John, incident in early life of, 21; views of, concerning living and dying, 370; inscription on monument to, in Westminster Abbey, 449.
West Point, academy at, illustration from, 263.
Wilberforce, Rt. Rev. Samuel, D.D., "Heroes of Hebrew History," quoted from, 456, 464, 467.
Wilderness of Paran, 292, 323, 358.
Wilderness of Shur, 128.
Wilderness of Sin, 133.
William the Silent, parallel between, and Moses, 30, 455.

Williams, Rev. Isaac, "Characters of the Old Testament," referred to, 467.

Wines, Rev. E. C., D.D., LL.D., "Commentaries on the Laws of the Ancient Hebrews," referred to, 271.

Wrong, always wrong, 206; consequences of doing, always more serious than were at first supposed, 212; consequences of, cannot be arrested, 212.

www.ingramcontent.com/pod-product-compliance
Lightning Source LLC
Chambersburg PA
CBHW071232300426
44116CB00008B/1008